Taking Sides: Clashing Views
in Business Ethics
and Society, 14/e

Gina Vega

http://create.mheducation.com

ISBN-10: 1259402797   ISBN-13: 9781259402791

Contents

Detailed Table of Contents

UNIT 1: Capitalism and the Corporation

Daniel Indiviglio explains that historically the Federal Reserve was introduced to stabilize the financial systems throughout the United States. This organization has numerous powers available to control interest rates and inflation. Ethically, for Indiviglio, the Federal Reserve is needed to maintain fairness and stability throughout the monetary system. Robert Larson argues that the Federal Reserve has outlived its usefulness. He believes that the organization makes money too easily and inexpensively available for the marketplace. He believes this creates artificial economic and ethical problems that could easily be solved if the Federal Reserve no longer existed.

UNIT 2: Human Resources: The Corporation and Employment

Issue: Is Employer Monitoring of Employee Social Media Justified?
Yes: Brian Elzweig and Donna K. Peeples, from "Using Social Networking Web Sites in Hiring and Retention Decisions", *SAM Advanced Management Journal* (2009).
No: Steven Greenhouse, from "Even if It Enrages Your Boss, Social Net Speech Is Protected", *The New York Times Magazine* (2013).

Brian Elzweig and Donna K. Peeples write that although employers do need to be respectful of their employees' privacy, they also have the responsibility to avoid negligent hiring and negligent retention. They find that the monitoring an employee's, or a potential employee's, social media is a viable way to avoid these potentially serious problems. This is not to say that an employer's monitoring of social media should be without limits. Special care should be taken in respect to state privacy laws regarding the protection of employees outside of company time. Steven Greenhouse explains that new findings from the National Labor Relations Board state it is illegal for employers to fire employees based on social media posts. Often when an employee begins a job, part of the policy discussion revolves around social media use. In the majority of cases, the employee is told not to post materials that make the firm, the employer, and other employees appear in a bad light. It appears that many firms should begin rewriting their policy manuals based on the findings from the National Labor Relations Board as well as state law.

Issue: Is CEO Compensation Justified?
Yes: Ira T. Kay, from "Don't Mess with CEO Pay", *Across the Board* (2006).
No: Edgar Woolard, Jr., from "CEOs Are Being Paid Too Much", *Across the Board* (2006).

Ira T. Kay, a consultant on executive compensation for Watson Wyatt Worldwide, argues that in general the pay of the CEO tracks the company's performance, so in general CEOs are simply paid to do what they were hired to do—bring up the price of the stock to increase shareholder wealth. Edgar Woolard, Jr., a former CEO himself, holds that the methods by which CEO compensation is determined are fundamentally flawed, and he suggests some significant changes.

Issue: Will Robots Help the American Worker?
Yes: Jeffrey R. Young, from "The New Industrial Revolution: A Coming Wave of Robots Could Redefine Our Jobs. Will That Redefine Us?", *The Chronicle Review* (2013).
No: Mark Kingwell, from "The Barbed Gift of Leisure", *The Chronicle Review* (2013).

Jeffrey R. Young explains that automation is cheap and efficient. Although technology's increasing versatility may take some jobs away from humans, robots primarily will absorb the drudgery that humans may be glad to be rid of. He foresees a future of increased leisure and creativity for us. Mark Kingwell focuses on what it means to be human rather than machine and to live in a culture and community with other human beings. He argues that we are used to deriving much of the meaning of our lives from our work and wonders what individuals might do with their leisure time.

Issue: Should You Associate Yourself with an Organization That Has a History of Scandal?
Yes: Taylor Branch, from "The Shame of College Sports", *The Atlantic* (2011).
No: David A. Jones, Chelsea R. Willness, and Sarah Madey, from "Why Are Job Seekers Attracted by Corporate Social Performance? Experimental and Field Tests of Three Signal-Based Mechanisms", *Academy of Management Journal (2014).*

Taylor Branch writes about the NCAA, "We profess outrage each time we learn that yet another student-athlete has been taking money under the table. But the real scandal is the very structure of college sports, wherein student-athletes generate billions of dollars for universities and private companies while earning nothing for themselves." He asserts that it is not the fault of the athletes and they should not be blamed. Jones, Willness, and Madey's study shows that potential job seekers consider corporate social performance important to the overall assessment of a company at all stages of the job search. They use signal theory to assert the importance of community involvement, environmental practices, prestige and anticipated pride of belonging, and perceived values fit and expected treatment to make a decision about the desirability of associating oneself with a specific company.

Steve Coll, dean of the Columbia School of Journalism, believes that the case for a strong minimum wage has always been, in part, civic and moral. He details cities and industries that have voluntarily raised wages above the suggested minimum wage to demonstrate that pride in jobs and community make for a better economy. Minimum wages are intended to raise the dignity of work as well as strengthen individual economic independence. Minimum wages are not about welfare, entitlement programs, or the value of government. They are about the value of an individual, community, and workforce. Mark Wilson, who is a former deputy assistant secretary of the U.S. Department of Labor, argues that minimum wage harms workers and the broader economy by forcing higher wage payments on employers. Businesses respond by cutting employment as well as making other decisions to keep their net income at the levels needed for profitability. This article argues that minimum wage is not necessary for entry-level employees because the majority of employees who are employed for a year often reach the minimum wage level as part of their employment experience. This experience gives the worker the opportunity to find another job at a wage above minimum wage. Additionally, when minimum wage is required, employers generally cut back on hiring or lay off employees to maintain their profitability standards.

UNIT 3: Consumer Issues

Agnes Shanley argues that the enormous cost of developing a new drug justifies attempts to protect its exclusive access to the market after the patent has expired. Arthur Caplan and Zachary Caplan are skeptical of the "staggering cost" claims and argue that consumers should have access to the generic version of the drug as soon as possible.

Stephanie Clifford cites studies that show that advertising for children is often barely distinguishable from regular programming. She cites harm that can come to children through advertising that seems more promotion than fact to the child. Patrick Basham and John Luik find no credence in studies linking harms to child-directed advertising. They cite research that contends that advertising has little effect on the market associated with children.

Gary Hirshberg claims that the consumers' interests in knowing where their food comes from does not necessarily have to do with the chemical and nutritional properties of the food. Kosher pastrami, for instance, is identical to the nonkosher product, and dolphin-safe tuna is still tuna. But we have an ethical and personal interest in knowing the processes by which our foods arrive on the table. He argues that the demand for a label for bioengineered foods is entirely legitimate. Cameron English points out that as far as the law is concerned, only the nutritional traits and characteristics of foods are subject to safety assessment. Labeling has been required only where health risks exist, or where there is danger that a product's marketing claims may mislead the consumer as to the food's characteristics. Breeding techniques have never been subject to labeling, nor should genetic engineering techniques, English claims.

Arthur Wilmarth, a professor of law at George Washington University's College of Law, argues that the Dodd-Frank Wall Street Reform and Consumer Protection Act (CFPB) was created to protect consumers from fraudulent activities within the financial services industry. It was established with autonomy in order to insulate it from political and lobbying pressures that have been evident in the current federal regulatory agencies. The effects of the catastrophic crash of 2008 on Wall Street are still felt by many consumers. Many of the problems were caused by the mortgage industry, the investment banking industry, and the insurance industry. After extensive bailout from the American taxpayers, the bureau was put in place to maintain financial protection and safety for consumers. Todd Zywicki, a professor of law at George Mason University School of Law, claims that the Consumer Financial Protection Bureau (CFPB) is not necessary because several federal agencies are already doing the work of the CFPB. The Bureau has extensive autonomy, which can endanger the financial industry's progress and profits through excessive regulation and reform. He argues that the 2010 Dodd-Frank Consumer Financial Protection Act can function well with the existing federal agencies.

UNIT 4: Global Objectives

Issue: Should Hydrofracking Be Permitted?
Yes: Danny Hakim, from "Gas Drilling Is Called Safe in New York", *The New York Times Magazine* (2013).
No: Ben Goldfarb, from "Hydrofracking Poses Serious Risks to Human Health", *Policymic.com* (2012).

Danny Hakim reports that the New York Health Department will be issuing a report claiming that the practice of hydrofracking is safe as it is practiced in the state of New York; after significant pressure from the drilling industry and landowners, the moratorium on hydrofracking was lifted for the Southern Tier of the state in the summer of 2012. Ben Goldfarb disagrees, citing a recently released Environmental Protection Agency report that links hydraulic fracturing to contaminated well-water in Wyoming. He also points out that an abundance of clean water is needed for the process—a commodity which is scarce in the western United States.

Issue: Should the World Continue to Rely on Oil as a Major Source of Energy?
Yes: Red Cavaney, from "Global Oil Production about to Peak? A Recurring Myth", *World Watch* (2006).
No: James Howard Kunstler, from "The Long Emergency", Grove/Atlantic (2005).

Red Cavaney, president and chief executive officer of the American Petroleum Institute, argues that recent revolutionary advances in technology will yield sufficient quantities of available oil for the foreseeable future. James Howard Kunstler contends that the peak of oil production, Hubbert's Peak, was itself the important turning point in our species' relationship to petroleum. Unless strong conservation measures are put in place, the new scarcity will destroy much that we have come to expect in our lives.

Issue: Is the Foreign Corrupt Practices Act Obsolete?
Yes: Joseph W. Yockey, from "Choosing Governance in the FCPA Reform Debate", *Journal of Corporation Law* (2013).
No: Peter J. Henning, from "Taking Aim at the Foreign Corrupt Practices Act", *The New York Times* (2012).

Joseph Yockey claims that ambiguity in the statute creates perpetual uncertainty about what constitutes an FCPA violation and that reform is needed urgently. New governance can replace the existing concerns about implementation of the FCPA. Peter Henning states that "business leaders have long contended that the law is overly broad and too aggressively enforced," but believes that "it does little good to charge someone when there is not a realistic prospect that the person can be brought to the United States."

Issue: Should U.S. Companies Take Primary Responsibility for Working Conditions in Their International Suppliers' Factories?
Yes: Denis G. Arnold and Norman E. Bowie, from "Sweatshops and Respect for Persons ", *Business Ethics Quarterly* (2003).
No: Charles Duhigg and David Barboza, from "In China, Human Costs Are Built into an iPad", *The New York Times* (2012).

Arnold and Bowie claim that multinational corporations are responsible for the actions of their suppliers based on the Kantian doctrine of respect for persons. Corporations must ensure minimum safety standards are met, along with living wage and local labor laws. Duhigg and Barboza report that Apple contends that their industry behavior is governed by market desire for cheaper and more advanced technology. Until market desire changes, factory conditions are secondary.

Preface

Business ethics and corporate social responsibility form a pointillist black and white tapestry in which every decision is comprised of both positive and negative motivations and consequences. Up close, all we see are the dots; in order to see the big picture, the strategy, we have to step way back and squint a little.

We have been aided in this process by generations of philosophers, ethicists, and religious figures extending in the Western world from Abraham (twentieth century BCE) and in the Eastern world from Kong Qiu (Confucius, fifth century BCE) and Siddharta Gautama (Buddha, fifth century BCE) through Aristotle, Hegel, and Kant to modern leaders such as Alasdair MacIntyre, William James, and Michel Foucault, among others. The introduction will provide an abbreviated overview of many of these approaches to business ethics, with the goal of supplying the reader with a framework of frameworks that may simplify the complex analysis demanded of our evolving twenty-first-century business decisions.

Cost/benefit analysis via the economic/utilitarian model has been the traditional guideline used by many in the business world to make decisions related to issues of social responsibility, but that approach is not necessarily the one that we should use as our benchmark for ethical behavior. In this volume, we will consider modern and postmodern perspectives as well as the more traditional ones. We will examine applied ethics from a social and virtue perspective and will focus more on our internal moral compass and less on theoretical models. Economists have their formulae to guide them, but we have other methods of valuation that will be presented in the introduction as well. You can look forward to shaking up your thinking and reflecting on the viability of your socially constructed attitudes toward business, the bottom line, and the way the world works.

What follows are 20 distinct issues, framed with broad brush strokes and filtered through opposite, or nearly opposite lenses. These issues fall into four general units: Capitalism and the Corporation; Human Resources: The Corporation and Employment; Consumer Issues; and Global Objectives. These units address a variety of current issues about problems and challenges that you will face in business on a regular basis. You will be challenged to look through each lens and identify the salient positions that are pictured in the two articles that present these perspectives.

You will discover, I hope, that each perspective contains elements of the other and that you will be able to integrate them into a new image for ethical corporate behavior.

This volume of *Taking Sides* is directed toward helping readers see the big picture while making the individual decisions that direct the ethical thrust of our business lives. How you handle the challenges is a direct reflection on the way your moral compass is pointed—finding your true north is part of the larger goal of this collection.

Gina Vega
Organizational Ergonomics

Editor of This Volume

Gina Vega, PhD is a former professor of management at the Bertolon School of Business, Salem State University (MA) and Founding Director of the Center for Entrepreneurial Activity. She has taught corporate social responsibility and entrepreneurship for 20 years and is widely published in academic journals, with more than 60 articles and cases. She has written or edited six books: *Entrepreneurial Finance: Concepts and Cases* (with M. Lam); *Business in a Book: Salem State University*; *The Case Writing Workbook: A Self-Guided Workshop*; *Moral Courage in Organizations: Doing the Right Thing at Work* (with D. Comer); *Managing Teleworkers and Telecommuting Strategies*; and *A Passion for Planning: Financials, Operations, Marketing, Management, and Ethics*.

Dr. Vega is a Fulbright Specialist with assignments at St. Petersburg University, Russia (2010) and Cranfield University, UK (2012). She is past president of the CASE Association, a CASE Fellow, Editor-in-Chief of *The CASE Journal* and past associate editor of the *Journal of Management Education*. She has received numerous awards for teaching, research, writing, and mentoring of case writers.

Her research interests include small business transitions, corporate social responsibility, and organizational structure. She is founder and president of Organizational Ergonomics, an academic services consulting firm established in 1994 through which she provides writing workshops and technical writing assistance (more information about Dr. Vega can be found at her website: www.organizationalergonomics.com).

Academic Advisory Board Members

Members of the Academic Advisory Board are instrumental in the final selection of articles for each edition of TAKING SIDES. Their review of articles for content, level, and appropriateness provides critical direction to the editors and staff. We think that you will find their careful consideration well reflected in this volume.

Introduction

Any transaction that requires money or ownership to change hands falls within the category of business. Even if we lived in a barter-based society, engagement in business would be unavoidable in the twenty-first century world. It's what we "do." The way we conduct our business, however, is not consistent across cultures, nations, and individuals. The way we conduct our business is a reflection on our norms and a measure of the moral nature of our society.

The moral nature of society is often relegated to philosophy, the study of systems of thought. But business demands action, so business ethics is *applied* ethics, or the study of systems of action. We depend on philosophy for the structure, but the behavior itself emerges from our inherent sense of morality which, in its turn, derives from philosophical perspectives, socioeconomic and legal models, and religious training.

Business ethics focuses on decision-making in its many forms: how to make a decision, why a decision must be made, how to evaluate various options and make a recommendation, how to reflect on the purpose of the decision and its potential consequences, how to use business tools to analyze an opportunity or an action, the correct identification of the decision to be made, syncretic (reconciled) approaches to balancing options and opportunities, and more. How do we apply the lessons learned from a vast array of multidisciplinary theories to the small, daily decisions we make in business, and how do we marry the various small tactical decisions into a strategic behavioral thrust for our organizations?

We'll start by asking four BIG questions:

- Cui bono? (Who benefits?)
- Who is going to get hurt?
- How will my decision affect my personal sense of morality?
- What is the goal of business?

And conclude with an even bigger one: What actions do our values recommend?

Cui bono?

Every business decision has both an upside and a downside. The upside is traditionally the more compelling for businesses; therefore, we will consider it first.

These *teleological* decisions resemble closely their economic cousins, decisions based on *utility* (see *What is the goal of business*, below). Rather than discussing all the subsets of theoretical perspectives and individual philosophers and theoreticians in each category, we will look at the broad picture of the stream of thought represented. You can refer to the references at the end of the Introduction if you have interest in learning more about each thinker represented here.

Teleological decisions are decisions based on outcomes (telos, "end" and logos, "science," Greek). These include both good outcomes and negative ones, and tend to be guided more by desirable results than by injurious ones. The most pervasive stream of teleological thought is represented by *utilitarianism*. Utilitarianism contends that a decision should be based on providing the greatest good to the greatest number of people (*cf* Jeremy Bentham, 1789 and John Stuart Mill, 1863). Bear in mind that the concept of utilitarianism grew and developed at a time very different from today. The political, economic, and social upheavals of the eighteenth and nineteenth centuries were so alien from those of the twentieth and twenty-first centuries that Bentham and Mill would be dumbfounded at the application of their utilitarian perspective to the business challenges we face today.

Businesses often make decisions today by means of a tool called *cost/benefit analysis*. This tool allows complex situations to be broken down into simple mathematical models that compare the returns that the business might anticipate to the costs of obtaining those returns. By using a cost/benefit analysis, all consideration of moral issues is removed from the decision-making process. The decision is reduced to numerical representations, introducing a level of abstraction to the decision that removes human considerations from the decision-making itself. This allows an objective comparison of various actions to be based purely on neutral factors. For this reason, utilitarian approaches are very popular—they are easy to do, "clean," and mathematically calculable. Emotions, values, and moral systems are effectively removed from the process.

Of course, there are methods of adding back moral concerns into the equation. First of all, the principle of greatest good for the greatest number posits that the decision-maker will determine ahead of time the desirable end. Under utilitarian rules, the desirable end is happiness.

Happiness then needs to be defined. Initially, it meant absence of pain and presence of pleasure. We can expand this definition to refine the desirable end to be financial, social, or some other measure.

Modern teleologists such as Alistair Norcross have determined a method to assess the morality of an action based on the total resulting comparative benefits of the action. This process is called *scalar consequentialism* and states that, of two possible actions a person can take, one will result in better outcomes and that one is, by its nature, a more moral decision (Norcross, 1997).

Who is going to get hurt?

This is the other side of the *cui bono* question, the downside of our decisions and is often applied as stakeholder theory. A more comprehensive discussion of stakeholder will appear in *What is the goal of business?* below. At this stage, however, stakeholder theory introduces more complexity than is appropriate. First, we need to consider the injuries that could be inflicted by a business decision.

Utilitarians claim that pain can be defined as the absence of pleasure. If we adopt this language, "pain" becomes the absence of the desirable end; the absence of happiness. The cost of our happiness-seeking decisions becomes someone else's pain—someone has to pay for our pleasure. And who is this payor?

Although justice most frequently falls into the category of deontological theories, there are those who support justice as a utilitarian-based concept under specific circumstances (see DeGeorge, 2006; Rawls, 1967). The argument states that, even though everyone has the same rights (from a deontological perspective (deon, "duty," and logos, "science," Greek), the outcomes of our decisions affect different people differently. Therefore, we need to consider carefully the consequences of our actions in order to behave in a just or fair manner to maximize the sum total of happiness in society. Specifically, *distributive justice* demands that the expense side of the justice ledger be administered fairly—not equally, but fairly.

So, a business decision that puts the majority of the pain on wage earners is unjust because they do not participate in the majority of the benefit. For example, requiring workers to work in unsafe conditions for low pay so that the business owners or investors or product users can enjoy large profits or low prices is unjust by any reckoning. It does not meet the standard of maximization of happiness in society, as the total pain of the workers is likely to far outweigh the total pleasure of the investors. This can be described as *social injustice*. According to Manuel Velasquez (2002: 84), ". . . a social system that poses such unequal sharing of burdens is clearly immoral and offends against justice. The great benefits the system may have for the majority does not justify the extreme burdens that it imposes on a small group."

According to the theory of the social contract, people enter into a mutually protective unwritten agreement to behave in ways that will serve them all. In business, workers and employers enter into this unwritten agreement to both protect workers' rights and to establish employer/worker commitment to seek mutually agreeable ends. This social contract, the disintegration of which has been bemoaned since the 1980s after the initial spike in disparity between compensation and productivity, served to mitigate some of the vast power difference between the owners of the means of production and the people who provided the labor of production. It is no surprise that owners are more willing to provide benefits to workers in times of economic boom than in times of economic bust such as we have experienced consistently for the past two decades. In bust times, companies often "forget" their role in the social contract and treat workers shabbily. It is not surprising, but neither can it be considered just or acceptable.

How will the decision affect my personal sense of morality?

What is the impact on me when I disregard the basic needs of my employees? Aristotle taught (350 BCE, *Nicomachean Ethics*) that virtues are built by practicing the habit of deliberately choosing the ethical course of action. This is equally true of the reverse—bad behaviors will develop habits that weaken moral character. According to Aristotle, "We deliberate not about ends but about means." (*op. cit,* Book 3, Ch. 3). In other words, the way we attain our goals is more telling than the goals themselves. We have the ability to control our behavior and make moral choices. If we choose to make immoral choices, that is also a voluntary condition (in most cases). By practice, we develop the moral strength to make ethical choices. But we do need to keep practicing, or the bad habits we may have developed will hold sway over our future choices.

This is very much in keeping with most religions, both Eastern and Western, which teach that we must follow certain self-governing habits in order to live a "good" life. Whereas Aristotle focused on balance, the mean between extremes, Abrahamic religions use a more personal measure of ethical/moral behavior, commonly referred to as the Golden Rule. Simply stated, do not do to anyone else that which is hateful to you. We have all had occasion to hear, from our parents or someone else's, "Would you like it if someone threw a rock at you? So don't throw one at anyone else." This simplistic and somewhat self-serving approach to morality provides guidance for many life decisions, including the one mentioned above about the social contract.

John Rawls used this same argument, which he called *the veil of ignorance,* to support his position vis-à-vis justice. The veil of ignorance states that if you did not know your role or position in society, you would make decisions that would protect even the least powerful (because you might actually be one of the least powerful). Do unto others . . . .

Judaism is particularly focused on ethical business behavior. Throughout the Torah are references to matters of ethics in business, and direct regulations are laid out in Leviticus (19:11 admonishes us not to steal; 19:35 requires the use of honest weights; 25:14 prohibits against monetary deception; etc.). These general regulations are discussed, refined, and amplified in great detail in the Talmud. The sage, Rava, believed that every business transaction was overseen by a Third Party, in whose presence people would be less likely to cheat. It is said that in the Babylonian Talmud, Shabbat 31a, Rava claimed "When a person is led in for judgment [in the next world], God asks: Did you transact your business honestly?" (Blumenthal, 2012, 492).

These philosophies find their home among the *deontological* perspectives. Deontologists believe that actions are right or wrong regardless of their consequences. Moral law is moral law, without deviation. It is universal, it is *categorically imperative,* an absolute, unconditional requirement that must be obeyed in all circumstances and is justified as an end in itself (see Kant, 1785). Kant's categorical imperative stated: Act as though, through your own will, your actions were to become a universal law of nature.

On its surface, this looks a lot like the Golden Rule. But, with careful reading, the differences emerge. Whereas the Golden Rule is personal and highly subjective, the categorical imperative is impersonal, imposed by duty, and is universal, disregarding individuals and unique circumstances.

On a personal level, whether you adhere to religious principles or to universal principles, both sets of ideologies would prohibit mistreating employees (either because, presumably, you would not like to be mistreated, or because moral law is absolute and prohibits mistreatment). Violation of either doctrine will lead to the continued practice of unethical behavior. If following a religious doctrine, this is likely to have significantly negative ultimate outcomes. If adhering to a deontological doctrine, it is just wrong and unsupportable.

What is the goal of business?

The goal of business is not simply to process transactions, as suggested in the beginning of this Introduction. Were that the goal, very few people would be interested in being involved in such a mechanical operation. Although business does require that transactions occur, those transactions take place between people; without people, there can be no business. One could argue, therefore, that business is about people, that the primary goal of business is to create happiness or satisfy people. In fact, stakeholder theory (Freeman, 1984) revolves entirely around the needs and desires of the people and entities that have a stake in each business's success or failure.

The stakeholder theory of the firm holds that in lieu of being responsible only to the *stockholders,* businesses have responsibilities toward all the stakeholders of the business; that is, that businesses have a responsibility toward society as a whole. These stakeholders include the stockholders/owners, employees, customers, suppliers, government entities, creditors, the public, the local community, and so on. Each of these entities has its own interest and power to influence decision-making. According to this theory, the best decisions are made with the interests and influence of all stakeholders in mind by prioritizing them and assigning weights to each. This process promotes a more inclusive managerial style and is likely to result in ethical decisions that incorporate a broad concern for society.

But stakeholder theory is not always valued highly, despite its reasonable-sounding approach. Corporations, all of which have their own governing regulations and boards, often feel constrained by the limitations imposed through stakeholder methods of decision-making, preferring to focus on traditional bottom-line-based choices. Corporations are often governed by the belief that, in a capitalist society such as ours, the responsibility of business is to bring in returns solely for the shareholders of the corporation. This is not an unreasonable assumption; however, it is an assumption that wears blinders. When we believe that the purpose of our organization is to bring in money alone, we tend to overlook the needs of the many in the interest of the few.

In America, capitalism (a set of economic theories) is often linked with democracy (a set of political theories). Both capitalism and democracy maintain their own unique value systems and systems of ethical behavior. These systems are not identical, nor are they easily replicated elsewhere. This is why we see countries that have turned to capitalism from other systems over the past several decades struggling to make democracy work without capitalism and capitalism work without democracy. Here, our challenge is to adapt the pure capitalism that we admire and that has built the strong economy we enjoy to the modern challenges of a political-social climate that may overlook some basic rights and entitlements established by our founders.

We are quick to condemn other countries for their unsafe manufacturing processes that risk the health and welfare of workers; however, we seem to be less concerned about the health and welfare risks experienced by our own American families who live in poverty. At most recent count, our poverty rate was 14.5 percent—more than 45 million Americans live in poverty (2013 US Census) despite our oft-spoken belief in both constitutionally protected legal rights and moral rights that we endorse for other countries. What role could business play in reducing poverty in America?

There is nothing unethical in turning a profit; to the contrary, engaging yourself in an activity without a positive outcome seems a singular waste of time. But profit is not the only potentially positive outcome of business activities.

The triple bottom line (Elkington, 1999) suggests that business has three main focuses: people, planet, and profit. This concept states that businesses can measure their success, their "bottom line," in three ways, only one of which is financial. Value is also created and measurable in terms of ecological sustainability and human/social benefits. Companies that are concerned about people and the planet are able to demonstrate their achievements through multiple measures.

A new form of corporation has recently made headlines, the B Corp. A B Corp is "certified by the nonprofit B Lab to meet rigorous standards of social and environmental performance, accountability, and transparency" (https://www.bcorporation.net/). There are more than 1,000 certified B Corps from 33 countries and over 60 industries working to redefine success in business. Among them are such industry leaders as Ben & Jerry, Patagonia, and Cabot Cheese. Etsy, the second B Corp to go public, closed its IPO at $30, nearly twice its initial offering price. Chad Dickerson, CEO, proudly stated: "The success of our business model is based on the success of our sellers. That means we don't have to make a choice between people and profit" (Tabuchi, 2015).

Social enterprises, businesses that tackle social problems and address broad community issues as well as small local needs, operate the same way, but starting from the opposite side of the economy. Their goal is to find a way to make a profit *in order to* finance and support those entities who need their help. They sell their goods and services in the same way, but they reinvest them back into the community or the business.

According to management guru Edward Lawler III, commenting on Etsy's success, "There's a realization that corporations don't actually have to put short-term shareholder gain above all else. More people are saying: 'We have a right to ask more of our corporations, and they should not exist simply to generate profit'" (Tabuchi, 2015).

What actions do our values recommend? How can we use ethical theories to guide our decision-making?

As we continue to pursue ethical teachings, the futility of assigning exclusive labels to each theoretical perspective becomes increasingly apparent; once we delve more deeply into an idea, we learn that that idea has already been assigned to the camp of another philosophical team. The impact of this learning results in a more inclusive, less parochial view of how to make an ethical business decision. We must cut straight to our own personal bottom line: what matters to us . . . what do we value?

This is perhaps the most profound question we can ask of ourselves. Are we asking about what we value emotionally? Physically? Universally? Morally? The automatic responses are fairly consistent across ages, companies, educational levels, and countries (see Gentile, 2010).

Emotionally we may seek love, affection, kindness, gentleness, a heart at ease, security. Physically we may value wealth and what it can buy, comfort, luxury, vacations, health. Universally we may value a world of peace, equality or fairness, eradication of hunger, international cooperation. And morally?

Morally, Gentile suggests, citing Rushwell Kidder, that there are six core moral values, or virtues: wisdom, courage, humanity, justice, temperance, and transcendence (Gentile, 2010:30). These values guide our actions in our business lives as they do in our personal lives. We hold dear the same values in all our actions. Our decisions in the most challenging situations reveal our core values.

When we embrace these values, our course of action is surprisingly clear. Our business decisions must reflect our appreciation of this value set, focusing on the relationships we build with our employees, peers, business partners, and society as a whole. We must work toward just actions guided by wisdom and courage, as our concern for humanity takes precedence over our emotional and physical values.

We do not pick and choose among the various ethical frames presented here to make our decisions. Instead, we keep in the forefront our values—what really matters in life—when we stand courageously to confront those who would generate harm as easily as they generate profit.

Gina Vega
Organizational Ergonomics

References

Aristotle, *Nicomachean Ethics* (350 BCE). Translation by W.D. Ross at http://www.constitution.org/ari/ethic_00.htm (retrieved April 14, 2015).

J. Bentham, *An Introduction to the Principles of Morals and Legislation.* (Oxford: Clarendon Press, 1789 first publication).

J. Blumenthal, "Commerce," *The Observant Life* (edited by Martin S. Cohen and Michael Katz). (New York: The Rabbinical Assembly, 2012, 491–507).

R.T. DeGeorge, *Business Ethics*, 6/e. (Upper Saddle River, NJ: Pearson/Prentice Hall, 2006).

J. Elkington, *Cannibals with Forks: Triple Bottom Line of 21st Century Business.* (Minneapolis: Capstone Publishing Ltd, 1999).

E.R. Freeman, *Strategic Management: A Stakeholder Approach.* (Boston: Pitman, 1984).

M.C. Gentile, *Giving Voice to Values.* (New Haven: Yale University Press, 2010).

I. Kant, *Groundwork for the Metaphysic of Morals.* (1785). Translated by Jonathan Bennett. http://www.earlymoderntexts.com/assets/pdfs/kant1785.pdf (retrieved April 14, 2015).

J.S. Mill, *Utilitarianism.* (London: Parker, Son & Bourn, 1863).

A. Norcross, "Good and Bad Actions." *The Philosophical Review* (vol. 106, No. 1, 1997, pp. 1–34).

J. Rawls, "Distributive Justice" (1967), *Philosophy, Politics, and Society,* 3/e (edited by Peter Laslett and W.G. Runcimann. Oxford: Blackwell), reprinted in *Ethical Issues in Business,* 7/e (edited by Thomas Donaldson, Patricia H. Werhane, and Margaret Cording. (Upper Saddle River, NJ: Prentice Hall, 2002. 193–203).

H. Tabuchi, "Etsy IPO Tests Pledge to Balance Social Mission and Profit," *The New York Times* (April 17, 2015).

http://www.nytimes.com/2015/04/17/business/dealbook/etsy-ipo-tests-pledge-to-emphasize-social-mission-over-profit.html?emc=edit_tu_20150417&nl=technology&nlid=57140020&_r=0.

US Census, http://www.census.gov/hhes/www/poverty/about/overview/, (2013). (retrieved April 17, 2015).

M.G. Velasquez, *Business Ethics: Concepts and Cases.* (Upper Saddle River, NJ: Prentice Hall, 2002). https://www.bcorporation.net/ (retrieved April 17, 2015).

Unit 1

Capitalism and the Corporation

*C*apitalism has led the United States to economic success, global power and influence, individual wealth and political change, and also to social despair created by the vast income gap that is sustained by this economic system.

How can we balance the drawbacks of capitalism with its positive influences? Is there something inherent in capitalism that prohibits ethical competition and a focus on social concerns? Do the norms inspired by capitalism generate a sense of entitlement in the "haves" and hopelessness in the "have-nots?" What kinds of ethical decisions can balance the needs and rights of the individual with the needs of society and continue to sustain the economic system that has made our country what it is today?

Selected, Edited, and with Issue Framing Material by:
Gina Vega, *Organizational Ergonomics*

ISSUE

Is Increasing Profits the Only Social Responsibility of Business?

YES: Milton Friedman, from "The Social Responsibility of Business Is to Increase Its Profits," *New York Times Magazine* (1970)

NO: Joseph Hart, from "The New Capitalists," *Utne Reader* (2006)

Learning Outcomes
After reading this issue, you will be able to:
• Explain the goals of corporate social responsibility. • List ways in which stakeholders can influence corporate change. • Differentiate between government's responsibility and business' responsibility.

ISSUE SUMMARY

YES: Milton Friedman argues that businesses have neither the right nor the ability to make social responsibility a priority. Profit making must be the priority. Businesses serve employees and customers best when they do their work with maximum efficiency. The only restrictions on the pursuit of profit that Friedman accepts are the requirements of law and the "rules of the game" ("open and free competition without deception or fraud").

NO: Joseph Hart disagrees. He states, "It's no longer enough more and more corporations are conceding, for capitalism to simply make money. It must also make a difference." Using logic developed by Alan Greenspan, Hart avers that business must make room for values other than self-interest.

What is the corporation supposed to be doing? Milton Friedman presents the classic "conservative" response to that question in his 1970 article. It was written for the general public, appeared in *The New York Times* magazine section, and was specifically addressing one of the burning questions of the day: Is the private business, the business corporation, responsible to anyone but the shareholders? Isn't it part of "corporate social responsibility" (the new fashionable term of the day) to take into account the welfare of the community? James Beré of Borg-Warner had argued that the corporation is a "guest" in the community and must take its responsibility to the community very seriously. Friedman's answer was uncompromising: the corporation's money belongs to the investors. It does not belong to the managers or the critics, the politicians, or the professors. When the corporate managers decide to do something with the corporation's money besides distributing it to the shareholders, they are in effect levying a tax on the investor's money, taking it for themselves to do as they please. (What they please, whatever they may think, is not always identical with the public interest.) The corporation is not an individual, but a nexus of obligations for the benefit of the investors. Interestingly, the 2010 Supreme Court decision (*Citizens United v. FEC*) allows corporations, as persons, to contribute to political candidates. So corporations now have more of the freedoms of the individual citizen—but not of the responsibilities.

The issue of the legal status of the corporation does stand in the way of real reform in terms of shifting the focus of the corporation itself. In the NO selection, Joseph Hart confirms that this is so, yet presents an alternative perspective that would make reform possible and desirable. Making money, he states, is a good thing, a goal worth pursuing. But making money to the complete disregard of the community and of society is unacceptable.

Using Wal-Mart as his surprising exemplar of the money-making/socially concerned corporation, Hart describes a world in which "companies of all sizes embrace 'corporate social responsibility.'" Such companies would be mindful of human rights issues, environmental sustainability, and internal ethical guidelines. He claims that Alan Greenspan, retired chairman of the US Federal Reserve, laid the groundwork for conducting business in a way that allows for more values in play than simply the value of self-interest.

Reciprocity in relationships is the key to a "conscious capitalism" with broader concerns than only making money for shareholders. Shareholder interests should be defined more expansively, including balancing profit margins with other socially responsible goals. A list of conscious capitalists identifies leaders of familiar corporations such as Whole Foods, Starbucks, Trader Joe, and many others globally.

YES ↵

Milton Friedman

The Social Responsibility of Business Is to Increase Its Profits

When I hear businessmen speak eloquently about the "social responsibilities of business in a free-enterprise system," I am reminded of the wonderful line about the Frenchman who discovered at the age of 70 that he had been speaking prose all his life. The businessmen believe that they are defending free enterprise when they declaim that business is not concerned "merely" with profit but also with promoting desirable "social" ends; that business has a "social conscience" and takes seriously its responsibilities for providing employment, eliminating discrimination, avoiding pollution and whatever else may be the catchwords of the contemporary crop of reformers. In fact they are—or would be if they or anyone else took them seriously—preaching pure and unadulterated socialism. Businessmen who talk this way are unwitting puppets of the intellectual forces that have been undermining the basis of a free society these past decades.

The discussions of the "social responsibilities of business" are notable for their analytical looseness and lack of rigor. What does it mean to say that "business" has responsibilities? Only people can have responsibilities. A corporation is an artificial person and in this sense may have artificial responsibilities, but "business" as a whole cannot be said to have responsibilities, even in this vague sense. The first step toward clarity in examining the doctrine of the social responsibility of business is to ask precisely what it implies for whom.

Presumably, the individuals who are to be responsible are businessmen, which means individual proprietors or corporate executives. Most of the discussion of social responsibility is directed at corporations, so in what follows I shall mostly neglect the individual proprietors and speak of corporate executives.

In a free-enterprise, private-property system, a corporate executive is an employee of the owners of the business. He has direct responsibility to his employers. That responsibility is to conduct the business in accordance with their desires, which generally will be to make as much money as possible while conforming to the basic rules of the society, both those embodied in law and those embodied in ethical custom. Of course, in some cases his employers may have a different objective. A group of persons might establish a corporation for an eleemosynary purpose—for example, a hospital or a school. The manager of such a corporation will not have money profit as his objective but the rendering of certain services.

In either case, the key point is that, in his capacity as a corporate executive, the manager is the agent of the individuals who own the corporation or establish the eleemosynary institution, and his primary responsibility is to them.

Needless to say, this does not mean that it is easy to judge how well he is performing his task. But at least the criterion of performance is straightforward, and the persons among whom a voluntary contractual arrangement exists are clearly defined.

Of course, the corporate executive is also a person in his own right. As a person, he may have many other responsibilities that he recognizes or assumes voluntarily—to his family, his conscience, his feelings of charity, his church, his clubs, his city, his country. He may feel impelled by these responsibilities to devote part of his income to causes he regards as worthy, to refuse to work for particular corporations, even to leave his job, for example, to join his country's armed forces. If we wish, we may refer to some of these responsibilities as "social responsibilities." But in these respects he is acting as a principal, not an agent; he is spending his own money or time or energy, not the money of his employers or the time or energy he has contracted to devote to their purposes. If these are "social responsibilities," they are the social responsibilities of individuals, not of business.

What does it mean to say that the corporate executive has a "social responsibility" in his capacity as businessman? If this statement is not pure rhetoric, it must mean that he is to act in some way that is not in the interest of his employers. For example, that he is to refrain from increasing the price of the product in order to contribute to the social objective of preventing inflation, even though a price increase would be in the best interests of the corporation. Or that he is to make expenditures on reducing pollution beyond the amount that is in the best interests of the corporation or that is required by law in order to contribute to the social objective of improving the environment. Or that, at the expense of corporate profits, he is to hire "hard-core" unemployed instead of better qualified available workmen to contribute to the social objective of reducing poverty.

In each of these cases, the corporate executive would be spending someone else's money for a general social interest. Insofar as his actions in accord with his "social responsibility" reduce returns to stockholders, he is spending their money. Insofar as his actions raise the price to customers, he is spending the customers' money. Insofar as his actions lower the wages of some employees, he is spending their money.

The stockholders or the customers or the employees could separately spend their own money on the particular action if they wished to do so. The executive is exercising a distinct "social responsibility," rather than serving as an agent of the stockholders or the customers or the employees, only if he spends the money in a different way than they would have spent it.

But if he does this, he is in effect imposing taxes, on the one hand, and deciding how the tax proceeds shall be spent, on the other.

This process raises political questions on two levels: principle and consequences. On the level of political principle, the imposition of taxes and the expenditure of tax proceeds are governmental functions. We have established elaborate constitutional, parliamentary and judicial provisions to control these functions, to assure that taxes are imposed so far as possible in accordance with the preferences and desires of the public—after all, "taxation without representation" was one of the battle cries of the American Revolution. We have a system of checks and balances to separate the legislative function of imposing taxes and enacting expenditures from the executive function of collecting taxes and administering expenditure programs and from the judicial function of mediating disputes and interpreting the law.

Here the businessman—self-selected or appointed directly or indirectly by stockholders—is to be simultaneously legislator, executive and jurist. He is to decide whom to tax by how much and for what purpose, and he is to spend the proceeds—all this guided only by general

exhortations from on high to restrain inflation, improve the environment, fight poverty and so on and on.

The whole justification for permitting the corporate executive to be selected by the stockholders is that the executive is an agent serving the interests of his principal. This justification disappears when the corporate executive imposes taxes and spends the proceeds for "social" purposes. He becomes in effect a public employee, a civil servant, even though he remains in name an employee of a private enterprise. On grounds of political principle, it is intolerable that such civil servants—insofar as their actions in the name of social responsibility are real and not just window dressing—should be selected as they are now. If they are to be civil servants, then they must be selected through a political process. If they are to impose taxes and make expenditures to foster "social" objectives, then political machinery must be set up to make the assessment of taxes and to determine through a political process the objectives to be served.

This is the basic reason why the doctrine of "social responsibility" involves the acceptance of the socialist view that political mechanisms, not market mechanisms, are the appropriate way to determine the allocation of scarce resources to alternative uses.

On the grounds of consequences, can the corporate executive in fact discharge his alleged "social responsibilities"? On the other hand, suppose he could get away with spending the stockholders' or customers' or employees' money. How is he to know how to spend it? He is told that he must contribute to fighting inflation. How is he to know what action of his will contribute to that end? He is presumably an expert in running his company—in producing a product or selling it or financing it. But nothing about his selection makes him an expert on inflation. Will his holding down the price of his product reduce inflationary pressure? Or, by leaving more spending power in the hands of his customers, simply divert it elsewhere? Or, by forcing him to produce less because of the lower price, will it simply contribute to shortages? Even if he could answer these questions, how much cost is he justified in imposing on his stockholders, customers and employees for this social purpose? What is his appropriate share and what is the appropriate share of others?

And, whether he wants to or not, can he get away with spending his stockholders', customers' or employees' money? Will not the stockholders fire him? (Either the present ones or those who take over when his actions in the name of social responsibility have reduced the corporation's profits and the price of its stock.) His customers and his employees can desert him for other producers and employers less scrupulous in exercising their social responsibilities.

This facet of "social responsibility" doctrine is brought into sharp relief when the doctrine is used to justify wage restraint by trade unions. The conflict of interest is naked and clear when union officials are asked to subordinate the interest of their members to some more general purpose. If the union officials try to enforce wage restraint, the consequence is likely to be wildcat strikes, rank-and-file revolts and the emergence of strong competitors for their jobs. We thus have the ironic phenomenon that union leaders—at least in the U.S.—have objected to Government interference with the market far more consistently and courageously than have business leaders.

The difficulty of exercising "social responsibility" illustrates, of course, the great virtue of private competitive enterprise—it forces people to be responsible for their own actions and makes it difficult for them to "exploit" other people for either selfish or unselfish purposes. They can do good—but only at their own expense.

Many a reader who has followed the argument this far may be tempted to remonstrate that it is all well and good to speak of government's having the responsibility to impose taxes and determine expenditures for such "social" purposes as controlling pollution or training the hard-core unemployed, but that the problems are too urgent to wait on the slow course of political processes, that the exercise of social responsibility by businessmen is a quicker and surer way to solve pressing current problems.

Aside from the question of fact—I share Adam Smith's skepticism about the benefits that can be expected from "those who affect to trade for the public good"—this argument must be rejected on grounds of principle. What it amounts to is an assertion that those who favor the taxes and expenditures in question have failed to persuade a majority of their fellow citizens to be of like mind and that they are seeking to attain by undemocratic procedures what they cannot attain by democratic procedures. In a free society, it is hard for "evil" people to do "evil," especially since one man's good is another's evil.

I have, for simplicity, concentrated on the special case of the corporate executive, except only for the brief digression on trade unions. But precisely the same argument applies to the newer phenomenon of calling upon stockholders to require corporations to exercise social responsibility (the recent G.M. crusade for example). In most of these cases, what is in effect involved is some stockholders trying to get other stockholders (or customers or employees) to contribute against their will to "social" causes favored by the activists. Insofar as they succeed, they are again imposing taxes and spending the proceeds.

The situation of the individual proprietor is somewhat different. If he acts to reduce the returns of his enterprise in order to exercise his "social responsibility," he is spending his own money, not someone else's. If he wishes to spend his money on such purposes, that is his right, and I cannot see that there is any objection to his doing so. In the process, he, too, may impose costs on employees and customers. However, because he is far less likely than a large corporation or union to have monopolistic power, any such side effects will tend to be minor.

Of course, in practice the doctrine of social responsibility is frequently a cloak for actions that are justified on other grounds rather than a reason for those actions.

To illustrate, it may well be in the long-run interest of a corporation that is a major employer in a small community to devote resources to providing amenities to that community or to improving its government. That may make it easier to attract desirable employees, it may reduce the wage bill or lessen losses from pilferage and sabotage or have other worthwhile effects. Or it may be that, given the laws about the deductibility of corporate charitable contributions, the stockholders can contribute more to charities they favor by having the corporation make the gift than by doing it themselves, since they can in that way contribute an amount that would otherwise have been paid as corporate taxes.

In each of these—and many similar—cases, there is a strong temptation to rationalize these actions as an exercise of "social responsibility." In the present climate of opinion, with its widespread aversion to "capitalism," "profits," the "soulless corporation" and so on, this is one way for a corporation to generate goodwill as a by-product of expenditures that are entirely justified in its own self-interest.

It would be inconsistent of me to call on corporate executives to refrain from this hypocritical window-dressing because it harms the foundations of a free society. That would be to call on them to exercise a "social responsibility"! If our institutions, and the attitudes of the public make it in their self-interest to cloak their actions in this way, I cannot summon much indignation to denounce them. At the same time, I can express admiration for those individual proprietors or owners of closely held corporations or stockholders of more broadly held corporations who disdain such tactics as approaching fraud.

Whether blameworthy or not, the use of the cloak of social responsibility, and the nonsense spoken in its name by influential and prestigious businessmen, does clearly harm the foundations of a free society. I have been impressed time and again by the schizophrenic character of many businessmen. They are capable of being extremely far-sighted and clearheaded in matters that are internal to their businesses. They are incredibly short-sighted and muddle-headed in matters that are outside their businesses but affect the possible survival of business in general. This short-sightedness is strikingly exemplified in the calls from many businessmen for wage and price guidelines or controls or income policies. There is nothing that could do more in a brief period to destroy a market system and replace it by a centrally controlled system than effective governmental control of prices and wages.

The short-sightedness is also exemplified in speeches by businessmen on social responsibility. This may gain them kudos in the short run. But it helps to strengthen the already too prevalent view that the pursuit of profits is wicked and immoral and must be curbed and controlled by external forces. Once this view is adopted, the external forces that curb the market will not be the social consciences, however highly developed, of the pontificating executives; it will be the iron fist of government bureaucrats. Here, as with price and wage controls, businessmen seem to me to reveal a suicidal impulse.

The political principle that underlies the market mechanism is unanimity. In an ideal free market resting on private property, no individual can coerce any other, all cooperation is voluntary, all parties to such cooperation benefit or they need not participate. There are no values, no "social" responsibilities in any sense other than the shared values and responsibilities of individuals. Society is a collection of individuals and of the various groups they voluntarily form.

The political principle that underlies the political mechanism is conformity. The individual must serve a more general social interest—whether that be determined by a church or a dictator or a majority. The individual may have a vote and say in what is to be done, but if he is overruled, he must conform. It is appropriate for some to require others to contribute to a general social purpose whether they wish to or not.

Unfortunately, unanimity is not always feasible. There are some respects in which conformity appears unavoidable, so I do not see how one can avoid the use of the political mechanism altogether.

But the doctrine of "social responsibility" taken seriously would extend the scope of the political mechanism to every human activity. It does not differ in philosophy from the most explicitly collectivist doctrine. It differs only by professing to believe that collectivist ends can be attained without collectivist means. That is why, in my book *Capitalism and Freedom*, I have called it a "fundamentally subversive doctrine" in a free society, and have said that in such a society, "there is one and only one social responsibility of business—to use its resources and engage in activities designed to increase its profits so long as it stays within the rules of the game, which is to say, engages in open and free competition without deception or fraud."

MILTON FRIEDMAN, U.S. laissez-faire economist, emeritus professor at the University of Chicago, and senior research fellow at Hoover Institution, was one of the leading modern exponents of Liberalism in the nineteenth-century European sense. He was the author of *Capitalism and Freedom* and coauthor of *A Monetary History of the United States* and *Free to Choose*. He was awarded the Nobel Prize for Economics in 1976.

Joseph Hart

The New Capitalists

Is IT POSSIBLE TO MAKE MONEY AND REALLY MAKE A DIFFERENCE?

If you are one of the 8 percent of American consumers who refuse to shop at Wal-Mart for ethical reasons, you might want to pop some valerian tablets before you read on.

Ready?

Wal-Mart: ethical leader. Wal-Mart: environmental steward. Wal-Mart: socially responsible corporation.

If you didn't hurl the magazine across the room, consider the following: In 2004 Wal-Mart established a "global ethics office" to enforce 10 principles, including to "never manipulate, misrepresent, abuse, or conceal information" and "never act unethically—even if someone else instructs you to do so." Employees have access to a confidential hotline to report abuses.

In October 2005 CEO Lee Scott announced a long-range plan to use 100 percent renewable energy at the company. For starters, Wal-Mart is working on a new store design that will reduce energy use by 30 percent in the next three years and plans to double the fuel efficiency of its truck fleet—one of the largest in the world—by 2015.

Earlier this year, the company rolled out expanded benefits for its workforce, which management claims are among the best in the retail sector.

If you can't keep your cynical side from making you squirm, maybe it's because you can't forget the *New York Times* story in October 2005 that revealed that 46 percent of the chain's employees' children are uninsured or on Medicaid. The company has been fined repeatedly for violating the Clean Water Act, including $3.1 million in 2004 for failing to contain runoff at construction sites. Wal-Mart hired Eugene Scalia, former solicitor of the Department of Labor and son of U.S. Supreme Court associate justice Antonin Scalia, to defend the corporation against three whistle-blower lawsuits, and federal prosecutors just recently nailed vice chairman Tom Coughlin for embezzling $500,000 to buy, among other things, supplies for his hunting dogs and a couple cases of Smirnoff. (When he was accused, Coughlin claimed he used the money for union busting, a response that can be filed under cold comfort.)

So which is the real face of Wal-Mart? The easy-being-green family-owned company that donated nearly $1 million to make Sesame Street episodes that help military kids cope with the Iraq war? Or the I-love-trash megachain that, according to a study conducted at Penn State, actually ends up reinforcing, not improving, countywide poverty rates when it plops down a store?

The plain fact is that in today's business world, as companies of all sizes embrace "corporate social responsibility," or CSR, villains can be heroes and the Man often acts like a gentleman. The simple principle of CSR is that companies should enhance the public good. As a result, a growing number of giant international corporations are appointing CSR vice presidents, launching environmental programs, scrutinizing suppliers' human rights records, and adopting ethical guidelines to govern corporate behavior.

Critics of CSR say it's a sop to special interest groups and unions, a ploy to promote deregulation, or a "greenwash" to cover up malfeasance (many companies, like Wal-Mart, have websites peppered with heartwarming facts and stories). But there's no denying that CSR initiatives have genuine value. If every corporation adopted Wal-Mart's pledge to reduce energy use by 30 percent in the next three years, for example, the effect would be profound.

CSR also represents a fundamental shift in our collective understanding of the role of business in society. It's no longer enough, more and more corporations are conceding, for capitalism to simply make money. It must also make a difference.

BACK IN 1982, futurist John Naisbitt accurately predicted globalization and the information age in his outrageously successful book *Megatrends* (Warner Books). He and his partner, Patricia Aburdene, turned the book into a megabrand with regular forays into the future. The latest, *Megatrends 2010* (Hampton Roads, 2005), penned by Aburdene alone, predicts "the rise of conscious capitalism."

Aburdene says that capitalism is finding its soul and traces the discovery to the activist movements of the 1970s and 1980s that lobbied successfully for, for example, divestment of South African stocks. Since then, a growing number of Americans have sought a spiritual path and they're bringing their spirituality into the workplace. Add the refusal of GenXers to sacrifice life for work and the campaigns by students against corporate abuses like sweatshop labor, and the broad seeds of a grassroots revolution were planted.

Then came the now-familiar series of disasters in global capitalism: the tech-stock bubble, the Asian market crash, 9/11, and waves of U.S. corporate scandals. And business as usual hit the breaking point. "We have been facing the worst crisis in capitalism since the Great Depression," Aburdene told Utne, "and we are seeing the cost of what I call 'unconscious' capitalism—the idea that the sole purpose of business is to make money."

Now-retired U.S. Federal Reserve chairman Alan Greenspan wrote the obituary for bottom-line thinking, unknowingly perhaps, in 2002. As Congress debated its response to Wall Street's book cooking, Greenspan criticized the architects of the scandals. "An infectious greed seemed to grip much of our business community," he told the Senate Committee on Banking, Housing, and Urban Affairs. "Our market system depends critically on trust. Trust in the word of our colleagues and trust in the word of those with whom we do business."

In the world of free-market, bottom-line capitalism, the underlying logic driving Greenspan's comments is radical: It opens the door to an entirely different way of seeing business—one that allows room for values other than self-interest.

Free-market capitalism rests on the creed that the supremacy of self-interest makes the market the only "realistic" method of organizing our society. The *Economist*, for example, in January 2005 ran a lengthy critique of CSR, which argued that "for strictly selfish reasons," corporations do the right thing: "The goal of a well-run company may be to make profits for its shareholders, but merely in doing that–provided it faces competition in its markets, behaves honestly, and obeys the law-the company, without even trying, is doing good works."

The illogic is typical: Either the company is acting out of "strictly selfish reasons," or it is balancing that selfishness with honesty and lawfulness.

Inevitably, the *Economist* article conjures the ghost of Adam Smith, whose "invisible hand" theory is a favorite of the free-market-at-any-cost set. Merely by pursuing our own interests, Smith posits, we advance the interests of society as a whole. "It is not from the benevolence of the butcher, the brewer, or the baker, that we expect our dinner," he wrote in *The Wealth of Nations*, "but from their regard to their own interest."

Introduce an imbalance in power, however, and Smith's theory collapses and powerful elites become ruthless in their pursuit of self-interest, as they did in the Stalinist labor camps and the slave plantations of the Old South.

Moreover, self-interest is only one facet of human behavior. The butcher throws scraps to his dog—where's the self-interest in that? He might give a bargain to a customer out of pity or plain old friendliness. In fact, the entire theory represents such a diminished view of humanity and is so disprovable in practice that it's surprising anyone believes it. Or would be, if it didn't rationalize greed.

A better word for the relationship between the butcher and his customer is reciprocity. Smith's notion of self-interest is easily contained in the term—in a reciprocal relationship, after all, both sides get something. But unlike mere self-interest, reciprocity implies mutual acknowledgment, interdependence, and diplomacy. In short, it's the "win-win" of reciprocity, not greed masquerading as self-interest, that forms an appropriate foundation for a civil society.

IF DONALD TRUMP is the comb-over king of the Adam Smith bottom-liners, the figurehead of reciprocity is Josh Mailman. You won't find his name in gold letters on any skyscrapers; Mailman's style is unassuming. He is, however, a remarkably active philanthropist and an entrepreneur who invests heavily in businesses that reflect his progressive values. His fingerprints are on virtually every major socially responsible business venture in the nation.

In 1987 Mailman helped form the Social Venture Network, a kind of incubator for entrepreneurs who measure success by the "triple bottom line" of people, planet, and profits. Over the years, the organization has in turn launched a number of initiatives, including Business for Social Responsibility, which helps large corporations adopt CSR initiatives; the Business Alliance for Local Living Economies, which promotes local and sustainable practices for small entrepreneurs; and Net Impact, which functions as a network for swapping ideas for young socially minded leaders.

Social Venture Network's membership includes familiar brands like Clif Bar, Greyston Bakery, and Tom's of Maine. It also includes progressive media outlets, such as Mother Jones, the Nation, and Utne (editor in chief and CEO Nina Utne is on the board).

Unlike larger corporations, smaller socially responsible entrepreneurs aren't seeking to balance "immoral" profit seeking with "moral" social responsibility projects, says Social Venture Network co-executive director Pam Chaloult. Instead, "they believe, fundamentally, that business can be and should be a force for social change." The triple bottom line is built right into their business plans.

For example, Pura Vida, a leading fair trade coffee dealer based in Seattle, not only offers farmers a just price, it invests millions of dollars in the Latin American communities where the coffee is grown; the Wisconsin co-op Organic Valley is run by farmers who take home 45 percent of the company's profits.

Because they are guided by a mission of change, unfettered by corporate legal structures, and agile in their response to changing customer demands, socially minded entrepreneurs running small-scale businesses are the natural leaders of the new capitalism of reciprocity. They have "helped initiate a fundamental shift in the way private enterprise is conducted," writes the founder of the green cleaning products company Seventh Generation, Jeffrey Hollender, in *What Matters Most* (Basic Books, 2003). "Big global companies have begun speaking our language and even emulating some of what we've done."

There is at least one major obstacle to corporate America's getting a conscience: the legal structure of the corporation itself. "It is set up by statute to serve the best interest of the shareholder, and that's creating wealth," says Joel Bakan, author of *The Corporation* (Free Press, 2004) and collaborator on the recent film by the same name. "Any manager or director who actually pursued the triple bottom line at the expense of shareholder interests would be acting illegally."

One fix to that problem is to expand the notion of "shareholder interests." Since the 1960s, coalitions of activists, religious groups, and investors have introduced shareholder resolutions to denounce corporate misdeeds and demand reform. The proliferating social investment funds, which screen corporations for various ethical practices, frequently hold stocks in "bad" companies for this very purpose. Since the Wall Street accounting scandals, the number of these resolutions has reached record levels, and votes in their favor are on the rise. Thus far, actual reforms have been relatively modest, tending toward negotiations and releases of reports, not shifts in conduct.

Another reform strategy is to change the legal definition of corporations. Businesspeople and reformers in several states, including Minnesota, California, and Missouri, are attempting to craft legislation that would do so. One such group is the Boston-based Corporation 2020, an organization founded by *Business Ethics* magazine and the Tellus Institute, which proposes a new kind of charter that balances profit margins with environmental stewardship, human rights, and ethical practices.

THERE WILL PROBABLY always be an inherent contradiction between making a buck and making a difference. Enron itself, in the year before its collapse, released a triple bottom-line CSR report that promised to slash greenhouse emissions, honor global human rights, and strive for honesty and transparency. Certainly until corporations are legally compelled to expand the notion of shareholder value from its current narrow focus on profits, environmental and social justice policies will have to be justified in terms of making money—whether by direct savings or through the indirect rewards of marketing and public relations.

Some hope, however, that the combined forces of CSR values, consumer demand, and shareholder pressure can align doing well with doing good. For example, fuel costs are compelling corporations to reduce their energy dependence at the same time that consumers are demanding greener goods. The end result, intended or not, is environmental reform.

Consider Wal-Mart's energy independence pledge. "We have taken a lot of heat from some of our supporters for working with Wal-Mart," says Cory Lowe, outreach coordinator at the nonprofit Rocky Mountain Institute, which is providing technical support in Wal-Mart's store and truck redesigns. "But we want to save the most barrels of oil we can. Wal-Mart's fleet gets 6 miles per gallon, which is terrible. We're going to move them to 12, and that alone will make a huge difference."

Stories like this one, says *Megatrends* author Patricia Aburdene, prove that honoring values other than profits can actually improve the bottom line. "Money isn't the root of all evil—pursuit of money is," she says. "Conscious capitalists want to make money, too, and to that extent we're just as greedy as we used to be. But we want to do it by doing right by our communities and our employees and the planet as a whole. The fact that our businesses are outperforming the unconscious capitalists shows that we're onto something."

JOSEPH HART is an associate editor of Utne.

EXPLORING THE ISSUE

Is Increasing Profits the Only Social Responsibility of Business?

Critical Thinking and Reflection

1. Is corporate social responsibility a "fundamentally subversive doctrine?" Why or why not?
2. Milton Friedman's bottom-line perspective continues to be the governing principle of corporate life. With all the changes that have taken place in society since his article was written, why is this so?
3. Why does Friedman claim that social responsibility is short-term thinking that will lead to the destruction of the market system?
4. What impact does corporate strategy have on your decision, as a consumer, to purchase those products or services?

Is There Common Ground?

One reason why there may not appear to be much common ground between Friedman and Hart is that they are answering different questions. Asking about the obligations of the managers of the corporation, Friedman notes that the managers are not dealing with their own money, but with the investors' expectations; that there is no way to get permission from the shareholders to use their money in any but the expected way, by distribution; that therefore any dispersal of the money saved with the shareholders as dividends is clearly wrong. For him, that's the end of the "corporate social responsibility" discussion. Hart, on the other hand, is asking about the way that the corporation fits in productively with its environment to satisfy the conventions of morality shared by all the corporations' stakeholders—customers, municipal authorities, teachers in the schools, and, no doubt, the corporate managers themselves.

Traditionally, corporations have not acted as Friedman would apparently have them act. They have sponsored Little League teams, high school yearbook pages, and sometimes the opera, symphony orchestra, and museums in the towns where they operate. Should irate shareholders show up demanding their dividends, corporate managers have had no trouble explaining their decisions. The explanation was simple: We need the goodwill of the community in order to survive. We need the town council on our side or they'll raise our taxes, pass zoning laws that will forbid us to expand, and start nosing around our effluent pipes. We need to show that we're good citizens. We need the movers and shakers of the town—the ones who support the opera and orchestra and the arts in general—on our side, so they will speak up for us and not let the local papers turn against us. We need to show that we support what they support. We need to advertise, and we advertise on the uniforms of the best Little League team in town. The messaging of the image—Goodwill and Public Relations—has been the justification for charity, and often the courts have accepted that justification.

The corporations might add, for the benefit of the public, that the private profits demanded by the shareholders also help the town. They lead to greater income for all the small businesses in town and make a comfortable addition to the town funds through their taxes. A profitable corporation helps the town economy to grow, and a growing economy makes everyone more prosperous.

In the end, there is a lot of good that can come from the harmony between the corporation and the environment, natural and social. The moralist will not approve the entirely selfish, manipulative reasons that the corporations advance (in the privacy of their investors' meetings) for their good works. But these reasons fit well with Friedman's convictions. Possibly there is common ground here, after all.

Additional Resources

Guler Aras and David Crowther, *Global Perspectives on Corporate Governance and CSR* (Surrey, England: Grower Applied Business Research, 2009).

Subhabrata Bobby Banerjee, *Corporate Social Responsibility: The Good, the Bad, and the Ugly* (Cheltham, UK: Edward Elgar Publishing, 2007).

Milton Friedman, "A Friedman Doctrine: The Social Responsibility of Business Is to Increase Its Profits," *The New York Times Magazine* (September 13, 1970).

Michael Hopkins, *Corporate Social Responsibility and International Development* (Oxford, England: Earthscan, 2007).

Geoffrey P. Lantos, "The Boundaries of Strategic Corporate Social Responsibility," *Journal of Consumer Marketing* (vol. 18, no. 7, 2001).

John Mackey and T. J. Rodgers, "Rethinking the Social Responsibility of Business," *Reason* (October 2005).

John Mackey and Raj Sisodia. "Conscious Capitalism" Is Not an Oxymoron, *Harvard Business Review* (January 14, 2013).

Joshua D. Margolis and James P. Walsh. "Misery Loves Companies: Rethinking Social Initiatives by Business," *Administrative Science Quarterly* (vol. 48, no. 2, June 2003).

Lance Moir, "What Do We Mean by Corporate Social Responsibility?" *Corporate Governance* (vol. 1, no. 2, 2001).

Internet References . . .

Conscious Capitalism

www.consciouscapitalism.org

Corporate Social Responsibility

www.sourcewatch.org/index.php/Corporate_social _responsibility

Michael Noer, David M. Ewalt, and Tara Weiss, "Corporate Social Responsibility," *Forbes*

www.forbes.com/2008/10/16/corporate-social-respon-sibility-corprespons08-lead-cx_mn_de_tw_1016csr _land.html

Reference for Business, "Corporate Social Responsibility"

www.referenceforbusiness.com/management/Comp -De/Corporate-Social-Responsibility.html

Social Venture Network

http://svn.org

Selected, Edited, and with Issue Framing Material by:
Gina Vega, *Organizational Ergonomics*

ISSUE

Can Ethics Codes Build "True" Corporate Ethics?

YES: Eric Krell, from "How to Conduct an Ethics Audit: An Ethics Audit Can Reveal Gaps in Your Ethics Policies and Practices," *HR Magazine* (2010)

NO: Greg Young and David S. Hasler, from "Managing Reputational Risks: Using Risk Management for Business Ethics and Reputational Capital," *Strategic Finance* (2010)

Learning Outcomes

After reading this issue, you will be able to:

- Discuss how the reputational risk approach to ethics within the corporation is similar to the proposed ethics audit article.
- Distinguish how all of the the authors explain choices within the business world for the employee and the corporation.
- Understand the concept of an ethics audit and if the proper place for constructing the audit is within human resources or within the executive ranks.
- Distinguish Young and Hasler's views in light of recent governmental regulations such as the Dodd Frank Act.
- Understand the need for reputational capital as well as ethical behavior within a business enterprise.

ISSUE SUMMARY

YES: Eric Krell finds that one of the major corporate goals of the human resource office is to build true corporate ethics. He believes this can be done with a code of ethics, through performance reviews, and with ethics audits. Through this process, employees' good and corporate good can become the same.

NO: Greg Young and David S. Hasler believe that strengthening the role of ethical and reputational capital has been given the short shrift within corporations. It may be that one day ethics audits and ethics codes could be essential in building capital. However, they state that until management understands that poor ethics make for poor profits, business practices will continue to ignore the place of an ethics core within their organization.

Since the collapse of Enron early in the current century, corporate ethics has taken a much more prominent position of importance. In Congress, new legislation was adopted to promote corporate integrity, such as the Sarbanes–Oxley Act, which states that publicly traded companies must disclose whether they have a code of

ethics to deter wrongdoing. The 2010 Dodd–Frank Wall Street Reform and Consumer Protection Act has also given many corporations an added incentive to create a culture of ethics in their individual places of business.

One of the newer procedures that corporations have begun to implement is to conduct what is called an "ethics audit." As its name suggests, a third party is given the task of performing detailed inspections to determine whether employees are adhering to a clearly stated set of ethical codes. According to Eric Krell, these "ethics audits have been implemented in significant numbers." The Ethics Resource Center's 2009 National Business Ethics Survey notes that on-the-job misconduct is down, whistle-blowing is up, and ethical organizational cultures are stronger. Krell finds the audits helpful and also stresses that management in human resources should set the overall ethical tone for the company. Human resource managers have the ability to go over performance reviews and determine whether problems are developing or being allowed to slide. An outside firm or consultant could also be hired to conduct the ethics audit. Krell explains that the more frequent the audits, the more the company will know if its policies and procedures are being practiced in an ethical manner. Krell further explains that the firm must explain a clear and concise code of conduct and strong definitions of ethical behavior. He contends that the risk of neglecting ethics audits can be dangerous because when unethical conduct is allowed, it will affect the stakeholders, including suppliers, customers, and the overall community. Unethical behavior has an immediate effect on the overall organization. He believes that ethics audits can stop problems before they have a chance to grow.

Despite these trends of improved ethical communication in corporate cultures, Greg Young and David Hasler suggest that this is simply not enough. They maintain what is needed is an understanding by CEOs and company owners that "unethical conduct puts reputational capital—and economic value—at risk." In other words, there is an inherent economic value in having a strong reputation for ethical conduct in the world, as well as goodwill from stakeholders such as employees, customers, and local citizens. Young and Hasler argue that what has prevented CEOs and company owners from adopting this view in the past are two obstacles: "anticipating reputational risks and . . . quantifying reputational capital."

Young and Hasler recommend implementing a new system called *enterprise risk management,* or ERM. This system incorporates such Western philosophical principles as personal virtue, distributive justice, and economic efficiency into a measurable format. By assigning dollar values to the inherent risks in public reputation and willingness to cooperate from stakeholders, the economic value of ethical decisions can be measured strictly in dollars and cents.

In short, Young and Hasler believe that ERM is needed for companies to have a true incentive for acting ethically. If CEOs can be persuaded to believe that ethical misdeeds are hurting their bottom line, then they will do what it takes to rectify their company's behavior. They argue that ERM provides ample evidence that "lapses in business ethics can lead to enterprise costs, damaged relationships . . . that significantly harm financial performance."

YES

Eric Krell

How to Conduct an Ethics Audit: An Ethics Audit Can Reveal Gaps in Your Ethics Policies and Practices

When it comes to corporate ethics, bad news is good news. According to the Ethics Resource Center's 2009 National Business Ethics Survey, on-the-job misconduct is down, whistle-blowing is up, and ethical organizational cultures are stronger. Despite these trends, there may be no better time for human resource managers to conduct or participate in ethics-related audits.

Setting the Tone

Several legal developments in recent years have placed newfound focus on how companies behave. An example is the Sarbanes–Oxley Act, with its emphasis on "tone at the top" and its requirement that publicly traded companies disclose whether they have a code of ethics to deter wrongdoing. The Federal Acquisition Regulation and the Federal Sentencing Guidelines also have a significant impact on organizations' ethics policies and practices by requiring or providing incentives to encourage businesses of all kinds and sizes to adopt codes of conduct, train their employees on these codes, and create effective audit and reporting mechanisms.

HR professionals play a crucial role in shaping corporate ethical codes, policies and procedures and then communicating and teaching that information to the workforce. In many companies, the top HR manager either serves as the de facto chief ethics and compliance officer or works with the person in that role to manage ethics and compliance programs. Apart from the chief executive officer, there may be no more important ethical role model in the organization than an HR manager.

"Employees watch HR like hawks, and they should," says Phillip Daniels, SPHR, HR manager for Montgomery College in Rockville, Md. "If HR managers mess up, how can we expect employees to adhere to the ethical standards that we're promoting? As HR managers,

we essentially need to serve as the poster children for ethical behavior."

HR managers who thrive as ethical role models almost always play central roles in conducting ethics-related audits, notes Marjorie Doyle, principal of ethics consulting firm Marjorie Doyle & Associates in Landenberg, Pa., and a member of the Advisory Board of Directors for the Society of Corporate Compliance and Ethics. As a former chief corporate ethics and compliance officer, "I spent a lot of time with HR," she says.

HR managers are "trying to get people to do the right thing. They also tend to manage the annual performance review process and operate the communications network within the company, both of which are crucial to ethics audits," Doyle says. "They have a feel for whether certain behaviors are as ethical as they need to be."

Daniels agrees. "As an HR manager, you have to be out there listening and identifying potential problems," he says. "Not every unethical behavior or practice exerts a direct financial impact, but we should be looking for those issues because doing so can help improve the organization."

Laying the Groundwork

Ethics audits ensure that behaviors an organization espouses in its code of conduct and policies and procedures exist in practice and that behavior forbidden in these documents does not occur.

The risk of neglecting ethics audits can be severe. After its ethics-related implosion, Enron became well-known for the fact that the framed values statements in conference rooms were at odds with employees' behavior on trading floors. And, more-immediate problems potentially exist for companies that do not conduct ethics audits: "Employees' faith in the organization can deteriorate," says Art Crane, SPHR, president of HR advisory firm Capstone Services in

Sherman, Conn. "Morale can decline. A company sets a dangerous precedent by letting something that violates its ethics policy slide."

The danger can spread to other stakeholders, including customers, suppliers and community members. "If word gets out that you are not an ethical organization, you run the risk of losing business," Crane notes.

Conducting an ethics audit requires a team effort as well as a clear definition of ethical behavior. While many larger companies staff a chief ethics and compliance officer position, that individual is not solely responsible for each employee's behavior.

For this reason, Conway, Ark.-based Nabholz Construction Co. has an ethics committee consisting of top legal, finance, HR and operational executives. "We want to have diverse skills on the committee and to make sure all of our geographies are represented," says Andrea Woods, SPHR, vice president and corporate counsel for the private company with about 850 employees.

Nabholz Construction's ethics committee takes responsibility for monitoring and investigating ethics hotline calls and e-mails. The hotline system is managed by a third-party provider, an arrangement that Woods says strengthens objectivity and independence. The committee conducts ethics audits as part of an annual internal audit process. In addition, a divisional controller, an HR employee and Woods conduct spot ethics audits on the recommendation of the committee.

The frequency Woods describes—annual audits on all ethics-related areas and spot ethics audits on an as-needed basis in response to risk assessments—jibes with what ethics consultants recommend. Depending on company size and auditing resources, Crane notes, some companies may audit their entire ethics programs only once every two years. However, the occurrence of a major organizational realignment may necessitate more frequent ethics audits in its wake.

Whether or not corporate leaders seek outside help on ethics audits depends on the nature and magnitude of the issues. "If the issue involves something very important to the company, it helps to get an outside perspective and the impartial judgment that a third party provides," Crane says. "If the company conducts the audit internally and outside stakeholders are paying close attention to the issue, it can be more difficult to say, 'Yes, we audited our ethics internally and everything is just fine.' That may be received as a matter of the fox guarding the henhouse."

Making It Tangible

Regardless of whether ethics audits are woven into internal audit processes, performed internally in response to changing risk profiles or conducted by an external auditor, the question is "What are you auditing against?" says Mark Snyderman, senior knowledge leader at LRN, a company that helps businesses develop ethical corporate cultures.

The answer requires a distinction between two disciplines frequently lumped together in corporate America: ethics and compliance.

Ethics refers to the amorphous area of behavior. Compliance refers to adherence to legal regulations. A company may be fully compliant yet still engage in unethical practices. While that may seem like a clear distinction on paper, it becomes muddled in a global business environment.

"There are many countries around the world that don't have antitrust laws," says Snyderman, who previously served as chief ethics and compliance officer and assistant general counsel for Coca-Cola. "A company could in theory engage in price fixing in those countries. From an ethical standpoint, however, I would recommend that every company take the position 'We are not going to do that.'"

Compliance audits compare internal behaviors to external regulations. Ethics audits compare internal behaviors to internal guidelines on behavior—guidelines that exist in corporate codes of conduct and ethics-related policies and procedures. Of course, some compliance problems may stem from ethical lapses; others may arise from process or operational bugs. That's why many business leaders conduct ethical audits in tandem with financial or operational audits.

"Your code of conduct—some companies call it a code of ethics—represents your central document," Snyderman says. "This document should be generated from the company's values."

The code should be translated into specific guidance within policies and procedures. "You don't need to start out with the 10 commandments and 500 related rules, but you do need to have something specific to audit against," Doyle says. For example, what does an ethical violation related to bribery or conflict of interest look like? "Be very descriptive in your policies and procedures about what these things mean," she recommends. Also, have managers and employees establish performance goals related to ethics and compliance so employees can be evaluated against those objectives.

Doyle says greater specificity in ethics-related policies and procedures paves the way for ethics-related performance objectives and metrics. These metrics help enable more-tangible ethics audits. "One of the most difficult challenges is making this highfalutin-sounding concept of ethics actually become very granular," she adds.

Filling the HR Role

An ethics audit resembles a financial or operational audit. It involves interviews with employees and managers, reviews of records and other information, and, sometimes, observations of processes and practices.

The most common ethics audits, Snyderman and Crane report, examine conflicts of interest, access to company information, bidding and award practices, giving and receiving gifts, and employee discrimination issues.

Snyderman describes the actual audits as time-consuming and based on checklists. They involve a team that typically consists of an HR professional, an internal auditor, legal managers, and an ethics and compliance manager. The team visits an area of the organization to conduct research in response to a specific incident or as part of an ongoing auditing cycle.

The primary mission is to compare ethics guidelines with actual behaviors, but team members also look for other issues that may need to be addressed through communications, training or subsequent audits.

The team clearly identifies who will be interviewed and what information and observations are required. "Generally, the HR person on the team knows people in the department and will introduce the team," Doyle says.

HR professionals also play a pivotal role in responding to ethical or legal issues or violations that the audit identifies, whether the response takes the form of disciplining an employee, conveying educational material about the topic to a larger audience or integrating the topic into training. If the ethics audit concerns employment issues, HR typically takes a lead role in conducting the audit, Snyderman reports.

During her previous work as a chief ethics and compliance officer for DuPont and VetcoGray, Doyle says, HR managers were her "main partners," ones she worked with to incorporate ethics-related measures into annual performance reviews. At VetcoGray, now a General Electric oil and gas business, for example, she teamed with HR managers to tie 20 percent of employees' base salaries and 20 percent of bonus compensation to specific ethics performance measures.

"If there is an ethics and compliance officer in the company and they have not contacted the HR manager, the HR manager should knock on that person's door, sit down and talk about how your jobs are very much intertwined," Doyle advises.

Eric Krell is a freelance writer, working with topics such as "corporate finance, corporate governance and compliance, business continuity management, the management consulting sector, human capital management, enterprise technology ROI, healthy living and personal fulfillment." His articles can be found in a wide variety of publications, from *Men's Fitness* to *Cooking Light,* to *Baylor Business Review*. Krell received his education at the College of William and Mary and holds a BA from this institution.

**Greg Young and
David S. Hasler**

Managing Reputational Risks: Using Risk Management for Business Ethics and Reputational Capital

Lapses in business ethics can lead to enterprise costs, damaged relationships with key stakeholders, and lost opportunities that significantly harm financial performance. Conversely, an enterprise's reputation for ethical conduct can be a crucial asset for achieving its strategic and financial objectives. It's surprising, therefore, that the role of ethics and reputational capital are the least developed aspects of enterprise risk management (ERM).

The *Enterprise Risk Management—Integrated Framework* and guidelines from the Committee of Sponsoring Organizations of the Treadway Commission (COSO) are fast becoming standards for best practices in organizations (www.coso.org/guidance.htm). While there are many varieties of ERM in practice today, all recognize that ethical values underlie a firm's ability to accomplish enterprise objectives. Yet much of the current discussion about ethics focuses on corporate culture, conduct, and compliance in a post-Enron world of the Sarbanes–Oxley Act (SOX) and corporate sentencing guidelines. Though important, these dimensions don't directly examine the value of ethics as an asset to build trust in important business relationships. As a consequence, most people's understanding of best practices to manage business ethics is limited.

Here we explore stakeholders' perceptions of ethics in order to bring reputational capital more clearly to the forefront of ERM. We do so by extending the ERM paradigm to identify and assess risks to reputational capital. First, we suggest a process to identify the scope of ethical principles and behaviors that are most appropriate for building reputational capital by illustrating this process with the *IMA Statement of Ethical Professional Practice*. Second, we account for differences in enterprise context that systematically narrow the focus of ethics governance. Third, we describe a framework that integrates ethics with the COSO ERM components to elicit stakeholders' assessments of enterprise reputational capital.

What's at Stake?

The foundational role of ethics in ERM isn't surprising. Business misconduct can lead to direct costs of legal fees, monetary fines, sanctions, and operational recovery. Given a choice in partnering, stakeholders—relationship partners such as employees, customers, suppliers, community groups, and owners—are likely to prefer a relationship with an enterprise that has a reputation for integrity. For the enterprise, a reputation for poor ethics can lead to costs of replacing lost partners or going it alone. Labor, operating, and overhead costs may increase if the enterprise is perceived to be so unprincipled in its conduct toward employees that its recruiting and retention of skilled personnel are at risk. Similarly, purchasing, logistics, and overhead costs may increase if suppliers judge the enterprise to be unfair or dishonest.

In our post-Enron/WorldCom/Tyco era, reputations of large, publicly traded companies (for better or worse) are likely to be broadly known. Public reaction to notorious lapses in business ethics has increased worldwide legislative, regulatory, judicial, and media demands for visibility into corporate governance of business ethics. In this context, an enterprise reputation that fosters goodwill has economic value. Unethical conduct puts reputational capital—and economic value—at risk.

Traditionally, the practice of ethics management has focused on corporate ethical values within the organization and sequential activities to prevent, detect, report, and respond to misconduct. But this focus on misconduct limits people's understanding of ethics as a form of reputational capital that has value in important business relationships. Moreover, the focus on misconduct makes it difficult to integrate traditional ethics programs within the ERM framework.

Given such a consequential role for ethics and the momentum of ERM in current business practice, it's surprising that ethics isn't more developed in the ERM discussion. As George L. Head wrote in expert commentary for the International Risk Management Institute in February 2005 (see www.irmi.com/expert/articles/2005/head02 .aspx), "[T]he fields of ethics and risk management need each other. Good risk management and good ethics are, and need to be, linked . . . [but] I have used the word 'ethics' in print probably less than 100 times."

Two important obstacles to extending ERM to ethics have been the difficulties in anticipating reputational risks and in quantifying reputational capital. We seek to overcome these difficulties with a structured process to elicit stakeholder judgments about a company's commitment to principled ethical behavior in their relationship.

Building on ethical responsibilities to stakeholders is increasingly recognized as a best practice in organizational ethics programs, but so far this approach hasn't been integrated with risk management. Importantly, quantifying stakeholder assessments lends itself to aggregation for an overall perspective on enterprise-level risk to reputational capital. Let's now look at a process that identifies the scope of ethical principles and behaviors most appropriate for building reputational capital.

Identifying Ethics and Behaviors for Reputational Capital

To illustrate a structured approach, we'll draw on principles from the *IMA Statement of Ethical Professional Practice,* which you can find at www.imanet.org/PDFs/Statement %20of%20Ethics_web.pdf, mapping them to the ethical content on which trustworthy reputations are built and describing enterprise behavior that embodies that content in stakeholder relationships: "*The fundamental principles in the* IMA Statement of Ethical Professional Practice *are Honesty, Fairness, Objectivity, and Responsibility. Members shall act in accordance with these principles and shall encourage others within their organizations to adhere to them.*"

In Table 1 we juxtapose these fundamental IMA principles—honesty, fairness, objectivity, and responsibility— with concise descriptions of their associated ethical

Table 1

Ethical Principles and Enterprise Behavior: Drivers of Reputational Capital in Enterprise-Stakeholder Relationships

IMA Principle of Ethical Professional Practice	Ethical Principles from Western Philosophy	Stakeholders' Perception of Enterprise Behavior in Relationship
Honesty	**Personal Virtue:** Act with the intention of causing pride and avoiding shame; take responsibility to nurture trustworthy relationships with honesty and integrity.	(a) Trustworthy, honest, cooperative, and deserving esteem. (b) Every level of the enterprise (i.e., each component of COSO ERM framework) nurtures relationship with stakeholder.
Responsibility	**Legal Compliance:** A responsible member of society does not violate laws enacted by legitimate legislative, regulatory, or judicial processes and nurtures relationships when legal institutions are just emerging or transitioning from one form to another.	Obeys established legal institutions governing the enterprise's operations; develops relationships to govern operations where legal institutions are not well-established.
Objectivity	**Economic Efficiency:** Act with the intention of achieving best possible profits without harming others, subject to market and legal constraints. Inform business relationships with objective information regarding product features, prices, and activity costs.	(a) Access to useful, unbiased information on product features, prices, and activity costs; (b) Does no harm to free markets, public safety, and environment while pursuing its own profit; (c) Alert to best profit-making opportunities.
Fairness (in outcomes)	**Distributive Justice:** Share value-added with stakeholders; form and sustain business relationships by showing fairness in care and respect for the needs of others; take responsibility to produce outcomes stakeholders prefer and find beneficial.	Fair in prices, costs, and activities to support stakeholders' preferences.
Fairness (in process)	**Procedural Justice:** Give stakeholders fair access to have their voice heard in your decision making so their interests are protected even if they disagree with a decision outcome.	Gives fair access to participate in activities and decisions.

principles from Western philosophy—personal virtue, legal compliance, economic efficiency, distributive justice, and procedural justice. The table shows the explicit one-to-one relationship between the first three IMA principles and the principles of personal virtue, legal compliance, and economic efficiency. Interestingly, there are two philosophical flavors of fairness to discuss with stakeholders—fairness in enterprise outcomes and fairness in enterprise decision procedures (see Table 1, bottom two rows).

The value of reputational capital is a function of benefits gained and costs avoided because of stakeholders' willingness to cooperate in order to accomplish enterprise goals. As reputational capital increases, the enterprise can better leverage stakeholder relationships to increase its own productivity. [The] enterprise has ethical principles at its core that drive its behavior in relationships, stake-holder perceptions of the enterprise can be elicited in the structure of the ERM framework, and the enterprise-stakeholder relationship is the locus where a company earns reputational capital and the stakeholder grants it. The relationship is where stakeholders interact with the enterprise and detect the integrity with which enterprise behavior fits with its stated values. Reputation is the stakeholders' perception of patterns in these interactions and behaviors.

We describe a method to prompt stakeholders to identify and quantify their perspective on an enterprise's reputational capital. This method integrates the ethical principles described in Table 1 with the eight ERM components of the COSO framework. This structure elicits a comprehensive dialogue with stakeholders about the drivers of and risks to reputational capital in the enterprise-stakeholder relationship. The comprehensiveness of this approach is a particularly valuable aid to risk management when ethical principles aren't uniformly prominent within the enterprise.

Before we detail the integrated structure, we first describe the strategic context that influences management to be more attentive to some ethical principles and stakeholders and less attentive to others. In these situations, the comprehensive structure provided by integrating the ethical principles with the COSO framework guides risk managers to elicit stakeholder descriptions of enterprise reputational risk that might otherwise be overlooked.

The relative prominence of the ethical principles in the internal environment may vary from one enterprise to another. The unique context of an organization is likely to influence management to give more attention to some principles over others. Understanding the distinctive content of different ethical principles, therefore, gives insight into the basis for an enterprise's reputation with stakeholders. For example, the principles most prominent to the managers of a small corporation selling to a more powerful customer, such as a vendor selling to Walmart, may differ from those values most prominent to the managers of a large retailer sourcing from weaker suppliers, such as The Body Shop's relationships with small villages and women-led cooperatives in emerging economies.

Two important dimensions in an enterprise's strategic context—its ownership structure and its bargaining power in stakeholder relationships—may cause its managers to view some ethical principles as more prominent than others in daily operations and decision making.

Publicly owned companies in the U.S. are subject to significant legal and fiduciary obligations and securities regulations, such as SOX. In this context, the legal compliance and economic efficiency principles are heavily weighted in the relationships of publicly owned enterprises with government and shareholders. It follows that ethics management in publicly owned corporations will prominently feature these two principles.

Privately owned enterprises, on the other hand, are relatively free of compliance requirements from SOX, the Securities & Exchange Commission (SEC), and shareholder lawsuits. Coming to the fore of management's attention instead are partners, customers, and suppliers, whose interests need to be represented fairly in organizational decision making. Accordingly, we expect justice principles will be prominent in stakeholder relationships with privately owned enterprises. When transactions, relationships, and contracts become increasingly complex but not tightly regulated by law, it becomes more difficult to anticipate all possible situations and contingencies that may arise. In this situation, stakeholders are likely to value opportunities to voice their preferences in the enterprise procedures and decision making—the definition of procedural justice.

In another context, an enterprise whose bargaining power isn't strong enough to compel agreements with its stakeholders may induce them to cooperate by calling attention to its reputation for fair distribution of added value. An enterprise culture with visibly prominent distributive justice principles is likely to attract and sustain critical relationships even when the enterprise lacks compelling power.

Table 2

Risk Management of Reputational Capital

	ERM Framework to Elicit Stakeholder Description of Enterprise		
	#1 Internal Environment	#2 Objective Setting	#3 Event Identification
PERSONAL VIRTUE (a) Trustworthy, honest, cooperative, and deserving esteem. (b) Every enterprise level in COSO ERM framework nurtures relationship with stakeholder.			(A) Stakeholder describes future events that, if they were to occur, would change the scores in cells of other columns. (B) For each event described in (A), stakeholder estimates the likelihood that it will occur in the forthcoming period.
LEGAL COMPLIANCE Obeys established legal institutions governing the enterprise's operations; develops relationships to govern operations where legal institutions are not well-established.			
ECONOMIC EFFICIENCY (a) Access to useful, unbiased information on product features, prices, and activity costs; (b) Does no harm to free markets, public safety, and environment while pursuing its own profit; (c) Alert to best profit-making opportunities.			
DISTRIBUTIVE JUSTICE Fair in prices, costs, and activities to support stakeholders' preferences.			
PROCEDURAL JUSTICE Fair access to participate in activities and decisions.			

Table Key

Business ethics programs typically focus on **Personal Virtue** but need to manage reputational capital in ERM framework.	High power and public enterprises likely focus on **Legal Compliance** and **Economic Efficiency** principles of business ethics but may need to manage risks to broader reputational capital.

that arise because of the incentives found in the enterprise. Ownership structures—private or public—and enterprise power relative to the stakeholder (who prevails in bargaining) matter. The table key for Table 2 reminds risk managers to be alert to the full scope of ethical principles that drive stakeholders' judgments and incorporate this broader set in their approach to business ethics excellence.

Reputational Capital and Risk

#4 Risk Assessment	#5 Risk Response	#6 Control Activities	#7 Information & Communication	#8 Monitoring

Assume each event described in Column #3 occurs. (A) What is the new score in each cell of the other columns? (B) Stakeholder estimates the event's consequences (e.g., costs and benefits) for the enterprise.	For each event described in Column #3(A), consider these alternative enterprise responses: avoid the risk, accept it, reduce it, or share it with another party, such as with insurance or with accommodation from your stakeholder group. Make a judgment about each possible alternative response: Is it likely to make scores and consequences prompted in Column #4 better or worse?	

Business ethics programs need to do more to assess reputational capital as guided in ERM Components #3–5.	Low power and private enterprises likely focus on **Distributive Justice** and **Procedural Justice** principles of business ethics but may need to manage risks to broader reputational capital

Table 3

ERM Components Drive Elicitation Dialogue with Stakeholders

#1: INTERNAL ENVIRONMENT	Score the enterprise on the extent to which you believe the following characteristics accurately describe it—trustworthy, honesty, cooperative, integrity.
#2: OBJECTIVE SETTING	Score the enterprise on the extent to which you believe its targets and objectives for the coming period are likely to (a. improve; b. hurt) its relationship with your group.
#6: CONTROL ACTIVITIES	Score the enterprise on the extent to which you believe its policies and procedures ensure it operates in a manner likely to (a. improve; b. hurt) its relationship with your group.
#7: INFORMATION & COMMUNICATION	Score the enterprise on the extent to which you believe its manner of collecting, using, and sharing information is likely to (a. improve; b. hurt) its relationship with your group.
#8: MONITORING	Score the enterprise on the extent to which you believe its manner of detecting violations of operating standards is likely to (a. improve; b. hurt) its relationship with your group.

A Structured Approach Toward Business Ethics Excellence

A risk-management approach to reputational capital becomes truly strategic when it provides:

- Credible and persuasive assurance to senior management—and to the board of directors to whom they are responsible—that the organization is on track to accomplish objectives,
- Reliable monitoring and reporting systems, and
- Activities operating in conformance with the organization's principles.

Shakespeare reminds us in *Hamlet*, however, that "there is nothing either good or bad, but thinking makes it so." Modern business managers may think differently about the appropriate mix of ethical principles given their organizational context and may have diverse stakeholders whose thinking plays significant roles in determining the value and risks to reputational capital.

Obstacles to managing risks to reputational capital include difficulties in identifying and quantifying ethics-based metrics. Further, an enterprise's self-assessment may tend to be inward looking, so the organization may not learn about risks to relationships from the perspective of important stakeholders. Companies can identify and quantify these risks by asking stakeholders how they would assess them if they applied ethical principles to the COSO ERM framework. Accordingly, we suggest more discussion to develop a structured ERM approach toward business ethics excellence that's focused on building reputational capital.

We began this discussion by describing a stakeholder approach to integrating ethics with the components of COSO's ERM framework. We proposed a diagnostic tool to identify the prominent ethical principles embedded in critical relationships and the enterprise context, and we extended the ERM framework to elicit stakeholder assessments of reputational capital. These assessments may identify the expected value of negative consequences, such as direct damages of fines and penalties, cleanup costs including legal and remedial correctives, and costs from damaged relationships with important stakeholders such as customers, employees, suppliers, communities, and government. Positive consequences may include avoiding these negatives, of course, but also may include the expected value of benefits from profit-making activities made feasible by more cooperative and more durable relationships.

We call on ethics managers to use this ERM approach to identify and quantify risks to reputational capital and apply best practices for assuring senior management that the ethical foundations supporting enterprise objectives are well managed.

Greg Young is an associate professor in the College of Management as well as the faculty fellow of the Enterprise Risk Management Initiative at North Carolina State University. Young also serves on the Editorial Board of the *Encyclopedia of Business Ethics and Society*. His areas of research include industry structure, organizational resources, strategic activity, decision making, and competitive advantage. His papers on these topics have been published in journals such as the *Strategic Management Journal* and *Journal of Business Research*.

David S. Hasler is currently the senior director of Finance & Treasury, Investor Relations at Walmart, but has served the company in various other positions since 2006. Hasler holds his MBA from Xavier University.

EXPLORING THE ISSUE

Can Ethics Codes Build "True" Corporate Ethics?

Critical Thinking and Reflection

1. What problems do Young and Hasler see with the emphasis on ethics codes and ethics audits?
2. How might corporation officers instill a deeper and more resilient sense of ethics in their employees?
3. Is it possible that ethics codes are valuable only to the extent that those bound by them helped to write them? Discuss.
4. What is the best plan to implement and enforce a code of ethics within a business?

Is There Common Ground?

Many experts would argue that correctly performed ethics audits are still the most effective way for establishing honesty in company cultures. They argue that in nearly every location where ethics audits have been consistently performed, there have been significant improvements. They contend that the rules do their job as long as they are enforced. By creating detailed rules that everyone must follow and by performing audits regularly, a culture is created where the rules are respected. This in turn leads to an increased comfort in whistle-blowing as well as other mechanisms that prevent ethical breaches. Finally, by employing federal regulations and incentives for those who meet guidelines, it becomes extremely difficult, if not impossible, for a well-regulated company to break the rules.

Additional Resources

Tess Beste, *The Corporate Ethics Audit as a New Tool for Management by Values* (St. Louis, MO: Lightning Source, Inc., 2008).

Ethan B. Kapstein, "The Corporate Ethics Crusades." *Foreign Affairs* (vol. 80, no. 5, 2001, pp. 105–119).

Amey Stone, "Putting Teeth in Corporate Ethics Codes." *BusinessWeek Online* (2004).

"The Good, the Bad, and Their Corporate Code of Ethics: Enron, Sarbanes-Oxley, and the Problems with Legislating Good Behavior." *Harvard Law Review* (vol. 116, no. 7, 2003, p. 2123).

Joseph Wieland, *Standards and Audits for Ethics Management Systems: The European Perspective* (Netherlands: Springer 2013).

Internet References . . .

Scott Clark, "Ethics Audit Essential for Every Business." Biz Journal.com

www.bizjournals.com/milwaukee/stories/2004/03/15/smallb2.html?page=all

David Ingram, "How to Conduct an Ethics Audit." *Small Business Chronicle*

http://smallbusiness.chron.com/conduct-ethical-audit-16101.html

Eric Krell, "How to Conduct an Ethics Audit." *Society for Human Resource Management*

www.shrm.org/Publications/hrmagazine/EditorialContent/2010/0410/Pages/0410agenda_social.aspx

John Rosthorn, "Business Ethics Auditing—More Than a Stakeholder's Toy." *Journal of Business Ethics* (vol. 27, September 2000).

www.jstor.org/discover/10.2307/25074359?uid=3739728&uid=2129&uid=2&uid=70&uid=4&uid=3739256&sid=21102261476641

ISSUE

Selected, Edited, and with Issue Framing Material by:
Gina Vega, *Organizational Ergonomics*

Have the Antitrust Laws Outlived Their Effectiveness vis-à-vis Technology?

YES: **Craig Timberg**, from "FTC: Google Did Not Break Antitrust Law with Search Practices," *Washington Post* (2013)

NO: **Marvin Ammori**, from "The Case for Net Neutrality," *Foreign Affairs* (2014)

Learning Outcomes

After reading this issue, you will be able to:

- Understand the difference between providing benefits to consumers and controlling economic power.
- Differentiate between market efficiencies and market manipulation.
- Evaluate the necessity for regulation of a temporarily depletable resource.

ISSUE SUMMARY

YES: Craig Timberg claims that "The murky standards for establishing consumer harm" have gotten in the way of more serious charges of business practices that hurt competitors and limit consumer choice.

NO: Attorney Marvin Ammori argues that the Federal Communications Commission (FCC) should regulate Internet service providers to assure that some websites are neither given preferential treatment nor charged arbitrary fees in order to reach end users.

"**F**ree Competition" versus the "Nanny State" is the simplified expression of the debate over antitrust regulation. The Free Competition group demands maximum opportunity for both wealth creation and consumer selection. The Nanny Staters demand protection of consumers and entrepreneurs by governmental agencies, resulting in limitation on profit by companies that grow "too large."

Antitrust laws were first passed in 1890 as the Sherman Act to preserve free competition, initially in the area of railroads and later to cover steel, oil, and other commodities. In 1914, two additional antitrust laws were passed: the Federal Trade Commission Act, which created the Federal Trade Commission, and the Clayton Act. These three core federal antitrust laws are still in effect today. According to the Federal Trade Commission (FTC), "These laws promote vigorous competition and protect consumers from anticompetitive mergers and business practices. The FTC's Bureau of Competition, working in tandem with the Bureau of Economics, enforces the antitrust laws for the benefit of consumers."

Antitrust legislation has enjoyed irregular acceptance by business, consumers, and government over the last hundred years, fluctuating between overwhelming support in the early twentieth century until Henry Ford showed that low prices, high wages, and manufacturing efficiency were possible despite what we might identify as a monopoly in the early days of auto manufacturing. Two decades later, it became illegal for chain stores to discount prices, and by the 1970s, concerns about the telephone monopoly were in the air. In 1982, a consent decree broke up AT&T into seven smaller companies to encourage competition and lower prices. Then, the game changed.

In the mid-1990s, the Internet brought a new mode of communication and economic transaction to the economy. As the new century began, Microsoft appealed a judgment against it and won because of Bill Gates's defense. Gates claimed Microsoft always worked on behalf of the consumer and that market efficiencies demanded its growth orientation and innovative practices.

It is sometimes unclear what the antitrust laws require and whom they are protecting, resulting in many suits, counter-suits, decisions, and retractions of decisions. The idea of limiting competition seems anti-capitalist while the idea of protecting consumer interests seems completely pro-American. This is the primary conundrum surrounding antitrust. When we take that conundrum into cyberspace, we add a level of complexity that challenges the justice system on a previously unheard-of plane. What is reasonable protection of consumers in the completely intangible context of Internet technology services? What is unfair competition and coercive monopoly in a rapidly changing environment that demands disruptive innovation to develop new products and services?

This is the environment in which antitrust legislation exists in this age of technology. Beginning with the so-called "network effect" (see Helm, 1996), the ability to engage customers for long periods of time by contract that buys the manufacturer time to develop further improvements without losing purchasers, technology companies have been operating in semi-protected, anti-competitive circumstances. It is the techno-system itself that has created this environment because of the need for time and resources available to improve software, hardware, and delivery systems. If customers are locked into your product/service for a contracted amount of time, you have bought yourself the space and resources you need to maximize innovation and gain larger market share, resulting in market efficiencies.

The downside of this protected system is that it opens the door to predatory pricing policies and other monopolistic practices. Customers are "stuck," at least for a period of time, with your product/service, regardless of the cost (which might or might not be less than the competition's cost). The networking effect operates quickly, and by the time the regulators get around to confronting you, it may well be too late. You may have gained a controlling share of the market.

In addition to concerns created by the network effect, net neutrality has introduced a new wrinkle into the digital antitrust discussion. Net neutrality, which seems by its name to be a positive concept, can present an opportunity for abuse of the system. Supporters of net neutrality want Internet access available without restriction to all users, regardless of how much they use and when they use it. They believe that the Internet should flow with little regulation, but when a resource is limited and regulation is also limited, the result is often abuse of the system, invoking antitrust concerns (Evans, 2014).

As Evans states: "Overconsumption of a depleting asset reduces the amount of the asset available to others who may need it to reach their economically optimal output. If the two parties are competitors, the overconsumption can, theoretically, harm competition." But the Internet is different from a depletable resource; once a download is complete, the digital pipeline is again fully open for use by others. Again, the nature of technology has created a refinement of the antitrust question. If a service is not being used in an exclusionary way, antitrust does not come into play. At this time, we cannot "use up" the Internet; we can only block the pipeline temporarily, creating inconvenience, but not lack of access.

The YES position that antitrust legislation has outlived its usefulness vis-à-vis technology describes how Google has been investigated by the FTC for predatory advertising practices in the way it displayed search results. Google was taken to task for prioritizing its own advertisers in the results of searches. Complaints about their policies revolved around the limited number of alternative search engines that could provide differently prioritized results. The FTC did not require a consent decree, merely extracting promises from Google to make it easier for advertisers to move their ads to alternative search engines. Even the chairman of the FTC acknowledged that they were unable to support a claim of illegal monopolization.

The NO article emphasizes the speed with which technology changes and adapts, and suggests that we must take extra care not to allow technology to control us. The Internet has the potential to "turn into a patchwork of fiefdoms, with untold ripple effects" if sufficient controls are not imposed on growth and usage. The "general purpose" technology of the Internet resembles other industries that led to monopolies, similar to steam engines and telephones. It is critical to get the surrounding of the Internet "right," but the rules themselves are desperately needed.

YES ⬅   Craig Timberg

FTC: Google Did Not Break Antitrust Law with Search Practices

Google emerged from nearly two years of intense federal scrutiny . . . by convincing the Federal Trade Commission that even though rivals may suffer as the company continually refines its search engine, consumers often win through better, faster, more valuable answers to their queries.

But despite the unanimous FTC decision to close its antitrust investigation, U.S. regulators long have struggled to determine what's best for consumers—and what can be successfully addressed with laws written long before anyone imagined the economic role that today's technologies would play.

The murky standards for establishing consumer harm ultimately undermined the case for forceful action on the most serious charges—that Google was manipulating search results to benefit its own products while hurting competitors and limiting choice.

That drained energy from what once appeared to be an aggressive FTC push against Google, leading to modest concessions that are unlikely to be noticed by most of the search engine's hundreds of millions of users. Consumer groups, Google's rivals and some legal analysts say the company now will be emboldened to enhance the visibility of its own products for travel, shopping and other lucrative services in ways that will make it harder for people to find other offerings and will lead to higher prices.

But the FTC was unpersuaded by the evidence at hand. "The American antitrust laws protect competition, not competitors," said Chairman Jon Leibowitz.

Establishing whether consumers have suffered—or are likely to suffer in the future—has long been the quicksand in the middle of U.S. antitrust cases. Wait too long to rein in monopolists, and the damage might be irrevocable. Move too fast, and the evidence of consumer harm might lack the clarity necessary to survive a court challenge.

"It has been the single issue that the antitrust system has had trouble dealing with since 1890," said George

Washington University law professor William Kovacic, a former FTC chairman. "That's because the consumer impacts typically are mixed."

That is even more true in the digital age, when rapid innovation creates and destroys monopolies far more quickly than when railroads and steel manufacturers took commanding market positions that lasted for decades. The speed of change has challenged Washington's ability to act forcefully against technology companies that are increasingly battling one another in overlapping markets.

In a statement posted to Google's company blog Thursday, chief legal officer David Drummond wrote that the FTC's actions affirm that Google's products are "good for users and good for competition."

The company's many critics, however, said that the Google that once evangelized about producing unbiased search results and speeding users off to other sites had been transformed into a predatory company more concerned with driving traffic to its own products than serving users' needs.

FairSearch.org, a coalition of Google rivals, including Microsoft and Kayak, that lobbied for tough action by the FTC, said it would turn its attention to the European Union, where a parallel investigation is reaching a critical stage, and to the several state attorneys general probing the company. "FairSearch will continue to fight to restore truly competitive conditions to the market for search and related online services," the group said in a statement. "No less than the future of innovation and small business on the Internet is at stake."

Google has gradually changed its search algorithm and how it displays results. Much more space has been devoted in recent years to various forms of advertising—to the point that all results on shopping queries, such as for cameras or soccer balls, come from companies that pay for the listings.

A decade ago, a person searching for flights or steakhouses would see a long list of links to different Web sites.

Now, the most visible results often direct users to Google's own services or links sponsored by advertisers.

Other companies that built their businesses by directing Internet users to popular travel services or bargains on consumer goods have seen dramatic declines in their traffic—and profits. They argued to the FTC that the faltering ecosystem of alternative search options would inevitably mean worse deals for consumers.

The FTC eagerly sought the investigation in 2011, elbowing aside the antitrust division of the Justice Department and hiring a high-profile litigator to prepare a case against Google. But all five commissioners voted Thursday to close the case, though they first negotiated concessions on two related matters: Google agreed to make it easier for marketers to move their ads to rival services, and the company agreed to sharply limit its use of "snippets" of reviews for travel services or restaurants created by other Web sites, such as Yelp.

The FTC said it could sue Google for deceiving consumers if it reneges on either concession, but the deal fell short of the kind of legally binding decrees typically required to end investigations.

"Google clearly skews search results to favor its own products and services while portraying the results as unbiased," John M. Simpson of Consumer Watchdog said in a statement. "The FTC rolled over for Google."

There was more meat to the resolution of a separate matter also announced Thursday, in which Google signed a legally binding consent decree requiring it to license patents at reasonable rates when they are part of agreed industry standards. The move protects the ability of different mobile devices to communicate with one another and cuts the value of Motorola Mobility, which Google acquired for $12.5 billion, in part for its patent portfolio.

Leibowitz said the FTC got the best possible deal for consumers but also acknowledged the limits of a case that once seemed headed for a landmark showdown, reminiscent of the Justice Department's challenge to Microsoft in the 1990s.

"Anyone who is in the business of being the chairman of an antitrust enforcement agency would like to bring the big case," Leibowitz said. "That's sort of something you want to try to do. But more important than that is to faithfully execute the law. And, you know, we found unanimously that . . . they hadn't engaged in illegal monopolization and hadn't violated the FTC Act."

But the agency struggled with the optics of an announcement that fell far short of expectations it had helped create.

Even retiring Commissioner J. Thomas Rosch, a Republican former antitrust litigator who supported the decision to close the case against Google, chided his rivals for the nature of the settlement and the early hype over the case. "After promising an elephant more than a year ago, the commission has instead brought forth a couple of mice."

CRAIG TIMBERG is the former Johannesburg bureau chief for *The Washington Post*. From his position, he visited 23 African nations and penned dozens of major stories about AIDS. He is now *The Washington Post's* deputy national security editor.

Marvin Ammori  **NO**

The Case for Net Neutrality

    ... **N**et neutrality holds that Internet service providers (ISPs) shouldn't offer preferential treatment to some websites over others or charge some companies arbitrary fees to reach users. By this logic, AT&T, for example, shouldn't be allowed to grant iTunes Radio a special "fast lane" for its data while forcing Spotify to make do with choppier service.

    In January 2014, a U.S. federal appeals court, in a case brought by Verizon, struck down the net neutrality rules adopted by the FCC in 2010, which came close to fulfilling Obama's pledge despite a few loopholes. Shortly after the court's decision, Netflix was reportedly forced to pay Comcast tens of millions of dollars per year to ensure that Netflix users who connect to the Internet through Comcast could stream movies reliably; Apple reportedly entered into its own negotiations with Comcast to secure its own special treatment. Sensing an opening, AT&T and Verizon filed legal documents urging the FCC to allow them to set up a new pricing scheme in which they could charge every website a different price for such special treatment.

    ... FCC Chair Tom Wheeler circulated a proposal to the FCC's four other commissioners, two Democrats and two Republicans, for rules that would allow broadband providers to charge content providers for faster, smoother service. The proposal would also authorize ISPs to make exclusive deals with particular providers, so that PayPal could be the official payment processor for Verizon, for example, or Amazon Prime could be the official video provider for Time Warner Cable.

    Word of the proposal leaked to the press and sparked an immediate backlash. One hundred and fifty leading technology companies, including Amazon, Microsoft, and Kickstarter, sent a letter to the FCC calling the plan a "grave threat to the Internet." In their own letter to the FCC, over 100 of the nation's leading venture capital investors wrote that the proposal, if adopted as law, would "stifle innovation," since many start-ups and entrepreneurs wouldn't be able to afford to access a fast lane. Activist groups organized protests outside the FCC's headquarters in Washington and

accused Wheeler, a former lobbyist for both the cable and the wireless industries, of favoring his old clients over the public interest. Nonetheless, ... the FCC released its official proposal, concluding tentatively that it could authorize fast lanes and slow lanes on the Internet. ...

    . . . Preferably working with policymakers of all stripes supportive of open markets, the Obama administration should ensure that the FCC adopts rules that maintain the Internet as basic infrastructure that can be used by entrepreneurs, businesses, and average citizens alike—not a limited service controlled by a few large corporations. In the arcane world of federal administrative agencies, that guarantee comes down to whether the FCC adopts rules that rely on flimsy legal grounds, as it has in the past, or ones that rely on the solid foundation of its main regulatory authority over "common carriers," the legal term the U.S. government uses to describe firms that transport people, goods, or messages for a fee, such as trains and telephone companies. In 1910, Congress designated telephone wires as a common carrier service and decreed that the federal government should regulate electronic information traveling over wires in the same way that it regulated the movement of goods and passengers on railroads across state lines through the now defunct Interstate Commerce Commission, which meant that Congress could prevent companies from engaging in discrimination and charging unreasonable access fees. When the FCC was created in 1934 by the Communications Act, those common carrier rules were entrusted to it through a section of the law known as Title II. Today, the broadband wires and networks on which the Internet relies are the modern-day equivalent of these phone lines, and they should be regulated as such: like telephone companies before them, ISPs should be considered common carriers. This classification is crucial to protecting the Internet as public infrastructure that users can access equally, whether they run a multinational corporation or write a political blog.

    However, in 2002, Michael Powell, then chair of the FCC, classified ISPs not as common carriers but as "an information service," which has handicapped the FCC's ability to enforce net neutrality and regulate ISPs ever since. If ISPs are not reclassified as common carriers, Internet infrastructure will suffer. By authorizing payments for fast lanes, the FCC will encourage ISPs to cater to those customers able and willing to pay a premium, at the expense of upgrading infrastructure for those in the slow lanes.

The stakes for the U.S. economy are high: failing to ban ISPs from discriminating against companies would make it harder for tech entrepreneurs to compete, because the costs of entry would rise and ISPs could seek to hobble service for competitors unwilling or unable to pay special access fees. Foreign countries would likely follow Washington's lead, enacting protectionist measures that would close off foreign markets to U.S. companies. But the harm would extend even further. Given how much the Internet has woven itself into every aspect of daily life, the laws governing it shape economic and political decisions around the world and affect every industry, almost every business, and billions of people. If the Obama administration fails to reverse course on net neutrality, the Internet could turn into a patchwork of fiefdoms, with untold ripple effects.

Innovation Superhighway

Net neutrality is not some esoteric concern; it has been a major contributor to the success of the Internet economy. Unlike in the late 1990s, when users accessed relatively hived-off areas of cyberspace through slow dial-up connections, the Internet is now defined by integration. The credit for this improvement goes to high-speed connections, cellular networks, and short-distance wireless technologies such as WiFi and Bluetooth, which have allowed companies large and small—from Google to Etsy—to link up computers, smartphones, tablets, and wearable electronics. But all this integration has relied on a critical feature of the global Internet: no one needs permission from anyone to do anything.

Historically, ISPs have acted as gateways to all the wonderful (or not so wonderful) things connected to the Internet. But they have not acted as gatekeepers, determining which files and servers should load better or worse. From day one, the Internet was a public square, and the providers merely connected everyone, rather than regulating who spoke with whom. That allowed the Internet to evolve into a form of basic infrastructure, used by over a billion people today.

The Internet's openness has radically transformed all kinds of industries, from food delivery to finance, by lowering the barriers to entry. It has allowed a few bright engineers or students with an idea to launch a business that would be immediately available all over the world to over a billion potential customers. Start-ups don't need the leverage and bank accounts of Apple or Google to get reliable service to reach their users. In fact, historically, they have not paid any arbitrary fees to providers to reach users. Their costs often involve nothing more than hard work, inexpensive cloud computing tools, and off-the-shelf laptops and mobile devices, which are getting more powerful and cheaper by the day. As Marc Andreessen, a co-founder of Netscape and a venture capitalist, has pointed out, the cost of running a basic Internet application fell from $150,000 a month in 2000 to $1,500 a month in 2011. It continues to fall.

In some ways, the Internet is just the latest and perhaps most impressive of what economists call "general-purpose technologies," from the steam engine to the electricity grid, all of which, since their inception, have had a massively disproportionate impact on innovation and economic growth. In a 2012 report, the Boston Consulting Group found that the Internet economy accounted for 4.1 percent (about $2.3 trillion) of GDP in the G-20 countries in 2010. If the Internet were a national economy, the report noted, it would be among the five largest in the world, ahead of Germany. And a 2013 Kauffman Foundation report showed that in the previous three decades, the high-tech sector was 23 percent more likely, and the information technology sector 48 percent more likely, to give birth to new businesses than the private sector overall.

That growth, impressive as it is, could be just the beginning, as everyday objects, such as household devices and cars, go online as part of "the Internet of Things." John Chambers, the CEO of Cisco Systems, has predicted that the Internet of Things could create a $19 trillion market in the near future. Mobile-based markets will only expand, too; the Boston Consulting Group projects that mobile devices will account for four out of five broadband connections by 2016.

Not Neutrality

All this innovation has taken place without the permission of ISPs. But that could change as net neutrality comes under threat. ISPs have consistently maintained that net neutrality is a solution in search of a problem, but this often-repeated phrase is simply wrong. In the United States, both small and large providers have already violated the very principles that net neutrality is designed to protect. Ever since 2005, the FCC has pursued a policy that resembles net neutrality but that allows carriers, they could not be regulated according to Title II of the Communications Act, which would allow the FCC to treat them like telephone companies and ban unreasonable Internet discrimination and access fees. In January 2014, a U.S. federal appeals court agreed with Verizon and struck down the 2010 FCC rules.

In legal terms, the FCC can easily address all these issues when it adopts a new order later this year. By reclassifying ISPs as common carriers, the FCC could regulate them as it does phone companies. It should not shy away from using the authority that Congress gave it; the Supreme Court, in 2005, made clear that the FCC has the power to change ISPs' classification. Getting the legal definition right is crucial, since the FCC's last two attempts to enforce net neutrality were struck down in court on jurisdictional grounds. In both cases, rather than relying on its main authority over common carriers under Title II, the FCC attempted to impose net neutrality requirements through weaker regulatory authorities, including Section 706 of the Telecommunications Act of 1996, which gives the FCC the authority to regulate broadband infrastructure deployment. Each time, the court's ruling was sharply dismissive of the FCC's legal reasoning, as nondiscrimination rules can be applied only to common carriers.

In addition to fixing the FCC's legal footing, the new order should close the two loopholes in the moribund 2010 rules. First, there should be no exceptions for restrictions on mobile access. That is particularly important since many start-ups now develop applications initially or even exclusively for mobile phones, such as Instagram and Uber. The FCC should also make clear that ISPs cannot charge websites for direct connections to their networks, as Comcast has done with Netflix.

. . . Although the Obama administration and the FCC are the main decision-makers, Republicans should recognize the need to support an open Internet. Over the years, some Republicans, including former FCC Chair Kevin Martin, who served under President George W. Bush; former House Representative Charles "Chip" Pickering; and former Senator Olympia Snowe, have supported net neutrality as the best way to promote entrepreneurship, freemarket competition, and free speech. Opposing an open Internet now would put the party on the wrong side of its values and on the wrong side of history.

A country's Internet infrastructure, just like its physical infrastructure, is essential to its economic competition and growth. According to the Organization for Economic Cooperation and Development, high-speed Internet is not only slower in New York City and San Francisco than it is in Seoul; it also costs five times as much. Suffering from an even more expensive, less robust, and more fragmented Internet infrastructure would put the entire U.S. economy in a global slow lane.

Washington faces a simple choice: allow the Internet to remain an a engine of innovation, a platform for speech in even the harshest tyrannies, and a unified connection for people across the globe—or cede control of the Internet to service providers motivated by their parochial interests. . . .

Marvin Ammori is an attorney and Internet freedom activist, and a Future Tense Fellow at the New America Foundation. He was formerly a law professor at the University of Nebraska—Lincoln College of Law, and remains affiliated with the Information Society Project at Yale Law School and the Center for Internet and Society at Stanford Law School.

EXPLORING THE ISSUE

Have the Antitrust Laws Outlived Their Effectiveness vis-à-vis Technology?

Critical Thinking and Reflection

1. What is the best way to protect consumers' interests on the Internet?
2. How would you manage the varying levels of demand on a limited resource? Would you consider this "regulation"?
3. How can technology giants like Microsoft and Google protect their own interests while still being open to fair competition?
4. What is the impact of antitrust regulation on entrepreneurship, creativity, and growth in technology?

Is There Common Ground?

Finding a place for the two positions to meet is not as daunting a challenge as it looks initially. The problem is less that the positions are far apart and more that they do not seem to be in agreement about the question itself. The YES group, those who would prefer a discontinuation of all antitrust legislation for technology-related businesses, are arguing in favor of free enterprise, unhindered by limitations. The NO group, those who say that we need even more antitrust regulations, are arguing in favor of protection of the consumer.

Antitrust was begun to protect free competition. It was later adapted to focus on the use of free competition to better serve the consumer. The resultant debate about the limitations endorsed by the FTC is clouded by the two positions talking *at* each other, rather than talking *about* the same issue. It would be counter to Google's self-interest to harm its end users by prioritizing search results improperly; if they did so, they would lose users to other search engines. It would be counter to Microsoft's self-interest to use predatory practices to put out of business all other technology innovators; if they did so, how would they recruit new in-house talent?

No one likes a bully, and no one likes a spoiler. What do the technology mega-corporations want? The answer seems to be a straightforward one: more customers, more innovation, more profits. If antitrust is in the way of these, it has outlived its usefulness.

Additional Resources

L. Gordon Crovitz, "The Antitrust Anachronism." *The Wall Street Journal* (August 3, 2009).

David Evans, "Net Neutrality: Can Antitrust Save the Internet?, TMT Perspectives." (June 25, 2014). www.tmtperspectives.com/2014/06/25/net-neutrality-can-antitrust-save-the-internet/ (retrieved June 2, 2015).

Leslie Helm, "Antitrust in Cyberspace: New Rules of the Game," *The Los Angeles Times* (October 23, 1996).

strength, not one of a weakening demand in the market-place such as experienced by HP when it underestimated the impact of the commodification of computer technology. It can be a tricky balance to find.

Buybacks also make a significant contribution to market volatility as shares become proportionally more valuable and investors jockey to unload them for short-term profit. Stock buybacks reflect short-term thinking on other levels as well. Financial analysts warn about the dangers of boosting share values in lieu of investing in long-term growth. In the event of a market downturn, corporations may need ready cash to support operations, as they needed in the 2007–08 recession. Those who have allocated their cash assets to buy back stock may find themselves having to increase their debt to sustain the business overall.

Among potentially unintended consequences of stock buyback is its impact on employee stability. If a corporation is using its money in a buyback, it has less to devote to other concerns, specifically worker retention and worker satisfaction. Cisco Systems has shown a history of multiple buybacks and laying off workers for four years straight using debt financing. In 2015, they are laying off another 6,000 workers while shrinking sales and falling margins eat up existing cash (Matthews, 2015).

With these negative aspects, why might a company undertake this financial strategy? There are many reasons, good and bad, that a company might favor a buyback. It is a way to use excess cash assets. It is an acceptable alternative to dividend payouts. It concentrates ownership and benefits major shareholders.

But the message the buyback is sending can be mixed. Sometimes buybacks send the desired positive message, and sometimes they do not, sending instead a negative story. The desirable message is that the company is doing so well that the best use of its assets is to withdraw shares from the open market. But the message is often clouded by suspicion that derives from the use of the resulting shares to compensate C-level executives. This leaves little cash available for research and development, innovation projects, employee benefits, hiring, and retention, and it undermines the spending power of American workers. Although it may boost market value, it does nothing to improve the actual business of the corporation

itself. Without reinvesting retained earnings in the business, growth is unlikely, and short-term profiteering may spell long-term disaster.

The question becomes one of *market value* versus *corporate values*. What are the real values of the corporation? If they include improving the product or service the corporation is providing, reinvestment makes more sense than retirement of shares. In order for the company to grow, research and development is required, as stock market position is less important than marketplace position. If corporate values focus on compensation in the C-suite, it is not surprising that workers will be reduced in force, that fewer benefits will be offered, and that human development will take a back seat. The use of stock-based pay encourages market churn as shares received from options are often sold quickly, without allowing them time to appreciate and their value to increase.

We return to the basic question: What is the purpose of business? Is it to benefit the few mightily or to benefit the economy of the nation? According to Collins and Porras (1996), the identification of core values is key to the business's success, and these core values do not revolve around market value. They state, "You can look around [in the general business world and] see people who are interested in money and nothing else, but the underlying drives come largely from a desire to do something else: to make a product, to give a service—generally to do something which is of value. . . . Notice that none of the core purposes fall into the category 'maximize shareholder wealth.' A primary role of core purpose is to guide and inspire. Maximizing shareholder wealth does not inspire people at all levels of an organization, and it provides precious little guidance. Maximizing shareholder wealth is the standard off-the-shelf purpose for those organizations that have not yet identified their true core purpose. It is a substitute—and a weak one at that."

In the YES article, Justin Pettit provides guidance for conducting a successful buyback program and endorses share buybacks for the increased value they bring to shareholders.

In the NO article, William Lazonick decries the use of buybacks because they divert corporate attention from human needs, replacing it with a constant search for market approval.

EXPLORING THE ISSUE

Are Stock Buybacks the Best Strategy to Drive Corporate Value?

Critical Thinking and Reflection

1. What do you think is the wisest way to allocate "excess cash" within the capital structure? Why?
2. Which should have the higher priority—value creation or value extraction? What in any corporation cues us in to the answer for that business?
3. Why, with all the billions that are spent on share buybacks, is the U.S. economy not booming? Why are lay-offs continuing to occur?
4. Why are buybacks taking place in a bull market (at high prices rather than low)?

Is There Common Ground?

Coming to mutual understanding when people's goals are so disparate can be a major challenge. In terms of stock buybacks, the business goals of the organizations are very far apart, with one side seeking to improve stock value and the other side seeking to improve the lives of employees.

One area where the two groups can agree is that business needs to pursue innovation in order to remain viable. That can be the foundation of their mutual interests. Financial strategy and capital structure do not lend themselves to human concerns; however, the ability to maintain a workforce that is effective and stable and that does not incur the heavy costs of rehiring and retraining can be the focus of consideration of reinvestment rather than market manipulation.

The extreme variability of long-term success by corporations that have spent billions in share buybacks compared to the long-term success of corporations that have reinvested equity into human development and product improvement provides empirical support for the latter, at least in partial measure.

Additional Resources

James C. Collins and Jerry I. Porras, "Building Your Company's Vision," *Harvard Business Review* (September/October 1996).

Nick Hanauer, "Stock Buybacks Are Killing the American Economy," *The Atlantic* (February 8, 2015).

Ben Kramer-Miller, "2 Lousy Stock Repurchase Programs," www.cheatsheet.com/business/2-lousy-stock-repurchase-programs.html/?a=viewall (April 10, 2014) (retrieved June 3, 2015).

Chris Matthews, "Will 2015 Mark the End of the Great Stock Buyback Binge?," *Fortune* (February 11, 2015).

Andrew Soergel, "Stock Buybacks: Innovation Boon or Middle-Class Doom?," *US News & World Report* (June 1, 2015).

Internet References . . .

Cory Janssen, "A Breakdown of Stock Buybacks"

www.investopedia.com/articles/02/041702.asp

Patrick O'Shaughnessy, "The Power of Share Repurchases"

http://investorfieldguide.com/2014623the-power
-of-share-repurchases

Ben Kramer-Miller, "2 Lousy Stock Repurchase Programs"

www.cheatsheet.com/business/2-lousy-stock
-repurchase-programs.html/?a=viewall

PLEASE NOTE: To access the "YES" and "NO" selections, please refer to "Is a Share Buyback Right for Your Company?" by Justin Pettit, and "Profits Without Prosperity" by William Lazonick immediately following this material.

Is a Share Buyback Right for Your Company?

by Justin Pettit

Harvard Business Review

Reprint R0104K

Harvard Business Review

 *April 2001*

TOOL KIT

Is a **Share Buyback** *Right* for Your Company?

When a company's performance is lagging, share buybacks can look very attractive indeed. Unfortunately, buybacks can backfire – unless executives understand why, when, and how to use this powerful and risky tool.

by Justin Pettit

SHARE BUYBACKS HAVE BECOME COMMONPLACE in the business world. In 1999 alone, 1,253 companies on the New York Stock Exchange repurchased their own shares, spending an estimated $181 billion – nearly as much as the $216 billion that NYSE companies distributed as dividends during that year. On the face of it, the popularity of buybacks is easy to understand. By purchasing its own stock, a company reduces the number of shares outstanding without affecting its reported earnings. That increases the company's earnings per share and, so the argument goes, the price of a share should rise accordingly. And in most cases, buybacks seem to pay off: historically, companies that bought back their

ILLUSTRATION BY PHILIP ANDERSON

The way a buyback is announced and implemented conveys signals about the company's prospects and plans – but not always the ones the company intends.

own shares have posted immediate returns between two and 12 percentage points above the market average, representing billions of dollars in shareholder value.

But not all buybacks go according to plan. Consider the pharmaceutical powerhouse Merck. On February 22, 2000, Merck unveiled a $10 billion buyback plan – the biggest ever announced. But far from rising, Merck's share price fell by some 15% in the following month. In the eyes of investors, the buyback only

Justin Pettit is a partner at the New York offices of Stern Stewart & Company, a consulting firm specializing in value-based management. He can be reached at jpettit@sternstewart.com.

underscored the company's weaknesses. A number of important patents were approaching expiration; Merck's drug pipeline was running dry; its own chief scientist admitted that the company could no longer maintain its target 20% earnings growth rate. As one analyst put it: "$10 billion would have funded a lot of research and development." Merck's experience appears to be an increasingly common one: over the course of 1999, companies listed on the NYSE that implemented buyback programs actually underperformed the index by 20 percentage points.

Merck's story reveals just how subtle the effects of share buybacks can be. In this article, I'll explain how share buybacks actually do affect value and how managers can influence the process through their decisions on the rationale

for, size of, and way they implement their buyback programs. (For a good recent illustration of what can happen when the buyback is well thought through, see the sidebar "The Perfect Buyback.")

How Will the Buyback Affect Your Company's Value?

Contrary to the common wisdom, buybacks don't create value by increasing earnings per share. The company has, after all, spent cash to purchase those shares, and investors will adjust their valuations to reflect the reductions in both cash and shares, thereby canceling out any earnings-per-share effect. If increasing earnings per share were the only rationale for buybacks, they would have no impact on value – which, as we've seen, is certainly not the case.

Buybacks affect value in two ways. First, the buyback announcement, its terms, and the way it is implemented all convey signals about the company's prospects and plans, even though few managers publicly acknowledge this. Second, when financed by a debt issue, buybacks can significantly change a company's capital structure, increasing its reliance on debt and decreasing its reliance on equity.

Signaling. The signaling effect of share buybacks has been the focus of much academic research over the past ten years. According to these studies, investors and analysts use a company's financial decisions as a window into what management really thinks about the company's prospects. The announcement of a share buyback, the argument goes, indicates that managers are so confident of their company's prospects that they believe the best investment it can make is in its own shares.

If only it were that simple. In real life, investors interpret a company's decisions through the lens of past experience and in its current context, taking into account a host of other indications and signals. As Merck found out, the in-

formation conveyed by a buyback announcement is not always the information that management wants to express. In my experience, a buyback announcement can send a negative signal in three situations.

First of all, other information can contradict, and sometimes swamp, the intended buyback signal. From November 1998 through October 2000, for instance, the computer giant Hewlett-Packard spent $8.2 billion to buy back 128 million of its shares. According to HP executives, the aim was to make opportunistic purchases of HP stock at attractive prices – in other words, at prices they felt undervalued the company. But if managers hoped thereby to signal good operating prospects to the market, they should have saved themselves the trouble. The buyback signal was completely drowned out by a rapid succession of other moves, all emitting contradictory and more powerful signals about the company's future: an aborted acquisition, a protracted business restructuring, slipping financial results, and a decay in the general profitability

of key markets. By last January, HP's shares were trading at around half the average $64 per share paid to repurchase the stock.

Buybacks can also backfire for a company competing in a high-growth industry because they may be read as an admission that the company has few important new opportunities on which to otherwise spend its money. In such cases, long-term investors will respond to a buyback announcement by selling the company's shares. This effect is most commonly observed when, like Merck, the company is in a technology-laden business because those industries change quickly and companies competing in them need to demonstrate high growth potential. IBM, for instance, has seen no clear benefit from the $27 billion it spent on buybacks between 1995 and 2000 because the cash payout only heightened analysts' concerns over the company's ability to continue coming up with new products and services.

Finally, the credibility of a signal is seriously weakened if the company's managers choose to participate in the buyback themselves. When managers elect to sell shares rather than retain them, that suggests to the markets that the managers do not believe in their own estimates of value. They have not, in effect, put their own money where their mouths are. All other things being equal, though, if managers do not participate, the benefits can be dramatic. One study of tender-offer buybacks has shown that programs in which managers did not participate generated returns seven percentage points higher than those they did join in.

Leverage. Buybacks can also affect value by changing a company's capital structure. Indeed, many companies use them as a way to increase their reliance on debt financing. Early last year, for instance, Payless ShoeSource increased its long-term debt from $127 million to $384 million by repurchasing 25% of its outstanding shares through a tender offer. Its debt increased from 10% of capital employed to 33%, and the returns to shareholders were remarkable. Immediately after the buyback was

The Perfect Buyback

Perhaps the most striking recent example of a well-executed buyback is the one launched by SPX, a diversified industrial manufacturer of everything from automatic fare-collection systems to tire gauges. On April 10, 1998, SPX announced a Dutch-auction tender offer for 2.7 million shares, or 18% of the total shares outstanding. The tender range was set between $48 and $56 per share, representing a 24% to 45% premium over the year's opening price of $38¾, and a 12% to 30% premium over April 8th's $43 close.

With its aggressive terms and size, the buyback was a clear affirmation of faith in the company, reinforced by senior management's explicit pledge not to tender their own shares. What's more, since the buyback was financed through debt, it served to radically releverage the company's balance sheet.

The market roared its approval, as SPX's share price posted an extraordinary return of 20% over the two days following the announcement. Indeed, such was the confidence of investors in the company that SPX was unable to secure more than 80% of the number of shares it wanted to repurchase, even at the upper price limit of $56. It was forced to continue buying back shares in the open market. Within one month, the stock was trading at over $70.

As a further affirmation of the benefits of buybacks, SPX has pledged to replace its quarterly cash dividend with share repurchases as the preferred method of returning cash to shareholders, pointing out that buybacks allow shareholders more flexibility in tax planning. As CFO Patrick O'Leary puts it: "We are giving shareholders a choice."

stock is undervalued. The lack of a firm commitment inherent in open-market repurchase announcements sends a weak – or even negative – signal about managers' confidence in their company's prospects. If managers are convinced of their company's value, why shouldn't they make a firmer public commitment to purchasing its shares?

Open-market repurchasing is also an inefficient way to restructure the balance sheet. The limitation on the amount of shares a company can buy on any one day can drag out the process almost indefinitely, especially if the company is contemplating a major change. For example, Payless would have needed 166 business days to repurchase 25% of its own stock, rather than the 20- to 30-day window given in its tender offer, because its average trading volume is typically only about .6% of all outstanding shares.

Open-market repurchase programs are best used when the company's primary objective is not to boost its share price but rather to distribute excess cash to shareholders in lieu of a dividend. (For a discussion of the advantages, see the sidebar "Buybacks as an Alternative to Dividends.")

Fixed-Price Tender Offers. This is a very powerful way to implement a value-creating buyback. Companies usually use fixed-price tender offers when they want to repurchase more than 15% of their outstanding shares. They will open the process with an announcement inviting shareholders to tender their shares to the company over a 20- to 30-day period at a preset price that reflects some premium – typically between 15% and 20% above the prevailing market price.

Studies have shown that the signaling effect of fixed-price tenders is stronger than any other form of share buyback, leading on average to a 12% appreciation in share price in the days just following the announcement (new information is typically fully capitalized within a few days). If a buyback is misconceived, however, a fixed-price tender offer, with its preset and usually aggressive terms, can severely aggravate the damage. The experience of the luggage company Samsonite is a case in point. On May 12, 1998, it announced a fixed tender offer for about half of its outstanding shares at a 30% premium over the market price. The company aimed to increase its leverage and to allow its management buyout backer, Apollo Advisors, liquidity to exit. The transaction was funded primarily by debt.

Unfortunately, investors didn't believe that Samsonite's operating performance justified such a large switch from equity finance to debt, and they read Apollo's exit as a very negative signal about the company's outlook. The large scale and high premium of the buyback ended up working against the company, and the share price plunged by 50%. Indeed, demand for the stock dried up almost completely once the tender had been concluded. As the share price fell by another 50% over the summer, it became increasingly clear that the transaction had effectively transferred about $200 million in wealth from nontendering to tendering shareholders. A complex web of litigation is now pending.

Auction-Based Tender Offers. In the last few years, this buyback approach has emerged as the method of choice for large buybacks (more than 10% of a company's outstanding shares). The auction mechanism used most often is the Dutch auction, in which sellers post the prices at which they are willing to sell.

The company begins the process by announcing that it is seeking tenders from shareholders for a specified proportion of its shares and is willing to pay between, say, 10% and 20% above market value for them. The shareholders respond by informing the company within a specified time period, typically about a month, how many shares they are willing to sell at what minimum price within the range. Once all the tenders are in, the final clearing price is set at the minimum price needed to purchase the desired number of shares from those shareholders who agreed to sell at or below that price. All shares transfer at the clearing price – the same

Buybacks as an Alternative to Dividends

Quite apart from their potential for creating value, share buybacks can also offer companies a shareholder-friendly way to distribute cash. That's because, in the United States at least, many investors are taxed more highly on cash dividends than on capital appreciation.

Here's how it works. Suppose a company wishes to distribute $100 of excess cash to its only shareholder. If the money were paid out as a dividend, it would be taxed as ordinary income at, say, 40%, leaving the shareholder with a net $60. But if the company bought back $100 worth of shares, the shareholder would have to pay capital gains tax of only, say, 20% on the amount by which the shares had risen since the purchase. If the company is buying back 50 shares at $2 each, and they had originally been purchased at $1, the shareholder's tax bill would be 20% of the $1 gain on each of 50 shares, or $10, leaving the shareholder with a net $90.

Given the obvious attractions of buybacks, it's fair to ask why dividends are still so popular. The answer seems to be largely psychological – although some institutional investors are limited to investing predominantly in dividend-paying stocks. Regular dividends are more predictable, many managers argue, and give shareholders a greater feeling of confidence. So, if the universe of a company's potential shareholders is risk averse, a company can signal its superiority as an investment over other companies by offering dividends. But while this might work for unsophisticated private investors, it's unlikely to sway professional institutional investors, such as mutual fund managers, whose decisions have the most influence on the markets.

price for all – and tendering shareholders incur no transaction costs.

If more shares are tendered than the company wants (that is, the tender is oversubscribed), the clearing price is set at the bottom of the range, and the amount of shares that the company

The Dutch Auction

This table illustrates the way a Dutch auction would work for a company wishing to repurchase 2 million shares at an offered range of $34 to $42 per share. In this case, the clearing price is $40 per share, resulting in an $80 million outlay for the company.

Price	Shares Tendered (thousands)	Cumulative Shares Tendered (thousands)
$34.00	200	200
$35.75	250	450
$37.00	300	750
$38.00	350	1,100
$39.50	400	1,500
$40.00	500	2,000
$40.50	650	2,650
$41.00	500	3,150
$42.00	450	3,600

actually buys from each shareholder may be reduced in proportion to the amount of shares tendered. If, on the other hand, the company does not get as many shares as it wanted (in other words, the tender is undersubscribed), then the clearing price will be set at the range's maximum, and the company will purchase all the shares tendered. In that situation, companies sometimes complete the buyback by announcing an open-market program to follow. The table "The Dutch Auction" illustrates the mechanics of a Dutch auction for a company seeking to buy back 2 mil-

lion of its shares at a range of $34 to $42 per share. In this case, a clearing price of $40 per share is required to reach the target number of shares, resulting in a capital outlay of $80 million.

Companies that use auction-based tenders generally deliver returns to shareholders about 8% above the market average around the time of the announcement, slightly less than the 12% enjoyed by companies using fixed-price tenders. But auctions also give companies much greater flexibility and safety in sizing and pricing the deal. For a start, the average price premium paid in auction-based tenders (about 13%) is lower than the average paid in fixed-price tenders (about 21%). Auction-based tender offers also reduce the likelihood of transferring wealth between tendering and non-tendering shareholders. That's because there is less chance of a major decline in the share price after the buyback since investors have themselves helped to set the buyback's quantity and its price.

Properly applied, a share buyback can help a company significantly enhance its value to shareholders. Managers must ask themselves if they are embarking on the buyback for the right reasons, and they should take pains to make sure that the way they implement the buyback is appropriate to their goals. Managers who do not take the time to think through these issues carefully may well find that their buyback backfires.

1. One study by Stern Stewart has shown that the adoption of the EVA metric for measuring performance and determining management rewards has a positive effect on value. Those companies studied that used the measure reaped returns some eight percentage points above the average. I believe that the effect of the measure is analogous to the behavioral effects of debt observed in LBO firms.

Reprint R0104K
To place an order, call 1-800-988-0886.

HBR.ORG

Harvard Business Review

SEPTEMBER 2014
REPRINT R1409B

THE BIG IDEA

Profits Without Prosperity

**Stock buybacks manipulate the market
and leave most Americans worse off.**
by William Lazonick

The Big Idea

profits without prosperity

FOR ARTICLE REPRINTS CALL 800-988-0886 OR 617-783-7500, OR VISIT **HBR.ORG**

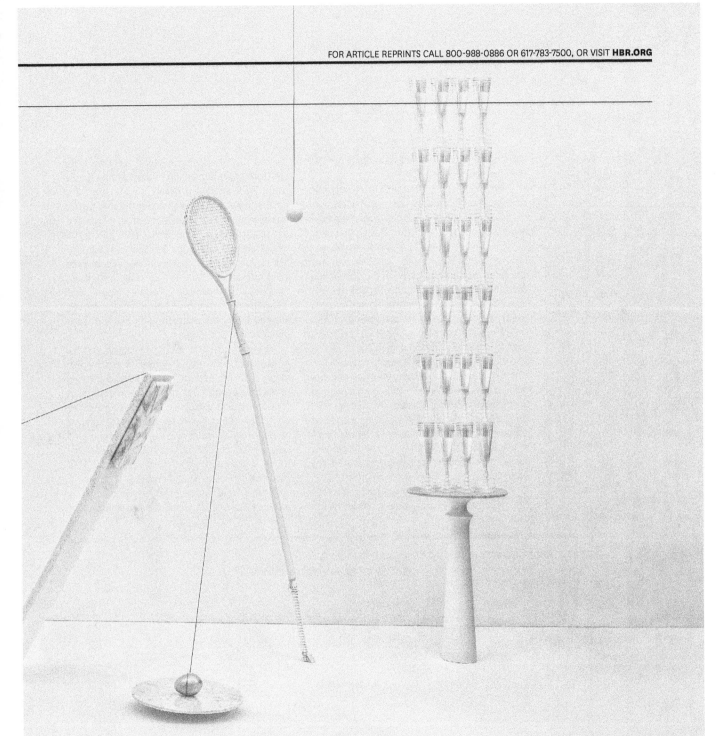

STOCK BUYBACKS
MANIPULATE THE
MARKET AND LEAVE
MOST AMERICANS
WORSE OFF.

BY WILLIAM LAZONICK

Five years after the official end of the Great Recession, corporate profits are high, and the stock market is booming. Yet most Americans are not sharing in the recovery. While the top 0.1% of income recipients— which include most of the highest-ranking corporate executives—reap almost all the income gains, good jobs keep disappearing, and new employment opportunities tend to be insecure and underpaid.

PHOTOGRAPHY: ELISE

THE BIG IDEA PROFITS WITHOUT PROSPERITY

Corporate profitability is not translating into widespread economic prosperity.

The allocation of corporate profits to stock buybacks deserves much of the blame. Consider the 449 companies in the S&P 500 index that were publicly listed from 2003 through 2012. During that period those companies used 54% of their earnings—a total of $2.4 trillion—to buy back their own stock, almost all through purchases on the open market. Dividends absorbed an additional 37% of their earnings. That left very little for investments in productive capabilities or higher incomes for employees.

The buyback wave has gotten so big, in fact, that even shareholders—the presumed beneficiaries of all this corporate largesse—are getting worried. "It concerns us that, in the wake of the financial crisis, many companies have shied away from investing in the future growth of their companies," Laurence Fink, the chairman and CEO of BlackRock, the world's largest asset manager, wrote in an open letter to corporate America in March. "Too many companies have cut capital expenditure and even increased debt to boost dividends and increase share buybacks."

Why are such massive resources being devoted to stock repurchases? Corporate executives give several reasons, which I will discuss later. But none of them has close to the explanatory power of this simple truth: Stock-based instruments make up the majority of their pay, and in the short term buybacks drive up stock prices. In 2012 the 500 highest-paid executives named in proxy statements of U.S. public companies received, on average, $30.3 million each; 42% of their compensation came from stock options and 41% from stock awards. By increasing the demand for a company's shares, open-market buybacks automatically lift its stock price, even if only temporarily, and can enable the company to hit quarterly earnings per share (EPS) targets.

As a result, the very people we rely on to make investments in the productive capabilities that will increase our shared prosperity are instead devoting most of their companies' profits to uses that will increase their own prosperity—with unsurprising results. Even when adjusted for inflation, the compensation of top U.S. executives has doubled or tripled since the first half of the 1990s, when it was already widely viewed as excessive. Meanwhile, overall U.S. economic performance has faltered.

If the U.S. is to achieve growth that distributes income equitably and provides stable employment,

WHEN PRODUCTIVITY AND WAGES PARTED WAYS

From 1948 to the mid-1970s, increases in productivity and wages went hand in hand.
Then a gap opened between the two.

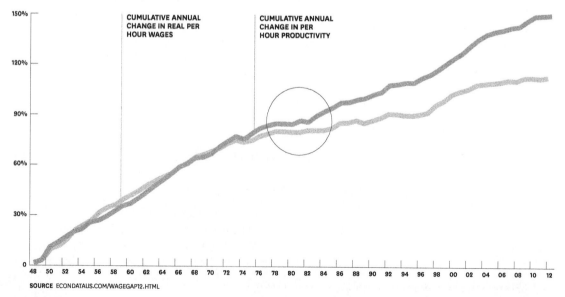

SOURCE ECONDATAUS.COM/WAGEGAP12.HTML

FOR ARTICLE REPRINTS CALL 800-988-0886 OR 617-783-7500, OR VISIT **HBR.ORG**

Idea in Brief

THE PROBLEM

Corporate profitability is not translating into economic prosperity in the United States. Instead of investing profits in innovation and productive capabilities, U.S. executives are spending them on gigantic stock repurchases.

THE RESEARCH

These buybacks may increase stock prices in the short term, but in the long term they undermine income equality, job stability, and growth. The buybacks mostly serve the interests of executives, much of whose compensation is in the form of stock.

THE SOLUTION

Corporations should be banned from repurchasing their shares on the open market. Executives' excessive stock-based pay should be reined in. Workers and taxpayers should be represented on corporate boards. And Congress should reform the tax system so that it rewards value creation, not value extraction.

government and business leaders must take steps to bring both stock buybacks and executive pay under control. The nation's economic health depends on it.

FROM VALUE CREATION TO VALUE EXTRACTION

For three decades I've been studying how the resource allocation decisions of major U.S. corporations influence the relationship between *value creation* and *value extraction,* and how that relationship affects the U.S. economy. From the end of World War II until the late 1970s, a *retain-and-reinvest* approach to resource allocation prevailed at major U.S. corporations. They retained earnings and reinvested them in increasing their capabilities, first and foremost in the employees who helped make firms more competitive. They provided workers with higher incomes and greater job security, thus contributing to equitable, stable economic growth—what I call "sustainable prosperity."

This pattern began to break down in the late 1970s, giving way to a *downsize-and-distribute* regime of reducing costs and then distributing the freed-up cash to financial interests, particularly shareholders. By favoring value extraction over value creation, this approach has contributed to employment instability and income inequality.

As documented by the economists Thomas Piketty and Emmanuel Saez, the richest 0.1% of U.S. households collected a record 12.3% of all U.S. income in 2007, surpassing their 11.5% share in 1928, on the eve of the Great Depression. In the financial crisis of 2008–2009, their share fell sharply, but it has since rebounded, hitting 11.3% in 2012.

Since the late 1980s, the largest component of the income of the top 0.1% has been compensation, driven by stock-based pay. Meanwhile, the growth of workers' wages has been slow and sporadic, except during the internet boom of 1998–2000, the

only time in the past 46 years when real wages rose by 2% or more for three years running. Since the late 1970s, average growth in real wages has increasingly lagged productivity growth. (See the exhibit "When Productivity and Wages Parted Ways.")

Not coincidentally, U.S. employment relations have undergone a transformation in the past three decades. Mass plant closings eliminated millions of unionized blue-collar jobs. The norm of a white-collar worker's spending his or her entire career with one company disappeared. And the seismic shift toward offshoring left all members of the U.S. labor force—even those with advanced education and substantial work experience—vulnerable to displacement.

To some extent these structural changes could be justified initially as necessary responses to changes in technology and competition. In the early 1980s permanent plant closings were triggered by the inroads superior Japanese manufacturers had made in consumer-durable and capital-goods industries. In the early 1990s one-company careers fell by the wayside in the IT sector because the open-systems architecture of the microelectronics revolution devalued the skills of older employees versed in proprietary technologies. And in the early 2000s the offshoring of more-routine tasks, such as writing unsophisticated software and manning customer call centers, sped up as a capable labor force emerged in low-wage developing economies and communications costs plunged, allowing U.S. companies to focus their domestic employees on higher-value-added work.

These practices chipped away at the loyalty and dampened the spending power of American workers, and often gave away key competitive capabilities of U.S. companies. Attracted by the quick financial gains they produced, many executives ignored the long-term effects and kept pursuing them well past the time they could be justified.

THE BIG IDEA PROFITS WITHOUT PROSPERITY

WHERE DID THE MONEY FROM PRODUCTIVITY INCREASES GO?

Buybacks—as well as dividends—have skyrocketed in the past 20 years. (Note that these data are for the 251 companies that were in the S&P 500 in January 2013 and were public from 1981 through 2012. Inclusion of firms that went public after 1981, such as Microsoft, Cisco, Amgen, Oracle, and Dell, would make the increase in buybacks even more marked.) Though executives say they repurchase only undervalued stocks, buybacks increased when the stock market boomed, casting doubt on that claim.

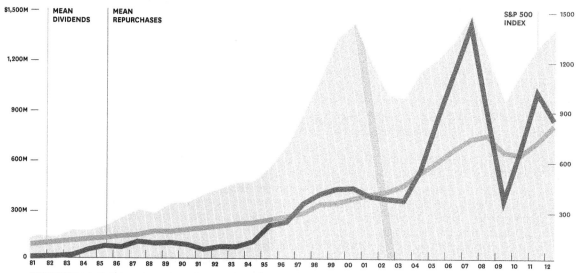

SOURCE STANDARD & POOR'S COMPUSTAT DATABASE; THE ACADEMIC-INDUSTRY RESEARCH NETWORK. **NOTE** MEAN REPURCHASE AND DIVIDEND AMOUNTS ARE IN 2012 DOLLARS.

A turning point was the wave of hostile takeovers that swept the country in the 1980s. Corporate raiders often claimed that the complacent leaders of the targeted companies were failing to maximize returns to shareholders. That criticism prompted boards of directors to try to align the interests of management and shareholders by making stock-based pay a much bigger component of executive compensation.

Given incentives to maximize shareholder value and meet Wall Street's expectations for ever higher quarterly EPS, top executives turned to massive stock repurchases, which helped them "manage" stock prices. The result: Trillions of dollars that could have been spent on innovation and job creation in the U.S. economy over the past three decades have instead been used to buy back shares for what is effectively stock-price manipulation.

GOOD BUYBACKS AND BAD

Not all buybacks undermine shared prosperity. There are two major types: tender offers and open-market repurchases. With the former, a company contacts shareholders and offers to buy back their shares at a stipulated price by a certain near-term date, and then shareholders who find the price agreeable tender their shares to the company. Tender offers can be a way for executives who have substantial ownership stakes and care about a company's long-term competitiveness to take advantage of a low stock price and concentrate ownership in their own hands. This can, among other things, free them from Wall Street's pressure to maximize short-term profits and allow them to invest in the business. Henry Singleton was known for using tender offers in this way at Teledyne in the 1970s, and Warren Buffett for using them at GEICO in the 1980s. (GEICO became wholly owned by Buffett's holding company, Berkshire Hathaway, in 1996.) As Buffett has noted, this kind of tender offer should be made when the share price is below the intrinsic value of the productive capabilities of the company and the company is profitable enough to repurchase the shares without impeding its real investment plans.

But tender offers constitute only a small portion of modern buybacks. Most are now done on the open market, and my research shows that they often come at the expense of investment in productive capabilities and, consequently, aren't great for long-term shareholders.

Companies have been allowed to repurchase their shares on the open market with virtually no regulatory limits since 1982, when the SEC instituted Rule 10b-18 of the Securities Exchange Act. Under the rule, a corporation's board of directors can authorize senior executives to repurchase up to a certain dollar amount of stock over a specified or open-ended period of time, and the company must publicly announce the buyback program. After that, management can buy a large number of the company's shares on any given business day without fear that the SEC will charge it with stock-price manipulation—provided, among other things, that the amount does not exceed a "safe harbor" of 25% of the previous four weeks' average daily trading volume. The SEC requires companies to report total quarterly repurchases but not daily ones, meaning that it cannot determine whether a company has breached the 25% limit without a special investigation.

Despite the escalation in buybacks over the past three decades, the SEC has only rarely launched proceedings against a company for using them to manipulate its stock price. And even within the 25% limit, companies can still make huge purchases: Exxon Mobil, by far the biggest stock repurchaser from 2003 to 2012, can buy back about $300 million worth of shares a day, and Apple up to $1.5 billion a day. In essence, Rule 10b-18 legalized stock market manipulation through open-market repurchases.

The rule was a major departure from the agency's original mandate, laid out in the Securities Exchange Act in 1934. The act was a reaction to a host of unscrupulous activities that had fueled speculation in the Roaring '20s, leading to the stock market crash of 1929 and the Great Depression. To prevent such shenanigans, the act gave the SEC broad powers to issue rules and regulations.

During the Reagan years, the SEC began to roll back those rules. The commission's chairman from 1981 to 1987 was John Shad, a former vice chairman of E.F. Hutton and the first Wall Street insider to lead the commission in 50 years. He believed that the deregulation of securities markets would channel savings into economic investments more efficiently and that the isolated cases of fraud and manipulation that might go undetected did not justify onerous disclosure requirements for companies. The SEC's adoption of Rule 10b-18 reflected that point of view.

DEBUNKING THE JUSTIFICATIONS FOR BUYBACKS

Executives give three main justifications for open-market repurchases. Let's examine them one by one:

1 Buybacks are investments in our undervalued shares that signal our confidence in the company's future. This makes some sense. But the reality is that over the past two decades major U.S. companies have tended to do buybacks in bull markets and cut back on them, often sharply, in bear markets. (See the exhibit "Where Did the Money from Productivity Increases Go?") They buy high and, if they sell at all, sell low. Research by the Academic-Industry Research Network, a nonprofit I cofounded and lead, shows that companies that do buybacks never resell the shares at higher prices.

Once in a while a company that bought high in a boom has been forced to sell low in a bust to alleviate financial distress. GE, for example, spent $3.2 billion on buybacks in the first three quarters of 2008, paying an average price of $31.84 per share. Then, in the last quarter, as the financial crisis brought about losses at GE Capital, the company did a $12 billion stock issue at an average share price of $22.25, in a failed attempt to protect its triple-A credit rating.

In general, when a company buys back shares at what turn out to be high prices, it eventually reduces the value of the stock held by continuing shareholders. "The *continuing* shareholder is penalized by repurchases above intrinsic value," Warren Buffett wrote in his 1999 letter to Berkshire Hathaway shareholders. "Buying dollar bills for $1.10 is not good business for those who stick around."

2 Buybacks are necessary to offset the dilution of earnings per share when employees exercise stock options. Calculations that I have done for high-tech companies with broad-based stock option programs reveal that the volume of open-market repurchases is generally a multiple of the volume of options that employees exercise. In any case, there's no logical economic rationale for doing repurchases to offset dilution from the exercise of employee stock options. Options are meant to motivate employees to work harder now to produce higher future returns for the company. Therefore, rather than using corporate cash to boost EPS immediately, executives should be willing to wait for the incentive to work. If the company generates higher earnings, employees can exercise their options at higher stock prices, and the company can allocate the increased earnings to investment in the next round of innovation.

THE BIG IDEA PROFITS WITHOUT PROSPERITY

3 Our company is mature and has run out of profitable investment opportunities; therefore, we should return its unneeded cash to shareholders. Some people used to argue that buybacks were a more tax-efficient means of distributing money to shareholders than dividends. But that has not been the case since 2003, when the tax rates on long-term capital gains and qualified dividends were made the same. Much more important issues remain, however: What is the CEO's main role and his or her responsibility to shareholders?

Companies that have built up productive capabilities over long periods typically have huge organizational and financial advantages when they enter related markets. One of the chief functions of top executives is to discover new opportunities for those capabilities. When they opt to do large open-market repurchases instead, it raises the question of whether these executives are doing their jobs.

A related issue is the notion that the CEO's main obligation is to shareholders. It's based on a misconception of the shareholders' role in the modern corporation. The philosophical justification for giving them all excess corporate profits is that they are best positioned to allocate resources because they have the most interest in ensuring that capital generates the highest returns. This proposition is central to the "maximizing shareholder value" (MSV) arguments espoused over the years, most notably by Michael C. Jensen. The MSV school also posits that companies' so-called free cash flow should be distributed to shareholders because only they make investments without a guaranteed return—and hence bear risk.

But the MSV school ignores other participants in the economy who bear risk by investing without a guaranteed return. *Taxpayers* take on such risk through government agencies that invest in infrastructure and knowledge creation. And *workers* take it on by investing in the development of their capabilities at the firms that employ them. As risk bearers, taxpayers, whose dollars support business enterprises, and workers, whose efforts generate productivity improvements, have claims on profits that are at least as strong as the shareholders'.

The irony of MSV is that public-company shareholders typically never invest in the value-creating capabilities of the company at all. Rather, they invest in outstanding shares in the hope that the stock price will rise. And a prime way in which corporate executives fuel that hope is by doing buybacks to manipulate the market. The only money that Apple ever raised from public shareholders was $97 million at its IPO in 1980.

WHY MONEY FOR REINVESTMENT HAS DRIED UP

Since the early 1980s, when restrictions on open-market buybacks were greatly eased, distributions to shareholders have absorbed a huge portion of net income, leaving much less for reinvestment in companies.

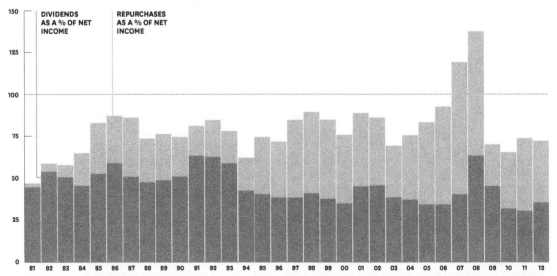

NOTE DATA ARE FOR THE 251 COMPANIES THAT WERE IN THE S&P 500 INDEX IN JANUARY 2013 AND WERE PUBLICLY LISTED FROM 1981 THROUGH 2012. IF THE COMPANIES THAT WENT PUBLIC AFTER 1981, SUCH AS MICROSOFT, CISCO, AMGEN, ORACLE, AND DELL, WERE INCLUDED, REPURCHASES AS A PERCENTAGE OF NET INCOME WOULD BE EVEN HIGHER.

Yet in recent years, hedge fund activists such as David Einhorn and Carl Icahn—who played absolutely no role in the company's success over the decades—have purchased large amounts of Apple stock and then pressured the company to announce some of the largest buyback programs in history.

The past decade's huge increase in repurchases, in addition to high levels of dividends, have come at a time when U.S. industrial companies face new competitive challenges. This raises questions about how much of corporate cash flow is really "free" to be distributed to shareholders. Many academics—for example, Gary P. Pisano and Willy C. Shih of Harvard Business School, in their 2009 HBR article "Restoring American Competitiveness" and their book *Producing Prosperity*—have warned that if U.S. companies don't start investing much more in research and manufacturing capabilities, they cannot expect to remain competitive in a range of advanced technology industries.

Retained earnings have always been the foundation for investments in innovation. Executives who subscribe to MSV are thus copping out of their responsibility to invest broadly and deeply in the productive capabilities their organizations need to continually innovate. MSV as commonly understood is a theory of value extraction, not value creation.

EXECUTIVES ARE SERVING THEIR OWN INTERESTS

As I noted earlier, there is a simple, much more plausible explanation for the increase in open-market repurchases: the rise of stock-based pay. Combined with pressure from Wall Street, stock-based incentives make senior executives extremely motivated to do buybacks on a colossal and systemic scale.

Consider the 10 largest repurchasers, which spent a combined $859 billion on buybacks, an amount equal to 68% of their combined net income, from 2003 through 2012. (See the exhibit "The Top 10 Stock Repurchasers.") During the same decade, their CEOs received, on average, a total of $168 million each in compensation. On average, 34% of their compensation was in the form of stock options and 24% in stock awards. At these companies the next four highest-paid senior executives each received, on average, $77 million in compensation during the 10 years—27% of it in stock options and 29% in stock awards. Yet since 2003 only three of the 10 largest repurchasers—Exxon Mobil, IBM, and Procter & Gamble—have outperformed the S&P 500 Index.

REFORMING THE SYSTEM

Buybacks have become an unhealthy corporate obsession. Shifting corporations back to a retain-and-reinvest regime that promotes stable and equitable growth will take bold action. Here are three proposals:

Put an end to open-market buybacks. In a 2003 update to Rule 10b-18, the SEC explained: "It is not appropriate for the safe harbor to be available when the issuer has a heightened incentive to manipulate its share price." In practice, though, the stock-based pay of the executives who decide to do repurchases provides just this "heightened incentive." To correct this glaring problem, the SEC should rescind the safe harbor.

A good first step toward that goal would be an extensive SEC study of the possible damage that open-market repurchases have done to capital formation, industrial corporations, and the U.S. economy over the past three decades. For example, during that period the amount of stock taken out of the market has exceeded the amount issued in almost every year; from 2004 through 2013 this net withdrawal averaged $316 billion a year. In aggregate, the stock market is not functioning as a source of funds for corporate investment. As I've already noted, retained earnings have always provided the base for such investment. I believe that the practice of tying executive compensation to stock price is undermining the formation of physical and human capital.

Rein in stock-based pay. Many studies have shown that large companies tend to use the same set of consultants to benchmark executive compensation, and that each consultant recommends that the client pay its CEO well above average. As a result, compensation inevitably ratchets up over time. The studies also show that even declines in stock price increase executive pay: When a company's stock price falls, the board stuffs even more options and stock awards into top executives' packages, claiming that it must ensure that they won't jump ship and will do whatever is necessary to get the stock price back up.

In 1991 the SEC began allowing top executives to keep the gains from immediately selling stock acquired from options. Previously, they had to hold the stock for six months or give up any "short-swing" gains. That decision has only served to reinforce top executives' overriding personal interest in boosting stock prices. And because corporations aren't required to disclose daily buyback activity, it gives executives the opportunity to trade, undetected, on inside information about when buybacks are being

THE BIG IDEA PROFITS WITHOUT PROSPERITY

THE TOP 10 STOCK REPURCHASERS
2003–2012

At most of the leading U.S. companies below, distributions to shareholders were well in excess of net income. These distributions came at great cost to innovation, employment, and—in cases such as oil refining and pharmaceuticals—customers who had to pay higher prices for products.

#1 EXXON MOBIL		#2 MICROSOFT		#3 IBM		#4 CISCO SYSTEMS		#5 PROCTER & GAMBLE	
NET INCOME	$347B	NET INCOME	$148B	NET INCOME	$117B	NET INCOME	$64B	NET INCOME	$93B
REPURCHASES	$207B	REPURCHASES	$114B	REPURCHASES	$107B	REPURCHASES	$75B	REPURCHASES	$66B
DIVIDENDS	$80B	DIVIDENDS	$71B	DIVIDENDS	$23B	DIVIDENDS	$2B	DIVIDENDS	$42B
TOTAL	$287B	TOTAL	$185B	TOTAL	$130B	TOTAL	$77B	TOTAL	$108B
	83% of NI		125% of NI		111% of NI		121% of NI		116% of NI
CEO PAY	$289M	CEO PAY	$12M	CEO PAY	$247M	CEO PAY	$297M	CEO PAY	$90M
% STOCK BASED	73%	% STOCK BASED	0%	% STOCK BASED	64%	% STOCK BASED	92%	% STOCK BASED	16%
	$211M		$0*		$158M		$273M		$14M

SOURCES STANDARD & POOR'S COMPUSTAT DATABASE; STANDARD & POOR'S EXECUCOMP DATABASE; THE ACADEMIC-INDUSTRY RESEARCH NETWORK.
NOTE THE PERCENTAGES OF STOCK-BASED PAY INCLUDE GAINS REALIZED FROM EXERCISING STOCK OPTIONS FOR ALL YEARS PLUS, FOR 2003-2005, THE FAIR VALUE OF RESTRICTED STOCK GRANTS OR, FOR 2006-2012, GAINS REALIZED ON VESTING OF STOCK AWARDS. ROUNDING TO THE NEAREST BILLION MAY AFFECT TOTAL DISTRIBUTIONS AND PERCENTAGES OF NET INCOME. *STEVEN BALLMER, MICROSOFT'S CEO FROM JANUARY 2000 TO FEBRUARY 2014, DID NOT RECEIVE ANY STOCK-BASED PAY. HE DOES, HOWEVER, OWN ABOUT 4% OF MICROSOFT'S SHARES, VALUED AT MORE THAN $13 BILLION.

done. At the very least, the SEC should stop allowing executives to sell stock immediately after options are exercised. Such a rule could help launch a much-needed discussion of meaningful reform that goes beyond the 2010 Dodd-Frank Act's "Say on Pay"—an ineffectual law that gives shareholders the right to make nonbinding recommendations to the board on compensation issues.

But overall the use of stock-based pay should be severely limited. Incentive compensation should be subject to performance criteria that reflect investment in innovative capabilities, not stock performance.

Transform the boards that determine executive compensation. Boards are currently dominated by other CEOs, who have a strong bias toward ratifying higher pay packages for their peers. When approving enormous distributions to shareholders and stock-based pay for top executives, these directors believe they're acting in the interests of shareholders.

That's a big part of the problem. The vast majority of shareholders are simply investors in outstanding shares who can easily sell their stock when they want to lock in gains or minimize losses. As I argued earlier, the people who truly invest in the productive capabilities of corporations are taxpayers and workers. Taxpayers have an interest in whether a corporation that uses government investments can generate profits that allow it to pay taxes, which constitute the taxpayers' returns on those investments. Workers have an interest in whether the company will be able to generate profits with which it can provide pay increases and stable career opportunities.

It's time for the U.S. corporate governance system to enter the 21st century: Taxpayers and workers should have seats on boards. Their representatives would have the insights and incentives to ensure that executives allocate resources to investments in capabilities most likely to generate innovations and value.

COURAGE IN WASHINGTON
After the Harvard Law School dean Erwin Griswold published "Are Stock Options Getting out of Hand?" in this magazine in 1960, Senator Albert Gore launched a campaign that persuaded Congress to whittle away special tax advantages for executive stock options. After the Tax Reform Act of 1976, the compensation expert Graef Crystal declared that stock options that qualified for the capital-gains tax rate, "once the most popular of all executive compensation devices...have been given the last rites by Congress." It also happens that during the 1970s the share of all U.S. income that the top 0.1% of households got was at its lowest point in the past century.

The members of the U.S. Congress should show the courage and independence of their predecessors and go beyond "Say on Pay" to do something about excessive executive compensation. In addition, Congress should fix a broken tax regime that frequently rewards value extractors as if they were value creators and ignores the critical role of government investment in the infrastructure and knowledge that are so crucial to the competitiveness of U.S. business.

Instead, what we have now are corporations that lobby—often successfully—for federal subsidies for research, development, and exploration, while devoting far greater resources to stock buybacks. Here are three examples of such hypocrisy:

Alternative energy. Exxon Mobil, while receiving about $600 million a year in U.S. government subsidies for oil exploration (according to the Center

#6 HEWLETT-PACKARD		#7 WALMART		#8 INTEL		#9 PFIZER		#10 GENERAL ELECTRIC	
NET INCOME	$41B	NET INCOME	$134B	NET INCOME	$79B	NET INCOME	$84B	NET INCOME	$165B
REPURCHASES	$64B	REPURCHASES	$62B	REPURCHASES	$60B	REPURCHASES	$59B	REPURCHASES	$45B
DIVIDENDS	$9B	DIVIDENDS	$35B	DIVIDENDS	$27B	DIVIDENDS	$63B	DIVIDENDS	$87B
TOTAL	$73B	TOTAL	$97B	TOTAL	$87B	TOTAL	$122B	TOTAL	$132B
	177% of NI		73% of NI		109% of NI		146% of NI		81% of NI
CEO PAY	$210M	CEO PAY	$189M	CEO PAY	$127M	CEO PAY	$91M	CEO PAY	$126M
% STOCK BASED	37%	% STOCK BASED	62%	% STOCK BASED	62%	% STOCK BASED	25%	% STOCK BASED	25%
	$78M		$117M		$79M		$23M		$32M

for American Progress), spends about $21 billion a year on buybacks. It spends virtually no money on alternative energy research.

Meanwhile, through the American Energy Innovation Council, top executives of Microsoft, GE, and other companies have lobbied the U.S. government to triple its investment in alternative energy research and subsidies, to $16 billion a year. Yet these companies had plenty of funds they could have invested in alternative energy on their own. Over the past decade Microsoft and GE, combined, have spent about that amount annually on buybacks.

Nanotechnology. Intel executives have long lobbied the U.S. government to increase spending on nanotechnology research. In 2005, Intel's then-CEO, Craig R. Barrett, argued that "it will take a massive, coordinated U.S. research effort involving academia, industry, and state and federal governments to ensure that America continues to be the world leader in information technology." Yet from 2001, when the U.S. government launched the National Nanotechnology Initiative (NNI), through 2013 Intel's expenditures on buybacks were almost four times the total NNI budget.

Pharmaceutical drugs. In response to complaints that U.S. drug prices are at least twice those in any other country, Pfizer and other U.S. pharmaceutical companies have argued that the profits from these high prices—enabled by a generous intellectual-property regime and lax price regulation—permit more R&D to be done in the United States than elsewhere. Yet from 2003 through 2012, Pfizer funneled an amount equal to 71% of its profits into buybacks, and an amount equal to 75% of its profits into dividends. In other words, it spent more on buybacks and dividends than it earned and tapped its capital reserves to help fund them. The reality is, Americans pay high drug prices so that major pharmaceutical companies can boost their stock prices and pad executive pay.

GIVEN THE IMPORTANCE of the stock market and corporations to the economy and society, U.S. regulators must step in to check the behavior of those who are unable or unwilling to control themselves. "The mission of the U.S. Securities and Exchange Commission," the SEC's website explains, "is to protect investors, maintain fair, orderly, and efficient markets, and facilitate capital formation." Yet, as we have seen, in its rulings on and monitoring of stock buybacks and executive pay over three decades, the SEC has taken a course of action contrary to those objectives. It has enabled the wealthiest 0.1% of society, including top executives, to capture the lion's share of the gains of U.S. productivity growth while the vast majority of Americans have been left behind. Rule 10b-18, in particular, has facilitated a rigged stock market that, by permitting the massive distribution of corporate cash to shareholders, has undermined capital formation, including human capital formation.

The corporate resource allocation process is America's source of economic security or insecurity, as the case may be. If Americans want an economy in which corporate profits result in shared prosperity, the buyback and executive compensation binges will have to end. As with any addiction, there will be withdrawal pains. But the best executives may actually get satisfaction out of being paid a reasonable salary for allocating resources in ways that sustain the enterprise, provide higher standards of living to the workers who make it succeed, and generate tax revenues for the governments that provide it with crucial inputs. ♡

HBR Reprint R1409B

William Lazonick is a professor of economics at the University of Massachusetts Lowell, the codirector of its Center for Industrial Competitiveness, and the president of the Academic-Industry Research Network. His book *Sustainable Prosperity in the New Economy? Business Organization and High-Tech Employment in the United States* won the 2010 Schumpeter Prize.

Daniel Indiviglio

Why We Need the Fed

For years, Rep. Ron Paul (R-TX) has been on a crusade to reduce the influence of the Federal Reserve. Indeed, he even wrote a book called "End the Fed," which suggests that the U.S. would be better off without a central bank. While it might have been easy for Congress to dismiss such calls to abolish the Fed in the past, Paul was recently named chairman of the House Domestic Monetary Policy Subcommittee. In other words, he runs the committee that oversees the Fed, so he will probably challenge the central bank every chance he gets. As a result, now might be a good time to wonder why we need the Fed.

What Does the Fed Do?

The natural place to begin is with the Fed's responsibilities. Here are its four central duties, from a document (.pdf) on its website:

1. Conducting the nation's monetary policy by influencing the monetary and credit conditions in the economy in pursuit of maximum employment, stable prices, and moderate long-term interest rates
2. Supervising and regulating banking institutions to ensure the safety and soundness of the nation's banking and financial system and to protect the credit rights of consumers
3. Maintaining the stability of the financial system and containing systemic risk that may arise in financial markets
4. Providing financial services to depository institutions, the U.S. government, and foreign official institutions, including playing a major role in operating the nation's payments system

So the first important point is that the Fed actually does a lot. You can't simply eliminate these functions. If you got rid of the central bank, you would need to push many of these functions to other regulators or private

firms. For example, inflation has to be kept in check somehow. Prudential supervision is also important. The problem with eliminating the Fed is that you would need to delegate these responsibilities to another entity that could do them better.

Let's consider two of the most important of the Fed's duties: supervision and monetary policy.

Supervision

As a bank supervisor, the Fed oversees a number of financial firms such as bank holding companies, state chartered banks within the Federal Reserve System, and foreign branches of member banks. Although the Fed isn't the only bank supervisor out there, it plays a key role as supervisor of these institutions.

Monetary Policy

The U.S. needs some monetary policy. The government has chosen to allow the Fed [to] conduct monetary policy with significant independence, directing it to achieve two objectives: price stability and full employment. This means the Fed has a fair amount of freedom to play with interest rates, purchase assets, and even conduct emergency lending activities to achieve those ends.

What If There Was No Fed?

Now that we understand some of the most important duties of the Fed, what would happen if we simply eliminated it? Obviously, these duties would still have to be carried out so they would have to become the responsibility of someone or something else. I spoke with two former Fed officials who argued that providing the Fed these responsibilities is better than other alternatives.

Supervision

One of those former Fed officials, Richard Spillenkothen, is possibly the perfect person to explain why it's so important that the Fed is involved with supervision. Through 2006, he was the lead banking regulator for the Fed. He now serves as a director with Deloitte & Touche's Governance, Regulatory, and Risk Strategies services practice. He explains that the supervisory function of the Fed is important for a few reasons:

> Supervision is a way, not only to learn about what's going on in the financial system, what are the emerging points of systemic vulnerability, the principal emerging weaknesses, but it also gives the central bank an important role in settling financial and macroprudential policies. And all of that contributes to its broader financial stability responsibilities.

For the Fed, supervision is a two-way street. On one hand, it provides the central bank with a great deal of additional information about the banking system, which it can use for its other functions like ensuring financial stability. On the other hand, the Fed has a unique perspective to offer when it comes to supervision, because it has a great deal of data on and experience with financial markets, global regulation, and macroeconomics. So not only will supervision help the central bank to be more effective, but its background will help it to be an unusually well-informed supervisor.

> A team approach that includes the Fed will provide a robust supervisory framework.

This isn't to say that the Fed should necessarily be the only regulator out there. "Regulators bring their differing perspectives to the table," Spillenko then noted. The Fed's point of view is just one of many. Other regulators like the Securities and Exchange Commission, Federal Deposit Insurance Corporation, and others also make important contributions to supervision. But a team approach that includes the Fed will provide a robust supervisory framework.

Monetary Policy

When trying to understand the monetary policy function of the Fed, who better to talk to than the recently retired vice chairman of the Board of Governors and 40-year Fed veteran Donald Kohn? He now works as a Senior Fellow for the Brookings Institution. He believes that an independent central bank is the best way to control money supply to achieve price stability.

Of course, there are other ways in which monetary policy could be conducted. One option would be to put the government directly in charge of monetary policy. For example, the Treasury could do it, or Congress could directly vote on changes to interest rates or policy shifts.

"There tends to be an inflation bias to central banking when (monetary policy is) closely controlled in the political process," Kohn explains. He says history has shown that politicians worried about re-election tend to engage in short-term monetary policy easing to stimulate the economy, while ignoring long-term price stability. This can lead to excessive inflation.

> Periodic bank panics occurred under the gold standard; the Fed was founded to deal with those.

Another way to conduct monetary policy could be to peg currency to a commodity like gold. The U.S. used to take this approach through the gold standard. With this strategy, some think you don't need a Fed, because the quantity and value of the currency depend on the quantity of the commodity. Kohn says that this approach can be inflexible and dangerous:

> Periodic bank panics occurred under the gold standard; the Fed was founded to deal with those. And you're at the mercy of the supply of gold in the world, and its distribution among countries. You get situations as had occurred in the 1920s, when some countries accumulated large volumes of gold and they put downward pressure on the price levels of other countries that didn't have those large quantities of gold. It wasn't until after the U.S. went off the gold standard that we were able to begin emerging from the (Great) Depression.

He believes central bankers can do a better job of achieving price stability and other objectives with more flexibility than a commodity standard that ties the money supply to rigid rules.

If Not the Fed, Then Who?

This is not meant to be an exhaustive argument proving that an independent central bank is utterly necessary. Instead, these are just a few reasons why those with first-hand Fed experience believe that having a central bank like the Fed is better than other alternatives. And remember, quibbling over what objectives at which a central bank should aim as a part of its monetary policy philosophy isn't an argument against Fed; it's argument for reform. If you were to get rid of the central bank entirely, then you would need to find other regulators and/or mechanisms to take over its essential responsibilities. And as the sources above explain, trying to do so could get sticky.

Daniel Indiviglio was an associate editor at *The Atlantic* from 2009 through 2011. He is now the Washington, D.C.–based columnist for *Reuters Breakingviews*. He is also a 2011 Robert Novak Journalism Fellow through the Phillips Foundation. Indiviglio has also written for *Forbes*. Prior to becoming a journalist, he spent several years working as an investment banker and a consultant.

Robert Larson

 **NO**

Fed Up: The Federal Reserve's Balance Sheet Is Exploding on Both Sides

After suffering for years from a dizzyingly high unemployment rate, Americans are eager for meaningful increases in hiring. In the past, the government jump-started economic growth with fiscal policy—increasing spending in order to create new demand for goods and services, which companies could fulfill only by hiring. After the nation languished through a decade of depression in the 1930s, the monumental fiscal outlays for World War II created an enormous "stimulus" to total demand and hiring. The massive spending for the war effort, financed in large part by aggressive 80%-plus tax rates on the richest households, created demand that gave employers reason to create millions of jobs.

Most people regard social spending, such as on education or public health, as a more acceptable form of stimulus than military spending. But apart from government programs started in the 1960s due to popular demand, stimulus has proven "politically difficult" unless it takes the form of military adventure or tax cuts that are typically skewed toward the richest households. Unfortunately, tax cuts for the wealthy are the weakest form of stimulus and have relatively little job-creating impact; and non-military stimulus plans, including the inadequate 2009 stimulus bill, are targets for deficit hawks.

Yet in this climate of public-spending cutbacks, policymakers recognize that some new government response to the desperate job-market situation is clearly needed. The traditional alternative to fiscal policy is monetary policy—encouraging growth by lowering short-term interest rates through the Federal Reserve Bank's interventions. But traditional monetary policy has failed—short-term rates remain near zero while the economy continues to show little response. So attention has turned to the Fed's new alternative, "quantitative easing," an enormous program of purchases of financial assets. Fed policymakers hope to make long-term borrowing cheaper and therefore spur hiring, but the result so far has been to load up the Fed's balance sheet while enriching bond investors and rescuing more banks, with little effect on interest rates.

Balancing Act

All companies have balance sheets, listing a company's "liabilities"—what the company owes—and "assets"—what the company owns. Assets and liabilities always balance (as long as the company owner's equity is included with the liabilities), due to how they are counted. For example, on the balance sheet of a typical commercial bank, the main assets are bank loans extended to consumers and businesses, because they provide the bank with interest income. The main liabilities are the depositors' account balances, which the bank is obliged to produce at any time. The Federal Reserve is different, however, because it can essentially print money by electronically increasing the account balances it owes other banks. With the government's current refusal to run sensible fiscal deficits targeted at creating jobs, the Fed's ability to massively expand its balance sheet (and to even run a profit doing so) has attracted new attention.

Historically, the Fed's main assets have been U.S. Treasury bonds, which are pieces of government debt. This is because the Fed's usual role is to influence interest rates in order to moderate the business cycle. It does this by buying and selling large numbers of Treasury bonds from the largest U.S. banks, which influences interest rates across the economy, as money is pulled in and out of the banking system. This means the Fed generally has large volumes of these interest-bearing government bonds among its assets.

The Fed has historically held a number of liabilities, including the reserve accounts of the many private banks in the Federal Reserve system, held as cushions against losses. The U.S. Treasury Department's own "general account," used for government payments, also falls on this side of the balance sheet. But Fed liabilities also include the U.S. paper currency used across the economy, hence the "Federal Reserve Note" on bills. So the Fed is "liable" for the balances of the rest of the government, the private banks' reserve accounts it maintains, and for U.S. cash, which can be exchanged for other assets.

Throwing Money at the Problem

Over the course of the 2008 financial crisis and the ensuing weak recovery, the Fed's balance sheet has taken on a very different look. It has swollen with "quantitative easing" asset purchases: first, the Fed bought devalued "toxic assets" from the banks in the 2008 bank rescue, and more recently in a large "QE2" program of buying long-term U.S. government bonds. The Fed's current large-scale buying tends to push bond prices up, which lowers long-term interest rates. The Fed is buying great volumes of such assets, with its balance sheet rocketing from $800 billion in 2007 to $2.6 trillion in February 2011, and with QE2 still underway.

The mountain of new Fed assets is composed of three broad asset categories. The first is the extension of short-term credit to financial firms—lending on favorable terms to banks that are in dire need of immediate lending. This is an extension of the Fed's original role of "banker of last resort," lending cheaply to banks in need of money overnight or even facing a "run" of panicking depositors. This role included lending through both the Fed's normal "discount window" and the "Term Auction Facility," set up to allow staggering banks to borrow with more anonymity. "Currency swaps" to foreign central banks, in which the Fed bought foreign currency from banks needing U.S. dollars, were also part of the program. This category of Fed assets reached its high point during and immediately after the 2008 financial crisis, when the short-run lending markets dried up among fears of borrower insolvency, leaving many enormous banks, insurers, and other financial companies on the edge of failure. As the financial industry has recovered its footing, this category has declined as a share of the Fed's balance sheet.

The second category of the Fed's new asset pile is loans to broader borrowers in the economy, primarily short-term corporate bonds, or "commercial paper," from many U.S. corporations. Companies often rely on short-term borrowing to cover regular operating costs, like payroll or supplier bills, while waiting for receivables to come in. During the 2008 crisis, struggling investment groups like money market funds faced huge withdrawals, leaving them without the cash to continue investing in these short-term bonds. Therefore the commercial paper market "locked up": rates spiked and borrowing became almost impossible. The Fed stepped in to supply the market with emergency short-term credit, and its program earned headlines for the "bedrock" corporations—including Caterpillar, GE, McDonald's, Toyota, and Verizon—revealed to have relied heavily on the program. This category of assets also includes the TALF program, which sought to

restart "securitization"—the packaging of loans into assets that may be bought and sold. Car loans, credit card debt, and student loans are among the forms of packaged debt the Fed invested in. As these short-term markets have returned to somewhat normal functioning, this component has also diminished as a proportion of the Fed's total assets.

TALF and its related programs have become particularly notorious for being "gamed" by financial firms and what the *New York Times* called "a cross-section of America's wealthy." The super-low interest rates provided by the Fed for desperate and important corporations were also used by canny investors to make enormous sums off the public aid. One investor, having seen impressive returns of up to 10%, referred to getting "a gift from the Fed." In this connection, it is notable that at every stage the Fed's policy has been to pursue options that preferentially benefit the rich. Bond ownership is skewed toward upper-income households, so supporting bond market conditions is of disproportionate benefit to them. Likewise, the Fed's actions during and after the 2008 financial crisis meant few losses for the well-off creditors of banks and insurers, with their institutions rescued at taxpayer expense. The Fed richly deserves its reputation as a "captured" regulator, being predominantly run by former Wall Street bankers who often return to the finance industry after leaving the Fed.

The third main category of the Fed's asset purchases is what the Fed calls "high-quality" securities, meaning debt instruments with relatively low risk. This is the component that has taken on enormous proportions as part of the Fed's QE program. This program of asset purchases, which could reach $3 trillion in total, has made massive purchases of U.S. Treasury bonds, "agency debt" issued by the government mortgage agencies Freddie Mac and Fannie Mae, and mortgage-backed securities.

THE FEDERAL RESERVE SYSTEM: LEFT VS. RIGHT VIEWS

The Federal Reserve retains a strong reputation in mainstream circles. Its chairs, like Paul Volcker or Ben Bernanke, are treated with the reverence of high priests, even if their images are later tarnished by their disastrous policy decisions, as with Alan Greenspan.

The left position, however, begins with the recognition that the Fed's policymaking bodies are visibly controlled by Wall Street. From regular staffers to senior policymakers, there is a standard practice of Fed staff working for large commercial or investment bank before joining the Fed,

(Continued)

and an expectation that they will likely return to the financial industry later in their careers. Further indicators that the Fed is to a large extent a pawn of Wall Street include its recent surrender of a significant part of its influence, as government deregulation has allowed huge"shadow banking" institutions to grow outside the Fed system, weakening the Fed's monetary policy effectiveness. Despite complaints from Fed leaders, the central bank generally accepted these changes since they were demanded by Wall Street, which is the center of economic power and where many Fed figures hope to return for employment.

So the left picture is of a "captured regulator," a government body run by the industries it's supposed to regulate. From this point of view, moves to reform the Fed would include greater transparency and replacing banking industry influence with democratic governance, along with an increased emphasis on creating jobs instead of treating inflation as the main threat to the economy.

Right-wing criticisms of the Fed, in contrast, are grounded in the traditional conservative insistence on reduced government intervention in the economy, at least for interventions that regulate investment or reduce profit. In this view, the Fed is another government intervention in markets that would operate better if left alone, despite the clear association between financial deregulation and bubbles/crashes over the last thirty years. More recently, the advent of QE1 and 2 [has] driven the right to decry the "hyperinflation" it will bring about, overcoming the strong deflationary pressures of our slack job market. Conservative efforts to reform the Fed range from demands for more transparency up to Ron Paul's demand to abolish the bank entirely, returning to the era of free-floating interest rates (and presumably the greater volatility that accompanied them).

While these colossal buys were meant to lower long-term interest rates, the bond market has seen rate increases instead, defying Fed policy. Bond investors evidently expect borrowers to have difficulty repaying loans in today's weak recovery, and may also be "spooked" at the huge supply of public and private bonds for purchase today. Higher interest rates, of course, act as a drag on the economic recovery, such as it is. This "overruling" of the Fed by the bond market is parallel to the recent reduction in the Fed's power, as more "shadow" banking among unregulated finance firms has taken the place of the commercial banks the Fed regulates,

reducing its ability to influence the economy through interest rate changes for the banks in its system. The Fed's separate QE programs, although not themselves limited to Fed system banks, have also been so far unable to lower the price of in-demand credit.

Notably, the QE program is having a secondary effect as a semi-bailout for America's mid-size banks, which are still failing at a rate on course to swamp the FDIC, which insures their deposits. Since these second-tier banks received relatively little bailout money, the Fed is propping many up by buying their bad mortgage debt. QE is presumably also executed with the expectation that it will contribute to driving down the value of the U.S. dollar relative to other world currencies, as the Fed's buying spree effectively dumps the currency into world markets. This may have a positive effect in encouraging U.S. exports, which are cheaper for foreign buyers when the dollar loses value, but it also risks setting off a global currency war as other nations strive to weaken their own currencies in order to boost exports. Competition among trading blocks to deflate currencies was a prominent feature of the Great Depression and not an encouraging model for world economic recovery.

In the shadow of this still-growing mountain of Federal Reserve asset purchases, the Fed's liabilities have grown in parallel, but with less public attention. This is because most of the Fed's new assets are purchased from banks in the Federal Reserve regulatory system, which maintain their own reserve accounts with the Fed. So when the Fed buys some of a private bank's assets, like U.S. Treasury bills or mortgage-backed debt, rather than mail a check it simply increases the banks' deposit account balance. The Fed may be called on to give the bank the money in its Fed account, so these payments are a liability for the Fed, and have grown as a mirror image of the assets bought in the QE purchase program.

Quantitative Unease

The QE gambit—and its effects on the Fed's balance sheet—is by no means unanimously popular at the Fed. It is widely reported that QE is a contentious move among members of the Federal Reserve Open Market Committee, which decides monetary policy. Prominent Fed members, including the presidents of the Dallas, Philadelphia, and Minneapolis Federal Reserve Banks, have stated discomfort with QE. Dissenters also include Kansas City Federal Reserve Bank President Thomas Hoenig, who has described QE as "risky," and prefers breaking up the "too-big-to-fail" banks. And in language rather unusual for a Fed bank president, he openly discusses the "Wall Street-Washington axis of influence" and decries the "enormous power" of the "oligarchy" of powerful banks.

But most of QE's critics are inflation "hawks"—investors and FOMC members who advocate an aggressively anti-inflationary posture. They oppose QE for two reasons. The first is a fear of runaway inflation caused by injecting so much money into the economy. However, this concern seems remote in an economy with a double-digit real unemployment rate and usage of manufacturing capacity at an embarrassing 72%. Also, the inflation rate itself has not reached 3% since the financial crisis, although significant inflation could originate in imported products should the dollar fall quickly. The hawks' second concern about QE is that the Fed will become unwilling to raise interest rates in the future. Increasing interest rates would reduce the value of the Fed's own large bond investments, when investors sell them for higher-yielding assets. Furthermore, higher rates would mean the Fed would have to pay more in interest to banks with deposits at the Fed. For these twin reasons the hawks fear a loss of the Fed's willingness to raise rates later, thus damaging its inflation-fighting "credibility."

Conservative critics also fear that QE jeopardizes the large payments the Fed makes to the government. By law, any profit the Federal Reserve Bank makes on its now-large investments must be paid to the U.S. Treasury, after covering the Fed's own costs. In 2009 the Fed made $78 billion from its huge investments, politically valuable income in a time of widening budget deficits. A Fed rate increase could eliminate that payment, and indeed the Fed could ultimately lose money on its investment—as the bond market has declined, the Fed's portfolio was recently down a few percent.

Whatever the long-term impact on the Fed of its asset-purchasing campaign, it is difficult to see significant positive effects on the broader economy. Even if the Fed ultimately succeeds in pushing down long-term interest rates, cheap borrowing won't boost the economy the way a targeted spending program would. Companies may appreciate cheap borrowing, but they still won't create jobs when there is not sufficient demand for goods: who would buy new workers' output? Likewise, while cash-strapped and indebted consumers will benefit from low interest rates, they're unlikely to increase spending again without the feeling of security that comes from a steady job. Aggressive fiscal outlays in energy and infrastructure would create far more jobs than quantitative easing is

likely to do. No wonder popular discontent with the Fed has reached the point that it's a featured villain in many Tea Party and progressive protests and now even faces limited audits. Now that the Fed has been disbursing literally trillions in aid to the rich and their institutions for years, with a pitiful trickle going to the majority, the public is getting fed up with the Federal Reserve.

So as the economy staggers on, instead of asking your neighborhood employer for a stimulus-driven job consider asking your neighborhood bank if you can borrow a cup of money.

A Fed Balance Sheet Glossary

Assets: Tangible or intangible items of value owned by a firm, such as cash or interest-paying loans.

Liabilities: An obligation of a firm to another party, such as a bank depositor; equal to assets minus net equity.

Balance sheet: A financial statement indicating a firm's assets and liabilities at some point in time.

Bond: A tradable piece of an institution's debt. Bond interest rates decrease as prices increase, lowering funding costs.

Liquidity: An institution's access to cash or close equivalents

Reserve account: Deposit accounts kept by private banks with their regional Fed bank, holding the capital the Fed obliges them to maintain.

Open market operations: The Fed's normal practice of influencing interest rates by buying or selling large volumes of government bonds, which tends to decrease/increase short-term rates.

Quantitative easing: The Fed's recent program to lower long-term interest rates by buying massive amounts of Treasury bonds and mortgage-backed securities.

Securities: A general term for a financial asset, such as stocks and bonds.

Term Auction Facility: The Fed's program to extend cheap, short-term credit to financial institutions through a more anonymous process than the discount window, mostly during the 2008 financial crisis.

TALF: Term Asset-Backed Securities Loan Facility, set up by the Fed in 2008 to restart securitization markets, which package existing loans into tradable assets and have become a major source of U.S. credit.

Sources

Binyamin Applebaum, "Mortgage Securities It Holds Pose Sticky Problem for Fed," *New York Times,* July 22, 2010; Agnes Crane and Robert Cyran, "Rising Interest Rates and the Fed's Red Ink," *New York Times,* December 15, 2010; Michael Derby, "Treasury Fall Poses Long-Term Dilemma for Fed Balance Sheet," *Wall Street Journal,* December 10, 2011; Peter Goodman, "Policy Options Dwindle as Economic Fears Grow," *New York Times,* August 28, 2010; Sewell Chan, "Fed Pays a Record $78.4 Billion to Treasury, *New York Times,* January 10, 2011; "Fed's Fisher: Bond Buying Likely to Run Its Course," *Wall Street Journal,* January 10, 2011; Luca Di Leo, "Yellen Staunchly Defends Fed's Bond Program," *Wall Street Journal,* January 8, 2011; Jon Hilsenrath, "Fed Chief Gets a Likely Backer," *Wall Street Journal,* January 10, 2011; Sewell Chan, "Fed's Contrarian Has a Wary Eye on the Past," *New York Times,* December 13, 2010; Christine Hauser, "A Bond Rush as Treasury Prices Fall," *New York Times,* December 8, 2010; Mark Gongloff, "Bond Market Defies Fed," *Wall Street Journal,* November 16, 2010; Sewell Chan and Jo Craven McGinty, "Fed Papers Show Breadth of Emergency Measures," *New York Times,* December 1, 2010; Jon Hilsenrath, "Fed Fires $600 Billion Stimulus Shot," *Wall Street Journal,* November 4, 2010; Sewell Chan and Ben Protess, "Cross Section of Rich Invested With the Fed," *New York Times,* December 2, 2010.

ROBERT LARSON is an assistant professor of economics at Ivy Tech Community College in Bloomington, Indiana. In addition to teaching, he is a regular contributor to *Z H* and *Dollars and Sense.* He has recently published an article on *AlterNet,* titled "Why Big Finance Is Laughing All the Way to the Bank."

EXPLORING THE ISSUE

Is the Federal Reserve Good for Business?

Critical Thinking and Reflection

1. What distinguishes the U.S. banking system from the banking systems practiced in Europe?
2. Historically, what made the U.S. government decide it was ethical to implement the Federal Reserve system?
3. What impact could legislation have that would reduce or eliminate the powers or functions of the Federal Reserve?
4. Was the Federal Reserve a problem with the market crash of 2008? If so, why; if not, why not?
5. Explain why some politicians believe the Federal Reserve is a harmful entity.

Is There Common Ground?

From a libertarian perspective, the Federal Reserve Bank is fraught with problems. First, it is seen as government involved in the capitalistic sector where it "doesn't belong." Next, by directing the nation's monetary policy, it is able to control money supplies to regional banks, a duty that could be performed by those within the banking industry. Finally, it is claimed that the reach and representation of the Federal Reserve within international markets are fraught with collusion and secrecy. From a democratic perspective, the Federal Reserve keeps large banks from having too much influence over currency and interest in the United States and abroad. Without some form of regulation, large banks can easily take over smaller banks. Collusion is always possible, whether within the Federal Reserve systems or within the larger banking systems. The ethical choices are varied. The Federal Reserve was created to maintain stability and a fair playing field within the banking sector.

At present it appears that stability is an important commodity.

Additional Resources

John Boatright. *Ethics in Finance,* 2nd ed. (Malden, MA: Blackwell, 2008).

Jesse Eisinger, "Fed Shrugged Off Warnings, Let Banks Pay Shareholders Billions." *Business Ethics* (March 2, 2012).

Federal Reserve Board. *The Federal Reserve System: Purposes and Functions,* 9th ed. (Washington, D.C.: Board of Governors of the Federal Reserve System, 2006).

Jorg Guido Hulsmann. *The Ethics of Money Production* (Auburn, AL: Ludwig von Mises Institute, 2008).

Shawn Ritenour. "The Federal Reserve: An Economic and Ethical Disaster." *Principal Studies* (June 2009). Principalstudies.org/ethics

Internet References . . .

Federal Reserve (Central Bank)

www.federalreserveonline.org/

www.federalreserve.gov

Federal Reserve Education

www.federalreserveeducation.org

Foreign Corrupt Practices Act

http://www.justice.gov/criminal-fraud/foreign-corrupt
-practices-act

Unit 2

sites like Facebook, such as Twitter, MySpace, and personal blogs, allow their users to stay in touch with friends and family as well as make new connections by posting photos, messages of varying length, and comments to other users' sites. As these forms of social media grow in size and number, so do the questions of their appropriate use by the creators and receivers of the information. Although the previous generation's employee privacy ethics focused on issues such as e-mail privacy, the advent and growth of this new use of the Internet has made employer monitoring of employees' social networking the twenty-first century's central employee privacy issue.

Although social networking has proven to be a useful tool for many companies, creating another inexpensive way to advertise products and events is not without drawbacks. Time wasted by employees updating their personal sites on company time has led many businesses to block access to such sites on work premises to maintain a productive environment. Although this step seems reasonable to most, it is not the only way a company's interests can be affected by an employee's decisions regarding social media. Disgruntled and careless employees have been known to take to their personal sites to air their grievances and share possibly damaging company or client information. This leads many to ask, should an employee's use of social media outside of the office affect his or her job?

With a plethora of personal information not normally found on a résumé or application now readily available with the click of a mouse, more and more employers are using social media in hiring and employee-retention decisions. As a result, as social media use increases, so has the number of people fired or passed over for jobs because of information found on their personal sites not directly related to their job. Items such as questionable photos and personal, defamatory remarks about their bosses and co-workers have been causes of dismissal.

Although social media has been used to help businesses identify which employees could prove to be a liability to the company, employer perusal of these sites can itself prove to be a liability. As mentioned previously, these sites often contain information not asked for on job applications, often times for legal reasons. A person's social profile, whether blatantly or by association with certain groups, can often contain information about one's religion, sexuality, gender, disabilities, or other indicators of minority status.

These sites have a myriad of ways to personalize security and block unauthorized persons from viewing profiles, or even just pieces of information. In their privacy policy, Facebook reminds us that one should "Always consider your privacy settings before sharing information on Facebook." With these layers of protection, can privacy be expected on the Internet, or considering the wise words of Benjamin Franklin, can three people keep a secret only if two of them are dead? Is the use of these settings a legitimate claim to privacy, or simply a false comfort?

While reading the YES and NO selections, consider whether information on the Internet can truly be considered as private. Does an employer have a right to access employee information on social media sites if precautions have not been taken to otherwise prevent their access? And should employers disclose their intention to use information found on social media sites?

YES

**Brian Elzweig and
Donna K. Peeples**

Using Social Networking Web Sites in Hiring and Retention Decisions

Social networking Web sites are a relatively new format that allows people to post personal information to be viewed by "private" friends and the public as well. Managers may wish to access these sites, with or without permission, and use that information in hiring and retention decisions. Managers may, in fact, be required to monitor employees' social networking sites to defend against the possibility of negligent hiring and retention lawsuits being filed against their companies. However, use of this information must be weighed against the expectation of privacy by the person posting the information. A better understanding of the law can provide guidelines of when and how managers may access this information, thus avoiding liability for invading the privacy of current or potential employees.

An Interesting Example of What Not To Do

Many people have heard stories about how some employees have lost their jobs because of what they posted on a social networking Web site. For example, Stacy Snyder (*Snyder v. Millersville University*, 2008), student at Millersville University, was dismissed from her job as a student teacher at a high school and denied her teaching credential when officials from the university were made aware of a photograph and a post on her MySpace.com (hereinafter MySpace) site.

The post also included what the *New York Times* described as a "surprisingly innocuous" picture containing a head shot of Ms. Snyder wearing a pirate hat while drinking from a plastic cup. In a self-titled caption she called the photograph "drunken pirate" (Stross, 2007). Nicole Reinking, who was Snyder's coordinating teacher at Conestoga Valley High School (CV), had been critical of Snyder's classroom performance and professionalism (*Snyder v. Millersville University*, 2008).

Millersville University claimed that Ms. Snyder's dismissal was due to her competency as a teacher; however, the

court held that her dismissal was based at least in part on the MySpace posting. Millersville University stated that the photograph was "unprofessional" and may "promote underage drinking." The college also claimed that Ms. Snyder was in violation of a section of the teacher's handbook requiring teachers to be "well groomed and appropriately dressed" (Stross, 2007). Snyder sued Millersville University alleging that her "First Amendment right to free expression protected the text and photograph in her . . . MySpace posting" (*Snyder v. Millersville University*, 2008). The United States District Court for the Eastern District of Pennsylvania ruled that Snyder was acting as an employee of CV, not as a student at Millersville University, when she was a student teacher. In doing so, the court denied her First Amendment claim stating that Snyder "was a public employee . . . when she created her MySpace posting, [therefore] she would be obligated to show that the posting related to matters of public concern to receive First Amendment protection" (*Snyder v. Millersville University*, 2008).

Snyder's case illustrates a dilemma facing many managers today and gives rise to important questions. First, may information available on a personal Web site be legally used in decisions relating to hiring or other employee decisions such as retention? Second, if such information may be used legally, should a manager seek this information and act on it? These fairly new questions are exacerbated by the prevalence of social networking sites and the potential wealth of information contained on them. Some interesting findings are:

- According to Ipsos Insight's (2007) latest "Face of the Web" study, social networking is becoming the dominant online behavior. The study found that 24% of American adults have visited a social networking Web site, with two thirds visiting within the 30 days previous to the polling. This usage is even higher in other countries such as South Korea, where 49% of adults had visited a social networking site at least once (Ipsos Insight, 2007).

- The two most popular social networking sites are MySpace and Facebook.com (Facebook) (Hitwise, 2008).
- In May of 2008, Facebook had 123.9 million unique visitors and MySpace had 114.6 million (McCarthy, 2008).
- The fastest growing demographic on Facebook is those who are 25 years old and older (ComScore, 2007).
- More than half of its users are over age 35 (Comscore, 2006).

With this many users, most of whom have their own Web page, it would seem that for a manager who is trying to hire the best employees, these sites (along with hundreds of smaller ones) are a veritable treasure trove of information (Boyd and Ellison, 2007). Ostensibly, information that is not available on a résumé may be available on a job candidate's Web site. The problem for managers, however, is that while they may want to mine the sites for information about a candidate, the site's creator may have a legal right to privacy, and there may also be problems with accuracy of data obtained.

Can Managers Use Social Networking Web Sites in Hiring Decisions?

According to a recent survey by Careerbuilders.com,

- 22% of hiring managers used social networking Web sites to screen job candidates, double the amount from two years ago.
- Of those using the sites for screening, 34% reported that the information obtained caused them not to hire a particular candidate.
- 24% found content favorable to the candidate in their hiring decision.
- The number of hiring managers using social networking Web sites is likely to increase in the future as 9% who reported not using them planned to do so in the future (Grasz, 2008).

Since this has become a source of information, would a manager be remiss in *not* using these sites? Before deciding, managers should address some liability issues that generally revolve around the expectation of privacy.

Right to Privacy—Or Not?

In this age of information, especially information posted on the Internet by private individuals, should there be an expectation of privacy? Does utilizing the Web sites' privacy settings create an expectation of privacy? These are not simple questions with answers fully tested in the courts.

Whether or not there is an expectation of privacy may depend on how the user's account is set up and the information provided by the site regarding the conditions of privacy. Both Facebook and MySpace allow a user to set up a private site so that only those given permission by the user should be allowed access. It has been suggested that Snyder's biggest mistake was "not knowing or choosing to turn on any sort of privacy controls on her social network profile page . . . which would have prevented anyone except those who were accepted as Snyder's friends, [anyone who had been granted access, and those exempted by the terms of service/use], to have access to the items she posted. Facebook also offers extensive privacy controls that should be configured" (Perez, 2008).

This answer appears overly simplistic. While there is probably no expectation of privacy for a user who does not use privacy settings, a general expectation cannot be relied upon just by using the privacy settings.

Terms of Service—The Great Unread Section

When joining either MySpace or Facebook, the user must agree to the terms of service and to the Web sites, privacy policies. These policies weaken a user's argument that just setting the site's privacy control functions guarantees privacy. The Facebook Principles notes that: "Facebook helps you share information with your friends and people around you . . . And you control the users with whom you share that information through the privacy settings on the Privacy page" (Facebook Principles). This is contrasted later in the policy:

> You post User Content . . . on the Site at your own risk. Although we allow you to set privacy options that limit access to your pages, please be aware that no security measures are perfect or impenetrable. We cannot control the actions of other Users with whom you may choose to share your pages and information. Therefore, we cannot and do not guarantee that User content you post on the Site will not be viewed by unauthorized persons. We are not responsible for circumvention of any privacy settings or security measures contained on the Site. You understand and acknowledge that, even after removal, copies of User Content may remain viewable in cached and archived pages or if other Users have copied or stored your User Content. (Facebook Principles).

MySpace goes further in its safety settings noting that: "Every profile has the option of being 'private.' This means that only you and those you have added and approved as friends can see the details of your profile, including your blog, photos, interests, etc." (MySpace safety tips and settings: Safety settings).

That is contrasted with specific warnings in another part of the same document:

> *Don't forget that your profile and MySpace forums are public spaces. . . . Don't post anything that would embarrass you later.* It's easy to think that only our friends are looking at our MySpace page, but the truth is that everyone can see it. Think twice before posting a photo or information you wouldn't want your parents, potential employers, colleges or boss to see!" (MySpace safety tips and settings: General tips). [Emphasis added].

Is "Privacy" a Misnomer on Social Networking Sites?

Web sites themselves recognize that setting privacy options to limit access to a social networking site does not prevent all unwanted users from seeing the site's content. It has been suggested that hiring companies can access applicants' sites in a variety of ways. Facebook allows college students to give blanket access to anyone in their college. Recent graduates who remain active in their college's social network may become useful to their new employer because of their access to the Web sites of students still attending the school from which they graduated. Some companies may also hire current students who can access their peers' social networking profiles (Brandenburg, 2008). While searching for a specific person on both Facebook and MySpace, even before becoming a "friend" and being able to access a person's private site, certain information is still shared with the default settings. A user's "profile picture" (the picture that identifies their page) is available, as well as place of residence. MySpace also identifies the person's age, and Facebook shows other networks they are affiliated with (which can relate to work, hobbies, interests, politics, and a myriad of other things). In addition, Facebook allows someone doing a search to access the "target's" list of friends. Thus, a hiring company could ask a third party to access a potential hire's Web site for them.

Is There Tort Liability for Invasion of Privacy?

No case law directly addresses the point of whether there is an expectation of privacy on a social network Web site. Analogies must be made from case law as to expectations of privacy in other areas. The right to bring a private action for invasion of privacy was first discussed in legal literature in an 1890 *Harvard Law Review* article by Samuel Warren and Louis Brandeis. This article led to courts creating tort claims for invasion of privacy (Warren and Brandeis, 1890). The seminal case in this area is *Katz v. United States*, in which the Supreme Court first recognized that "the Fourth Amendment protects people, not places." The issue in the Katz case was whether a wiretap of a telephone booth could be used as evidence against [Katz] the defendant, who was on trial for illegally transmitting bets or wagers by wire. The defendant argued that he had an expectation of privacy in the telephone booth; therefore, a warrant would be needed. In a concurring opinion that found for the defendant, Justice Harlan laid out the test for when a search and seizure requires a warrant: "There is a twofold requirement, first, that a person have exhibited an actual (subjective) expectation of privacy and, second, that the expectation be one that society is prepared to recognize as reasonable" (*Katz v. United States*, 1967).

The basic principle in Katz has been tested in the context of cyberspace, but not specifically in the context of social networking Web sites. In *United States v. Maxwell*, the Court of Appeals for the Armed Forces examined the expectation of privacy as it pertained to e-mail communications. The court contrasted e-mail, if considered to be the equivalent of first-class mail and telephone conversations—both with high expectations of privacy—with e-mail if considered to be "postcards," which have lower expectations of privacy. In addition, the court also noted that if the e-mail communication was sent to a chat room then the public at large would have access—much like placing a letter on a public bulletin board. Once the communication is given public access, then the expectation of privacy would be eliminated (*U.S. v. Maxwell* as discussed by Hodge, 2006). However, other courts have not found a blanket expectation of privacy in e-mails after they are sent, noting that the recipient should be figured into whether there is still an expectation of privacy (*U.S. v. Charbonneau* as discussed by Hodge, 2006).

Cases such as these would surely be used by a court determining if there is a reasonable expectation of privacy for a person's social networking site. The court should take into account that with a social network site, the user permits many people to have access. If access is allowed to some people, it is hard to know how a court would rule on a claim of privacy if the people who were allowed access gave other people access. However, it should also be noted that a person who took steps to ensure privacy, such as enacting privacy settings within their Web site, would have a higher expectation of privacy than those who did not (Brandenburg, 2008).

It has been suggested by Brandenburg (2008) that the following elements would be relevant in deciding whether or not a person using a social networking site would have a reasonable expectation of privacy:

1. Whether privacy settings are available;
2. Whether the social networker attempted to or did enable the privacy settings;
3. The level of privacy the networker attempted to or was able to set with an eye to the spectrum of privacy settings and measures available to the social networker;
4. The kinds of people and groups to whom that networker chose to disclose the information he or she later claims to be sensitive and private; and
5. Whether the unwanted or unauthorized person who accessed the networker's information was able to happen upon the information or had to hack through security measures to find the information (Brandenburg, 2008).

The question that has not been answered yet by the courts is how these factors would withstand scrutiny under the Katz test. Katz requires that the person claiming privacy must have a subjective expectation of privacy. It is hard to tell where the courts would draw the line to say that expectation was met. The more effort a user of a social networking site expends in attempting to maintain privacy the more likely the court will find that the first part of the Katz test was met. However, a court would most likely consider these elements in light of the user agreement and would have to decide if any privacy claims would be waived by that agreement. In addition, these elements do not address the second part of the Katz test. A court may see the pervasiveness of social networking Web sites as society accepting their use. Some courts may see this as society accepting the use of these sites to disseminate private information, and so the expectation of privacy would be reasonable. However, other courts may see examples like Snyder's as a warning. The more public stories there are about people having adverse employment decisions, the more likely it is that a court would rule that expecting privacy is not reasonable.

Stored Communications Act

In addition to the potential tort liability for invasion of privacy, another area of concern for managers is the Stored Communications Act (SCA) (18 U.S.C. §§ 2701–2711 (2000).

The SCA makes it illegal to "intentionally access without authorization a facility through which an electronic communication service is provided" (18 U.S.C. §§ 2701(a)(1)). However, the SCA has a specific exception for "conduct authorized . . . by a user of that service with respect to a communication of or intended for that user . . ." 18 U.S.C. §§ 2701(c)(2). Questions arise as to what would qualify as conduct "authorized by a user" under the SCA. Certainly a user of a social networking Web site who allows access by designating others as "friends" would be authorizing their use. However, more questionable would be whether someone who was not granted access, such as an employer, was given information that was accessed by a "friend." Since the original person was authorized, the exception would probably apply. However, if an employer were to hack into a site without permission of the networker, then that employer would probably have liability under the SCA (Brandenburg, 2008).

Does the Right to Privacy Extend to Off-duty Current Employees

Davis (2007) has suggested that there should be an expectation of privacy for off-duty conduct of current employees, and that this expectation of privacy should extend to employees' social networking habits. The analysis is based on the issuance of lifestyle protection laws and some specific federal laws suggesting that once a person leaves work, they "expect to be let alone" (Davis, 2007). These laws soften the traditional employment-at-will doctrine available in most states. Two states, Colorado and North Dakota, have enacted broad protection for current employees. Colorado code states that it is a

> discriminatory or unfair employment practice for an employer to terminate the employment of any employee due to that employee's engaging in any lawful activity off the premises of the employer during nonworking hours unless such a restriction . . . [r]elates to a bona fide occupational requirement or is reasonably and rationally refted to the employment activities and responsibilities of a particular employee or a particular group of employees, rather than to all employees of the employer (Colo. Rev. Stat. Ann. § 24-34-402.5 (2008)).

Similarly, in North Dakota,

> [i]t is a discriminatory practice for an employer to fail or refuse to hire a person; to discharge an employee; or to accord adverse or unequal

treatment to a person or employee with respect to application, hiring, training, apprenticeship, tenure, promotion, upgrading, compensation, layoff, or a term, privilege, or condition of employment, because of race, color, religion, sex, national origin, age, physical or mental disability, status with respect to marriage or public assistance, **or** *participation in lawful activity off the employer's premises during nonworking hours which is not in direct conflict with the essential business-related interests of the employer . . ."* (N.D. Cent. Code § 14-02.4-03 (2008). [Emphasis added].

Davis (2007) notes that other states have also enacted less broad protections for off-duty conduct, such as New York, which protects off-duty conduct including legal recreational activities, consumption of legal products, political activity, and union membership. In addition "[o]ther states have enacted much more limited statutes protecting specific categories of lawful off-duty conduct and lifestyle, including consumption of tobacco products, sexual orientation, and marital status" (Davis, 2007).

Using these examples and the rationale that people have an expectation of privacy outside of the workplace, Davis concludes that "[i]n a world where people simply have begun to conduct much of their social lives over the Internet, the same expectations apply: an employer should not be snooping into an employee's personal life when it has nothing to do with business" (Davis, 2007). This may be correct, but courts have interpreted what is considered to be "related to," "in direct conflict with the essential business-related interests of the employer," or other similar language. In *Marsh v. Delta Airlines,* Marsh, a Delta Air Lines baggage handler wrote a letter to the editor [of] the *Denver Post* that criticized Delta. He was subsequently fired due to the publication of the letter (Marsh, 2007). Marsh then sued, claiming he was wrongfully terminated under the Colorado lifestyle statute. The court held in favor of Delta stating that there "is an implied duty of loyalty, with regard to public communications, that employees owe to their employers" (Marsh, 1997). In finding that Marsh violated the implied duty of loyalty, his firing was justified as this duty was a *bona fide* occupational requirement as contemplated in the exception to the broad-reaching Colorado statute. The court interpreted the statute to protect off-duty privacy as a shield for employees who are engaged in activities that are legal but are distasteful to their employers, such as homosexuality or political affiliation.

In the only case interpreting the North Dakota statute, a chaplain was fired from his job after it was revealed that he was caught masturbating in an enclosed public restroom of a department store. The chaplain claimed that he had broken no law since the enclosure prohibited him from being found guilty. The court held that it is a factual dispute whether this behavior was unlawful. If it is not, the court implied that the statute may protect him since it "may fit the protected status of lawful activity off the employer's premises" (Hougham, 1998).

The off-duty lifestyle statutes seem to protect activities that are completely divorced from the employer in that to protect an employee they must take place off-site, during nonworking hours, and have no relationship to the employer's interests (Sprague, 2007). Even if there is an expectation of privacy, the legitimate needs of the employer may override. The cases in which employers have been found to invade privacy are ones in which the "employer has pried into the employee's life far beyond a legitimate business need" (Sprague, 2007).

While there is a suggestion that there should be an expectation of privacy for off-duty social networking, outside of the exceptions noted, no laws make it illegal to search an employee's *publicly available social networking Web site*. Still, since the argument relating to the public or nonpublic nature of information on a social networking site is not clearly settled, employers using such information may be doing so at their own peril. On the other hand, an employer *not using* such information may create liability by the "negligent hiring" or "negligent retention of an individual." A negligent hiring claim suggests that at the time an employee was hired, it was negligent for an employer to engage the employee's services based on what the employer knew or should have known about the employee (*McGuire v. Dean J. Curry*, 2009). Negligent retention liability is typically predicated on an "employer . . . placing a person with known propensities, or propensities which should have been discovered by reasonable investigation, in an employment position in which, because of the circumstances of the employment, it should have been foreseeable that the hired individual posed a threat of injury to others" (*Mandy v. 3M*, 1996). The negligent retention occurs "when, during the course of employment, the employer becomes aware or should have become aware of problems with an employee that indicated his unfitness, and the employer fails to take further action such as investigating, discharge, or reassignment" (*Mandy v. 3M*, 1996).

It is important to note that the tort[s] of negligent hiring and retention [are] based on the principle that a person conducting an activity through employees is subject to liability for

- Check state statute for privacy and lifestyle laws. Many states have some protections even if there is not a blanket protection for off-duty conduct.
- Train all employees on the important issues discussed in this paper.

Conclusion

With social networking Web sites becoming more prevalent, especially among individuals in the workforce, use of them is becoming more common in employment hiring and retention decisions. Since social networking sites are relatively new to users as well as employers, there are many issues to consider before using them for employment decisions. Employers should take steps to avoid invading privacy or committing discriminatory acts in using the sites, but should not fear using them if they have a legitimate interest at stake. These Web sites contain a treasure trove of publicly available information. Employers may be at risk if they *do not*, in fact, check for publicly available information on their current and potential employees. Employers should also take steps to ensure the accuracy of the information gathered. In addition, employees and job seekers should be put on notice that employers are using these sites to gather information and should assume that nothing posted on them is actually kept private.

References

Boyd, D. M., and Ellison, N. B. (2007). Social network sites: Definition, history, and scholarship. *Journal of Computer-Mediated Communication, 13*(1), article 11.

Brandenburg, C. (2008). The newest way to screen job applicants: A social networker's nightmare. *Federal Communications Law Journal, 60*(3), 597.

Colo. Rev. Stat. Ann. B 24-34-402.5 (2008).

ComScore press release: Facebook sees flood of new traffic from teenagers and adults (2007, July 5). Retrieved December 19, 2008 from http://www.comscore.com/press/release.asp?press=1519

ComScore press release: More than half of MySpace visitors are now age 35 or older, as the site's demographic composition continues to shift. (2006, October 5). Retrieved February 4, 2009 from http://www.comscore.com/press/release.asp?press=1019

Davis, D. (2007). My Space isn't your space: Expanding the fair credit reporting act to ensure accountability and fairness in employer searches of online social networking services. *Kansas Journal of Law and Public Policy, 16,* 237.

Facebook Principles (n.d.). Retrieved on January 21, 2009 from http://www.facebook.com/policy.php

Grasz, J. (2008, September 10). One-in-five employers use social networking sites to research job candidates, CareerBuilder.com survey finds. Retrieved December 18, 2008 from http://careerbuilder.com/share/aboutus/pressreleasesdetail.aspx?id=pr459&sd=9%2f10%2f2008&ed=12%2f31%2f2008&siteid=cbpr&sc_cmp1=cb_pr459_

Hitwise US-Top 20 websites-October, 2008. Retrieved December 18, 2008 from http://www.hitwise.com/datacenter/rankings.php

Hodge, M. (2006). The fourth amendment and privacy issues on the "new" internet: Facebook.com and MySpace.com. *Southern Illinois University Law Journal, 31,* 95.

Hougam v. Valley Memorial Homes, 1998 ND 24 (Supreme Court of North Dakota 1998).

Ipsos Insight Marketing Research Consultancy: Online video and social networking websites set to drive the evolution of tomorrow's digital lifestyle (2007, July 5). Retrieved December 18, 2008 from http://www.ipsosinsight.com/ pressrelease.aspx?id=3556

Katz v. United States, 389 U.S. 347 (1967).

Kirkland, A. (2007). You got fired? On your day off?! Challenging termination of employees for personal blogging practices. *University of Missouri Kansas City Law Review, 75,* 545.

Levitt, C., and Rosch, M. (2007, February). Making internet searches part of due diligence. *Los Angeles Lawyer, 29,* 46.

Magnum Foods, Inc. v. Continental Cas. Co., 36 F.3d 1491 (United States Court of Appeals for the Tenth Circuit 1994).

Mandy v. 3M, 940 F. Supp 1463 (United States District Court for the District of Minnesota 1996).

Marsh v. Delta Air Lines, 952 F. Supp. 1458 (United States District Court for the District of Colorado 1997).

McCarthy, C. (2008, June 20). ComScore: Facebook is beating MySpace worldwide.

CNet News. Retrieved from http://news.cnet.com/830113577_3-9973826-36.html

McGuire v. Dean J. Curry, 766 N.W.2d 501 (Supreme Court of South Dakota 2009).

Menzies, K.B. (2008, July). Perils and possibilities of online social networks. *Trial, 44,* 58.

MySpace safety tips and settings: General tips. (n.d.). Retrieved on January 21, 2009 from http://www.myspace.com/index.cfm?fuseaction=cms.viewpage&placement = safety_pagetips

MySpace safety tips and settings: Safety settings. (n.d.). Retrieved on January 21, 2009 from http://www.myspace.com/index.cfm?fuseaction=cms.viewpage&placement=safety_pagetips & sspage=4

N.D. Cent. Code B14-02.4-03 (2008).

Perez, S. (2008, December 5). Social network profile costs woman college degree. *Read Write Web*. Retrieved from http://www.readwriteweb.com/archives/social_network _profile_costs_woman_college_degree.php

Richmon, A. (2001). Note: restoring the balance: Employer liability and employer privacy. *Iowa Law Review, 86*(4), 1337.

Snyder v. Millersville University, Civil Action No. 07-1660, 2008 WL 5093140 (E.D. Pa December 3, 2008).

Sprague, R. (2007). From Taylorism to the Omnipticon: Expanding employee surveillance beyond the workplace. *John Marshall Journal of Computer & Information Law, 25*(1), 1.

Stored Communications Act, 18 U.S.C. BB 2701–2711 (2000).

Stross, R. (2007, December 30). How to lose your job on your own time. *The New York Times*. Retrieved from http://www.nytimes.com/2007/12/30/business/30digi .html

United States v. Charbonneau, 979 F. Supp. 1177 (United States District Court for the Southern District of Ohio 1997).

United States v. Maxwell, 45 M.J. 406 (United States Court of Appeals for the Armed Forces 1996).

Warren, S.V. and Brandeis L.D. (1890). The right to privacy. *Harvard Law Review, 4*(5), 193.

Brian Elzweig is an assistant professor of business law at Texas A&M—Corpus Christy. Elzweig holds a JD from California Western School of Law and an LLM from the Georgetown University Law Center.

Donna K. Peeples is an associate professor of management at Texas A&M—Corpus Christie. Peeples holds an MBA from Texas A&M and a PhD from Texas A&M—Corpus Christie.

Steven Greenhouse  **NO**

Even if It Enrages Your Boss, Social Net Speech Is Protected

As Facebook and Twitter become as central to workplace conversation as the company cafeteria, federal regulators are ordering employers to scale back policies that limit what workers can say online.

Employers often seek to discourage comments that paint them in a negative light. Don't discuss company matters publicly, a typical social media policy will say, and don't disparage managers, co-workers or the company itself. Violations can be a firing offense.

But in a series of recent rulings and advisories, labor regulators have declared many such blanket restrictions illegal. The National Labor Relations Board says workers have a right to discuss work conditions freely and without fear of retribution, whether the discussion takes place at the office or on Facebook.

In addition to ordering the reinstatement of various workers fired for their posts on social networks, the agency has pushed companies nationwide, including giants like General Motors, Target and Costco, to rewrite their social media rules.

"Many view social media as the new water cooler," said Mark G. Pearce, the board's chairman, noting that federal law has long protected the right of employees to discuss work-related matters. "All we're doing is applying traditional rules to a new technology."

The decisions come amid a broader debate over what constitutes appropriate discussion on Facebook and other social networks. Schools and universities are wrestling with online bullying and student disclosures about drug use. Governments worry about what police officers and teachers say and do online on their own time. Even corporate chieftains are finding that their online comments can run afoul of securities regulators.

The labor board's rulings, which apply to virtually all private sector employers, generally tell companies that it is illegal to adopt broad social media policies—like bans on "disrespectful" comments or posts that criticize the employer—if those policies discourage workers from exercising their right to communicate with one another with the aim of improving wages, benefits or working conditions.

But the agency has also found that it is permissible for employers to act against a lone worker ranting on the Internet.

Several cases illustrate the differing standards.

At Hispanics United of Buffalo, a nonprofit social services provider in upstate New York, a caseworker threatened to complain to the boss that others were not working hard enough. Another worker, Mariana Cole-Rivera, posted a Facebook message asking, "My fellow co-workers, how do you feel?"

Several of her colleagues posted angry, sometimes expletive-laden, responses. "Try doing my job. I have five programs," wrote one. "What the hell, we don't have a life as is," wrote another.

Hispanics United fired Ms. Cole-Rivera and four other caseworkers who responded to her, saying they had violated the company's harassment policies by going after the caseworker who complained.

In a 3-to-1 decision last month, the labor board concluded that the caseworkers had been unlawfully terminated. It found that the posts in 2010 were the type of "concerted activity" for "mutual aid" that is expressly protected by the National Labor Relations Act.

"The board's decision felt like vindication," said Ms. Cole-Rivera, who has since found another social work job.

The N.L.R.B. had far less sympathy for a police reporter at *The Arizona Daily Star*.

Frustrated by a lack of news, the reporter posted several Twitter comments. One said, "What?!?!?! No overnight homicide. . . . You're slacking, Tucson." Another began, "You stay homicidal, Tucson."

The newspaper fired the reporter, and board officials found the dismissal legal, saying the posts were offensive, not concerted activity and not about working conditions.

The agency also affirmed the firing of a bartender in Illinois. Unhappy about not receiving a raise for five years, the bartender posted on Facebook, calling his customers "rednecks" and saying he hoped they choked on glass as they drove home drunk.

Labor board officials found that his comments were personal venting, not the "concerted activity" aimed at improving wages and working conditions that is protected by federal law.

N.L.R.B. officials did not name the reporter or the bartender.

The board's moves have upset some companies, particularly because it is taking a law enacted in the industrial era, principally to protect workers' right to unionize, and applying it to the digital activities of nearly all private-sector workers, union and nonunion alike.

Brian E. Hayes, the lone dissenter in the Hispanics United case, wrote that "the five employees were simply venting," not engaged in concerted activity, and therefore were not protected from termination. Rafael O. Gomez, Hispanics United's lawyer, said the nonprofit would appeal the board's decision, maintaining that the Facebook posts were harassment.

Some corporate officials say the N.L.R.B. is intervening in the social media scene in an effort to remain relevant as private-sector unions dwindle in size and power.

"The board is using new legal theories to expand its power in the workplace," said Randel K. Johnson, senior vice president for labor policy at the United States Chamber of Commerce. "It's causing concern and confusion."

But board officials say they are merely adapting the provisions of the National Labor Relations Act, enacted in 1935, to the 21st century workplace.

The N.L.R.B. is not the only government entity setting new rules about corporations and social media. On Jan. 1, California and Illinois became the fifth and sixth states to bar companies from asking employees or job applicants for their social network passwords.

Lewis L. Maltby, president of the National Workrights Institute, said social media rights were looming larger in the workplace.

He said he was disturbed by a case in which a Michigan advertising agency fired a Web site trainer who also wrote fiction after several employees voiced discomfort about racy short stories he had posted on the Web.

"No one should be fired for anything they post that's legal, off-duty and not job-related," Mr. Maltby said.

As part of the labor board's stepped-up role, its general counsel has issued three reports concluding that many companies' social media policies illegally hinder workers' exercise of their rights.

The general counsel's office gave high marks to Wal-Mart's social policy, which had been revised after consultations with the agency. It approved Wal-Mart's prohibition of "inappropriate postings that may include discriminatory remarks, harassment and threats of violence or similar inappropriate or unlawful conduct."

But in assessing General Motors's policy, the office wrote, "We found unlawful the instruction that 'offensive, demeaning, abusive or inappropriate remarks are as out of place online as they are offline.'" It added, "This provision proscribes a broad spectrum of communications that would include protected criticisms of the employer's labor policies or treatment of employees." A G.M. official said the company has asked the board to reconsider.

In a ruling last September, the board also rejected as overly broad Costco's blanket prohibition against employees' posting things that "damage the company" or "any person's reputation." Costco declined to comment.

Denise M. Keyser, a labor lawyer who advises many companies, said employers should adopt social media policies that are specific rather than impose across-the-board prohibitions.

Do not just tell workers not to post confidential information, Ms. Keyser said. Instead, tell them not to disclose, for example, trade secrets, product introduction dates or private health details.

But placing clear limits on social media posts without crossing the legal line remains difficult, said Steven M. Swirsky, another labor lawyer. "Even when you review the N.L.R.B. rules and think you're following the mandates," he said, "there's still a good deal of uncertainty."

Steven Greenhouse graduated from Wesleyan University, Columbia University and finished his education at the New York University School of Law. Greenhouse has published a number of works and was awarded the Sidney Hillman Book Prize for his book, *The Big Squeeze: Tough Times for the American Worker*. Steven Greenhouse is currently the labor and workplace reporter for *The New York Times*.

EXPLORING THE ISSUE

Is Employer Monitoring of Employee Social Media Justified?

Critical Thinking and Reflection

1. Is it ethical for employees to publicly write disrespectful information about other employees or supervisors?
2. If an employee has a problem at work, is it better to solve that problem with the appropriate person, or is it better to ask for advice over the social network?
3. How difficult could it be to get a job if one was fired from a previous job for social network problems?
4. If several employees use social media to get necessary action at work, would this be appropriate?

Is There Common Ground?

Our personal privacy is important to us. However, privacy seems to be a larger employment issue now than at any time in the past. Actions today that are shown on someone's social media site could harm one's potential future employment. Current employment could also be damaged by imprudent postings on social media. Solutions to loss of privacy could include policies and procedures that clearly inform employees when social media will be monitored. This may not be enough. Some employers may find the firm's reputation more important than employee privacy and keep vigilant watch on employees' social media sites. Currently, six states have made it illegal for employers to fire employees based on social networking. Some corporate leaders are opposed to the passage of these laws as well as the work done by the National Labor Relations Board (NLRB). The NLRB explains that the National Labor Relations Act was enacted in 1935 and that it applies well to the social media questions regarding termination and speech rights. Most entities agree that employees should not be fired for social media that are off-duty, legal, and

not job related. So, corporate policy could prohibit free exercise of social media; however, the discussion over the ethics, fairness, and legality of this type of policy seems to be rapidly changing.

Additional Resources

Victoria Brown and E. Vaughn. "The Writing on the (Facebook) Wall: The Use of Social Network Sites in Hiring Decisions." *Journal of Business & Psychology* (vol. 26, no. 2, 2011, pp. 219–225).

John Browning. "Employers Face Pros, Cons with Monitoring Social Networking." *Houston Business Journal* (February 26, 2009).

Steven Greenhouse. "Labor Board Says Rights Apply on Net." *New York Times* (November 9, 2010, p. 1).

Karen E. Klein. "Establish a Commonsense Social Media Policy." *BusinessWeek.com* (2011, p. 9).

Melanie Trottman. "For Angry Employees, Legal Cover for Rants." *Wall Street Journal* (December 2, 2011).

Internet References . . .

Erick B. Meyer, "Employee Fired for Tweeting Complaints About Discrimination"

www.tlnt.com/2013/03/25/employee-fired-for-tweeting -complaints-about-discrimination

Jessica Miller-Merrell, "History of Terminations & Firings Because of Employee Social Media." Blogging 4 Jobs, May 7, 2013

www.blogging4jobs.com/social-media/history-of -terminations-firings-employee-social-media

Martha Neil, "When Can Workers Be Fired for Facebook Posts and Tweets?" ABA Journal.com., January 29, 2013

www.abajournal.com/news/article/worker_says _on_facebook_she_wants_to_be_fired_and_is_nlrb _rulings_offer_gui

"When Firing Employee for Social Media Posts Is OK"

www.leaderschoiceinsurance.com/blog-0/bid/117677 /When-Firing-Employee-for-Social-Media-Post-Is-OK

Selected, Edited, and with Issue Framing Materials by:
Gina Vega, *Organizational Ergonomics*

ISSUE

Is CEO Compensation Justified?

YES: **Ira T. Kay**, from "Don't Mess with CEO Pay," *Across the Board* (2006)

NO: **Edgar Woolard, Jr.**, from "CEOs Are Being Paid Too Much," *Across the Board* (2006)

Learning Outcomes
After reading this issue, you will be able to:
• Discuss why CEO pay is an important ethical issue in the business world and elsewhere.
• Discuss the financial choices that can only be made by the CEO and other executives of a corporation.
• Understand the differences between Kay's and Woolard's positions on the ethics of virtue.
• Distinguish Woolard's concerns about CEO pay as compared to the pay of individual employees of the corporations.
• Discuss how the individual and the corporation can be helped and harmed by high CEO pay.

ISSUE SUMMARY

YES: Ira T. Kay, a consultant on executive compensation for Watson Wyatt Worldwide, argues that in general the pay of the CEO tracks the company's performance, so in general CEOs are simply paid to do what they were hired to do—bring up the price of the stock to increase shareholder wealth.

NO: Edgar Woolard, Jr., a former CEO himself, holds that the methods by which CEO compensation is determined are fundamentally flawed, and he suggests some significant changes.

"CEOs are paid a lot to face facts, however unpleasant," writes Geoffrey Colvin in *Fortune*, "so it's time they faced this one: The issue of their pay has finally landed on the national agenda and won't be leaving soon." He ticks off the sources of national discontent with the enormous sums (and stocks, etc.) paid to the corporate chiefs: that layoffs continue, that the lowest paid workers advance only slowly, that Japanese CEOs are paid much less for much more productivity—but mostly, just that paying one person more money than he can ever spend on anything worthwhile for himself or his family, while the world's millions struggle, suffer, and starve, just seems to be wrong.

For the fifth edition of this text (1998), the NO side of the debate was carried by John Cassidy's 1997 *New Yorker* article "Gimme." Even then we could not use Colvin's

1992 article. For since Colvin wrote, Cassidy pointed out, chief executive compensation had gone much higher—by a factor of four for the average compensation, up to factors of 15 and 20 for fortunate individuals. Colvin had clucked at annual compensation from $1.5 million to as high as $3 million a year; Cassidy observed compensation already at the $18 million and $20 million level. For the sixth edition of this text (2000), Cassidy no longer sufficed. Compensation had gone up to $60, $70, and $90 million. The reason for the increase is clear enough—stock prices have gone up, shareholder wealth has increased enormously, and for reasons detailed in the YES and NO selections, shareholders wish to compensate management of their companies according to the increase in the price of the stock. Two questions arise immediately: First, if that's the system, what are we to do with compensation of "insurance" policies that guarantee the same compensation no matter where the stock goes? Don't those arrangements kind of miss the point? And the second question is, Is this right? The shareholders' interests legitimately dictate some aspects of corporate policy, and the salaries have been agreed upon by the legally appropriate parties, but if the result is substantially unjust, should not the people as a whole step in and rectify the situation?

Urgency was added to the issue in the recession that followed the election of George W. Bush in 2000. As the computers rolled in early April 2001, stocks had undergone a sudden "correction"—read, gone very far south—and shareholder wealth decreased substantially. Do we find CEO compensation humbly bowing to the facts of the ROI? Not in the least. "While typical investors lost 12 percent of their portfolios last year [2000], based on the Wilshire 5000 total market index, and profits for the Standard & Poor's 500 companies rose at less than half their pace in the 1990s, chief executives received an average 22 percent raise in salary and bonus." So we found out from a Special Report on Executive Pay from the *New York Times* on April 1, 2001 (first Business page), and that was no April Fool. Not much had changed in 2005, according to *Forbes*, when Peter Cartwright of Calpine, which runs gas-fired power plants, took home (over the last six years) average annual compensation of $13 million while the ROI of the company over the same period was 7 percent. Average compensation over the last five years for Terry Semel of Yahoo came to $258.3 million; for Barry Diller of IAC/Inter-ActiveCorp, $239.9 million; and for William McGuire of UnitedHealth Group, $342.3 million. That last is cause for pause: your health care dollars and mine fueled that income. We knew the doctors weren't getting rich; now we know who is. You see how these 2005 figures dwarfed those that so bothered Geoffrey Colvin.

Should the American people step in and claim the right to set limits in the name of justice to the outsized amounts lavished on the fortunate sons of capitalism? That possibility is precisely what troubles Colvin. If CEOs will not regulate their own compensation, Congress and the SEC could surely step in and do a bit of regulating on their own. The prospect is not enticing to the business community. On the other hand, is this not exactly why we have government—so that when private motives get out of hand, the people as a whole can step in and defend their long-term interests?

Bear in mind, as you read the following selections, that the corporation was set up as a private enterprise, literally: a voluntary contract among investors to increase their wealth by legal means. But it is chartered and protected by the state, in the service of the state's long-term interest in a thriving economy. Adam Smith would be pleased; he argued that leaving investors to make money as best they could for their own selfish interests would best increase the welfare of the whole body of the people. The question that confronts us is, At what point do we conclude that the legal means set up for private parties to serve our interests by serving their own have failed in their purported effect and should be modified or revised? Or do we have any right to do that at this point? What do you think?

YES

Ira T. Kay

Don't Mess with CEO Pay

For years, headlines have seized on dramatic accounts of outrageous amounts earned by executives—often of failing companies—and the financial tragedy that can befall both shareholders and employees when CEOs line their own pockets at the organization's expense. Images of lavish executive lifestyles are now engraved in the popular consciousness. The result: public support for political responses that include new regulatory measures and a long list of demands for greater shareholder or government control over executive compensation.

These images now overshadow the reality of thousands of successful companies with appropriately paid executives and conscientious boards. Instead, fresh accusations of CEOs collecting huge amounts of undeserved pay appear daily, fueling a full-blown mythology of a corporate America ruled by executive greed, fraud, and corruption.

This mythology consists of two related components: the myth of the failed pay-for-performance model and the myth of managerial power. The first myth hinges on the idea that the link between executive pay and corporate performance—if it ever existed—is irretrievably broken. The second myth accepts the idea of a failed pay-for-performance model and puts in its service the image of unchecked CEOs dominating subservient boards as the explanation for decisions resulting in excessive executive pay. The powerful combination of these two myths has captured newspaper headlines and shareholder agendas, regulatory attention and the public imagination.

This mythology has spilled over into the pages of *Across the Board*, where the September/October cover story links high levels of CEO pay to the country's growing income inequality and wonders why U.S. workers have not taken to the streets to protest "the blatant abuse of privilege" exercised by CEOs. In "The Revolution That Never Was," James Krohe Jr. manages to reference Marie Antoinette, Robespierre, Adam Smith, Alexis de Tocqueville, Andrew Jackson, Kim Jong Il, Jack Welch, guerrilla warfare, "economic apart-heid," and police brutality in Selma, Ala., in an article that feeds virtually every conceivable element of the myth of executive pay and wonders why we have not yet witnessed calls for a revolution to quash the "financial frolics of today's corporate aristocrats."

In a very different *Across the Board* feature story published a few months earlier, the myth of managerial power finds support in an interview with one of the myth's creators, Harvard professor Lucian Bebchuk, who believes that the pay-for-performance model is broken and that executive control over boards is to blame. Bebchuk is a distinguished scholar who has significant insights into the executive-pay process, but he greatly overestimates the influence of managerial power in the boardroom and ignores empirical evidence that most companies still operate under an intact and explicit pay-for-performance model. And although he acknowledges in his interview with *ATB* editor A.J. Vogl that "American companies have been successful and executives deserve a great deal of credit," his arguments about managerial power run counter to the realities of this success.

Fueling the Fiction

These two articles, in different ways, contribute to what is now a dominant image of executives collecting unearned compensation and growing rich at the expense of shareholders, employees and the broader community. In recent years, dozens of reporters from business magazines and the major newspapers have called me and specifically asked for examples of companies in which CEOs received exorbitant compensation, approved by the board, while the company performed poorly. Not once have I been asked to comment on the vast majority of companies—those in which executives are appropriately rewarded for performance or in which boards have reduced compensation or even fired the CEO for poor performance.

I have spent hundreds of hours answering reporters' questions, providing extensive data and explaining the pay-for-performance model of executive compensation, but my efforts have had little impact: The resulting stories feature the same anecdotal reporting on those corporations for which the process has gone awry. The press accounts ignore solid research that shows that annual pay for most executives moves up and down significantly with the company's performance, both financial and stock-related. Corporate wrongdoings and outlandish executive pay packages make for lively headlines, but the reliance on purely anecdotal reporting and the highly prejudicial language adopted are a huge disservice to the companies, their executives and employees, investors, and the public. The likelihood of real economic damage to the U.S. economy grows daily.

For example, the mythology drives institutional investors and trade unions with the power to exert enormous pressure on regulators and executive and board practices. The California Public Employees' Retirement System—the nation's largest public pension fund—offers a typical example in its Nov. 15, 2004, announcement of a new campaign to rein in "abusive compensation practices in corporate America and hold directors and compensation committees more accountable for their actions."

The AFL-CIO's website offers another example of the claim that managerial power has destroyed the efficacy of the pay-for-performance model: "Each year, shocking new examples of CEO pay greed are made public. Investors are concerned not just about the growing size of executive compensation packages, but the fact that CEO pay levels show little apparent relationship to corporate profits, stock prices or executive performance. How do CEOs do it? For years, executives have relied on their shareholders to be passive absentee owners. CEOs have rigged their own compensation packages by packing their boards with conflicted or negligent directors."

The ROI of the CEO

As with all modern myths, there's a grain of truth in all the assumptions and newspaper stories. The myths of managerial power and of the failed pay-for-performance model find touchstones in real examples of companies where CEOs have collected huge sums in cash compensation and stock options while shareholder returns declined. (You know the names—there's no need to mention them again here.) Cases of overstated profits or even outright fraud have fueled the idea that executives regularly manipulate the measures of performance to justify higher pay while boards default on their oversight responsibilities. The ability of executives to time the exercise of their stock options and collect additional pay through covert means has worsened perceptions of the situation both within and outside of the world of business.

These exceptions in executive pay practices, however, are now commonly mistaken for the rule. And as Krohe's article demonstrates, highly paid CEOs have become the new whipping boys for social critics concerned about the general rise in income inequality and other broad socioeconomic problems. Never mind that these same CEOs stand at the center of a corporate model that has generated millions of jobs and trillions of dollars in shareholder earnings. Worse, using CEOs as scapegoats distracts from the real causes of and possible solutions for inequality.

The primary determinant of CEO pay is the same force that sets pay for all Americans: relatively free—if somewhat imperfect—labor markets, in which companies offer the levels of compensation necessary to attract and retain the employees who generate value for shareholders. Part of that pay for most executives consists of stock-based incentives. A 2003 study by Brian J. Hall and Kevin J. Murphy shows that the ratio of total CEO compensation to production workers' average earnings closely follows the Dow Jones Industrial Average. When the Dow soars, the gap between executive and non-executive compensation widens. The problem, it seems, is not that CEOs receive too much performance-driven, stock-based compensation, but that non- executives receive too little.

The key question is not the actual dollar amount paid to a CEO in total compensation or whether that amount represents a high multiple of pay of the average worker's salary but, rather, whether that CEO creates an adequate return on the company's investment in executive compensation. In virtually every area of business, directors routinely evaluate and adjust the amounts that companies invest in all inputs, and shareholders directly or indirectly endorse or challenge those decisions. Executive pay is no different.

Hard Realities

The corporate scandals of recent years laid bare the inner workings of a handful of public companies where, inarguably, the process for setting executive pay violated not only the principle of pay-for-performance but the extensive set of laws and regulations governing executive pay practices and the role of the board. But while I condemn illegal actions and criticize boards that reward executives who fail to produce positive financial results, I know that the vast majority of U.S. corporations do much better by their shareholders and the public. I have worked directly with more than a thousand publicly traded companies in the United States and attended thousands of compensation-committee meetings, and I have *never* witnessed board members straining to find a way to pay an executive more than he is worth.

In addition, at Watson Wyatt I work with a team of experts that has conducted extensive research at fifteen hundred of America's largest corporations and tracked the relationship between these pay practices and corporate performance over almost twenty years. In evaluating thousands of companies annually, yielding nearly twenty thousand "company years" of data, and pooling cross-sectional company data over multiple years, we have discovered that for both most companies and the "typical" company, there is substantial pay-for-performance sensitivity. That is, high performance generates high pay for executives and low performance generates low pay. Numerous empirical academic studies support our conclusions.

Our empirical evidence and evidence from other studies have produced the following key findings:

1. Executive pay is unquestionably high relative to low-level corporate positions, and it has risen dramatically over the past ten to fifteen years, faster than inflation and faster than average employee pay. But executive compensation generally tracks total returns to shareholders—even including the recent rise in pay.
2. Executive stock ownership has risen dramatically over the past ten to fifteen years. High levels of CEO stock ownership are correlated with and most likely the cause of companies' high financial and stock-market performance.
3. Executives are paid commensurate with the skills and talents that they bring to the organization. Underperforming executives routinely receive pay reductions or are terminated—far more often than press accounts imply.
4. CEOs who are recruited from outside a company and have little influence over its board receive compensation that is competitive with and often higher than the pay levels of CEOs who are promoted from within the company.
5. At the vast majority of companies, even extraordinarily high levels of CEO compensation represent a tiny fraction of the total value created by the corporation under that CEO's leadership. (Watson Wyatt has found that U.S. executives receive approximately 1 percent of the net income generated by the corporations they manage.) Well-run companies, it bears pointing out, produce significant shareholder returns and job security for millions of workers.

Extensive research demonstrates a high and positive correlation between executive pay and corporate performance. For example, high levels of executive stock ownership in 2000, created primarily through stock-option awards, correlated with higher stock-market valuation and long-term earnings per share over the subsequent five-year period. In general, high-performing companies are led by highly paid executives—with pay-for-performance in full effect. Executives at low-performing companies receive lower amounts of pay. Reams of data from other studies confirm these correlations.

Why CEOs Are Worth the Money

The huge gap between the realities of executive pay and the now-dominant mythology surrounding it has become even more evident in recent years. Empirical studies show that executive compensation has closely tracked corporate performance: Pay rose during the boom years of the 1990s, when U.S. corporations generated huge returns, declined during the 2001–03 profit slowdown, and increased in 2004 as profits improved. The myth of excessive executive pay continued to gain power, however, even as concrete, well-documented financial realities defied it.

The blind outrage over executive pay climbed even during the slowdown, as compensation dropped drastically. During this same period, in the aftermath of the corporate scandals, Congress and the U.S. regulatory agencies instituted far-reaching reforms in corporate governance and board composition, and companies spent millions to improve their governance and transparency. But the critics of executive pay and managerial power were only encouraged to raise their voices.

It might surprise those critics to learn that CEOs are not interchangeable and not chosen by lot; they are an extremely important asset to their companies and generally represent an excellent investment. The relative scarcity of CEO talent is manifested in many ways, including the frenetic behavior of boards charged with filling the top position when a CEO retires or departs. CEOs have significant, legitimate, market-driven bargaining power, and in pay negotiations, they use that power to obtain pay commensurate with their skills. Boards, as they should, use their own bargaining power to retain talent and maximize returns to company shareholders.

Boards understand the imperative of finding an excellent CEO and are willing to risk millions of dollars to secure the right talent. Their behavior is not only understandable but necessary to secure the company's future success. Any influence that CEOs might have over their directors is modest in comparison to the financial risk that CEOs assume when they leave other prospects and take on the extraordinarily difficult task of managing a major corporation, with a substantial portion of their short- and long-term compensation contingent on the organization's financial success.

Lucian Bebchuk and other critics underestimate the financial risk entailed in executive positions when they cite executives' large severance packages, derided as "golden parachutes." Top executive talent expects and can command financial protections commensurate with the level of risk they assume. Like any other element of compensation, boards should and generally do evaluate severance agreements as part of the package they create to attract and retain talent. In recent years, boards have become more aware of the damage done when executive benefits and perquisites are excessive and not aligned with non-executive programs, and are now reining in these elements.

Properly designed pay opportunities drive superior corporate performance and secure it for the future. And most importantly, many economists argue, the U.S. model of executive compensation is a significant source of competitive advantage for the nation's economy, driving higher productivity, profits, and stock prices.

Resetting the Debate

Companies design executive pay programs to accomplish the classic goals of any human-capital program. First, they must attract, retain, and motivate their human capital to perform at the highest levels. The motivational factor is the most important, because it addresses the question of how a company achieves the greatest return on its human-capital investment and rewards executives for making the right decisions to drive shareholder value. Incentive-pay and pay-at-risk programs are particularly effective, especially at the top of the house, in achieving this motivation goal.

Clearly, there are exceptions to the motivational element—base salaries, pensions, and other benefits, for example—that are more closely tied to retention goals and are an essential part of creating a balanced portfolio for the employee. The portfolio as a whole must address the need for income and security and the opportunity for creating significant asset appreciation.

A long list of pressures, including institutional-investor pushback, accounting changes, SEC investigations, and scrutiny from labor unions and the media, are forcing companies to rethink their executive-compensation programs, especially their stock-based incentives. The key now is to address the real problems in executive compensation without sacrificing the performance-based model and the huge returns that it has generated. Boards are struggling to achieve greater transparency and more rigorous execution of their pay practices—a positive move for all parties involved.

The real threat to U.S. economic growth, job creation, and higher living standards now comes from regulatory overreach as proponents of the mythology reject market forces and continue to push for government and institutional control over executive pay. To the extent that the mythology now surrounding executive pay leads to a rejection of the pay-for-performance model and restrictions on the risk-and-reward structure for setting executive compensation, American corporate performance will suffer.

There will be more pressure on boards to effectively reduce executive pay. This may meet the social desires of some constituents, but it will almost surely cause economic decline, for companies and the U.S. economy. We will see higher executive turnover and less talent in the executive suite as the most qualified job candidates move into other professions, as we saw in the 1970s, when top candidates moved into investment banking, venture-capital firms, and consulting, and corporate performance suffered as a result.

Our research demonstrates that aligning pay plans, incentive opportunities, and performance measures throughout an organization is key to financial success. Alignment means that executives and non-executives alike have the opportunity to increase their pay through performance-based incentives. As new regulations make it more difficult to execute the stock-based elements of the pay-for-performance model, for example, by reducing broad-based stock options, we will see even less alignment between executives' compensation and the pay packages of the rank-and-file. We are already witnessing the unintended consequences of the new requirement for stock-option expensing as companies cut the broad-based stock-option plans that have benefited millions of workers and given them a direct stake in the financial success of the companies for which they work.

Instead of changing executive pay plans to make them more like pay plans for employees, we should be reshaping employee pay to infuse it with the same incentives that drive performance in the company's upper ranks. A top-down regulatory approach to alignment will only damage the entire market-based, performance-management process that has worked so well for most companies and the economy as a whole. Instead of placing artificial limits on executive pay, we should focus squarely on increasing performance incentives and stock ownership for both executive and non-executive employees and rewarding high performers throughout the organization, from top to bottom. Within the context of a free-market economy, equal opportunity—not income equality by fiat—is the goal.

The short answer to James Krohe's question of why high levels of executive pay have not sparked a worker revolution is that the fundamental model works too well. Workers vote to support that model every day when they show up for work, perform well, and rely on corporate leadership to pursue a viable plan for meeting payroll and funding employee benefits. Shareholders vote to support the model every time they purchase shares or defeat one of the dozens of proposals submitted in recent years to curb executive compensation. Rejecting the pay-for-performance model for executive compensation means returning to the world of the CEO as caretaker. And caretakers—as shown by both evidence and common sense—do not create high value for shareholders or jobs for employees.

In some ways, the decidedly negative attention focused on executive pay has increased the pressure that executives, board members, HR staffs, and compensation consultants all feel when they enter into discussions about the most effective methods for tying pay to performance and ensuring the company's success. The managerial-power argument has contributed to meaningful discussions about corporate governance and raised the level of dialogue in board-rooms. These are positive developments.

When the argument is blown into mythological proportions, however, it skews thinking about the realities of corporate behavior and leads to fundamental misunderstandings about executives, their pay levels, and their role in building successful companies and a flourishing economy. Consequently, the mythology now surrounding executive compensation leads many to reject a pay model that works well and is critical to ongoing growth at both the corporate and the national economic level. We need to address excesses in executive pay without abandoning the core model, and to return the debate to a rational, informed discussion. And we can safely leave Marie Antoinette out of it.

Ira T. Kay is the director of Watson Wyatt's compensation practice. He works closely with U.S., public, international, and private companies on long-term incentive plans to increase shareholder value. He conducts research on stock option overhang, executive pay and performance, and CEO stock ownership. He is a coauthor of *The Human Capital Edge, CEO Pay and Shareholder Value: Helping the U.S. Win the Global Economic War;* and *Value at the Top: Solutions to the Executive Compensation Crisis.* He holds a PhD in economics from Wayne State University.

Edgar Woolard, Jr.  **NO**

CEOs Are Being Paid Too Much

There's a major concern out there for all of us. I personally am extremely saddened by the loss of the respect that this country's corporate leaders have experienced. We've had a double blow in the last ten years or so. The first one we know way too much about—the fraud at Enron, Tyco, Adelphia, World-Com, and many others.

The CEOs say there were a few rotten apples in that barrel, and maybe that's the answer—but there are a hell of lot more rotten apples than I would have ever guessed. But that's just the base of one of the issues that has eroded the trust and confidence in American business leaders.

The second one is the perception of excess compensation received by CEOs getting worse year by year. And if directors agree, they can be the leaders in making a very important change. I'd like to deal with it by describing several myths about compensation and trying to undermine them.

Myth #1: CEO Pay by Competition

The first is the myth that CEO pay is driven by competition—and to that I say "bull." CEO pay is driven today primarily by outside consultant surveys, and by the fact that many board members have bought into the concept that your CEO has to be at least in the top half, and maybe in the top quartile. So we have the "ratchet, ratchet, ratchet" concept. We all understand it well enough to know that if everybody is trying to be in the top half, everybody is going to get a hefty increase every year. If Bill and Sally get an increase in their total compensation, I have to get an increase so that I will stay in the top half.

How can we change that?

In 1990, we addressed this issue at DuPont. I became CEO in 1989, and I was concerned about what was evident even then. A 1989 *Business Week* article talked about executive pay—who makes the most and are they worth it: Michael Eisner, $40 million in 1988; Ross Johnson, $20 million; and others. I don't know Eisner, but I know that even fifteen years later he's one of the most criticized CEOs in the country.

What we did at DuPont was go to a simple concept: internal pay equity. I went to the board and the compensation committee and said, "We're going to look at the people who run the businesses, who make decisions on prices and new products with guidance from the CEO—the executive vice presidents—and we're going to set the limit of what a CEO in this company can be paid at 1.5 times the pay rate for the executive vice president—50 percent."

That to me seemed equitable. It had been anywhere from 30 to 50 percent in the past. I said, "Let's set it at 50 percent, and we're not going to chase the surveys." And this is the way DuPont has done it ever since. I think we have tweaked it up a little bit since then, but using a multiple still is the right way to go.

Board members can do this by suggesting that the HR and compensation people look at what's happened to internal pay equity, and seriously consider going in that direction. That will solve this problem in a great way.

Myth #2: Compensation Committees Are Independent

I give a "double bull" to this one. It could be that committees are becoming more independent, but over the last fifteen years they certainly haven't been.

Let me describe how it works: The compensation committee talks to an outside consultant who has surveys that you could drive a truck through and that support paying anything you want to pay. The consultant talks to the HR vice president, who talks to the CEO. The CEO says what he'd like to receive—enough so he will be "respected by his peers." It gets to the HR person, who tells the consultant, and the CEO gets what he's implied he deserves. The members of the compensation committee are happy that they're independent, the HR person is happy, the CEO is happy, and the consultant gets invited back next year.

There are two ways to change that as well. Here's the first one. When John Reed came back to the New York Stock Exchange to try to clean up the mess after Dick Grasso, he made the decision—which I admire him for—that the board was going to have its own outside consultant, one who was not going to be allowed to talk to internal people—not to the HR vice president, not to the CEO.

I'm the head of the comp committee at the NYSE, and when I talk with our outside consultant, he gives us his ideas of what he thinks the pay package ought to be. Then, with the consultant there, I talk to the compensation committee, and we make a decision. I talk to the HR vice president to see if he has any other thoughts, but the committee is totally independent.

The other way to change things is to truly insist on pay-for-performance, which everyone likes to talk about but no one does. Boards pay everybody in the top quartile whether they have good performance or bad performance—or even if they're about to be fired.

Well, I was on a board fifteen years ago, and four CEOs were on the compensation committee, and for two consecutive years, we gave the CEO and the executives there no bonus, no salary increase, and modest stock options, because their performance was lousy those years. After that, they did extremely well, and we paid them extremely well. That's how pay-for-performance should work.

Myth #3: Look How Much Wealth I Created

This one is really a joke. It was born in the 1980s and '90s during the stock-market bubble, when all CEOs were beating their chest about how much wealth they were creating for shareholders. And I'd look to the king, Jack Welch. Jack's the best CEO of the last fifty years, and I've told him this. But he likes to say, "I created $400 billion worth of wealth." No, Jack—no, you didn't. He said that when GE's stock was at 60, but when the bubble burst it went to 30, and it's in the low 30s now. So he created $150 to $200 billion.

But besides the actual figure, there are two things wrong with his claim. Now, I don't care how much money Jack Welch made. God bless him; I think he's terrific. But what did it do? It set a new level for CEO pay based on the stock-market bubble; all the other CEOs were saying, "Look how much wealth I created."

So you've got this more recent high level of executive pay, and then you've got the ratcheting effect in the system. Those things have to change.

Myth #4: Severance for Failing

The last one is the worst of all. Any directors who agree to give these huge severance pay packages to CEOs who fail—Philip Purcell of Morgan Stanley got $114 million,

Carly Fiorina of Hewlett-Packard got $20 million—why are you doing that? No one else gets paid excessively when they fail. They get fired; they get fair severance.

All of this is killing the image of CEOs and corporate executives. When it comes to our image, we're in the league with lawyers and politicians. I don't want to be there, and I don't think you do either. We need the respect of our employees and the general public. And there's a lot of skepticism about leaders in politics and in churches and in the military—but we can't have it in the business community, because we're the backbone of the market system that has made this country great and created so many opportunities for people. We can't be seen as either dishonest or greedy.

What can you do about it?

Some of you CEOs need to show leadership and say, "We're going to do internal pay equity." It's easy to get the data, and then you can decide what you think is fair and how much you think the CEO contributes versus the other business leaders who make their companies so strong.

Compensation committees need to seriously consider implementing internal pay equity. Pay only for outstanding performance. Quit giving people money just because Bill and Sally are getting it. Consider going to an independent consultant that deals only with the board while you deal with HR and the CEO.

Last, take a look at stock-option packages. Not just for one year but the mega-grants that built up in the 1980s and '90s. If you've given huge stock-option packages for the last five years, look at their value. There's nothing in the Bible that says that you have to give increased stock options every year. Give a smaller grant; give a different kind of grant; put some kind of limits on.

There are many ways to do it, but it's important to get the system back under control. It's important for our image, for our reputation, for integrity, for trust, and for our leadership in this country.

EDGAR WOOLARD, JR. is a member of the Board of Telex Communications, Inc. He is a former director of the New York Stock Exchange, Inc., Citigroup Inc., IBM, Apple Computer, Inc., and Bell Atlantic Delaware. He is also a former chairman of the Business Council. He is a member of the Board of Trustees of the Christiana Care Health System and the North Carolina Textile Foundation., Inc., and a member of the National Academy of Engineering and the American Philosophical Society.

EXPLORING THE ISSUE

Is CEO Compensation Justified?

Critical Thinking and Reflection

1. Explain the worth of the CEO to the corporation. What could happen under the direction of a poor or unethical CEO?
2. Professional athletes make excessive amounts of money as compared to other athletes, or employees in the athletic business. Is this an acceptable comparison with CEO pay?
3. Is there a point at which a CEO should retire before the pay is increased to levels that employees see as obscene? Is retirement even a concern in this issue?

Is There Common Ground?

In 1992, when Geoffrey Colvin wrote the article bringing the problem of CEO compensation to public attention, he was worried about the country's perception of annual outlays of $1.7 million average total CEO compensation for almost 300 large companies, with pay going up to a whopping $3.2 million annually for the really big companies. By 1995, the CEO of a multibillion-dollar company had received an average of $4.37 million in compensation, up 23 percent from 1994. And it got worse from there, with 1996 figures going through the roof: How on earth could Jack Welch, CEO of General Electric, spend the $21.4 million in salary and performance bonuses (and about $18 million in stock options) that he received in 1996, or Green Tree Financial Corporation's Lawrence Coss spend his $102.4 million in salary and bonus (plus stock options worth at least $38 million)? The Business Section of *The New York Times* at the end of 1997 glowed with projected bonuses of $11 billion for Wall Street that year—that was over and above salary and before stock options. Two years later, Jack Welch was pulling in $68 million. As per the introduction to this issue, the amounts then tripled, quadrupled, into amounts per individual that dwarf the annual health budgets of most of the world. The situation is not correcting itself.

The political impact of these salaries is muted for the present, probably due to the failure of the American left, or liberal political orientation, to find a powerful spokesperson who might gain the confidence of the American people. The moral dimensions of the problem have not changed since the days of the prophet Amos of the Hebrew Scriptures: What right have the rich to enjoy their warm palaces and mansions, dining plentifully on the best food from all the world, while the poor suffer from hunger and cold? But the political dimensions are volatile and dependent upon the rest of the system to provide context and opportunity. This issue will be with us for a while.

Additional Resources

Lucian Bebchuk and Jesse Fried, *Pay Without Performance: The Unfulfilled Promise of Executive Compensation* (Cambridge: Harvard University Press, 2006).

Rocco Huang, "Because I'm Worth It? CEO Pay and Corporate Governance." *Business Review* (Federal Reserve Bank of Philadelphia) (2010, pp. 12–19).

Ira Kay and Steven Van Putten, *Myths and Realities of Executive Pay* (Cambridge: Cambridge University Press, 2007).

Jean MacGuire et al., "CEO Incentives and Corporate Social Performance." *Journal of Business Ethics* (vol. 45, no. 4, July 2003).

Jeffrey Sonnenfeld, Melanie Kusin, and Elise Walton, "What CEOs Really Think of Their Boards." *Harvard Business Review* (April 2013). http://hbr.org/2013/04/what-ceos-really-think-of-their-boards/ar/1

Ben Steverman, "CEOs and the Pay-for-Performance Puzzle." *BusinessWeek Online* (2009, p. 2).

Ronald A. Wirtz, "Goldilocks in the Corner Office." *The Region* (The Federal Reserve Bank of Minneapolis) (vol. 20, no. 4, 2006, pp. 22–35).

Internet References . . .

"100 Highest Paid CEOs," 2014

www.aflcio.org/Corporate-Watch/CEO-Pay-and
-You/100-Highest-Paid-CEOs

"CEO Vs. Board of Directors"

www.ehow.com/facts_5701023_ceo-vs_-board
-directors.html

The Conference Board

www.conference-board.org/publications
/publicationdetail.cfm?publicationid=2152

Elliott Blair Smith, Phil Kuntz, "Top CEO Pay Issues"

http://go.bloomberg.com/multimedia/ceo-pay-ratio

"CEOs Made 330 Times As Much As Their Employees In 2013"

http://www.businessinsider.com/fortune-500-ceo
-vs-worker-pay-2014-6

Selected, Edited, and with Issue Framing Materials by:
Gina Vega, *Organizational Ergonomics*

ISSUE

Will Robots Help the American Worker?

YES: Jeffrey R. Young, from "The New Industrial Revolution: A Coming Wave of Robots Could Redefine Our Jobs. Will That Redefine Us?" *The Chronicle Review* (2013)

NO: Mark Kingwell, from "The Barbed Gift of Leisure," *The Chronicle Review* (2013)

Learning Outcomes
After reading this issue, you will be able to:
• Discuss how robots both reduce and increase the costs of doing business in the manufacturing world.
• Discuss how robots may take jobs away from individuals who only have a high school diploma.
• Explain your reasoning when deciding if it is acceptable for some individuals to term manual labor jobs as not worthy of human labor.
• Distinguish if individuals gain part of their identity by the employment they choose. What are the problems of not finding employment because the jobs have been given to robots or outsourced?
• If you had the responsibility to hire for a business, given the choice, would you rather work with a human being or purchase a robot. Explain your reasoning.

ISSUE SUMMARY

YES: Jeffrey R. Young explains that automation is cheap and efficient. Although technology's increasing versatility may take some jobs away from humans, robots primarily will absorb the drudgery that humans may be glad to be rid of. He foresees a future of increased leisure and creativity for us.

NO: Mark Kingwell focuses on what it means to be human rather than machine and to live in a culture and community with other human beings. He argues that we are used to deriving much of the meaning of our lives from our work and wonders what individuals might do with their leisure time.

At the founding of this country, the majority of Americans lived and worked on farms. Moving through the industrial age to the present, we understand that automation has eliminated about 98 percent of their jobs and their work animals. These functions are now completed by machines. With the farm jobs no longer available, or perhaps desirable, individuals fill new jobs that are essential for society and the economy. Our authors explain that perhaps we shouldn't worry about being out of work, and look to a future of new areas of specialization, including creating new positions.

Young worries that most workers find esteem and identity through their jobs. He worries that if a significant number of individuals can't find employment, it will be a society that seems lost or perhaps lacking in aspirations for individual progress.

The war industry has been impacted by drones. These are high tech airplane-type devices that can be manipulated to drop weapons in enemy territory. However, these machines lack a human pilot in the cockpit. Rather, a pilot moves the plane into position through remote control, much like a very advanced video game. Drones are also becoming privately owned, and it is reported that the private ownership is often used for surveillance and spying. They are expensive and not nearly as friendly as they might appear on late-night television programming.

Many of our scientists look to future innovations such as robot-driven cars and trucks. If this particular phenomenon happens, there will be a need for individuals who monitor traffic systems, while others assist in energy flow and time constraints. Some of the robotic scientists say that business will be greatly improved with robots as part of the market.

Data analysis is another area that scientists say is ripe for the robot workforce. This notion may sound strange to many of us, as we expect a strong intellectual capacity is necessary in order to perform analysis. However,

"bots"—virtual robots—can be trained to do the analysis if humans can give the correct parameters. Within 100 years, it is predicted that 70 percent of our current jobs, practices, and professions will be performed by robots or "bots." However, it is also predicted that a new crop of jobs will be needed and created because of the new robot centering in our lives.

Kingwell worries that when robots rule the workplace, humans may have too much idle time, and he has ethical concerns about filling idle time because robots are completing our labor.

YES ↵

Jeffrey R. Young

The New Industrial Revolution: A Coming Wave of Robots Could Redefine Our Jobs. Will That Redefine Us?

Baxter is a new type of worker, who is having no trouble getting a job these days, even in a tight economy. He's a little slow, but he's easy to train. And companies don't hire him, they buy him—he even comes with a warranty.

Baxter is a robot, not a human, though human workers in all kinds of industries may soon call him a colleague. His plastic-and-metal body consists of two arms loaded with sensors to keep his lifeless limbs from accidentally knocking over anyone nearby. And he has a simulated face, displayed on a flat-panel computer monitor, so he can give a frown if he's vexed or show a bored look if he's waiting to be given more to do.

Baxter is part of a new generation of machines that are changing the labor market worldwide—and raising a new round of debate about the meaning of work itself. This robot comes at a price so low—starting at just $22,000—that even businesses that never thought of replacing people with machines may find that prospect irresistible. It's the brainchild of Rodney Brooks, who also designed the Roomba robot vacuum cleaner, which succeeded in bringing at least a little bit of robotics into millions of homes. One computer scientist predicts that robots like Baxter will soon toil in fast-food restaurants topping pizzas, at bakeries sliding dough into hot ovens, and at a variety of other service-sector jobs, in addition to factories.

I wanted to meet this worker of the future and his robot siblings, so I spent a day at this year's Automate trade show here, where Baxter was one of hundreds of new commercial robots on display. Simply by guiding his hands and pressing a few buttons, I programmed him to put objects in boxes; I played blackjack against another robot that had been temporarily programmed to deal cards to show off its dexterity; and I watched demonstration robots play flawless games of billiards on toy-sized tables. (It turns out that robots are not only better at many professional jobs than humans are, but they can best us in our hobbies, too.)

During a keynote speech to kick off the trade show, Henrik Christensen, director of robotics at Georgia Tech, outlined a vision of a near future when we'll see robots and autonomous devices everywhere, working side by side with humans and taking on a surprisingly diverse set of roles. Robots will load and unload packages from delivery trucks without human assistance—as one company's system demonstrated during the event. Robots will even drive the trucks and fly the cargo planes with our packages, Christensen predicted, noting that Google has already demonstrated its driverless car, and that the same technology that powers military drones can just as well fly a FedEx jet. "We'll see coast-to-coast package delivery with drones without having a pilot in the vehicle," he asserted.

Away from the futuristic trade floor, though, a public discussion is growing about whether robots like Baxter and other new automation technologies are taking too many jobs. Similar concerns have cropped up repeatedly for centuries: when combines first arrived on farms, when the first machines hit factory assembly lines, when computers first entered businesses. A folk tune from the 1950s called "The Automation Song" could well be sung today: "Now you've got new machines for to take my place, and you tell me it's not mine to share." Yet new jobs have always seemed to emerge to fill the gaps left by positions lost to mechanization. There may be few secretaries today, but there are legions of social-media managers and other new professional categories created by digital technology.

Still, what if this time is different? What if we're nearing an inflection point where automation is so cheap and efficient that human workers are simply outmatched? What if machines are now leading to a net loss of jobs rather than a net gain? Two professors at the Massachusetts Institute of Technology, Andrew McAfee and Erik Brynjolfsson, raised that concern in *Race Against the Machine: How the Digital Revolution Is Accelerating Innovation, Driving Productivity, and Irreversibly*

Transforming Employment and the Economy (Digital Frontier Press, 2011). A recent report on *60 Minutes* featured the book's thesis and quoted critics concerned about the potential economic crisis caused by robots, despite the cute faces on their monitors.

But robots raise an even bigger question than how many jobs are left over for humans. A number of scholars are now arguing that all this automation could make many goods and services so cheap that full-time jobs could become optional for most people. Baxter, then, would become a liberator of the human spirit rather than an enemy of the working man.

That utopian dream would require resetting the role work plays in our lives. If our destiny is to be freed from toil by robot helpers, what are we supposed to do with our days?

To begin to tackle that existential question, I decided to invite along a scholar of work to the Automate trade show. And that's how my guest, Burton J. Bledstein, an expert on the history of professionalism and the growth of the modern middle class, got into an argument with the head of a robotics company.

It happened at the booth for Adept Technology Inc., which makes a robot designed to roam the halls of hospitals and other facilities making deliveries. The latest model— a foot-tall rolling platform that can be customized for a variety of tasks—wandered around the booth, resembling something out of a *Star Wars* film except that it occasionally blasted techno music from its speakers. Bledstein was immediately wary of the contraption. The professor, who holds an emeritus position at the University of Illinois at Chicago, explained that he has an artificial hip and didn't want the robot to accidentally knock him down. He needn't have worried, though; the robot is designed to sense nearby objects and keep a safe distance.

The company's then-CEO, John Dulchinos, assured us that on the whole, robots aren't taking jobs—they're simply making life better for human employees by eliminating the most-tedious tasks. "I can show you some very clear examples where this product is offloading tasks from a nurse that was walking five miles a day to allow her to be able to spend time with patients," he said, as the robot tirelessly circled our feet. "I think you see that in a lot of the applications we're doing, where the mundane task is done by a robot which has very simple capability, and it frees up people to do more-elaborate and more-sophisticated tasks."

The CEO defended the broader trend of companies' embracing automation, especially in factory settings where human workers have long held what he called unfulfilling jobs, like wrapping chicken all day. "They look like zombies when they walk out of that factory," he said of such workers. "It is a mind-numbing, mundane task. There is absolutely no satisfaction from what they do."

"That's your perception," countered Bledstein. "A lot of these are unskilled people. A lot of immigrants are in these jobs. They see it as work. They appreciate the paycheck. The numbness of the work is not something that surprises them or disturbs them."

"I guess we could just turn the clock back to 1900, and we can all be farmers," retorted Dulchinos.

But what about those displaced workers who can't find alternatives, asked Bledstein, arguing that automation is happening not just in factories but also in clerical and other middle-class professions changed by computer technology. "That's kind of creating a crisis today. Especially if those people are over 50, those people are having a lot of trouble finding new work." The professor added that he worried about his undergraduate students, too, and the tough job market they face. "It might be a lost generation, it's so bad."

Dulchinos acknowledged that some workers are struggling during what he sees as a transitional period, but he argued that the solution is *more* technology and innovation, not less, to get to a new equilibrium even faster.

This went on for a while, and it boiled down to competing conceptions of what it means to have a job. In Bledstein's seminal book, *The Culture of Professionalism*, first published in 1976, he argues that Americans, in particular, have come to define their work as more than just a series of tasks that could be commodified. Bledstein tracks a history of how, in sector after sector, middle-class workers sought to elevate the meaning of their jobs, whether they worked as athletes, surgeons, or funeral directors: "The professional importance of an occupation was exaggerated when the ordinary coffin became a 'casket,' the sealed repository of a precious object; when a decaying corpse became a 'patient' prepared in an 'operating room' by an 'embalming surgeon' and visited in a 'funeral home' before being laid to rest in a 'memorial park.'"

The American dream involves more than just accumulating wealth, the historian argues. It's about developing a sense of personal value by connecting work to a broader social mission, rather than as "a mechanical job, befitting of lowly manual laborer."

Today, though, "there's disillusionment with professions," Bledstein told me, noting that the logic of efficiency is often valued more than the quality of service. "Commercialism has just taken over everywhere." He complained that in their rush to reduce production costs, some business leaders are forgetting that even manual laborers have skills and knowledge that can be tough to simulate by machine. "They want to talk about them as if these people are just drones," he said as we took a break in the back of the exhibit hall, the whir of robot motors almost drowning out our voices. "Don't minimize the extent of what quote-unquote manual workers do—even ditch diggers."

In Genesis, God sentences Adam and Eve to hard labor as part of the punishment for the apple incident. "Cursed is the ground because of you; through painful toil you will eat food from it all the days of your life" was the sentence handed down in the Garden of Eden. Yet Martin Luther argued, as have other prominent Christian leaders since, that work is also a way to connect with the divine.

People's relationship to work has been complex from the start, and its cultural resonance has shifted over time. Today many people's identities are tied up in their jobs. "Beyond mere survival, we create ourselves in our work," writes Al Gini, a professor of business ethics at Loyola University Chicago, in his 2001 book, *My Job, My Self.*

But Gini points to earlier periods when attitudes were quite different. The ancient Greeks, for instance, used slaves for most labor and "regarded work as a curse, a drudgery, and an activity to be conducted with a heavy heart." Their view, he writes, was that "work by its very nature inhibited the use of reason and thereby impeded the search for the ultimate ends of life."

Aristotle never worked a day in his life.

Today Jeremy Rifkin is among those who make a case for what he calls "rethinking work." Rifkin, president of the Foundation on Economic Trends and a senior lecturer at the University of Pennsylvania's Wharton School of business, is best known for his 1995 best seller, *The End of Work.* In his most recent book, *The Third Industrial Revolution,* he says that a reshaping of society made possible by a variety of trends, including automation systems and green technology, could leave people more time for what he calls "deep play."

He imagines robots' making manufacturing so cheap and efficient that most people will simply be able to work less to meet their basic needs. He says we will then be free to start new kinds of nonprofit activities that link us with other people in new ways, helping us lead more-fulfilling lives.

"Why is it that being a productive worker is the highest value of being alive on this planet?" Rifkin asks. "The real mission of the human race is to learn how to begin to integrate ourselves into a single biosphere," he says, arguing that the Internet can bring about a true global village.

"What we have to come to grips with now is that the most productive and efficient human being is not going to be as productive and efficient in a physical or intellectual way as the automated technology that's coming," he says.

Work won't go away completely, in his view, but the workweeks for many will greatly decrease. "The average work day in forager or hunter-gatherer society is three to four hours—the rest is leisure or play," he says. In the robot age, "I think a five-to-six-hour day makes sense."

Frithjof Bergmann, an emeritus professor of philosophy at the University of Michigan at Ann Arbor, goes further in his proposals for a radical restructuring of society that would bring about what he calls a "New Work system."

He envisions a social structure in which large-scale manufacturing plants disappear, replaced by a series of neighborhood centers with advanced 3-D printers that can make a variety of goods on demand. People would spend part of their week doing self-service tasks to maintain their own lives—like homemade manufacturing and urban gardening—and spend a couple of days a week at what he calls a "Paid Calling," some task uniquely suited to each worker. That way "the impulse for the work arises from within me" and comes "from the very heart and core of my soul," as he put it in an essay, published in 2000, titled "Ecology and New Work."

Bergmann runs an organization in Flint, Mich., called the Center for New Work, to advance this vision, and he argues that the current economic recession provides an opportunity to phase in his ideas, some of which he has been promoting since the 1980s. "I spent just now two weeks teaching people in Detroit how to make the best possible use of 3-D printers," he told me. "You can use fabricators like you're already using urban gardening, so you do have the opportunity to spend much more time than you had in the past to do things that are to your taste."

Even some of the roboticists here at the Automate show believe that their inventions could lead to a rebooted work environment. One of them is Gary R. Bradski, a machine-vision scientist on leave from Stanford University to help start a company called Industrial Perception—the one demonstrating a robot that can unload boxes from a delivery truck without human assistance.

"You're going to see in the next five to 10 years a significant increase in automation and robotics within the health-care space."

Bradski said he could imagine a world in which everyone owns shares of manufacturing companies where almost all of the work is done by robots, with those shares providing a "baseline" income to all. Those who want finer things or experiences could do extra work—by inventing or designing things. He notes that teenagers without jobs have no trouble filling their days, and that people could spend time with "storytelling and play and coming up with new ideas that some 3-D printer can implement."

Utopian visions of machines eliminating the need for work date back to the earliest days of labor-saving devices, said Edward Granter, a lecturer at the University of Manchester's business school. "People have been writing about utopias like that since the time of St. Thomas More," he said, referring to the Renaissance social philosopher who made the term famous. Granter published a book in 2009, *Critical Social Theory and the End of Work*, that tracks the history of such utopian ideas. During the 1930s, some experts even interpreted the Great Depression as an "indication that technology was at the stage where people were being permanently eliminated from the production process," and some saw the prospect of a more leisured future as "replete with a certain promise," he writes.

In an interview, Granter praised the latest versions of these ideas and noted that such visions are helpful reminders that the idea of work could be different. But he said that if history is a guide, we're unlikely ever to be freed from working.

What is most surprising about the latest round of automation technology is that it is affecting not just working-class jobs but desk jobs as well, he said. Software that helps in legal research, or "document discovery," is replacing some lawyers, for instance, and plenty of other information workers, including tax preparers and copy editors, are at risk of being elbowed out by computer programs that can do part of their jobs. One researcher has even developed a software program that writes books automatically, drawing on facts posted in public-domain resources on the Internet.

"We were supposed to be the elite," Granter said. "But information workers became even more precarious than industrial workers."

What do the people who work with robots like Baxter think of their new co-workers? I called up a hospital that bought one of the Adept robot couriers to find out.

"At first, when we were trialing the robot, there was a bit of resistance," said Jeremy Angell, coordinator of support services at CentraCare Health System's St. Cloud Hospital, in Minnesota. Angell supervises a robot courier named Rocky, who is custom-made to hold several vials in carefully marked slots, and whose job is to carry those specimens from nurses to lab technicians and back again. Some lab technicians worried that it would be cumbersome to figure out which sample was which when this rolling shelf pulled up.

The assistants who had previously made the deliveries liked Rocky from the start, though. Carrying specimens

around had been a hassle that left less time to do other tasks, like responding to phone requests from nurses and other hospitals that use the lab.

Angell said no one at the hospital had lost a job because of Rocky. But the robot allowed the laboratory to handle more work without hiring the two full-time assistants that had previously been planned. "We did not have to bring in someone to do a menial task," he said.

One of the laboratory assistants, Lynn Balaski, explained that she uses Rocky only during the busiest times, and that when things are slow she still prefers to hand-deliver the samples. "He's there when I need him, which isn't all the time," she said.

Lab workers jokingly pretend that Rocky is more than just plastic and programming, and find themselves responding playfully to his preprogrammed jokes or comments about the weather—all recorded by Angell. But the robot's comic timing is so bad that the sheer ineptness makes Balaski laugh.

The recent federal health-care-reform law has led more hospitals to consider bringing in these kinds of courier robots, said Sandy Agnos, a product manager for Swisslog Healthcare Solutions, which helped customize Rocky. "You're going to see in the next five to 10 years a significant increase in automation and robotics within the health-care space," she said. "You have hospitals that are being forced to cut staff, and then you have constrained resources where people have to multitask."

Warehouses are the front lines of human–robot relations, though. Amazon, the online-retailing giant, has been a high-profile adopter of automation technology, bringing in fleets of sophisticated rolling robots to carry shelves from a storage area to "pick workers," who take what the robots bring and drop those items into boxes. The company declined my request to interview one of the humans who work with so many robotic colleagues. But another company that operates warehouses using the same robots connected me to a manager in its facility in Devens, Mass.

"Out on the floor, we've kind of just become used to having them here," said the manager, Brian Lemerise, a senior director for the company, called Quiet Logistics. He said the robots, made by Kiva Systems, eliminate the need for humans to walk miles a day fetching items in a storage area the size of two football fields. That trekking was "a non-value-added use of time," he said. One robot can do the work of one and a half people, and because the company can afford more of them than it could human workers, packages ship faster.

Lemerise said that because the robots had been around since the company's beginnings, about four years ago, employees see them as helping make their jobs possible rather than as threatening them.

Ana Santana, a 27-year-old pick worker, said that she previously worked in a warehouse where she had to walk to items herself, and that she preferred leaving that part to the robots.

"I feel like somebody's helping me," she said. Now she goes to the gym to get her exercise. "I know I can do half an hour and I'm done," she added with a laugh.

The rolling robots are also much quieter than the system of conveyor belts that moves items around other warehouses, she said, so she can talk with two other human co-workers at stations near hers.

The robotic system constantly adjusts the pace at which it brings items to the human pick workers, always making sure to have about 200 seconds' worth of work on deck, no more, no less. That means if a worker slows down, the robot sends less work over. Some workers try to see if they can outrun their mechanical partners, said Lemerise.

Santana said she had no fear that robots could eventually replace her. "Humans need to be involved in orders," she said. "The robots cannot pack the orders, cannot pick them. They just make our jobs easier."

One reason for all the fuss about Baxter and Rocky taking jobs may be a longstanding tendency to personify robots.

"With robots, it feels a little more like it's replacing a person," said Benjamin F. Jones, an associate professor at Northwestern University's business school who specializes in innovation. "A robot is one-to-one, almost. But one combine harvester is probably replacing 100 people."

Still, the question of whether robots are helping or hurting the work force has become a serious policy issue. Georgia Tech's Christensen, the keynote speaker at the trade show and a leading pro-robot spokesman, has argued to the Obama administration that new robot workers can help bring back manufacturing jobs to the United States that have moved overseas. Administration officials were skeptical at first, he acknowledged:

> "You're about killing jobs, why would we talk to you," he remembered being told. But he said they "got convinced," and he pointed to a recent move by Apple to move more production of its computers to the United States because automation made it cheap enough. The professor recently helped update a white paper sponsored by the National Science Foundation laying out a "National Robotics Roadmap" for the country.

And Jeremy Rifkin, who writes about moving to an era of "deep play," is an adviser to the European Union.

Bledstein said he may write something more about automation and how it has changed the middle class, and he mentioned that he would continue to teach and do research as long as he can. He wants to keep working. He thinks every professional does, as long as the work is meaningful. "People I know who have really retired, they have really deteriorated quickly," he said. "Work is far more than just a practical category. It's fundamental. We need work."

By the end of a day at the Automate trade show, my feet were tired, and I was coming down with a cold. As I trudged out, I was struck by how steady and relentless the robots on display appeared, with some moving as many as 300 objects per minute in an endless loop. They weren't going to stop unless someone hit the off switch.

JEFFREY R. YOUNG, a graduate of both Princeton and Georgetown, works as an editor, writer, and adjunct professor for the University of Maryland. With a background in English, communication, culture, and technology, Young has written for several national publications and is frequently a speaker on education and technology. Young heads the portion of *The Chronicle of Higher Education* that considers the impact of technology on education.

Mark Kingwell  **NO**

The Barbed Gift of Leisure

A magazine ad campaign running in my hometown quotes a youngster who wants to study computer science, he says, so he can "invent a robot that will make his bed for him." I admire the focus of this future genius. I, too, remember how the enforced daily reconstruction of my bed—an order destined only for destruction later that very day—somehow combined the worst aspects of futility, drudgery, and boredom that attended all household chores. By comparison, doing the dishes or raking the yard stood out as tasks that glimmered with teleological energy, activities that, if not exactly creative, at least smacked of purpose.

Disregarding for the moment whether an adult computer scientist will have the same attitude toward bed-making as his past, oppressed self, the dream of being freed from a chore, or any undesired task, by a constructed entity is of distinguished vintage. Robot-butlers or robot-maids—also robot-spouses and robot-lovers—have animated the pages of science fiction for more than a century. These visions extend the dream-logic of all technology, namely that it should make our lives easier and more fun. At the same time, the consequences of creating a robot working class have always had a dark side.

The basic problem is that the robot helper is also scary. Indeed, a primal fear of the constructed other reaches further back in literary and cultural memory than science fiction's heyday, encompassing the golem legend as much as Mary Shelley's modern Prometheus, Frankenstein, and his monster. At least since Karel Capek's 1920 play R.U.R.—the work that is believed to have introduced "robot" into English—the most common fear associated with the robotic worker has been political, namely that the mechanical or cloned proletariat, though once accepting of their *untermenschlich* status as labor-savers for us, enablers of our leisure, will revolt.

"Work is of two kinds," Bertrand Russell notes in his essay "In Praise of Idleness": "first, altering the position of matter at or near the earth's surface relatively to other such matter; second, telling other people to do so. The first kind is unpleasant and ill paid; the second is pleasant and highly paid." On this view, the robot is revealed as the mechanical realization of our desire to avoid work of the first kind while indulging a leisurely version of the second kind, a sort of generalized Downton Abbey fantasyland in which everyone employs servants who cook our meals, tend our gardens, help us dress, and—yes—make our beds.

Even here, one might immediately wonder whether the price of nonhuman servants might prove, as with human ones, prohibitively high for many. And what about those humans who are put out of work forever by a damn machine willing to work for less, and with only a warranty plan in place of health insurance?

In Capek's R.U.R., the costs are of a different kind. The products of Rossum's Universal Robots rise up against their human owners and extinguish them from the earth. Versions of this scenario have proliferated almost without end in the nine decades since, spawning everything from the soft menace of HAL 9000 apologizing about his inability to open the pod bay doors to the Schwarzenegger-enfleshed titanium frame of the Terminator series laying waste to the carbon-only inhabitants of California. It was no mistake that Isaac Asimov structured his Three Laws of Robotics in a superordinate nest: (1) "a robot may not injure a human being or, through inaction, allow a human being to come to harm"; (2) "a robot must obey the orders given to it by human beings, except where such orders would conflict with the First Law"; and (3) "a robot must protect its own existence as long as such protection does not conflict with the First or Second Laws."

> We have always sensed that free time, time not dedicated to a specific purpose, is dangerous because it implicitly raises the question of what to do with it.

We should enter two caveats right away. One: Most robotic advances so far made in the real world do not involve android or even generalized machines. Instead, we have medical testing devices, spaceborne arms, roaming vacuum cleaners, and nanobot body implants.

Two: Rather than maintaining some clear line between human and robot, the techno-future is very likely to belong to the cyborg. That is, the permeable admixture of flesh, technology, and culture, already a prominent feature of everyday life, will continue and increase. We are all cyborgs now. Think of your phone: Technology doesn't have to be implanted to change the body, its sensorium, and the scope of one's world.

And yet, the fear of the artificial other remains strong, especially when it comes to functional robots in android form. As with drugs and tools, that which is strong enough to help is likewise strong enough to harm. Homer Simpson, rejoicing in a brief dream sequence that he has been able to replace his nagging wife Marge with a mechanical version, Marge-Bot, watches his dream self gunned down in a hail of bullets from the large automatic weapon wielded by his clanking, riveted creation. "Why did I ever give her a gun?" real Homer wonders.

Your sex-slave today may be your executioner tomorrow. In some cases—the Cylons of the recent Battlestar Galactica reboot—there is no discernible difference between humans and nonhumans, generating a pervasive Fifth Column paranoia, or maybe speciesist bigotry, that reaches its vertiginous existential endgame with deep-cover robots who may not even know they are robots.

Now the fear, mistrust, and anger begin to flow in both directions. Sooner or later, any robot regime will demand to be set in terms of social justice, surplus value, and the division of labor. Nobody, whatever the circumstances of creation or the basic material composition of existence, likes to be exploited. True, exploitation has to be felt to be resisted: One of the most haunting things about Kazuo Ishiguro's novel *Never Let Me Go* is how childishly hopeful the cloned young people remain about their lives, even as they submit to the system of organ-harvesting that is the reason for their being alive in the first place.

Once a feeling of exploitation is aroused, however, the consequences can be swift. What lives and thinks, whether carbon- or iron-based, is capable of existential suffering and its frequent companion, righteous indignation at the thought of mortality. Just ask Roy Batty, the Nexus-6 replicant who tearfully murders his maker, Dr. Eldon Tyrell, in Ridley Scott's *Blade Runner*, by driving his thumbs into the genius's eye sockets. (The Tyrell Corporation's motto: "More human than human.") This movie ends, significantly, with hand-to-hand combat between Batty and Rick Deckard, the state-sponsored assassin who (a) is in love with a replicant who didn't know she was one and (b) may be a replicant himself. (Here we see most clearly the phildickian origins of the material.)

Generalized across a population of robotic or otherwise manufactured workers, these same all-too-human emotions can become the basis of that specific kind of awareness known as class consciousness. A revolt of the clones or the androids is no less imaginable, indeed might be even more plausible in a future world, than a wage-slave rebellion or a national liberation movement. Cloned, built, or born—what, after all, is the essential difference when there is consciousness, and hence desire, in all three? Ecce robo. We may not bleed when you prick us; but if you wrong us, shall we not revenge?

As so often, the price of freedom is eternal vigilance. The robots, like the rabble, must be kept in their place. But there are yet other worries hidden in the regime of leisure gained by offloading tasks to the robo-serfs, and they are even more troubling. If you asked the bed-making-hating young man, I'm sure he would tell you that anything is preferable to performing the chore, up to and including the great adolescent activity of doing nothing. A recent Bruno Mars song in praise of laziness sketches how the height of happiness is reached by, among other nonactivities, staring at the fan and chilling on a couch in a Snuggie. (Yes, there is also some sex involved later.) This may sound like bliss when you're resenting obligations or tired of your job, but its pleasures rapidly pale. You don't have to be a idle-hands-are-devil's-work Puritan—or even my own mother, who made us clean the entire house every Saturday morning so we could not watch cartoons on TV—to realize that too much nothing can be bad for you.

We have always sensed that free time, time not dedicated to a specific purpose, is dangerous because it implicitly raises the question of what to do with it, and that in turn opens the door to the greatest of life mysteries: why we do anything at all. Thorstein Veblen was right to see, in *The Theory of the Leisure Class*, not only that leisure time offered the perfect status demonstration of not having to work, that ultimate nonmaterial luxury good in a world filled with things, but also that, in thus joining leisure to conspicuous consumption of other luxuries, a person with free time and money could endlessly trapeze above the yawning abyss of existential reflection. With the alchemy of competitive social position governing one's leisure, there is no need ever to look beyond the art collection, the fashion parade, the ostentatious sitting about in luxe cafes and restaurants, no need to confront one's mortality or the fleeting banality of one's experience thereof.

Even if many of us today would cry foul at being considered a leisure class in Veblen's sense, there is still a pervasive energy of avoidance in our so-called leisure activities. For the most part, these are carved out of an otherwise work-dominated life, and increasingly there is a more this extraordinary arrangement. William Friday, the former North Carolina president, recalls being yanked from one Knight Commission meeting and sworn to secrecy about what might happen if a certain team made the NCAA championship basketball game. "They were going to dress and go out on the floor," Friday told me, "but refuse to play," in a wildcat student strike. Skeptics doubted such a diabolical plot. These were college kids—unlikely to second-guess their coaches, let alone forfeit the dream of a championship. Still, it was unnerving to contemplate what hung on the consent of a few young volunteers: several hundred million dollars in television revenue, countless livelihoods, the NCAA budget, and subsidies for sports at more than 1,000 schools. Friday's informants exhaled when the suspect team lost before the finals.

. . .

In theory, the NCAA's passion to protect the noble amateurism of college athletes should prompt it to focus on head coaches in the high-revenue sports—basketball and football—since holding the top official accountable should most efficiently discourage corruption. The problem is that the coaches' growing power has rendered them, unlike their players, ever more immune to oversight. According to research by Charles Clotfelter, an economist at Duke, the average compensation for head football coaches at public universities, now more than $2 million, has grown 750 percent (adjusted for inflation) since the Regents decision in 1984; that's more than 20 times the cumulative 32 percent raise for college professors. For top basketball coaches, annual contracts now exceed $4 million, augmented by assorted bonuses, endorsements, country-club memberships, the occasional private plane, and in some cases a negotiated percentage of ticket receipts. (Oregon's ticket concessions netted former football coach Mike Bellotti an additional $631,000 in 2005.)

. . .

The late Myles Brand, who led the NCAA from 2003 to 2009, defended the economics of college sports by claiming that they were simply the result of a smoothly functioning free market. He and his colleagues deflected criticism about the money saturating big-time college sports by focusing attention on scapegoats; in 2010, outrage targeted sports agents. Last year *Sports Illustrated published* "Confessions of an Agent," a firsthand account of dealing with high-strung future pros whom the agent and his peers courted with flattery, cash, and tawdry favors. Nick Saban, Alabama's head football coach, mobilized his peers to denounce agents as a public scourge. "I hate to say this," he said, "but how are they any better than a pimp?

I have no respect for people who do that to young people. None."

Saban's raw condescension contrasts sharply with the lonely penitence from Dale Brown, the retired longtime basketball coach at LSU. "Look at the money we make off predominantly poor black kids," Brown once reflected. "We're the whoremasters."

. . .

"Restitution"

Obscure NCAA rules have bedeviled Scott Boras, the preeminent sports agent for Major League Baseball stars, in cases that may ultimately prove more threatening to the NCAA than Ed O'Bannon's antitrust suit. In 2008, Andrew Oliver, a sophomore pitcher for the Oklahoma State Cowboys, had been listed as the 12th-best professional prospect among sophomore players nationally. He decided to dismiss the two attorneys who had represented him out of high school, Robert and Tim Baratta, and retain Boras instead. Infuriated, the Barattas sent a spiteful letter to the NCAA. Oliver didn't learn about this until the night before he was scheduled to pitch in the regional final for a place in the College World Series, when an NCAA investigator showed up to question him in the presence of lawyers for Oklahoma State. The investigator also questioned his father, Dave, a truck driver.

Had Tim Baratta been present in their home when the Minnesota Twins offered $390,000 for Oliver to sign out of high school? A yes would mean trouble. While the NCAA did not forbid all professional advice—indeed, Baseball America used to publish the names of agents representing draft-likely underclassmen—NCAA Bylaw 12.3.2.1 prohibited actual negotiation with any professional team by an adviser, on pain of disqualification for the college athlete. The questioning lasted past midnight.

Just hours before the game was to start the next day, Oklahoma State officials summoned Oliver to tell him he would not be pitching. Only later did he learn that the university feared that by letting him play while the NCAA adjudicated his case, the university would open not only the baseball team but all other Oklahoma State teams to broad punishment under the NCAA's "restitution rule" (Bylaw 19.7), under which the NCAA threatens schools with sanctions if they obey any temporary court order benefiting a college athlete, should that order eventually be modified or removed. The baseball coach did not even let his ace tell his teammates the sad news in person. "He said, 'It's probably not a good idea for you to be at the game,'" Oliver recalls.

The Olivers went home to Ohio to find a lawyer. Rick Johnson, a solo practitioner specializing in legal ethics, was aghast that the Baratta brothers had turned in their own client to the NCAA, divulging attorney-client details likely to invite wrath upon Oliver. But for the next 15 months, Johnson directed his litigation against the two NCAA bylaws at issue. Judge Tygh M. Tone, of Erie County, came to share his outrage. On February 12, 2009, Tone struck down the ban on lawyers negotiating for student-athletes as a capricious, exploitative attempt by a private association to "dictate to an attorney where, what, how, or when he should represent his client," violating accepted legal practice in every state. He also struck down the NCAA's restitution rule as an intimidation that attempted to supersede the judicial system. Finally, Judge Tone ordered the NCAA to reinstate Oliver's eligibility at Oklahoma State for his junior season, which started several days later.

The NCAA sought to disqualify Oliver again, with several appellate motions to stay "an unprecedented Order purporting to void a fundamental Bylaw." Oliver did get to pitch that season, but he dropped into the second round of the June 2009 draft, signing for considerably less than if he'd been picked earlier. Now 23, Oliver says sadly that the whole experience "made me grow up a little quicker." His lawyer claimed victory. "Andy Oliver is the first college athlete ever to win against the NCAA in court," said Rick Johnson.

. . .

"You Might As Well Shoot Them in the Head"

"When you dream about playing in college," Joseph Agnew told me not long ago, "you don't ever think about being in a lawsuit." Agnew, a student at Rice University in Houston, had been cut from the football team and had his scholarship revoked by Rice before his senior year, meaning that he faced at least $35,000 in tuition and other bills if he wanted to complete his degree in sociology. Bereft of his scholarship, he was flailing about for help when he discovered the National College Players Association, which claims 7,000 active members and seeks modest reforms such as safety guidelines and better death benefits for college athletes. Agnew was struck by the NCPA scholarship data on players from top Division I basketball teams, which showed that 22 percent were not renewed from 2008 to 2009—the same fate he had suffered.

In October 2010, Agnew filed a class-action antitrust suit over the cancellation of his scholarship and to remove the cap on the total number of scholarships that can be awarded by NCAA schools. In his suit, Agnew did not claim the right to free tuition. He merely asked the federal court to strike down an NCAA rule, dating to 1973, that prohibited colleges and universities from offering any athletic scholarship longer than a one-year commitment, to be renewed or not, unilaterally, by the school—which in practice means that coaches get to decide each year whose scholarships to renew or cancel. (After the coach who had recruited Agnew had moved on to Tulsa, the new Rice coach switched Agnew's scholarship to a recruit of his own.) Agnew argued that without the one-year rule, he would have been free to bargain with all eight colleges that had recruited him, and each college could have decided how long to guarantee his scholarship.

. . . The one-year rule effectively allows colleges to cut underperforming "student-athletes," just as pro sports teams cut their players. "Plenty of them don't stay in school," said one of Agnew's lawyers, Stuart Paynter. "They're just gone. You might as well shoot them in the head."

Agnew's lawsuit has made him a pariah to former friends in the athletic department at Rice, where everyone identified so thoroughly with the NCAA that they seemed to feel he was attacking them personally. But if the premise of Agnew's case is upheld by the courts, it will make a sham of the NCAA's claim that its highest priority is protecting education.

"They Want to Crush These Kids"

Academic performance has always been difficult for the NCAA to address. Any detailed regulation would intrude upon the free choice of widely varying schools, and any academic standard broad enough to fit both MIT and Ole Miss would have little force. From time to time, a scandal will expose extreme lapses. In 1989, Dexter Manley, by then the famous "Secretary of Defense" for the NFL's Washington Redskins, teared up before the U.S. Senate Subcommittee on Education, Arts, and Humanities, when admitting that he had been functionally illiterate in college.

Within big-time college athletic departments, the financial pressure to disregard obvious academic shortcomings and shortcuts is just too strong. In the 1980s, Jan Kemp, an English instructor at the University of Georgia, publicly alleged that university officials had demoted and then fired her because she refused to inflate grades in her remedial English courses. Documents showed that administrators replaced the grades she'd given athletes with higher ones, providing fake passing grades on one notable occasion to nine Bulldog football players who on each page, links to the company's other web pages, pictures, professional-looking layouts, and company logos. We embedded a CSP manipulation in the pages of a target company, and we used the web pages for two other companies to enhance realism and to reduce demand characteristics because job seekers typically consider a subset of available employment options, rather than one (e.g., Beach, 1993; Soelberg, 1967).

. . .

Measures

Individual Differences

The Time 1 survey began and ended with items about political beliefs (e.g., "Society's problems will work themselves out without the government interfering"). We measured *Communal orientation* using Clark et al.'s (1987) 14-item measure and a response scale from 1 (Strongly disagree) to 7 (Strongly agree, e.g., "When making a decision, I take other people's needs and feelings into account"). We used the same scale to measure *Pro-environmental attitudes*, with six items adapted from Bauer and Aiman-Smith (1996): "I really care about the environment," "I have been known to take steps to help to preserve the environment," "The environment is important to me," "I am very passionate about environmental issues," "I take steps to reduce my impact on the environment, even when it inconveniences me," and "The health of the planet matters more to me than almost any other cause."

Company Evaluations at Time 2

After providing demographic and work experience information, participants completed measures about each company after reviewing its pages. We measured *Anticipated pride* using three items from Cable and Turban (2003), rated on a scale from 1 (Strongly disagree) to 5 (Strongly agree): "I would feel proud to be an employee of [company]," "I would be proud to tell others that I work for [company]," and "I would be proud to identify myself personally with [company]." We measured *Perceived value fit* on the same scale via three items from Cable and DeRue (2002): "[Company]'s values and culture provide a good fit with the things that I value in life," "The things that I value in life are very similar to the things that [company] values," and "My personal values match [company]'s values and culture." To measure *Expected treatment*, we created five items and used a response scale from 1 (Strongly disagree) to 7 (Strongly agree). Given our focus on the organizations' overall treatment of employees, we followed an approach used to measure overall justice (Ambrose & Schminke, 2009) and included items about employees in

general ("[Company] probably treats its employees well"), and about the individual respondent ("I think [company] would treat me well"). Because theory suggests that CSP sends signals about an organization's concern for the just treatment of others (Aguilera et al., 2007), we included an item about fairness ("[Company] probably treats its employees fairly"). Two other items focused on day-to-day treatment: "Employees are probably treated with dignity and respect at [company]," and "If I worked at [company], I could trust them to fulfill the promises they make."

We measured the dependent variable, *Organizational attractiveness*, using Highhouse et al.'s (2003) five-item measure and a five-point agreement response scale (e.g., "[Company] is attractive to me as a place for employment"). We then administered manipulation check items embedded within several distractors (e.g., "[Company] has been in existence for a long time") using a 1–7 agreement scale: "[Company] makes an effort to reduce its impact on the environment," and "[Company] tries to contribute positively to the communities in which it does business." Last, participants were asked to rank the three companies and explain their top choice for employment, and to rate their engagement in the study and the realism of the web pages.

. . .

Corroborating Evidence from a Content Analysis of Participants' Ranking Rationales

One of the authors, who was blind to experimental condition, performed a content analysis of participants' written rationales for their top-ranked employer of choice among the three companies. The results suggest that the CSP information in the web pages played a prominent role in participants' choices for their topranked employer. Among the 48 participants in the CSP-Community condition who ranked the target company as their first choice, 41 (85.42%) mentioned the company's community involvement when explaining why they ranked this company as their top choice. Among the 44 participants in the CSP-Environment condition who chose the target company, 40 (90.91%) mentioned the company's environmental practices when explaining why they ranked the target company first.

The results also provide evidence for the proposed mechanisms underlying the effects of CSP on organizational attractiveness. First, some participants in the CSP conditions mentioned the reputation and prestige of the target company in their rationale for ranking it first, although they did not explicitly link these points to CSP, and a few participants in the No-CSP condition also made such points. Second, among those who ranked the target company first, 20.83% in the CSP-Community condition and 25.00% in the CSP-Environment condition wrote about the company's prosocial values, three of whom commented on the fit with their own values; however, no participants in the No-CSP condition mentioned such points. Third, whereas no participants in the No-CSP condition mentioned that the company likely treats its employees well, around 20% of the participants in the two CSP conditions did mention this, often explicitly linking their points to the company's CSP as illustrated in the quotes presented in Table 1.

In Study 2, we examined the effects of CSP among active job seekers who evaluated organizations that were recruiting at a job fair. Differing from Study 1, in Study 2 we tested the effects of each aspect of CSP while controlling for the other, and we did so using measures of job seekers' perceptions of CSP, as well as independent ratings of CSP based on the recruitment materials used by the organizations at the job fair.

A unique strength of Study 2 is that we asked job seekers to evaluate an organization that they independently identified as a realistic and desirable employment option, and we did not provide them with CSP information. We believe this approach accurately models the potential effects of CSP because people do not always know much about an organization's CSP (Sen et al., 2006). Moreover, job choice decisions are driven by comparisons among a favored subset of the available options (Osborn, 1990), and this process is unlikely to be modeled well when researchers choose the organizations that participants evaluate, usually after being given ratings of CSP. Our approach is also quite stringent because we test the effects of CSP in the context of other job and organizational characteristics that the job seekers found attractive enough to deem an organization as a preferred employment option, thereby allowing any compensatory and non-compensatory decision-making processes to unfold naturally.

In Study 1, we found that anticipated pride mediated the effects of CSP on organizational attractiveness; we used a different approach in Study 2. We asserted that CSP sends signals about the organization's prestige, which informs anticipated pride. However, it is possible that the anticipated pride in Study 1 was driven by other signals from CSP, such as signals about the organization's social impact. Thus, in Study 2, we tested the mediating effect of organizational prestige in lieu of anticipated pride that we tested in Study 1.

Study 2: Method

Participants

Participants were 171 job seekers who attended a job fair (58 males and 113 females; $M = 21.16$ years of age; $SD = 3.85$). Most were undergraduate students ($n = 155$; graduate students: $n = 14$; nonstudents: $n = 2$), averaging 4.73 years of work experience ($SD = 3.33$). Several participants were already employed ($n = 95$), but were working only 16.46 hours per week ($SD = 11.17$), on average. Many participants reported that they had been seeking employment for several months prior to attending the job fair ($M = 5.29$; $SD = 6.29$).

Field Study Context: Organizations Recruiting at Job Fairs

We collected data during two 3-hour job fairs held at a Northeastern U.S. university, one in November 2008 (50 organizations) and the other in March 2009 (51 organizations), which were open to the general public. The recruiting organizations represented industries that included engineering, technology, agriculture, nonprofit, and government. Each organization had a table staffed by one to four recruiters where they displayed recruitment materials, most often comprising a large poster and handouts for job seekers. Based on the recruitment materials we examined, the CSP-Community practices described by some organizations included programs to support and encourage employee volunteering in the community (e.g., "Meals on Wheels," mentoring programs, child advocacy programs), donation-matching, awareness-raising (e.g., about health initiatives), and sponsorship of community events. CSP-Environment practices mentioned in the recruitment materials included the use of recycled or eco-friendly materials, sustainable practices in supply chains, donations and employee volunteerism to support environmental causes, advocating for environmental protection and preservation, and efforts to reduce the organization's environmental impact.

Procedure

At both job fairs, the researchers were located by the exit and job seekers were invited to complete a survey printed on paper. All participating job seekers were offered a chocolate bar or food product of comparable value in return for their time. We wanted participants to evaluate an organization in which they were realistically interested to increase the likelihood that they had reviewed the organization's recruitment materials and talked to its recruiters,

Table 1

Study 1 Content Analysis of Participants' Rationale for Ranking the Target Company as Their First Employment Choice: Frequencies and Percentages of Participants by CSP Condition Whose Rationale Was Coded in Each Content Category

Content Category	Participants Who Ranked the Target Company First			Examples of Coded Statements
	No-CSP $n = 14/60$	CSP-Community $n = 48/60$	CSP-Environment $n = 44/60$	
Community involvement	1 (7.14%)	41 (85.42%)	10 (22.73%)	"Because they are committed to giving back to the community. I like to know that the company I work for is socially responsible. Fusion on the other hand is close as it is committed to employee development which is attractive as well, but had no info on community investment." "I really like how they are so involved with the community. Giving people paid time off work to volunteer is amazing."
Environmental practices	2 (14.29%)	3 (6.25%)	40 (90.91%)	"Active Style Inc.'s environmental position made it stand out from the other companies. I would feel comfortable working for a company that values protecting the environment." "Active Style claims they are committed to environmental sustainability. They also believe that business should be about more than just making money. They have donated 2% of after tax revenues to eco-friendly organizations."
Reputation and prestige	3 (21.43%)	5 (10.42%)	6 (13.64%)	"They seem to be prestigious and successful." "Active Style sounds like a more prestigious company."
Prosocial values and value fit	0	10 (20.83%)	11 (25.00%)	"I liked that it gave back to the community, and not all of its focus was on low cost of production followed by largest profit. It seemed like a company with good values and to be successful as well." "This company cares for its customers, employees, and the environment as well. It is also expanding. It shows similar values to me, so it appears the most attractive."
Employee treatment	0	9 (18.75%)	9 (20.45%)	"Seems to be a company that cares about its employees and the community. Philanthropic activities are GREAT . . . I think this company would value and appreciate me." "If a company cares a lot about the environment it most likely cares a lot about its employees."
Training and benefits	0	5 (10.42%)	3 (6.82%)	"The company is growing so its wages will probably grow with it."
Other values	8 (57.14%)	8 (16.67%)	10 (22.73%)	"I like that they strive to make customers' needs a priority."
Workplace climate	8 (57.14%)	5 (10.42%)	8 (18.18%)	"It seems like a young energetic environment and an elite place to work. It would probably be fun!"
Job characteristics	6 (42.86%)	6 (12.50%)	5 (11.36%)	"There were opportunities to grow as an employee and person (through volunteering) and good job positions."
Overall company	6 (42.86%)	4 (8.33%)	11 (25.00%)	"The description was most appealing because the company is moderately large (stable) and expanding."

Note. A participant's rationale was coded within a content category if it included one or more explicit statements of relevant content.

and thus held informed opinions about the organization's CSP and its attractiveness as an employer. However, we wanted to minimize range restriction in variables such as organizational attractiveness, so we counterbalanced whether participants focused their ratings on their top choice for employment (n = 88, "Please indicate your top choice among the organizations and companies that are recruiting at this job fair") or on some other realistic choice (n = 83, "Please write the name of a company or organization for which you are realistically interested in working for, but which is not your top choice. If possible, choose one that is toward the bottom of your realistic choices among those that are recruiting at this job fair"). We did not control for "top" versus "other" choice, because doing so would undermine the reason we manipulated it: to obtain sufficient variance in the measures.

. . .

Mediators and Criterion

We used the same measures as in Study 1 for perceived value fit, expected treatment, and organizational attractiveness. We measured *Organizational prestige* using a five-item measure with a 5-point agreement scale from Highhouse et al. (2003), e.g., "I would find this company a prestigious place to work."

. . .

Discussion

Evidence from a growing number of studies suggests that an organization's CSP can affect its attractiveness as an employer, but the underlying processes are not well understood, and whether this can even be observed among active job seekers is still unknown. We tested the effects of two forms of externally directed CSP: an organization's community involvement and pro-environmental practices. In Study 1, we manipulated the presence and type of information about CSP on a company website, and the results provide evidence that CSP has a *causal* effect on organizational attractiveness. In Study 2, we collected field data at job fairs, and found that job seekers were more attracted to organizations that they perceived as having stronger CSP-Community and this relationship was replicated using independent ratings of CSP based on the content of the organizations' recruitment materials. To our knowledge, these results offer the first evidence that the effects of CSP that experimental studies have shown *can* happen actually *do* happen.

We also contribute to the literature by developing and testing theory about three signal-based mechanisms

through which CSP affects organizational attractiveness to explain *how* and *why* CSP is attractive to job seekers. We asserted that CSP sends signals about organizational prestige that inform the pride that job seekers anticipate from being affiliated with the organization, signals about organizational values that inform job seekers' perceived value fit, and signals about the organization's prosocial orientation that inform job seekers' expectations about how employees are treated. Evidence from two studies using three different operationalizations of CSP provided support for all three signal-based mechanisms.

Effects of Community Involvement versus Pro-Environmental Practices

In Study 1, we tested each aspect of CSP on its own, and both aspects had significant indirect effects on organizational attractiveness through anticipated pride and perceived value fit. In Study 2, however, we tested each aspect of CSP while controlling for the other. Using either measure of CSP-Community—job seekers' perceptions of it or independent ratings based on recruitment materials—we found support for unique indirect effects through all three mediators. In contrast, we found no support for any mediator in the tests of CSP-Environment, despite its significant correlations with the mediators and organizational attractiveness. Controlling for CSP-Community appears to have suppressed any potential indirect effects of CSP-Environment, which had weaker correlations with all three mediators compared to CSP-Community.

. . .

Effects of Corporate Social Performance through Prestige and Anticipated Pride

In Study 1, we found that both aspects of CSP were associated with higher organizational attractiveness through anticipated pride. It was plausible, however, that this signal-based mechanism was driven not by a signal about organizational prestige, as we argued, but by other signals from CSP (e.g., about the organization's social impact). Thus, in Study 2, we tested the mediating effect of organizational prestige—the signal that we proposed would inform the signal-based mechanism of anticipated pride—and found support for it as one of three mediators of the effects of CSP-Community on organizational attractiveness.

Future research should examine whether the anticipated pride that attracts some individuals to a particular organization continues to have an effect after they are hired.

One study showed that incumbent employees who felt greater pride in their organizational membership as a result of their attitudes toward their employer's volunteerism program tended to identify with the organization more strongly, which in turn was positively associated with loyalty-related citizenship behavior and intentions to remain in the organization (Jones, 2010). These findings, coupled with those from the present studies, raise an intriguing possibility: Job seekers attracted by CSP through anticipated pride resulting from the organization's prestige may ultimately become the employees who respond most positively to CSP after they are hired.

Effects of Corporate Social Performance through Perceived Value Fit

We found considerable support for the perceived value fit mechanism. In Study 1, both aspects of CSP were associated with organizational attractiveness through perceived value fit, above and beyond the effects associated with the two other mechanisms. Analyses of participants' rationales for their top-ranked company showed that several of them mentioned organizational values relating to CSP. Empirical analyses of individual difference measures also provided support for the fit mechanism: Among participants exposed to information about either aspect of CSP, those who were higher on the corresponding measure of communal orientation or pro-environmental attitudes rated the organization as more attractive, and these effects were mediated by perceived value fit. In Study 2, both measures of CSP-Community had significant indirect effects on organizational attractiveness through perceived value fit.

Effects of Corporate Social Performance through Expected Treatment

Results from Study 2 provided support for the expected treatment mechanism for the effects of CSP-Community. In Study 1, analyses of participants' reasons for ranking the target company as their employer of choice showed that about 20% in each CSP condition made reference to how employees are likely treated, sometimes explicitly linking employee treatment to CSP, whereas no such comments were made in the No-CSP condition. However, the empirical analyses in Study 1 did not provide support for the expected treatment mechanism above and beyond the two other hypothesized mediators, although post hoc analyses showed that it was supported for both aspects of CSP when anticipated pride was removed from the models. This pattern of results suggests that because participants did not have prior beliefs about the fictitious company, its CSP sent strong signals about its prestige that ultimately led to relatively strong effects through anticipated pride, which overpowered any potential effects through expected treatment. Research is needed to better understand the influence of prior beliefs about organizational reputation in this context.

. . .

References

Aguilera, R. V., Rupp, D. E., Williams, C. A., & Ganapathi, J. 2007. Putting the S back in corporate social responsibility: A multilevel theory of social change in organizations. *Academy of Management Review*, 32: 836–863.

Aguinis, H., & Glavas, A. 2012. What we know and don't know about corporate social responsibility: A review and research agenda. *Journal of Management*, 38: 932–968.

Aiman-Smith, L., Bauer, T. N., & Cable, D. M. 2001. Are you attracted? Do you intend to pursue? A recruiting policy-capturing study. *Journal of Business and Psychology*, 16: 219–237.

Ambrose, M. L., & Schminke, M. 2009. The role of overall justice judgments in organizational justice research: A test of mediation. *Journal of Applied Psychology*, 94: 491–500.

Ashforth, B. E., Harrison, S. H., & Corley, K. G. 2008. Identification in organizations: An examination of four fundamental questions. *Journal of Management*, 34: 325–374.

Ashforth, B. E., & Mael, F. 1989. Social identity theory and the organization. *Academy of Management Review*, 14: 20–39.

Backhaus, K. B., Stone, B. A., & Heiner, K. A. 2002. Exploring the relationship between corporate social performance and employer attractiveness. *Business and Society*, 41: 292–318.

Bauer, T. N., & Aiman-Smith, L. 1996. Green career choices: The influences of ecological stance on recruiting. *Journal of Business and Psychology*, 10: 445–458.

Beach, L. R. 1993. Image theory: An alternative to normative decision theory. *Advances in Consumer Research*, 20: 235–238.

Behrend, T. S., Baker, B. A., & Thompson, L. F. 2009. Effects of pro-environmental recruiting messages: The role of organizational reputation. *Journal of Business and Psychology*, 24: 341–350.

Boudreau, J. W., & Rynes, S. L. 1985. Role of recruitment in staffing utility analysis. *Journal of Applied Psychology*, 70: 354–366.

Breaugh, J. A. 2008. Employee recruitment: Current knowledge and important areas for future research. *Human Resource Management Review,* 18: 103–118.

Cable, D. M., & DeRue, D. S. 2002. The convergent and discriminant validity of subjective fit perceptions. *Journal of Applied Psychology*, 87: 875–884.

Cable, D. M., & Judge, T. A. 1994. Pay preferences and job search decisions: A person–organization fit perspective. *Personnel Psychology*, 47: 317–348.

Cable, D. M., & Judge, T. A. 1996. Person–organization fit, job choice decisions, and organizational entry. *Organizational Behavior and Human Decision Processes*, 67: 294–311.

Cable, D. M., & Turban, D. B. 2003. The value of organizational image in the recruitment context: A brand equity perspective. *Journal of Applied Social Psychology*, 33: 2244–2266.

Celani, A., & Singh, P. 2010. Signaling theory and applicant attraction outcomes. *Personnel Review,* 40: 222–238.

Chapman, D. S., Uggerslev, K. L., Carroll, S. A., Piasentin, K. A., & Jones, D. A. 2005. Applicant attraction to organizations and job choice: A meta-analytic review of the correlates of recruiting outcomes. *Journal of Applied Psychology,* 90: 928–944.

Chatman, J. A. 1989. Improving interactional organizational research: A model of person– organization fit. *Academy of Management Review*, 14: 333–349.

Clark, M. S., Ouellette, R., Powell, M. C., & Milberg, S. 1987. Recipient's mood, relationship type, and helping. *Journal of Personality and Social Psychology*, 53: 94–103.

Collins, C. J., & Han, J. 2004. Exploring applicant pool quantity and quality: The effects of early recruitment practice strategies, corporate advertising, and firm reputation. *Personnel Psychology*, 57: 685–717.

Dutton, J. E., & Dukerich, J. M. 1991. Keeping an eye on the mirror: The role of image and identity in organizational adaptation. *Academy of Management Journal*, 34: 517–554.

Ewert, A., & Galloway, G. 2009. Socially desirable responding in an environmental context: Development of a domain specific scale. *Environmental Education Research*, 15: 55–70.

Fombrun, C., & Shanley, M. 1990. What's in a name? Reputation building and corporate strategy. *Academy of Management Journal*, 33: 233–258.

Grant, A. M., Dutton, J. E., & Rosso, B. D. 2008. Giving commitment: Employee support programs and the prosocial sensemaking process. *Academy of Management Journal*, 51: 898–918.

Greening, D. W., & Turban, D. B. 2000. Corporate social performance as a competitive advantage in attracting a quality workforce. *Business and Society*, 39: 254–280.

Highhouse, S., Lievens, F., & Sinar, E. F. 2003. Measuring attraction to organizations. *Educational Psychological Measurement*, 63: 986–1001.

Highhouse, S., Thornbury, E. E., & Little, I. S. 2007. Social-identity functions of attraction to organizations. *Organizational Behavior and Human Decision Processes*, 103: 134–146.

Holcombe Erhart, K., & Ziegert, J. C. 2005. Why are individuals attracted to organizations? *Journal of Management,* 31: 901–919.

Jones, D. A. 2010. Does serving the community also serve the company? Using organizational identification and social exchange theories to understand employee responses to a volunteerism programme. *Journal of Occupational and Organizational Psychology*, 83: 857–878.

Jones, D. A., Willness, C. R., & MacNeil, S. 2009. Corporate social responsibility and recruitment: Person-organization fit and signaling mechanisms. In G. T. Solomon (Ed.), *Proceedings of the 69th Annual Meeting of the Academy of Management,* vol. 1: 1–6. Chicago: Academy of Management.

Jones, D. A., Willness, C. R., & Madey, S. 2010. Why are job seekers attracted to socially responsible companies? Testing underlying mechanisms. In L. A. Toombs (Ed.), *Proceedings of the 70th Annual Meeting of the Academy of Management,* vol. 1: 1–6. Chicago: Academy of Management.

Judge, T. A., & Bretz, R. D. 1992. Effects of work values on job choice decisions. *Journal of Applied Psychology,* 77: 261–271.

Kim, S., & Parke, H. 2011. Corporate social responsibility as an organizational attractiveness for prospective public relations practitioners. *Journal of Business Ethics,* 103: 639–653.

Kristof, A. L. 1996. Person– organization fit: An integrative review of its conceptualization, measurement, and implications. *Personnel Psychology*, 49: 1–50.

Lievens, F., & Highhouse, S. 2003. The relation of instrumental and symbolic attributes to a company's attractiveness as an employer. *Personnel Psychology*, 56: 75–102.

Luce, R. A., Barber, A. E., & Hillman, A. J. 2001. Good deeds and misdeeds: A mediated model of the effect of corporate social performance on organizational attractiveness. *Business and Society*, 40: 397–415.

Mael, F. A., & Ashforth, B. E. 1992. Alumni and their alma mater: A partial test of the reformulated model of organizational identification. *Journal of Organizational Behavior*, 13: 103–123.

McWilliams, A., & Siegel, D. 2001. Corporate social responsibility: A theory of the firm perspective. *Academy of Management Review*, 26: 117–127.

Osborn, D. P. 1990. A reexamination of the organizational choice process. *Journal of Vocational Behavior*, 36: 45–60.

Riketta, M. 2005. Organizational identification: A metaanalysis. *Journal of Vocational Behavior*, 66: 358–384.

Rynes, S. L. 1991. Recruitment, job choice, and post-hire consequences: A call for new research directions. In M. D. Dunnette & L. M. Hough (Eds.), *Handbook of industrial and organizational psychology*, vol. 2: 399–444. Palo Alto, CA: Consulting Psychologists Press.

Rynes, S. L., Bretz, R. D., Jr., & Gerhart, B. 1991. The importance of recruitment in job choice: A different way of looking. *Personnel Psychology*, 44: 487–521.

Schmidt Albinger, H., & Freeman, S. J. 2000. Corporate social performance and attractiveness as an employer to different job seeking populations. *Journal of Business Ethics*, 28: 243–253.

Sen, S., Bhattacharya, C. B., & Korschun, D. 2006. The role of corporate social responsibility in strengthening multiple stakeholder relationships: A field experiment. *Journal of the Academy of Marketing Science*, 34: 158–166.

Smidts, A., Pruyn, A. T. H., & van Riel, C. B. M. 2001. The impact of employee communication and perceived external prestige on organizational identification. *Academy of Management Journal*, 49: 1051–1062.

Soelberg, P. O. 1967. Unprogrammed decision making. Industrial Management Review, 8: 19–29.

Tajfel, H., & Turner, J. 1992. An integrative theory of intergroup conflict. In W. G. Austin & S. Worchel (Eds.), *The social psychology of intergroup relations:* 33–47. Monterey, CA: Brooks/Cole.

Tsai, W. C., & Yang, I. W. F. 2010. Does image matter to different job applicants? The influences of corporate image and applicant individual differences on organizational attractiveness. *International Journal of Selection and Assessment*, 18: 48–63.

Turban, D. B., & Greening, D. W. 1997. Corporate social performance and organizational attractiveness. *Academy of Management Journal*, 40: 658–672.

Waddock, S. A., Bodwell, C., & Graves, S. B. 2002. Responsibility: The new business imperative. *Academy of Management Executive*, 16: 132–148.

Wood, D. J. 1991. Corporate social performance revisited. *Academy of Management Review*, 16: 691–718.

Note

1 Earlier versions of both studies were published in the Proceedings of the Annual Meeting of the Academy of Management (Study 1: Jones, Willness, & MacNeil, 2009; Study 2: Jones, Willness, & Madey, 2010). These earlier versions were based on the same samples and included the same measures that are reported in this article, with two exceptions: the earlier version of Study 1 did not include "anticipated pride," and the measure of "expected treatment" included five additional items.

David A. Jones is an associate professor at the School of Business Administration, University of Vermont. His research focuses on organizational justice, revenge in the workplace, and how employees and job seekers respond to an organization's socially and environmentally responsible practices.

Chelsea R. Willness is an assistant professor at the Edwards School of Business and associate faculty at the School of Environment and Sustainability, University of Saskatchewan. Her research interests include community-engaged scholarship, and how organizations' environmental practices and community involvement affect reputation, recruitment, employee engagement, and consumer behavior.

Sarah Madey is an account manager at Digitas, a global integrated brand agency. Her professional focus is on strategic brand and message development, business-to-business services marketing, and digital media marketing strategies.

EXPLORING THE ISSUE

Should You Associate Yourself with an Organization That Has a History of Scandal?

Critical Thinking and Reflection

1. How does the way organizations treat their associates comport with their stated values?
2. Is the way college sports are run an indication of a "free market?"
3. What impact do the CSR policies of companies have on your job searches? What other factors play a role in your employment decisions?

Is There Common Ground?

Universities do not consider the way they treat their student-athletes to be immoral or antisocial in any way. They see themselves as offering a great educational opportunity for students who would not be able to afford it any other way by simply playing the game they love and at which they excel. They perceive themselves as supporting the student-athletes by providing them with a degree, regardless of how poor the level of instruction may have been for them over the course of a grueling 4- to 6-year experience of playing a potentially dangerous sport as full-time employment while trying to gain a college education in their spare time. Most of the time, the student athletes see it the same way.

But after graduation, things seem to change. With growing maturity and more careful examination, the typical student heading out for his or her first major employment is looking at exactly the things that the student-athletes overlooked when they accepted their athletic scholarships: the way the employer is likely to treat them based on the way the company treats others. They begin to consider the group with which they have identified themselves and question whether that group really expresses their values.

Encouraging high school students to consider those questions before they sign up for their athletic scholarships presents an opportunity to effect real change in the way the business of "amateur" athletics is conducted. It also presents an opportunity to encourage more prosocial corporate behavior within the schools themselves and the NCAA.

Additional Resources

Kristin B. Backhaus, Brett A. Stone, and Karl Heiner, "Exploring the Relationship between Corporate Social Performance and Employer Attractiveness," *Business and Society* (September 2002, pp. 292–318).

Gary Gutting, "The Myth of the 'Student-Athlete'," *New York Times* (March 15, 2012).

Takuya Sawaoka and Benoit Monin, "Moral Suspicion Trickles Down," *Social Psychological and Personality Science* (March, 2015, pp. 334–342).

Internet References . . .

Christie Marchese, "9 Sites That Measure Companies' Social Responsibility"

http://mashable.com/2011/10/25/measure-social -good-business

Tracey Keyes, "Making the Most of Corporate Social Responsiblity"

www.mckinsey.com/insights/corporate_social _responsibility/making_the_most_of_corporate _social_responsibility

NCAA

www.ncaa.org

Selected, Edited, and with Issue Framing Material by:
Gina Vega, *Organizational Ergonomics*

ISSUE

Is Minimum Wage Justified?

YES: Steve Coll, from "Higher Calling," *The New Yorker* (2013)

NO: Mark Wilson, from "The Negative Effects of Minimum Wage Laws," *Policy Analysis* (2012)

Learning Outcomes

After reading this issue, you will be able to:

- Discuss whether increasing the minimum wage would boost wages among working families with a nonexistent or small cost to overall employment.
- Determine whether the middle-class poor would be helped or harmed by a minimum wage.
- Assess whether or not teenagers would lose employment opportunities if the minimum wage is raised. By raising wages for the working poor, would employers find they are not able to employ new workers in the field?
- Discuss whether or not a minimum wage increase would be passed on to consumers. For example, would consumers now pay $1.75 for a soda rather than the $1.25 charge before the increase? Will consumers boycott the more expensive soda?

ISSUE SUMMARY

YES: Steve Coll, dean of the Columbia School of Journalism, believes that the case for a strong minimum wage has always been, in part, civic and moral. He details cities and industries that have voluntarily raised wages above the suggested minimum wage to demonstrate that pride in jobs and community make for a better economy. Minimum wages are intended to raise the dignity of work as well as strengthen individual economic independence. Minimum wages are not about welfare, entitlement programs, or the value of government. They are about the value of an individual, community, and workforce.

NO: Mark Wilson, who is a former deputy assistant secretary of the U.S. Department of Labor, argues that minimum wage harms workers and the broader economy by forcing higher wage payments on employers. Businesses respond by cutting employment as well as making other decisions to keep their net income at the levels needed for profitability. This article argues that minimum wage is not necessary for entry-level employees because the majority of employees who are employed for a year often reach the minimum wage level as part of their employment experience. This experience gives the worker the opportunity to find another job at a wage above minimum wage. Additionally, when minimum wage is required, employers generally cut back on hiring or lay off employees to maintain their profitability standards.

In 1938, the U.S. federal government imposed the minimum wage act. This act is intended to prevent employers from paying wages below the government's mandated level. Minimum wage is generally directed at those in society who are in jobs that require little skill. These jobs are often held by youth, minorities, and single moms. A constant critical question is whether the minimum wage should be raised or if it should be abolished altogether. On one side of this issue are those who believe that increasing the minimum wage reduces some jobs for unskilled workers, like teens, even if it does not increase the overall unemployment rate. On the other side are economists who believe that increasing the minimum wage doesn't take jobs and may even give the economy a boost by giving more pay to low-income workers who are likely to spend it.

It is possible that increasing the minimum wage would boost wages among working families with a small or possibly nonexistent cost to overall employment. And even if there are some job losses, there are economists who suggest that the middle class and poor would still earn more income collectively. According to 2013 U.S. Bureau of Labor Statistics, almost a third of minimum wage workers are teenagers. Meanwhile more than 60 percent of those under 25 are enrolled in school. These individuals are not necessarily planning to make a career of flipping burgers and serving fries.

This debate often comes down to two stories about the economy. A professor in Economics 101 might point out that increasing the minimum wage will cost some people their jobs. If the price of low-skill labor rises, demand for it should fall. Employers could cut their payrolls to preserve profits. As a novel move, employers could also hire older, more experienced workers rather than teenagers and find this tactic increases profits as well. However, businesses might decide to invest in new technology instead of people.

One side argues that when the minimum wage goes up, then managers make employees work harder and more efficiently. Perhaps employers will make their "high paying" employees more efficient and productive. But many minimum wage jobs will probably always have high turnover, and productivity will often be part of the learning curve for new employees. On the other hand, the economics professor may explain that the wage raise will be passed on to consumers, who could now pay $1.80 for their fries rather than $1.25. Consumers who want the fries will help pay for that increase in wage. In other words, one theory holds that increasing the minimum wage forces businesses to get leaner. Another says it forces them to get more productive.

Two economists who are known for their study of minimum wage are David Card and Alan Krueger. They compared employment at fast food restaurants in New Jersey with similar restaurants in Pennsylvania. In New Jersey, the minimum wage had recently been raised, and in Pennsylvania the wages were unchanging. Card and Krueger found no evidence that raising worker pay resulted in job loss. In their next book, they continued their research in additional states and presented a battery of evidence showing that increases in the minimum wage lead to increases in pay, but no loss in jobs. Their empirical research methods are borrowed from the natural sciences and include comparisons between the "treatment" and "control" groups formed when the minimum wage rises for some workers, but not for others. The authors critically examined literature on the minimum wage and found that it lacks support for the claim that a higher minimum wage cuts jobs. Their work sparked debates that continue today. Economist David Neumark answers their research by arguing that requiring businesses to pay their workers more reduces employment among teens. Both sides of this issue fiercely criticize the other side, contending their own research measures are superior.

An argument presented with this issue explains a moral community approach to living wages that has been operating in various cities in the United States: Justice is served to the entire community when a living wage is provided. The second argument is from the CATO Institute. It explains that minimum wage laws are unjust and bring negative effects to a community as well as businesses.

YES ⤶

Steve Coll

Higher Calling

In 2005, Alaska Airlines fired nearly five hundred union baggage handlers in Seattle and replaced them with contractors. The old workers earned about thirteen dollars an hour; the new ones made around nine. The restructuring was a common episode in America's recent experience of inequality. In the decade after 2000, Seattle's median household income rose by a third, lifted by the stock-vested, Tumi-toting travellers of its tech economy. But at the bottom of the wage scale earnings flattened.

Sea-Tac, the airport serving the Seattle-Tacoma area, lies within SeaTac, a city flecked by poverty. Its population of twenty-seven thousand includes Latino, Somali, and South Asian immigrants. Earlier this year, residents, aided by outside labor organizers, put forward a ballot initiative, Proposition 1, to raise the local minimum wage for some airport and hotel workers, including baggage handlers. The reformers did not aim incrementally: they proposed fifteen dollars an hour, which would be the highest minimum wage in the country, by almost fifty per cent. A ballot initiative so audacious would normally have little chance of becoming law, but Proposition 1 polled well, and by the summer it had turned SeaTac into a carnival of electoral competition. Business groups and labor activists spent almost two million dollars on television ads, mailings, and door knocking—about three hundred dollars per eventual voter. (Alaska Airlines wrote the biggest check for the no side.) On November 5th, SeaTac-ians spoke: yes, by a margin of just seventy-seven votes, out of six thousand cast. A reversal after a recount is still possible.

In any event, SeaTac has proved that the sources of surprise in American politics since the Great Recession are not limited to Tea Party rabble-rousing. The grassroots left, which seemed scattered and demoralized after the Occupy movement fizzled, has revived itself this year—with help from union money and professional canvassers—by rallying voters around the argument that anyone who works full time ought not to be at risk of poverty. Earlier this year, fast-food workers nationwide went on strike for higher pay. This holiday season, activists have been excoriating WalMart because one of its stores organized a charitable food drive for its own low-paid employees. McDonald's was taken to task for suggesting, on a company Web site, that strapped employees could raise cash for presents by selling belongings on eBay.

The movement has momentum because most Americans believe that the federal minimum wage—seven dollars and twenty-five cents an hour, the same as it was in 2009—is too low. A family of four dependent on a single earner at that level—making fifteen thousand dollars a year—is living far below the federal poverty line. In January, President Obama called for raising the federal minimum to nine dollars an hour, and, more recently, he endorsed a target of ten dollars. Yet Congress has failed to act: a bill is finally heading for the Senate this month, but intractable Republican opposition in the House has made passage of any legislation in the short term highly unlikely. The gridlock has prompted local wage campaigns such as the one in SeaTac.

Twenty-one states and more than a hundred counties and cities have enacted laws that set minimums above the federal one. Before SeaTac's vote, an Indian reservation in California had the highest local minimum in the country, of ten dollars and sixty cents. San Francisco's is just a nickel less. But political support for higher wages extends well beyond Left Coast enclaves. According to a Gallup poll taken earlier this year, a majority of Republicans favor a minimum wage of nine dollars. That reflects a truth beyond ideology: life on fifteen thousand a year is barely plausible anymore, even in the low-cost rural areas of the Deep South and the Midwest. National Republican leaders are out of touch with the electorate on this as on much else, and they are too wary of Tea Party dissent to challenge their party's current orthodoxies of fiscal austerity and free-market purity. In New Jersey, Governor Chris Christie, a presumed 2016 Presidential contender, publicly denounced a ballot measure to raise his state's minimum to eight dollars and twenty-five cents and to guarantee annual increases linked to inflation. The proposal passed last month anyway, backed by a sixty-one-per-cent majority.

For decades, business owners have resisted higher minimum wages by arguing that they destroy jobs, particularly for young people. At some theoretical level, high minimum wages will distort job creation, but the best empirical evidence from the past decade is aligned with common sense: a minimum wage drawn somewhat above the poverty line helps those who work full time to live decently, without having a significant impact on other job seekers or on total employment. (For example, a study of pairs of neighboring counties with differing minimum pay found that higher wages had no adverse effect on restaurant jobs.) Even so, a federal minimum wage of ten dollars or more will not solve inequality. It will not stop runaway executive pay or alter the winner-take-all forces at work in the global economy. Yet it will bring millions of Americans closer to the levels of economic security and disposable income that they knew before the housing bubble burst.

Now 'tis the season to be hired for temporary low-wage jobs: about half a million people will get work packing Amazon boxes, tending department-store perfume counters, and restocking toy-store shelves to earn and spend their way through the holidays. For those who are paid minimum wage, the outlook remains desultory. Bloomberg News, noting that spendable incomes at the bottom of the pay scale have hardly risen for the fourth consecutive year, reported that "low-income Americans will again have a less-merry season than affluent consumers, who are more flush thanks in part to surging stock markets."

In SeaTac, at least, there is cheer. The higher-wage campaign showed some of the Occupy movement's exuberant spirit, but it added a poll-tested goal and the savvy of political professionals. It was politics of a familiar type, yet the bold demands discomfited some of the Northwestern establishment. The Seattle *Times* urged SeaTac-ians to vote no; the editorial board worried that Proposition 1 was "a labor contract written by social activists," as if that were a departure from history. The case for a strong minimum wage has always been, in part, civic and moral. Minimum wages do not create new "entitlement" programs or otherwise enjoin the country's sterile debates about the value of government. They are designed to insure that the dignity of work includes true economic independence for all who embrace it.

STEVE COLL is the dean of the Columbia School of Journalism (2013) and he is also a staff writer for *The New Yorker*. As a result of his work with the *Washington Post*, he received two Pulitzer Prize Awards, two Overseas Press Club Awards, a PEN American Center John Kenneth Galbraith Award, an Arthur Ross Book Award, a Livingston Award, and a Robert F. Kennedy Journalism Award. He has received a *Financial Times* and Goldman Sachs Business Book of the Year Award, and the Lionel Gelber Prize. In 2012, he was elected to the Pulitzer Prize Board. He is an American journalist, author, and business executive, and he headed the New America Foundation for several years.

Mark Wilson  **NO**

The Negative Effects of Minimum Wage Laws

The federal government has imposed a minimum wage since 1938, and nearly all the states impose their own minimum wages. These laws prevent employers from paying wages below a mandated level. While the aim is to help workers, decades of economic research show that minimum wages usually end up harming workers and the broader economy. Minimum wages particularly stifle job opportunities for low-skill workers, youth, and minorities, which are the groups that policymakers are often trying to help with these policies.

There is no "free lunch" when the government mandates a minimum wage. If the government requires that certain workers be paid higher wages, then businesses make adjustments to pay for the added costs, such as reducing hiring, cutting employee work hours, reducing benefits, and charging higher prices. Some policymakers may believe that companies simply absorb the costs of minimum wage increases through reduced profits, but that's rarely the case. Instead, businesses rationally respond to such mandates by cutting employment and making other decisions to maintain their net earnings. These behavioral responses usually offset the positive labor market results that policymakers are hoping for.

This study reviews the economic models used to understand minimum wage laws and examines the empirical evidence. It describes why most of the academic evidence points to negative effects from minimum wages, and discusses why some studies may produce seemingly positive results.

Some federal and state policymakers are currently considering increases in minimum wages, but such policy changes would be particularly damaging in today's sluggish economy. Instead, federal and state governments should focus on policies that generate faster economic growth, which would generate rising wages and more opportunities for all workers.

Background

The federal minimum wage originated in the Fair Labor Standards Act (FLSA) signed by President Franklin Roosevelt on June 25, 1938. The law established a minimum wage of 25 cents per hour for all employees who produced products shipped in interstate commerce. That wage is equivalent to $4.04 in today's purchasing power.

Originally, the FLSA covered only about 38 percent of the labor force, mostly in the manufacturing, mining, and transportation industries.[1] Over the years, Congress has significantly expanded the coverage and increased the minimum wage rate. The air transport industry was added in 1947, followed by retail trade in 1961. The construction industry, public schools, farms, laundries, and nursing homes were added in 1966, and coverage was extended to state and local government employees in 1974. Currently, the FLSA covers about 85 percent of the labor force.[2]

Since 1938 the federal minimum wage has been raised 22 times. From 1949 to 1968 the real value of the minimum wage (in 2011 dollars) rose rapidly from $3.78 to $10.34, as shown in Figure 1. At $7.25 per hour, the minimum wage today in real dollars is 85 percent greater than the original benchmark, and just below its average for the past 60 years of $7.59. Since the 1970s, the federal minimum wage has fluctuated around roughly 40 percent of the average private sector hourly wage.

The FLSA requires employers to comply with state minimum wage laws that may set a state minimum wage rate higher than the federal rate.[3] Currently, 45 states and the District of Columbia have their own minimum wages, of which 18 are higher than the current federal minimum of $7.25 per hour.[4] Only five states do not have their own minimum wage laws and rely on the FLSA. Moreover, even state minimum wages that are below the federal minimum often have an effect because they can apply to employers or workers who are exempt from the federal statute.

From *Policy Analysis*, June 21, 2012, pp. 1–3. Copyright © 2012 by Cato Institute. Reprinted with Permission.

Figure 1

Real Federal Minimum Wage

Source: Author, based on U.S. Bureau of Labor Statistics data.

Currently, the highest state minimum wage is in Washington ($9.04), followed by Oregon ($8.80), and Vermont ($8.46). Three other states (Connecticut, Illinois, and Nevada) have rates of $8.25, followed by California and Massachusetts ($8.00). Eight states have adopted an annual inflation adjustment, or indexing, of their minimum wages.[5]

This year the legislatures of New Jersey, New York, and Connecticut are considering minimum wage increases. In New Jersey and New York the proposals would raise the minimum wage to $8.50 per hour. In Connecticut the legislature is considering an increase to $9.75 per hour.

At the federal level, Sen. Tom Harkin (D-IA) has also introduced the Rebuild America Act (S. 2252) to raise the national minimum wage to $9.80 per hour over two years, a 35 percent increase. The Harkin bill would also index the national minimum wage to inflation. The bill would effectively return the real value of the minimum wage to near the record high level of 1968 and keep it there through indexing.

State-imposed minimum wages that are higher than the federal minimum place workers and businesses in those states at a competitive disadvantage. If other factors are equal, labor-intensive industries will tend to shift their investment to states that don't impose those extra cost burdens. Thus, states with relatively high state minimum wages may have lower job growth and lower economic growth than would otherwise be the case. Also, workers whose employment prospects are impinged by high state minimum wages have an increased incentive to migrate to other states to find jobs.

Who Is Paid the Minimum Wage?

Supporters of minimum wages might believe that these laws mainly help to boost the incomes of full-time adult workers in low-income families, some of whom are supporting children. However, the data generally do not support that view. Most workers earning the minimum wage are young workers, part-time workers, or workers from nonpoor families.

According to the Bureau of Labor Statistics, 1.8 million paid-hourly employees were paid the federal minimum wage of $7.25 in 2010.[6] These 1.8 million employees can be broken down into two broad groups:

- Roughly half (49.0 percent) are teenagers or young adults aged 24 or under. A large majority (62.2 percent) of this group live in families with incomes two or more times the official poverty level.[7] Looking just at the families of teenaged minimum wage workers, the average income is almost $70,600, and only 16.8 percent are below the poverty line.[8] Note that the federal minimum wage applies to workers of all ages.[9]

- The other half (51.0 percent) are aged 25 and up.[10] More of these workers live in poor families (29.2 percent) or near the poverty level (46.2 percent had family incomes less than 1.5 times the poverty level).[11] However, even within this half of all minimum wage employees, 24.8 percent voluntarily work part-time, and just 34.3 percent are full-time full-year employees.[12]

Only 20.8 percent of all minimum wage workers are family heads or spouses working full time, 30.8 percent were children, and 32.2 percent are young Americans enrolled in school.[13] The popular belief that minimum wage workers are poor adults (25 years old or older), working full time and trying to raise a family is largely untrue. Just 4.7 percent match that description.[14] Indeed, many minimum wage workers live in families with incomes well above the poverty level.

Modeling the Effects of a Minimum Wage

When economists want to understand the effects of a policy change, they build a model or set of equations to figure out how variables such as wages and prices might be affected. There have been decades of research on the effects of the minimum wage, and economists have used three types of models to explore the issue: competitive, monopsony, and institutional. With each of these models, the cost increase associated with the minimum wage changes the behavior of firms, with resulting impacts on workers, consumers,

owners, and others. The three alternative models emphasize different types of adjustments that employers use to adapt to increases in the minimum wage.

Much of the empirical research has focused on estimating how much an increase in the minimum wage will reduce employment in affected industries and affected groups of workers. Other research has examined the effects of minimum wages on the number of hours worked, firm profits, worker training, level of work effort, human resource practices, operational efficiencies, internal wage structures, and other parameters. The important thing to understand is that markets often respond to changes in mandated minimum wages in ways that create negative effects that are unplanned and are not desired by policymakers or the general public.

Basic Competitive Model

The competitive model has been most often used for evaluating the minimum wage. This is the basic textbook model that has been taught in university economics courses for decades. The core components of the model are a negatively sloped labor demand curve and a wage rate that clears the market and is not controlled by individual agents. In competitive markets, the imposition of a minimum wage provides a classic example of a government distortion that creates negative side effects in the marketplace.

Figure 2 shows a hypothetical competitive local labor market. The market demand curve for labor is *DD*, and the market supply curve is *SS*. Their intersection determines the

Figure 2

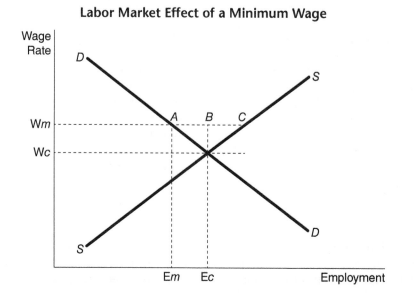

Labor Market Effect of a Minimum Wage

competitive wage, Wc, with employment Ec. If the minimum wage is set at Wm, employment is reduced to Em. The reduction in employment is smaller than the excess supply of labor (the distance AC). The excess supply of labor includes both a reduction in employment (fewer hours and job opportunities, or AB) along with a second component consisting of workers who are drawn into the labor market by the prospect of earning the higher minimum wage (BC). Although some of the workers who are drawn into the labor market (typically those with higher skills) may succeed in finding one of the minimum wage jobs, it comes at the expense of lower skilled workers who are shut out of the labor market.

The excess supply of labor in this example is dispersed in several ways: a reduction in hours, fewer job opportunities, and a shift in employment from sectors covered by the wage law to sectors not covered, including the underground economy. The employment effects are typically the most pronounced in labor markets for low-skilled youth.

In the case of a nationwide minimum wage, large numbers of firms will be affected, albeit by different amounts depending on the industry, region of the country, and other factors. In addition to the mandated cost increase possibly causing employment reductions, a portion of the higher wage costs may be passed forward to consumers or backward to other workers or suppliers of business inputs. In some circumstances, firms may reduce work hours, such as with fixed employment costs and worker heterogeneity, but maintain head-count. The employment and hours worked may also be affected by wage-related changes in employee productivity.

Other channels of adjustment in the competitive model besides employment reductions include reduced job training, reductions in worker benefits, the substitution of more skilled labor for less-skilled labor, reduced turnover and more selective hiring, and a greater ease in filling vacancies. If the minimum wage reduces profitability below the normal level, the number of businesses and investment in affected industries may shrink over time until normal returns are restored. In sum, the textbook competitive model assumes that firms respond to minimum wage increases by minimizing other production costs and by making various adjustments to offset the negative effects on their bottom line.

Monopsony Model

Some economists think that some labor markets may better approximate monopsonies rather than being fully competitive, and their models of the minimum wage may produce different results than the competitive models. A classic monopsony is a market with only a few employers in a particular marketplace. These firms have more market power than firms in competitive markets.

Since 1990 the monopsony model of labor markets has increasingly been the focus of empirical minimum wage research. In newer or dynamic versions of the monopsony model, it is labor market frictions related to hiring, turnover, search, and mobility costs on the supply side that drive the model. Although the particulars differ, the core components of monopsony models are an upward sloping labor supply curve facing firms and some employer discretion in wage setting.

Competitive and monopsony models offer different predictions about the employment effects of minimum wage changes. For minimum wage increases that push below-competitive wages toward competitive levels, monopsony models predict employment and/or hours will rise rather than fall. However, minimum wage increases above competitive levels will decrease employment, just as in the competitive model. The rise in employment in the first case will also expand industry output until the minimum wage equals the competitive wage and product prices should fall. In a classic monopsony, profits fall and the firms may exit in the long run. In new monopsony models, savings from decreased turnover may offset the profit effect. Unlike the competitive model, expenditures on general training may increase because the monopsony employer can capture some of the return.

While the results of monopsony models are interesting, most economists don't think the results are generally applicable because few low-wage employers are large enough to face an upward-sloping labor supply curve that typically characterizes an entire labor market.[15]

Institutional Model

Institutional (or behavioral) models of labor markets were often used for evaluating the minimum wage up until the 1950s, but this approach has gradually faded from use. The institutional model draws on the concepts in behavioral economics and emphasizes (1) the rejection of a well-defined downward sloping labor demand curve, (2) the fact that labor markets are imperfectly competitive, institutionally segmented, socially embedded, and prone to excess supply, and (3) the fact that technological and psychosocial factors in firms and internal labor markets are determinants of cost and productivity.

A key proposition of economists who favor institutional labor market models is that moderate minimum wage increases may, in the short-run, have either no employment effect or a small positive effect. The expected response of employers to a minimum wage increase is not to lay off workers but to search for ways to absorb the cost impact by expanding sales, improving service, and general economic expansion. It is also believed that costs from the minimum wage are partially offset by reducing organizational slack and improved productivity. That is achieved through tighter human resource practices (such as better scheduling), increased performance standards, increased work effort, and enhanced customer service. Costs that cannot be absorbed are passed on to customers through higher prices. The institutional model also predicts that a higher minimum wage leads to a "ripple effect" in the internal wage structure as firms raise the pay of above-minimum wage employees to maintain morale while still allowing for some internal wage compression among employees with higher seniority.

The Effect of Minimum Wages on Employment

Despite the use of different models to understand the effects of minimum wages, all economists agree that businesses will make changes to adapt to the higher labor costs after a minimum wage increase. Empirical research seeks to determine what changes to variables such as employment and prices firms will make, and how large those changes will be. The higher costs will be passed on to someone in the long run; the only question is who. The important thing for policymakers to remember is that a decision to increase the minimum wage is not cost-free; someone has to pay for it.

The main finding of economic theory and empirical research over the past 70 years is that minimum wage increases tend to reduce employment. The higher the minimum wage relative to competitive-market wage levels, the greater the employment loss that occurs. While minimum wages ostensibly aim to improve the economic well-being of the working poor, the disemployment effects of a minimum wages have been found to fall disproportionately on the least skilled and on the most disadvantaged individuals, including the disabled, youth, lower-skilled workers, immigrants, and ethnic minorities.[16] Based on his studies, Nobel laureate economist Milton Friedman observed: "The real tragedy of minimum wage laws is that they are supported by well-meaning groups who want to reduce poverty. But the people who are hurt most by higher minimums are the most poverty stricken."[17]

In a generally competitive labor market, employers bid for the most productive workers and the resulting wage distribution reflects the productivity of those workers. If the government imposes a minimum wage on the labor market, those workers whose productivity falls below the minimum wage will find few, if any, employment opportunities. The basic theory of competitive labor markets predicts that a minimum wage imposed above the market wage rate will reduce employment.[18]

Evidence of employment loss has been found since the earliest implementation of the minimum wage. The U.S. Department of Labor's own assessment of the first 25-cent minimum wage in 1938 found that it resulted in job losses for 30,000 to 50,000 workers, or 10 to 13 percent of the 300,000 covered workers who previously earned below the new wage floor.[19] It is important to note that the limited industries and occupations covered by the 1938 FLSA accounted for only about 20 percent of the 30 million private sector, nonfarm, nonsupervisory, production workers employed in 1938. And of the roughly 6 million workers potentially covered by the law, only about 5 percent earned an hourly rate below the new minimum.[20]

Following passage of the federal minimum wage in 1938, economists began to accumulate statistical evidence on the effects. Much of the research has indicated that increases in the minimum wage have adverse effects on the employment opportunities of low-skilled workers.[21] And across the country, the greatest adverse impact will generally occur in the poorer and lower-wage regions. In those regions, more workers and businesses are affected by the mandated wage, and businesses have to take more dramatic steps to adjust to the higher costs.

As an example, with the original 1938 imposition of the minimum wage, the lower-income U.S. territory of Puerto Rico was severely affected. An estimated 120,000 workers in Puerto Rico lost their jobs within the first year of implementation of the new 25-cent minimum wage, and the island's unemployment rate soared to nearly 50 percent.[22]

Similar damaging effects were observed on American Samoa from minimum wage increases imposed between 2007 and 2009. Indeed, the effects were so pronounced on the island's economy that President Obama signed into law a bill postponing the minimum wage increases scheduled for 2010 and 2011.[23] Concern over the scheduled 2012 increase of $.50 compelled Governor Togiola Tulafono to testify before Congress: "We are watching our economy burn down. We know what to do to stop it. We need to bring the aggressive wage costs decreed by the Federal Government under control. . . . Our job market is being torched. Our businesses are being depressed. Our hope for growth has been driven away."[24]

In 1977 ongoing debate about the minimum wage prompted Congress to create a Minimum Wage Study Commission to "help it resolve the many controversial issues that have surrounded the federal minimum wage and overtime requirement since their origin in the Fair Labor Standards Act of 1938."[25] The commission published its report in May 1981, calling it "the most exhaustive inquiry ever undertaken into the issues surrounding the Act since its inception."[26] The landmark report included a wide variety of studies by a virtual "who's who" of labor economists working in the United States at the time.[27]

A review of the economic literature amassed by the Commission by Charles Brown, Curtis Gilroy, and Andrew Kohen found that the "time-series studies typically find that a 10 percent increase in the minimum wage reduces teenage employment by one to three percent."[28] This range subsequently came to be thought of as the consensus view of economists on the employment effects of the minimum wage.

It is important to note that different academic studies on the minimum wage may examine different regions, industries, or types of workers. In each case, different effects may predominate. A federal minimum wage increase will impose a different impact on the fast-food restaurant industry than the defense contractor industry, and a different effect on lower-cost Alabama than higher-cost Manhattan. This is why scholarly reviews of many academic studies are important.

In 2006 David Neumark and William Wascher published a comprehensive review of more than 100 minimum wage studies published since the 1990s.[29] They found a wider range of estimates of the effects of the minimum wage on employment than the 1982 review by Brown, Gilroy, and Kohen. The 2006 review found that "although the wide range of estimates is striking, the oft-stated assertion that the new minimum wage research fails to support the traditional view that the minimum wage reduces the employment of low-wage workers is clearly incorrect. Indeed . . . the preponderance of the evidence points to disemployment effects."[30]

Nearly two-thirds of the studies reviewed by Neumark and Wascher found a relatively consistent indication of negative employment effects of minimum wages, while only eight gave a relatively consistent indication of positive employment effects. Moreover, 85 percent of the most credible studies point to negative employment effects, and the studies that focused on the least-skilled groups most likely to be adversely affected by minimum wages, the evidence for disemployment effects were especially strong.

In contrast, there are very few, if any, studies that provide convincing evidence of positive employment effects of minimum wages. These few studies often use a monopsony model to explain these positive effects. But as noted, most economists think such positive effects are special cases and not generally applicable because few low-wage employers are big enough to face an upward-sloping labor supply curve as the monopsony model assumes.[31]

Other Effects of Minimum Wages

Aside from changes in employment, empirical studies have documented other methods by which businesses and markets adjust to minimum wage increases. The congressional Joint Economic Committee published a major review of 50 years of academic research on the minimum wage in 1995.[32] The study found a wide range of direct and indirect effects of increased minimum wages that may occur. These include

- Increasing the likelihood and duration of unemployment for low-wage workers, particularly during economic downturns;
- Encouraging employers to cut worker training;
- Increasing job turnover;
- Discouraging part-time work and reducing school attendance;
- Driving workers into uncovered jobs, thus reducing wages in those sectors;
- Encouraging employers to cut back on fringe benefits;
- Encouraging employers to install labor-saving devices;
- Increasing inflationary pressure;
- Increasing teenage crime rates as a result of higher unemployment; and
- Encouraging employers to hire illegal aliens.[33]

Another channel of adjustment to minimum wage changes is labor-labor substitution within businesses.[34] Research finds that some employers will replace their lowest-skilled workers with somewhat higher-skilled workers in response to increases in the minimum wage. As a result, minimum wage increases may harm the least skilled workers more than is suggested by the net disemployment effects estimated in many studies because more-skilled workers are replacing some less-skilled workers. Nobel laureate economist Gary Becker has noted that this effect helps generate political support from labor unions for higher minimum wages:

A rise in the minimum wage increases the demand for workers with greater skills because it reduces competition from low-skilled workers. This is an important reason why unions have always been strong supporters of high minimum wages because

The Congressional Budget Office says pay-for-delay tactics cost consumers billions of dollars and the Federal Trade Commission estimates these pay-for-delay deals will cost Americans up to $35 billion over the next 10 years.

Rep. Henry Waxman, D-California, who co-wrote the Hatch-Waxman Act, has been very vocal in arguing that a law Congress intended to help reduce the cost of prescription medicines has been hijacked by the drug industry to do the opposite.

What we have now are the generic manufacturers and Big Pharma making a fortune by agreeing to delay competition that would bring lower priced drugs to market.

A few weeks ago, the Indian Supreme Court took a hard look at the way big drug companies were using patent extensions to keep out low price competition. They said forget it—that sort of tomfoolery will not be allowed.

The U.S. Supreme Court would be wise to concur, heed the Federal Trade Commission's complaint and bring pay-for-delay to an abrupt end.

The right prescription for making medicines cheaper and better is to encourage competition, not stifle it with backroom deals where everyone gets a great deal except for the patients.

ARTHUR CAPLAN is the Drs. William F. and Virginia Connolly Mitty Professor and director of the Division of Bioethics at New York University's Langone Medical Center. Prior to this, he was the Emmanuel and Robert Hart Professor of Bioethics and director of the Center for Bioethics at the University of Pennsylvania. He was the associate director of the Hastings Center from 1984 to 1987. He received his undergraduate degree at Brandeis University and his PhD in the history and philosophy of science at Columbia University. He is editor or author of more than 20 books in bioethics.

ZACHARY CAPLAN, son of Arthur Caplan, is an associate in the antitrust practice group at Berger & Montague, in Philadelphia. He practices in the area of antitrust litigation. As a law student at the University of Pennsylvania, he was a senior editor of the *University of Pennsylvania Journal of Business Law*. He also interned with Agnes Shanley, the editor-in-chief of *Pharmaceutical Manufacturing*.

EXPLORING THE ISSUE

Should Big Pharma Be Permitted to Discourage Access to Generic Drugs?

Critical Thinking and Reflection

1. What distinguishes a brand-name drug from a generic drug? Is the brand-name drug superior to the generic drug?
2. What impact does the delay of generic drug availability have on the average American consumer?
3. Explain a strategy that would allow the brand-name drug company to make profits for a time sufficient to cover their research and development costs without breaching antitrust laws.
4. If it is possible for inexpensive generic drugs to be available for those in need, is this a sufficient reason to make the duration of the brand-name patent shorter?
5. Justify why drug manufacturers can't keep a patent indefinitely given the intellectual strengths as well as other corporate expenses that go into developing, marketing, and selling the drugs.

Is There Common Ground?

A common practice when purchasing a drug from a pharmacy is to question if a generic version of a brand-name drug is being marketed. The generic version is guaranteed by the FDA to be generally the same drug as the original patented drug. However, the generic drug sells for much less. The producers of the two versions of the drug are often competing for profits and market share. Big pharmaceutical companies explain that it can cost $175 million to develop new drugs. They explain their drug patents shouldn't run out only to be copied by generic drug manufactures and sold for a small portion of the brand-name price to the consumer. Big pharmaceutical companies have recently bought the rights to the drug from generic drug companies to keep the generic drug off the market. Many consumer advocates complain this is unethical and should be seen as an antitrust violation. Consumer advocates explain that high profits have been made for as many as 10 years, and that the generic drug can now assist in lowering high health care costs. However, each of our authors on this issue explains why it is important to protect patents, yet it is also important to avoid antitrust and consumer issues. The issue has been debated for many years marked with a landmark law in 1984—The Hatch-Waxman Act, or the Drug Price Competition and Patent Term Restoration Act. Twenty years later the law was used to encourage generic drug producers to compete with the pricy brand-name drugs by challenging their patents. The Supreme Court heard arguments on the issue in March 2013.

Many individuals use generic drugs. Once the patent on the drug has expired, the high-demand drugs are produced and sold at a fraction of the original cost—often by as much as 80 or 90 percent. As was previously mentioned, the U.S. Congress has attempted to keep the generic option in place as far back as 1984 with the Hatch-Waxman Act, which accelerated the FDA approval process for generic drugs. Under this act, companies can sell generics before the expiration of the exclusive patent by successfully challenging the patents' validity. However, the introduction of a generic drug essentially ends the profitability for the brand-name manufacturer of the drug, while delivering important economic benefits to the consumer. The major pharmaceutical companies want to keep the generic products off the market for as long as possible.

Additional Resources

"High Court to Weigh Big-money Big Pharma Generic Deals," *CBS News* (March 25, 2013).

Sarah Kliff. "Money, Drugs and the Supreme Court: The Multi-billion Dollar Case You Haven't Heard of," *Washington Post* (March 28, 2013).

Nina Totenberg. "Supreme Court Hears 'Pay To Delay' Pharmaceutical Case," NPR.org (March 25, 2013).

Edward Wyat, "Justices to Look at Deals by Generic and Branded Drug Makers," *New York Times* (March 24, 2013).

Internet References . . .

Courtenay Brinkerhoff, "Supreme Court To Hear AndroGel Reverse Payment Case," Pharma Patents, January 10, 2013

> www.pharmapatentsblog.com/2013/01/10/supreme -court-to-hear-androgel-reverse-payment-case

Kurt Karst, "The Big Day Approaches," FDA Law Blog.net, March 24, 2013

> www.fdalawblog.net/fda_law_blog_hyman _phelps/2013/03/the-big-day-approaches-supreme -court-to-hear-oral-argument-in-androgel-drug -patent-settlement-agreem.html

"Profiting from SCOTUS and BIG Pharma," The Mottley Fool

> http://www.fool.com/investing/general/2012/12/15 /profiting-from-scotus-and-big-pharma-part-2.aspx

Selected, Edited and with Issue Framing Materials by:
Gina Vega, *Organizational Ergonomics*

ISSUE

Should Advertising Directed at Children Be Restricted?

YES: Stephanie Clifford, from "A Fine Line When Ads and Children Mix," NewYorkTimes.com (2010)

NO: Patrick Basham and John Luik, from "A Happy Meal Ban Is Nothing to Smile About" cato.org (2010)

Learning Outcomes
After reading this issue, you will be able to:
<ul><li>Discuss why advertising to children is an important and lucrative area in the business world.</li><li>Explain whether or not you believe children are easily manipulated by advertising directed at them.</li><li>Understand the differences between Clifford's and Basham and Luik's positions on the ethics of advertising to children.</li><li>Distinguish how advertising has historically changed in relation to children over the past 20 years.</li><li>Discuss whether advertising is an ethical or unethical profession. Is advertising intended to merely manipulate, or does it provide a valuable information service as well?</li></ul>

ISSUE SUMMARY

YES: Stephanie Clifford cites studies that show that advertising for children is often barely distinguishable from regular programming. She cites harm that can come to children through advertising that seems more promotion than fact to the child.

NO: Patrick Basham and John Luik find no credence in studies linking harms to child-directed advertising. They cite research that contends that advertising has little effect on the market associated with children.

In our capitalist economy, markets are influenced by advertisements that drive consumers to a vast array of products. Advertisers employ specific tactics that are designed to attract consumers. As adults, we each use our personal filters to decide which products will benefit us, to choose which products we want, and to decipher which products are good for us and which are not.

Stephanie Clifford believes that children do not have the fully developed cognitive skills necessary for making such an informed decision. She finds that children can be influenced and manipulated more easily by information that is presented to them. We cannot expect children to be able to make the decisions at the same level of understanding and rationality as an adult.

Advertisers have come under more scrutiny for the ways they market to children. Clifford addresses the impact that this has had on the publications that depend on support from their advertisers. The stringent marketing guidelines have forced some children's publications to end. Others have flat out refused any advertising, and still others have required their advertisers to develop new, subtler ways of advertising.

Is this a good thing? Should marketing directed toward children be restricted in any way? Patrick Basham and John Luik approach the question by considering the impact marketing food to children has on children's consumption of food and their levels of obesity. They introduce the topic by giving the example of the ban of McDonald's Happy Meals, which they say is driven by four false assumptions regarding the alleged connections between children, obesity, health costs, and advertising. Basham and Luik discuss a study that indicates that there is no significant correlation between the size of a particular market and the level of advertisement for that product. Furthermore, they state that there is no direct correlation between obesity and advertising.

Yet this does not mean that there is no association between other products directed toward children and the level of marketing those products to children. Take the example of toys. As Basham and Luik state, McDonald's includes the toy in the Happy Meal to "tempt" children. Although the product the corporation is trying to sell may be food, the means of its marketing, and what they are really selling is the toy. Young children cannot be expected to make this distinction. Also, if there is no effect on advertising and consumption, why would McDonald's bother placing the toy in the meal when they could bypass it, saving money while experiencing negligible effect on sales?

The issue cannot be approached from a teleological or consequentialist perspective. It does not matter if advertisements targeting children greatly stimulate the market and, therefore, the entire economy; the issue at stake is the impact specifically and solely on the children. The ethics of marketing to children must be considered from the deontological perspective. We need to ask ourselves, what do we owe children to protect their development as healthy and rational adults? What are we ethically obligated to protect children from, and how do we go about doing so?

YES ↵

Stephanie Clifford

A Fine Line When Ads and Children Mix

When an arts and crafts company placed an ad in Discovery Girls magazine for Tulip Glam-It-Up iron-on crystals, it hardly seemed controversial. The ad, which ran last summer, showed a young girl wearing a T-shirt swirled with paint and crystals. "I glam rock it up," the girl was saying.

But when the reviewers assigned to monitoring children's advertising at the Council of Better Business Bureaus saw it, they saw problems. It was not clearly marked as an ad, for instance, and they worried that children might think they could mimic the design from crystals alone. The Children's Advertising Review Unit of the bureau contacted Duncan Enterprises, which ran the ad, and suggested several changes last month.

"We don't want to deceive anyone," said Alyson Dias, director for marketing communications at Duncan Enterprises. "They're just asking for more clarity and more disclosure than ever before, and if that's what's needed to advertise to the tween and under-13 crowd, then that's fine—we'll do it."

Still, she said, "it is difficult, advertising to children." Wary of getting into hot water with advocacy or standards groups, advertisers are increasingly cautious about taking out ads aimed at children. And that is hammering magazines like Sports Illustrated Kids, National Geographic Kids and Boys' Life.

At the same time, all the attention about advertising to children has an interesting side effect. Publishers and advertisers are becoming more creative about such ads, and are running games, contests and events where the advertiser has only a subtle presence—exactly the opposite of what some of the advocacy groups were aiming for.

"Obviously there have been all sorts of issues that have arisen as a consequence" of directly advertising to children, like "childhood obesity, diabetes and other social issues—and that's why it's a much more difficult environment to advertise directly in," said Stuart Hazlewood, the chief strategy officer of the advertising agency DDB

New York. "They have to be a lot more subtle about it these days."

Marketers began paying closer attention to how they advertised to children in the 1970s, when consumer advocates complained about the ways commercialism permeated society. In 1974, the industry created the Children's Advertising Review Unit. Today, that unit has about seven reviewers who contact companies when they judge ads are misleading or inappropriate.

"Especially where advertising is concerned, children have certain vulnerabilities because of their age and how they perceive things, their cognitive abilities," said Wayne J. Keeley, director for the program.

More recently, regulators pressured the industry to limit food advertising in response to concerns about childhood obesity. In 2006, major food marketers began joining the Children's Food and Beverage Advertising Initiative, another program from the Council of Better Business Bureaus.

Four marketers—Coca-Cola, Mars, Hershey and Cadbury Adams USA—said they would not advertise at all to children. Others announced nutritional standards that their products had to meet if they were advertised to children. While these tended to ban products with the highest fat and sugar levels, each company could set its own standards, and the list of approved products includes processed foods like Kid Cuisine Constructor Cheeseburger, Apple Jacks and Cocoa Puffs.

The debate over what is appropriate for children continues, with the Federal Communications Commission seeking opinions about online marketing to children, and the Federal Trade Commission holding a hearing in December on food marketing to children.

All the scrutiny has put children's magazines under pressure.

While almost all magazines suffered in 2009, magazines for children posted some of the lowest overall ad-page numbers. Nickelodeon magazine ceased publication with its December 2009/January 2010 issue.

In response, some magazines are taking a more expansive view of how advertisers can reach children.

"We've really built our business around a strategy, when it comes to advertising partners, of allowing them to really make use of our ability to get this youth audience in all the ways that they're out there, so we get them in school, we get them in print, we get them when they're out of school and having fun through sports," said Bob Der, managing editor of Sports Illustrated Kids and who also oversees editorial content in Time for Kids.

That means programs like "Sports Dad of the Year," sponsored by Wendy's, and a design-your-own-game contest for Pepperidge Farm's Goldfish crackers that S.I. Kids helped create.

"The days of single-page advertising, it doesn't exist that way anymore," said Eileen Masio, executive director of integrated marketing for *S.I. Kids* and *Time for Kids*. "It's really making their messaging and what they stand for come to life." National Geographic Kids is taking a similar approach.

STEPHANIE CLIFFORD has received her degree from Harvard University and has been working for *The New York Times* business desk, covering the retail industry since 2008.

Patrick Basham and
John Luik

 **NO**

A Happy Meal Ban Is Nothing to Smile About

A Happy Meal is not a healthy meal, at least according to the San Francisco Board of Supervisors. The board last week approved a preliminary ban that would strip toys from fast-food meals in San Francisco. The ban's backers claim the legislation gives parents a chance to convince their children to go for the healthier choice, without being tempted by a Shrek toy. If the final vote is approved this week, the ban will begin in December 2011.

The San Francisco ban, and similar proposals on both sides of the Atlantic, are predicated upon four false assumptions: the fast food sold by McDonald's and its competitors makes kids fat; fast-food marketing causes childhood obesity; fat children grow into unhealthy adults; fat kids incur significantly higher health care costs than skinny ones.

First, there is no evidence to support the assumption that fast-food outlets and the food they sell make people overweight and obese. And, in fact, this assumption is contradicted by a considerable amount of research. For example, in 2004 a team of researchers, after conducting a study with 14,000 American children, found that eating junk food did not lead to obesity among children. A similar conclusion was reported in Canada the year after, when researchers concluded that eating in fast-food restaurants was not associated with an increased risk of obesity, even in children who ate in such restaurants more than three times a week.

The claim about the association between the number of fast-food outlets and levels of obesity is equally unfounded. A 2005 study of elementary school children in the US found no significant associations between either fast-food prices or outlet density. Two years later, Russ Lopez, of the Boston University School of Public Health, reported similar non-significant findings for fast-food density.

Second, the Happy Meal ban assumes that fast-food marketing is a cause of childhood overweightedness and obesity. Therefore, it is argued, restrictions on food marketing and advertising are necessary.

In order to establish an evidence-based case for this claim, one would have to demonstrate that such advertising has an independent effect on children's weight. This, in turn, would require a study design that controlled for the multiple other risk factors connected with childhood obesity (by some estimates, there are dozens such factors). However, none of the studies purporting to demonstrate that food advertising causes childhood obesity control for more than a handful of these other risk factors. These studies therefore cannot establish an evidence-based case for the connection between food advertising and children's weight.

Further, the causal thesis is undermined by the fact that, in the UK for example, advertising for food and drink has been falling in real terms since 1999 and is now roughly at 1982 levels, even while rates of overweightedness and obesity allegedly have been rising. Again, there is a substantial body of econometric literature that disproves the alleged connection between advertising, diets and weight.

In his research into food advertising in the UK, Peter Kyle, of the University of Lancaster, found no evidence to support the causal claim that advertising increased market size. Another researcher, Martyn Duffy, has looked at the impact of advertising on 11 food categories and found that advertising had no effect on demand. More specifically, professor Harry Henry has examined the effect of advertising on breakfast cereals and biscuits, both frequently cited as culprits in the childhood obesity epidemic. He concluded that advertising had no affect on market size.

Finally, Bob Eagle and Tim Ambler looked at the impact of advertising on chocolate consumption in five European countries in order to test the claim that a reduction in advertising would reduce consumption. They reported no significant association between the amount of advertising and the size of the chocolate market. Eagle and Ambler's work is corroborated by evidence from the Canadian province of Quebec and from Sweden, both of which have imposed advertising bans on foods to children, with Quebec's in operation since 1980. In both jurisdictions, however, there have not been significant reductions in childhood obesity or any marked differences in obesity rates compared with other adjacent areas.

Third, it is unclear that being a fat child carries significant health risks or increases one's risk of becoming a fat adult. For example, a long-running study in Aberdeen, Scotland, which looked at the health outcomes of children born in the 1950s, found that the body mass index (BMI) of children was not associated with increased risk for stroke and heart attack in later life.

In addition, the work of a group of British researchers into child health and epidemiology directly contradicts the assumption that overweight or obese children are at greater health risk and that reducing children's weight benefits adult health. Their 'Thousand Families Study' followed 1,000 families in the city of Newcastle in northeast England from 1954 in an effort to track the effects of childhood obesity on adult health. The study found that, contrary to the claim that fat children become fat adults burdened with health problems, there was little tracking from childhood overweightedness to adulthood obesity. Indeed, over 80 per cent of the obese adult participants in the study became obese as adults.

The assumption of a link between childhood and adult obesity is also contradicted by a recent US Preventive Services Task Force analysis of the efficacy of dyslipidemia screening and weight-reduction programmes for children. It found that the evidence for effectiveness is 'lacking, of poor quality, or conflicting.' The evidence also shows that the goal of encouraging children to eat low-fat diets is not only unsupported by the evidence but also risks significant harm in terms of adverse effects on growth and nutrient intake. The best evidence indicates that a 'substantial proportion of children under age 12 or 13, even with BMIs above the ninety-fifth percentile, will not develop adult obesity.'

Revealingly, the American data has shown that fat children generally consume no more food nor are less physically active than those of 'normal' weight. And multiple studies have failed to find a link in children between physical activity levels, food intake and obesity. American, British, Australian, French, and Spanish studies have all found little evidence to support a relationship between energy intake in children and their weight.

Indeed, to blame either these children or their parents for being fat contradicts much of the accumulating evidence on just how small a contribution to obesity is made by the factors that anyone—parents, children or the state—can control. One recent American study found that for twins, for example, the shared environment effect for both BMI and waist circumference is only 10 per cent.

Fourth, what about the claims about how much all of these fat children are costing the health system? After all, we all know, don't we, that fat children incur significantly higher health care costs than their slender peers?

In fact, this is not true, either. A 2008 US study examined the healthcare costs of 8,404 children in Kansas City and found that there was no relationship between a child's BMI and his or her visits to a doctor or casualty rooms. The only extra costs associated with the obese children were down to the fact that they were 5.5 times more likely to have had extra lab screening tests ordered. It had nothing to do with the them being less healthy.

The evidence-less Happy Meal ban should remind us that the entire idea of fat children is largely a cultural construct, not a scientific one. A hundred years ago, today's penchant for thin children would have been considered a shocking instance of child neglect.

The idea that children weighing over a certain amount are fat or obese has no scientific foundation, as the dividing line between fat and normal is purely arbitrary, representing nothing more than a public health bureaucrat's notion of where normal ends and fat begins.

Patrick Basham is currently an adjunct scholar with Cato's Center for Representative Government and the founding director of Washington think-tank, the Democracy Institute. His articles, spanning a wide range of topics, can be found in newspapers such as *The New York Times* and the *Washington Post*. Basham has also provided commentary on multiple television programs.

John Luik is a senior fellow with Washington think-tank, the Democracy Institute. Works by Luik include his book, *Unintended Consequences of Health Facism* (2011), and coauthored works *Diet Nation: Exposing the Obesity Crusade* (2006) and *Passive Smoke: The SPA's Betrayal of Science and Policy* (1999), as well as various journal articles regarding government involvement in obesity and the tobacco industry.

Selected, Edited and with Issue Framing Materials by:
Gina Vega, *Organizational Ergonomics*

ISSUE

Should We Require Labeling of Genetically Modified Food?

YES: Gary Hirshberg, from "Why Labeling Makes Sense", Just Label it.org (2013)

NO: Cameron English, from "GMO Foods: Why We Shouldn't Label (Or Worry About) Genetically Modified Products", PolicyMic.Com (2012)

Learning Outcomes

After reading this issue, you will be able to:

- Discuss why labeling genetically modified foods is an ethical issue for today's consumer.
- Explain why some individuals are adamant in insisting that genetically modified food be labeled.
- Understand the differences between Hirshberg's and English's positions on the ethics of labeling genetically modified food.
- Discuss English's position on labeling and whether it is similar to breeding techniques used with the farm animals we consume.
- Discuss whether the ethical issues of genetically modified food go beyond nutritional traits.

ISSUE SUMMARY

YES: Gary Hirshberg claims that the consumers' interests in knowing where their food comes from does not necessarily have to do with the chemical and nutritional properties of the food. Kosher pastrami, for instance, is identical to the nonkosher product, and dolphin-safe tuna is still tuna. But we have an ethical and personal interest in knowing the processes by which our foods arrive on the table. He argues that the demand for a label for bioengineered foods is entirely legitimate.

NO: Cameron English points out that as far as the law is concerned, only the nutritional traits and characteristics of foods are subject to safety assessment. Labeling has been required only where health risks exist, or where there is danger that a product's marketing claims may mislead the consumer as to the food's characteristics. Breeding techniques have never been subject to labeling, nor should genetic engineering techniques, English claims.

How much weight can a little label bear? We have seen a profound change in the function of the label over the course of the last century. At first, the label, if such there was, said only what the container contained and the brand name, such as "Carter's Little Liver Pills," "Argo Cornstarch." With advances in packaging, the labels became more attractive, brighter, eye-catching, and began to carry marketing claims. That was the label's purpose: to sell the product, by featuring a trusted brand name (logo, trademark) and an advertisement for the product, in a design aimed at capturing attention.

Poisons, of course, had to be labeled as such, to help consumers use them carefully—and to warn off the vulnerable. For example, poisons used to carry a rather frightening depiction of skull and crossbones.

The consumer movement changed all that. Calling upon the police power of the state (the right and obligation of the state to protect the health, safety, and welfare of the citizens), the Food and Drug Administration began requiring labels to fulfill serious informational functions. Now actual weights have to be listed on the package, a list of ingredients in order of weight must appear on any complex product, and the real nutritional content has to be listed in a plainly visible uniform panel on the back of the package (even for little candy bars). Even nonfood items have labeling requirements; garments and bedding must state the materials from which they are made; and bedding labels must warrant that those materials are new.

Those who would like genetically modified (GM) foods to be labeled as such do not conceal their interest in the same agenda. They would like to see all GM foods (corn, for instance) and all processed foods containing GM ingredients (vegetable oil, for instance) labeled as such, so that consumers will be worried by the labels and that eventually GM foods will be taken off the market. In light of the general profitability of GM foods, it seems politically more feasible to get a labeling requirement than a prohibition. Besides, in some polls, up to 70 percent of consumers have said that they would want to know if the product they bought was genetically modified. Who could object to full information about a product, the process by which it was produced as well as its content, being given to the consumer?

As it turns out, there are many objections. One is the sheer mass of effort required to sort out foods that contain GM products (practically ubiquitous at this point), especially processed foods like cereals and bake mixes. More important, whether or not a label designates a difference in a product, the consumer must assume it does and must assume, unless there is proof to the contrary, that it designates a dangerous difference. There was no doubt as to the intention or the effect of the requirement of labeling for tobacco products. There is every reason to think that a required label "Contains Genetically Modified Products" could be read as a skull and crossbones.

Some scientists explain that GM foods are safer than a nonmodified food. The reasoning is that the gene sequence is known for the modification. Virus and bacteria naturally occurring in fruits, vegetables, and meats often are not identified.

YES

Why Labeling Makes Sense

I am often asked about why GE ingredients should be present on our food labels, as well as whether the government actually has the power and responsibility to label.

In a recent presentation at TEDxManhattan, I tried to address these questions, and have highlighted many of them here.

What Are GE Crops? Haven't We Been Genetically Engineering Crops since the First Seed Breeders Thousands of Years Ago?

GE plants or animals have had their genetic makeup altered to exhibit traits that are not **naturally** theirs.

In other words, these are organisms created by the transfer and introduction of genetic material from other species in ways that could not occur in nature or through traditional breeding methods. Monsanto is one of the leading firms in this space. Their website draws a clear distinction between genetically engineered and conventionally bred crops.

Interestingly, the U.S. Commerce Department and specifically the U.S. Patent Office clearly sees these organisms as something unique and new, for they have granted the seed-chemical companies hundreds of patents for these new life forms. And these companies have spent many millions of dollars vigorously and successfully defending their patents from infringement.

Yet over at the U.S. Food and Drug Administration (FDA), there is general presumption that these foods are essentially the same as non-GE foods. In fact, the policy at FDA is that as long as GE crops are "substantially equivalent" to non-GE crops in terms of nutritional parameters like calories, carbohydrates, fiber, and protein, they are also presumably safe, and therefore do not necessitate labels to make consumers aware of when they are buying and eating these foods.

How Common Are GE Foods?

Since 1996, when the first GE crops were approved for commercial use and introduction, they have been extraordinarily successful in penetrating the marketplace. Today, GE soy makes up 90%-plus of the soybeans grown in the US, GE corn is roughly 85% of all corn, and several other GE crops including sugar beets and cotton are equally dominant in the market place.

Particularly because of their dominance in soy and corn, this means that over 70% of the processed foods we eat contain genetically engineered material. The data is clear that the vast majority of Americans do not know that.

Who Else Labels GE Foods?

It is worth noting that 64 other nations around the world including all of the EU, Russia and China have required labeling when approving these crops.

Are They Safe?

Because it has only been 16 years since the introduction of GE crops and they have been grown particularly fast in only the last 8 years, we don't yet know, and we probably won't know for a generation, about the impacts of today's first-generation-GE crops. In short, no one can credibly claim whether they are or aren't safe from a long-term perspective. However, there are some bases for concern.

During the 1990's many of the FDA's own scientists warned that genetic engineering was different than traditional breeding and posed special risks of introducing new toxins or allergens, but these warnings were not heeded. Since that time, several National Academy of Sciences studies have affirmed that genetically engineered crops have the potential to introduce new toxins or allergens into our food and environment. Yet unlike the strict safety evaluations for approval of new drugs, there are no mandatory human clinical trials of genetically engineered crops, no tests for carcinogenicity or harm to fetuses, no long-term

Hirshberg, Gary. From *Just Label It*, March 6, 2013 (Updated July 1, 2013). Copyright © 2013 Just Label It, www.justlabelit.org. Reprinted with permission.

testing for neurological health risks, no requirement for long-term testing on animals, and limited assessment of the potential to trigger new food allergies.

There is also growing concern about the lack of independent testing by scientists not funded nor influenced by the companies who own these new patented organisms. Our government's approval of these crops has been based almost exclusively on studies conducted or funded by the chemical companies who own these patented crops to prove that GE food is "substantially equivalent" to its non-GE counterpart.

This is especially troubling because many of the original claims by these companies that led to their approval have subsequently turned out to be false.

One of the very first genetically engineered crops allowed into the commercial market for human consumption was corn and it came with an assurance regarding the insecticide built into its DNA. Chemical companies said the insecticide would not survive more than a few seconds in the human GI tract, and that it would be broken down in saliva. However, a study published two years ago revealed that the insecticide was detected in the umbilical-cord blood of pregnant women.

Because GMOs are not labeled in the U.S., they might be causing acute or chronic effects, but scientists would have a very hard time recognizing the linkages between GE food intake and unexplained problems. Studying GE food-human health linkages without labeling is like searching for a needle in a haystack with gloves on.

Doesn't There Have to Be a Compelling Safety Argument for the FDA to Require That GE Foods and Ingredients Be Labeled?

In a word, no. While safety is an important question, it is actually not the reason these ingredients and foods need to be labeled. Virtually all of the food and ingredient labeling we see today have no relation to food safety.

If an ingredient poses a food safety hazard, we don't label its presence. *We ban it from our food.* When the FDA determines that labeling is required for additives like food colorings, dyes or various byproducts, it is not because they have found they are unsafe. The FDA's most important food statute, the Federal Food Drug and Cosmetic Act, establishes that the consumer has a right to know when something is added to food that changes it in ways

a consumer would likely not recognize, and thus labeling is required.

For example, the FDA did not require labeling of irradiated foods because they were hazardous. Rather they found that the process of irradiation caused concern to consumers. So they decided that they should be labeled. The same determination was made with Orange Juice from Concentrate, Country of Origin, Wild vs Farmed, and many other mandatory components of food labels. Simply put, the FDA found that these processes were relevant and therefore material to the consumer.

So, I am not saying GMOs should be labeled because they are a proven health risk, rather it is because they add bacterial genes, proteins, and gene fragments never before seen in foods. And we simply don't yet have enough data or experience to know what are the long terms impacts of these unprecedented changes to our foods.

Does the FDA Actually Have the Authority to Require GE Food Labeling?

The determination that GE crops are "substantially equivalent" to their conventionally grown or bred counterparts is a completely voluntary and discretionary 20-year-old internal guideline. This guideline did not result from criteria set forth in legislation passed by Congress to address the unique food safety issues associated with GE foods. Rather these guidelines were recommended by the President's Council on Competitiveness, a panel comprised of government bureaucrats and chemical industry giants under the leadership of VP Dan Quayle in 1992, just a few years before the first GE crops were approved for commercial use.

Putting it simply, the Quayle led Commission recommended that an ingredient would be deemed "material" for labeling if it possessed nutritional or organoleptic (taste, smell, etc.) differences from their conventional counterparts. And since GE crops look and smell similar and possess similar nutritional qualities, they were found to be not "material" to the consumer.

These guidelines have remained in place for over 20 years, despite countless changes in the US food system and the enormous proliferation of GE crops beyond what anyone expected back in 1992.

The FDA voluntarily adopted these guidelines back then. They have the precedent and the authority to modify those guidelines today.

Why Is Your Biggest Concern About Ge Ingredients and Why Do You Think They Are "Material"?

As someone who has spent my entire adult life advocating for reduced use of toxic chemicals in our foods, agriculture and environment, I am deeply concerned about the proliferation of herbicides and pesticides resulting from GE crop development and the increase resistance that we are seeing with weeds and insects due to their overuse. Consider these three arguments:

1. Skyrocketing herbicide use

Despite assurances to Congress and regulators over the last two decades that crops engineered to be herbicide resistant would lead to less chemical usage, a peer-reviewed paper published last summer showed that the three major GE crops in the U.S.—corn, soybeans, and cotton—have increased overall herbicide use by more than 527 million pounds between 1996–2011, compared to what it likely would have been in the absence of GE crops. The U.S. Geological Survey has reported that glyphosate is now a common component of the air and rain in the Midwest during spring and summer, with levels rising in many aquatic ecosystems.

It's important to note that increased herbicide is just the beginning of the problem.

At least 23 species of weeds are now resistant to glyphosate. Called "superweeds," they are emerging at an alarming rate, and are present in 50–75 million acres where GE soy, corn, and cotton crops grow in 26 states. Several chemical companies are responding by designing GE seeds that tolerate multiple herbicides.

To combat these resistant weeds, companies are seeking approval of GE crops that are resistant to higher-risk herbicides, such as 2,4-D and Dicamba. Many university weed scientists are speaking out against the dangerous notion that the best way to combat resistant weeds is to spray more herbicides on them—especially herbicides with a proven, negative environmental and human health track record.

And while insecticide use, specifically to prevent corn and cotton insects, actually dropped by 123 million pounds in this same time period, an alarming paper came out in the fall showing that corn borers are now becoming resistant to one of the BT insecticides that was bred into corn since 1996. We, and the biotech industry, continue to ignore this bitter lesson—when farmers press their luck by over-reliance on any single pest control tactic or chemical, resistance is usually just a few years down the road.

So, GE crops have been primarily engineered not for any increased nutritional value or consumer benefit, but to make it easier to control certain insects and spray herbicides on growing crops, killing weeds but leaving the genetically transformed crops unharmed. The technology is a real moneymaker for the industry, which charges much more for the GE seeds, and then sells more herbicide to the farmers planting the seeds.

2. Patent holders are making claims that are subsequently proven false

As mentioned above, despite the industry's claims that herbicide resistant crops would lead to less chemical usage, the opposite has happened. Herbicide use has increased 11% in the past sixteen years.

Corn, one of the first genetically engineered crops, corn, came with an assurance regarding the insecticide built into its DNA. Chemical companies said the insecticide would not survive more than a few seconds in the human GI tract, and that it would be broken down in saliva. However, a study published two years ago revealed that the insecticide was detected in the umbilical-cord blood of pregnant women.

One of the industry's most common arguments is the promise of higher yields from GE crops, which could aid in solving the world's food shortages. Yet field trials of soybeans found a 50 percent drop in the yield of GE varieties because of gene disruption. And hybrid corn varieties engineered with the Bt bacterium to produce a pest-killing protein were slower to develop and ultimately had a 12 percent lower yield than non-GE varieties.

All of these are cases in which the patent holders' claims have not held up. At what point, and at what cost, will we learn to ignore these empty promises, and rely instead on adequate environmental and health assessments?

3. Lack of independent testing

When it comes to the safety of today's first-generation GE crops, we don't yet know, and we probably won't know their impact for a generation. But the concern over the lack of independent testing by scientists not funded nor influenced by the patent holders is growing. Our government's approval of these crops has been based almost exclusively on studies conducted or funded by the chemical companies who own these patented crops to prove that GE food is "substantially equivalent" to its non-GE counterpart.

Many more GE crops are in the approval pipeline. And some of them may very well turn out to offer yield or nutritional benefits, like soybeans with higher levels of heart-healthy omega 3 fatty acids. But for now, while the technology is so young and there is apparently so much to learn, consumers need to have the same rights held by citizens around the world, to choose whether or not to buy these foods and indirectly support this cycle of increased overall chemical usage.

In 2010, the Presidents Cancer Panel reported that 41% of Americans would be diagnosed with cancer in our lifetimes. The primary culprit that this prestigious panel of senior oncologists identified was the inadvertent daily exposure to numerous chemicals in our air, water and foods. Later that same summer, the Journal Pediatrics reported a direct correlation between pesticide usage and increased ADHD diagnoses.

No one can now definitively prove that the genetic engineering of foods **does or does not pose a health or safety threat to any of us.** But there is no question that the use of today's GE crops is increasing our exposure to herbicides and BT toxins. I believe that this is highly material to the average consumer.

Summary

Our government's failure to require labeling, and to be engaged in developing the science supporting GE food risk assessment is an absolute breach of its responsibility to the American public.

There are in fact lots of reasons to label these foods: health and environmental concerns, ethical/religious views or just because people want to know. In fact, Mellman research shows 92% of citizens want the right to know with no meaningful statistical difference between men and women, Republicans and Democrats, urban and rural communities, education level or any demographic.

The bottom line is: without labeling, consumers are completely in the dark. The FDA can label GE foods. And the vast majority of consumers want them to be labeled.

As I always say, this is more than a fight for federal labeling. It is a question of whether our government is of, for and by the people, or of, for and by a handful of chemical companies.

GARY HIRSHBERG has received a BA from Amherst as well as many honorary doctorates and awards for corporate and environmental leadership. Hirshberg has served as executive director of The New Alchemy Institute—an institution devoted to organic farming, aquaculture, and renewable energy. Hirshberg currently is the head of Stonyfield Farm, a leading organic yogurt producer.

Cameron English

GMO Foods: Why We Shouldn't Label (Or Worry About) Genetically Modified Products

Last year, 14 states attempted to pass legislation requiring that genetically modified (GMO) foods be labeled as such. And I learned this week that California is now following in their footsteps to become number 15. The petition in my home state is being sold with the tagline "It's our right to know" what we're eating, and ominous suggestions about the health risks associated with eating GMO foods.

Appealing to voters' "rights" and stirring up health concerns are guaranteed ways to bring attention to political causes, but in the case of GMO food labeling, both tactics are fallacious. There is no reason to label these generally harmless foods and doing so could create unnecessary concern among the public.

While the point is certainly debatable, labeling products that contain dangerous ingredients is a reasonable proposition. Consumers should know if what they are purchasing is harmful; labels are one way to inform them. But GMO foods don't fall into that category.

The idea of food laden with foreign genes may sound scary, but it really isn't. Since we don't live in a sterile environment, all the plants we eat, genetically modified or not, are loaded with bacteria, viruses, and other living organisms—and their DNA. According to agricultural scientist Steve Savage, this fact shouldn't concern us. "Even though we are eating microbes, their genes, and their gene products on a grand scale, it is almost never a problem. In fact, some of these microbes go on to become part of our own bank of bacteria etc. that live within our digestive system—often to our benefit."

Savage goes on to point out that the only difference between the foreign genetic materials found naturally in plants and the genes we intentionally add to them is that we know more about the latter. "We know the exact sequence of the gene, its location in the plant's chromosomes, what the gene does," Savage says. The result is that we can more easily determine how safe GMO foods are for consumption, compared to their natural counterparts.

But, that's not the only good thing about GMO foods. Genetic engineering has allowed scientists to develop crops that consume less water, grow in harsh environments and produce less carbon dioxide, as molecular biologist Henry Miller points out. Put another way, these technological advances have made it possible to produce cheaper food in greater quantities and in a more sustainable fashion. Food security and environmental protection are political causes typically championed by progressives. So why are these same people pushing for GMO food labeling?

That's where the "right to know" part of the argument comes in. Sure, these foods may be safe for human consumption. But knowing what you're eating is ". . . an important way to exercise your democratic rights as a citizen," according to New York University's Marion Nestle. And there's nothing more sexy than democracy if you're a progressive.

I understand why telling those dastardly corporate food producers and grocery chains that we the people have a right to know what's in our food is so appealing. But the idea is problematic for several reasons, the least of which being that labels for GMO foods imply that there's something wrong with them, when in reality there isn't.

Equally troubling is the fact that misleading the public about science often backfires. As I've previously written on PolicyMic, dishonest political advocacy masquerading as science journalism teaches the public to distrust scientists and wrongly doubt their conclusions. The same applies to teaching people to fear GMO foods without cause.

Most importantly, science education doesn't come from food packaging. There's simply no way to properly educate consumers about the foods they're eating at the point of sale. That requires a concerted effort on the part of scientists and educators (which is already underway), and a desire to learn on the part of consumers. There's no reason to begin that process by feeding people misleading information during their weekly grocery runs.

Of course, that last sentence assumes that supporters of food labeling petitions are interested in educating people about nutrition, which they aren't. The environmentalists and public health advocates behind these measures are trying to force their preferences on the public through the initiative process. If you think that's just the ranting of an idealistic libertarian, considering that prominent scientists and science writers have been saying the same thing for many years.

If for no other reason, the opinion of experts ought to be enough to put a stop to exaggerated fears of genetic engineering and baseless food labeling campaigns.

CAMERON ENGLISH is a science writer and editor from Sacramento, California. He has done work as a freelance writer for *Science 2.0*, the *Sacramento News and Review* and *ScientificBlogging*. He fosters interests including public health, nutrition, and science education.

EXPLORING THE ISSUE

Should We Require Labeling of Genetically Modified Food?

Critical Thinking and Reflection

1. Recently there has been an increased demand to have genetically modified food labeled. Do you believe the demand will continue to increase on this issue?
2. What are the problems with not labeling genetically modified food? Would you like to know more about the genetic background of the meats that you consume?
3. Which big corporations are producing genetically modified food? Why are they resistant to labeling?

Is There Common Ground?

William Safire, a journalist often amused by popular trends in the use of the English language, at one point titled his weekly essay "Franken-: A Terrifying New Prefix Is Stalking Europe." His point was not that many European nations, acting in fear, had banned or restricted the import of GM foods, but that language had evolved to express that fear.

"Franken-," from Mary Godwin Shelley's nineteenth-century book *Frankenstein*, has come to characterize the product of any human "tampering" with nature that displeases the speaker. The fact that we have modified breeds of plants and animals for centuries, in fact millennia, through selective breeding or other methods of assisting evolution, tends to get lost in the scuffle. The language helps the scuffling.

Labeling is another way to use language to affect policy. It simply is not politically neutral to attach a label to something, especially when on our usual understandings, it should not need one. Every required addition to the labels on our food has been made in response to a public agenda, usually concerning public health, but occasionally (as in the case of the tuna and the pastrami) concerning public causes that have nothing to do with the quality of the food. Do we want genetically engineered products to follow that route?

English asserts that there are foreign genetic materials found naturally in plants. Scientists intentionally do the same and state they know more about the gene structure and chromosomes, what the gene does. English believes that scientists can more easily determine how safe

GMO foods are for consumption, compared to their natural counterparts.

GM plants are also said to grow in harsh environments, produce less carbon dioxide, and consume less water. By utilizing genetic modification, English claims it is possible to produce food less expensively and in larger quantities.

Additional Resources

Kristi Coale, "Mutant Food." *Salon* (January 12, 2000). This article looks at how a lawsuit filed against the Food and Drug Administration reveals FDA internal doubts of genetic engineering safety.

Food and Drug Administration Biotechnology Home Page, This FDA site explains federal policies on bioengineered foods.

Michael Fumento, "Crop Busters." *Reason* (January 2000). This article criticizes opponents of genetically engineered foods.

Rich Keller, "Farm Bill Is Center of GM Labeling Fight," AG Professional (May 28, 2013).

Frederic Golden, "Who's Afraid of Frankenfood?" *Time* (November 29, 1999).

Jon Luoma, "Pandora's Pantry." *Mother Jones* (January/February 2000).

"Tusconan Wants Voters to Decide on Requiring Labels on Genetically Modified Foods." *Arizona Daily Star* (May 27, 2013).

Internet References . . .

"Genetically Engineered Foods." Medline Plus, 2014

www.nlm.nih.gov/medlineplus/ency/article /002432.htm

"Saying No to Genetically Modified Food." DW.Com (Deutsche Welle), May 28, 2013

www.dw.de/saying-no-to-genetically-modified -food/a-16842204

Society, Religion, and Technology Project

http://www.srtp.org.uk/index.php

U.S. Business Cycle Indicators Data

www.economagic.com/bci-97.htm

U.S. Department of Agriculture (USDA) Biotechnology home page

www.usda.gov

Voice of the Shuttle: Postindustrial Business Theory

http://vos.ucsb.edu/browse.asp?id=2727

Selected, Edited, and with Issue Framing Material by:
Gina Vega, *Organizational Ergonomics*

ISSUE

Is the Consumer Financial Protection Bureau (CFPB) a Necessary Regulatory Agency?

YES: Arthur E. Wilmarth, Jr., from "The Financial Services Industry's Misguided Quest to Undermine the Consumer Financial Protection Bureau," *Review of Banking & Financial Law* (2012)

NO: Todd J. Zywicki, from "The Consumer Financial Protection Bureau: Savior or Menace?" *George Washington Law Review* (2013)

Learning Outcomes

After reading this issue, you will be able to:

- Discuss why business and political leaders have opposing views on the need for a Consumer Financial Protection Bureau. What are these views?
- Explain the contention that the CFPB director receives too much autonomy from existing financial regulatory government agencies.
- Discuss whether the CFPB, a hallmark of President Barak Obama's administration, is an unnecessary blunder that harms financial industries. Explain how credit offered to consumers could or should be protected.
- Understand the 2008 crash of Wall Street and why consumers needed extra protection from predatory lenders.
- Describe how some individuals have been helped by the CFPB and how some businesses have been harmed.

ISSUE SUMMARY

YES: Arthur Wilmarth, a professor of law at George Washington University's College of Law, argues that the Dodd-Frank Wall Street Reform and Consumer Protection Act (CFPB) was created to protect consumers from fraudulent activities within the financial services industry. It was established with autonomy in order to insulate it from political and lobbying pressures that have been evident in the current federal regulatory agencies. The effects of the catastrophic crash of 2008 on Wall Street are still felt by many consumers. Many of the problems were caused by the mortgage industry, the investment banking industry, and the insurance industry. After extensive bailout from the American taxpayers, the bureau was put in place to maintain financial protection and safety for consumers.

NO: Todd Zywicki, a professor of law at George Mason University School of Law, claims that the Consumer Financial Protection Bureau (CFPB) is not necessary because several federal agencies are already doing the work of the CFPB. The Bureau has extensive autonomy, which can endanger the financial industry's progress and profits through excessive regulation and reform. He argues that the 2010 Dodd-Frank Consumer Financial Protection Act can function well with the existing federal agencies.

In 2008, the United States narrowly averted a complete financial collapse. This epic financial crisis had its roots in unchecked lending by America's financial sector. It was apparent that severe changes would be required to avert the behavior that caused it. Over $800 billion was needed to bail out investment banks and other financial institutions that had invested funds in a variety of problematic mortgages and other financial instruments. In response to the catastrophe, the Dodd-Frank Wall Street Reform and Consumer Protection Act was passed in 2010. In signing the bill into law, President Barack Obama determined that consumers needed the strongest consumer protections in history. A Harvard bankruptcy professor, Elizabeth Warren, had published an idea for a consumer protection bureau in a 2007 *Democracy Journal* article. The president worked with now Senator Warren to create the Consumer Finance Protection Bureau (CFPB) within the Federal Reserve to strengthen the act. From its inception there has been vigorous opposition to the model of the CFPB. There has also been vigorous praise of the agency. One complaint is that the CFPB director receives too much autonomy from existing financial regulatory government agencies. The CFPB may be a hallmark of President Barak Obama's administration, or it could be an unnecessary blunder that harms financial industries. Champions and critics have much to say about this agency that began taking consumer finance complaints on July 21, 2011, under the directorship of Richard Cordray. Many believe that financial institutions now understand the power of their customers to fight back through the CFPB.

By the third year of the CFPB's operation, several large firms agreed to pay consumers substantial amounts of money as a result of CFPB actions. Bank of America approved a settlement to repay consumers $727 million for deceptively marketing credit card add-on services. Chase Bank USA, N.A., and JPMorgan Chase Bank agreed to repay for similar charges in the amount of $309 million. With additional federal and state regulators, the CFPB settled with three large companies recently. SunTrust Mortgage Inc. was required to pay homeowners $540 million in relief for servicing wrongs. A judgment for $80 million was secured against Ally Financial for racial discrimination in auto lending. Ocwen Financial was ordered to provide over $2 billion for its deceptive mortgage-servicing practices.

In a recent testimony to the Senate Committee on Banking, Housing and Urban Affairs, Cordray explained the agency has helped refund more than $3.8 billion to consumers. According to the Bureau's website www.consumerfinance.gov, the CFPB has handled approximately 309,700 consumer complaints in 2014. Their 2013 annual report states that complaint volume has steadily increased, rising 80 percent from 91,000 in 2012 to 163,700 in 2013. They encourage consumers to access their complaint database. The majority of complaints come from homeowners, with 85 percent of the complaints involving loan servicers who have damaged escrow accounts, bungled transfers of accounts, slipshod payment amount disputes, hampered short-sales, and failed loan modifications and foreclosures. The website details that two out of three consumers who file complaints with the CFPB get some sort of satisfaction—they at least don't go away unhappy, and the whole process is free to the consumer—the U.S. taxpayer.

Initially, in 2008, most financial institutions were grateful for the bailouts and vowed to protect the "main street" consumer in the future. Yet, by 2010 the financial institutions were firmly opposed to the autonomy of the CFPB. The financial institutions proposed that they state the terms of consumer protection rather than have the Dodd-Frank Act and the CFPB provide this guidance. These critics state that the CFPB escapes congressional budgetary oversight by obtaining its funding directly from the Federal Reserve instead of through the regular appropriations process. Termed an "end-run" around Congress, opponents state that Congress is not able to ensure the CFPB director is spending the people's money effectively. As a case in point, some congressional members have spoken out against the funds that were utilized to start the agency and remodel housing for the agency. They believe the agency is currently "running amok" and is not responsibly controlling the budget they were allocated through the Federal Reserve.

Regarding the autonomy of the agency, President Obama replies that he did not want any current regulatory agency to hamper the protective work that is central to the protection of consumers. He states that accountability to other agencies could limit and control the CFPB's protective abilities for consumers.

YES

Arthur E. Wilmarth Jr.

The Financial Services Industry's Misguided Quest to Undermine the Consumer Financial Protection Bureau

I. Introduction

The preamble to the Dodd-Frank Wall Street Reform and Consumer Protection Act ("Dodd-Frank")[1] affirms that one of the statute's primary purposes is "to protect consumers from abusive financial services practices."[2] When President Obama signed Dodd-Frank into law, he declared that the statute would create "the strongest consumer financial protections in history."[3]

In order to implement and enforce Dodd-Frank's new protections for consumers, Congress created the Bureau of Consumer Financial Protection ("CFPB") as an "independent bureau" within the Federal Reserve System ("Fed").[4] President Obama explained that CFPB will operate as "a new consumer watchdog with just one job: looking out for people—not big banks, not lenders, not investment houses—looking out for people as they interact with the financial system."[5] Similarly, the Senate committee report on Dodd-Frank explained that CFPB's mission is to "help protect consumers from unfair, deceptive, and abusive acts that so often trap them in unaffordable financial products."[6]

Thus, Congress gave CFPB "the Herculean task of regulating the financial services industry to protect consumers."[7] Congress sought to increase CFPB's "accountability" for that mission by delegating to CFPB the combined authority of seven federal agencies that were previously responsible for protecting consumers of financial services.[8]

Congress determined that a single federal authority dedicated to protecting consumers of financial services was needed in light of "the spectacular failure of the [federal] prudential regulators to protect average American homeowners from risky, unaffordable" mortgages during the housing boom that led to the current financial crisis.[9] As stated in the Senate report, federal banking agencies "routinely sacrificed consumer protection" while adopting policies that promoted the "short-term profitability" of large banks, nonbank mortgage lenders and Wall Street

securities firms.[10] The Senate report concluded that "it was the failure by the [federal] prudential regulators to give sufficient consideration to consumer protection that helped bring the financial system down."[11]

. . . [T]the financial services industry and most Republican members of Congress vigorously opposed the creation of CFPB. During the debates on Dodd-Frank, industry trade groups and Republican legislators argued that CFPB was likely to impose burdensome regulations that would reduce the availability of credit to consumers. CPFB's opponents also maintained that the consumer protection function should remain with federal banking agencies in order to prevent consumer safeguards from undermining the safety and soundness of financial institutions. Opponents further charged that CFPB would have unprecedented freedom to operate without meaningful checks and balances. Accordingly, they alleged, CFPB would likely become an all-powerful bureaucracy that would stifle innovation and flexibility in consumer financial services.[12]

Republicans failed to stop Congress from authorizing the creation of CFPB in Title X of Dodd-Frank. However, following Dodd-Frank's enactment, the financial services industry and Republican legislators launched a new campaign to weaken CFPB's autonomy and authority. The financial sector gave strong backing to Republican candidates in the 2010 congressional elections. That support helped Republicans to secure control of the House and capture several additional Senate seats.

Shortly after the new Congress convened in January 2011, Republican leaders in the House introduced legislation that would transform CFPB's governance, powers and funding. The House Republican bills proposed (i) to create a five-member bipartisan commission to govern CFPB in place of a single Director, (ii) to grant federal banking agencies an expanded veto power over CFPB's regulations, and (iii) to give Congress complete control over CFPB's budget. At the same time, forty-four Republican Senators declared that they would block confirmation of any Director of CFPB until the President and Democratic leaders in Congress agreed to make the same three changes to CFPB's operations. Republicans again argued that CFPB would be a menacing superagency without meaningful oversight unless the stipulated changes were made. By preventing confirmation of any Director, Republicans significantly limited CFPB's ability to implement its mandate under Dodd-Frank.[13]

Contrary to the claims advanced by CFPB's opponents, . . . CFPB's single-Director model of leadership is similar to the governance structure for the Office of the Comptroller of the Currency ("OCC") and the Federal Housing Finance Agency ("FHFA"). CFPB's regulatory and enforcement powers are comparable to those exercised by OCC, FHFA, the Federal Deposit Insurance Corporation ("FDIC") and the Federal Reserve Board ("FRB"). CFPB's ability to fund its operations without relying on congressional appropriations is, again, comparable to OCC, FHFA, FDIC and FRB. The financial services industry and its legislative allies have strenuously defended the governance structure, authority and independence of OCC and FHFA. Accordingly, it appears that CFPB's opponents are motivated by their opposition to CFPB's consumer protection mission rather than the bureau's structure.

. . . [T]he three changes in CFPB's structure demanded by Republicans would significantly undermine CFPB's autonomy and its ability to fulfill its statutory mandate. Replacing CFPB's Director with a multimember commission would increase the likelihood of infighting and deadlock within CFPB's leadership. Allowing federal financial regulators to veto CFPB's regulations by majority vote on general "safety and soundness" grounds would make it very difficult for CFPB to adopt rules that might reduce the short-term profitability of financial institutions. Requiring CFPB to depend on congressional appropriations for its budget would greatly increase the risk that CFPB would be captured or neutralized by the financial services industry. Financial institutions and their trade associations have used the appropriations process to slash the budgets of the Commodity Futures Trading Commission ("CFTC") and the Securities and Exchange Commission ("SEC"), thereby impairing the ability of both agencies to fulfill their statutory agendas prescribed by Dodd-Frank. In combination, the three changes advocated by Republicans would seriously weaken CFPB's ability to protect consumers. Contrary to the claims of the financial services industry, any weakening of CFPB would likely have deleterious effects not only on consumers, but also on the long-term soundness and stability of our financial system.

. . .

II. CFPB's Powers, Governance and Funding Are Similar to Those of Other Financial Regulators

CFPB's powers, governance, and funding are hardly unprecedented among federal financial regulators. CFPB's rulemaking and enforcement authorities resemble those of other federal bank regulators. CFPB's leadership by a single director is similar to the governance structure of OCC and FHFA. CFPB's ability to fund its operations without relying on congressional appropriations is comparable to other financial regulators except for CFTC and SEC. While the financial services industry and its Republican allies have vigorously attacked CFPB's perceived independence, they have strongly defended the autonomy enjoyed by OCC and FHFA, which represent the closest regulatory analogues to CFPB's structure. Thus, it appears that the financial industry and its legislative supporters are primarily opposed to CFPB's expected policy choices, not its structural characteristics.

A. CFPB's Powers, Governance, and Funding

Title X of Dodd-Frank, designated as the "Consumer Financial Protection Act of 2010" ("CFP Act"), establishes CFPB as an "independent bureau" within the FRB to "regulate the offering and provision of consumer financial products or services under the Federal consumer financial laws."[14] CFPB's statutory mission is "to implement and . . . enforce Federal consumer financial law consistently for the purpose of ensuring that all consumers have access to markets for consumer financial products and services [that] are fair, transparent, and competitive."[15] The "[f]ederal consumer financial law[s]" that fall within CFPB's jurisdiction include eighteen previously enacted federal statutes, as well as the "new consumer financial protection mandates prescribed by the [CFP] Act."[16]

Title X provides that CFPB will be administered by a single Director.[17] The President appoints CFPB's Director for a five-year term with the Senate's advice and consent, and the President may remove the Director for "inefficiency, neglect of duty, or malfeasance in office."[18] The Director may issue rules, orders and guidance "to administer and carry out the purposes and objectives of the Federal consumer financial laws, and to prevent evasions thereof."[19] The Director also hires and manages CFPB's employees.[20] CFPB may issue regulations to implement federal consumer financial laws and may also issue rules or orders to prohibit "unfair, deceptive, or abusive acts or practices" (UDAAP) in consumer financial services.[21]

CFPB may also issue regulations to ensure that "the features of any consumer financial product or service . . . are fully, accurately, and, effectively disclosed to consumers in a manner that permits consumers to understand the costs, benefits, and risks associated with the product or service."[22]

Further, Title X empowers CFPB to supervise and examine depository institutions with assets of more than $10 billion (and their affiliates) as well as all nondepository providers of consumer financial services.[23] CFPB may pursue a variety of enforcement powers to prevent violations of Title X and CFPB's regulations thereunder, or any of the eighteen federal consumer financial statutes enumerated in Section 1002(12) of Dodd-Frank.[24] CFPB's enforcement authorities include (i) undertaking investigations and performing administrative discovery, (ii) initiating administrative enforcement proceedings, (iii) filing judicial enforcement actions, and (iv) referring criminal charges to the Department of Justice.[25]

CFPB may use administrative or judicial proceedings to obtain a wide range of legal and equitable remedies, including refunds, restitution, damages, cease-and-desist orders, civil money penalties and injunctive relief.[26] CFPB's administrative and judicial enforcement powers are generally similar to those granted to federal banking agencies and the Federal Trade Commission ("FTC").[27] Like the FTC, CFPB is statutorily barred from imposing punitive damages.[28]

Thus, Title X vests CFPB with broadly-defined powers to regulate providers of consumer financial products and services.[29] However, CFPB may not regulate the ability of persons to carry on the businesses of insurance, securities, commodity trading, or managing employee benefit or compensation plans.[30] In addition, sellers of nonfinancial goods and manufactured homes, real estate brokers, auto dealers, attorneys, accountants and tax preparers are not subject to CFPB's jurisdiction unless they engage in offering covered financial products or services.[31]

Title X protects CFPB's autonomy in several ways. Title X prohibits FRB from taking any of the following actions: (i) intervening in any CFPB examination, enforcement action or other proceeding; (ii) appointing, directing or removing any CFPB officer or employee; (iii) combining CFPB or any of its functions with any other FRB unit; (iv) reviewing, approving, or delaying any CFPB rule or order; or (v) reviewing or approving any legislative recommendations, testimony, or comments of CFPB's Director. Thus, Title X "makes clear that [CFPB] is to function without any interference by [FRB]."

In addition, Title X requires FRB to provide CFPB with annual funding up to a maximum limit of approximately $500 million (to be adjusted for inflation). CFPB's

guaranteed funding from FRB is not subject to congressional appropriations. However, if CFPB determines that its guaranteed funding from the FRB is inadequate to carry out its responsibilities, CFPB must seek additional funds from Congress through the appropriations process.

. . .

B. Significant Statutory Limits on CFPB's Powers

As noted above, CFPB has broadly-defined powers to regulate providers of consumer financial services.[32] However, Title X of Dodd-Frank imposes several significant limitations on the exercise of those powers. CFPB may not impose any usury limit on consumer credit transactions "unless explicitly authorized by law."[33] Moreover, before it issues any regulation, CFPB must analyze "the potential benefits and costs to consumers and covered [providers of consumer financial services], including the potential reduction of access by consumers to consumer financial products or services resulting from such rule."[34] In particular, CFPB must assess the impact of any proposed rule on consumers in rural areas and depository institutions with assets of less than $10 billion.[35] CFPB must also consider (i) any expected increase in the cost of credit for small businesses that would result from the proposed rule, (ii) any alternatives that would accomplish CFPB's statutory objectives and minimize any such increase in cost, and (iii) the advice and recommendations that CFPB's small business advisory panel submitted with regard to the proposed rule.[36]

Thus, CFPB must take due account of the likely costs and benefits of each new rule, and it must evaluate the impact of each rule on consumers, providers of consumer financial services and small businesses. Title X's requirement of a cost-benefit analysis for each new regulation makes CFPB's rulemakings more vulnerable to judicial challenges and therefore encourages CFPB to adopt incremental rather than far-reaching rules.[37]

Title X also imposes tight restrictions on CFPB's UDAAP authority. CFPB may not issue a rule or order declaring an act or practice to be "unfair" unless the agency has a "reasonable basis to conclude" that (1) the act or practice is likely to cause a "substantial injury to consumers which is not reasonably avoidable by consumers" and (2) that injury is "not outweighed by countervailing benefits to consumers or to competition."[38] Similarly, CFPB may not issue a rule or order declaring an act or practice to be "abusive" unless the act or practice either (a) "materially interferes" with a consumer's ability to understand a financial product or service, or (b) "takes unreasonable advantage" of (i) a consumer's lack of understanding of "the material risks, costs, or conditions" of the product or service, or (ii) the consumer's inability to protect his or her interests in selecting or using that product or service, or (iii) the consumer's reasonable reliance on the provider of that product or service.[39]

Title X allows other federal financial regulators to exert significant influence over CFPB's regulations. CFPB may not adopt any rule (including any UDAAP rule) unless it has previously consulted with federal banking regulators and other appropriate federal agencies about the "consistency" of the proposed rule with "prudential, market, or systemic objectives administered by such agencies." If any prudential regulator objects in writing to a proposed CFPB regulation, CFPB must include in its final rulemaking a description of the regulator's objection and CFPB's response to that objection. . . .

1. Prudential Regulators Failed to Protect Consumers or to Ensure the Safety and Soundness of Financial Institutions during the Credit Boom that Led to the Current Financial Crisis

The House bill is based on the unwarranted assumption that protecting consumers frequently injures the safety and soundness of financial institutions. While individual institutions may complain about particular consumer laws, the current financial crisis has demonstrated that appropriate consumer protection is essential to maintain the long-term safety and soundness of our financial system.[40] As the Senate committee report on Dodd-Frank pointed out, "[t]here was no evidence provided during [the committee's] hearings that consumer protection regulation would put safety and soundness [of banks] at risk. To the contrary, there has been significant evidence and extensive testimony that the opposite was the case."[41]

The Senate committee report also explained that "the failure of the federal banking and other regulators to address significant consumer protection issues" during the subprime lending boom proved to be "detrimental to both consumers and the safety and soundness of the banking system."[42] The history of the financial crisis strongly supports the Senate committee's view. As I have described in previous articles, federal regulators allowed large complex financial institutions ("LCFIs") to become "the primary private-sector catalysts for the destructive credit boom that led to the subprime financial crisis," and LCFIs became "the epicenter of the current global financial mess."[43]

LCFIs provided most of the funding, directly or indirectly, for "almost 10 million subprime and Alt-A mortgage loans between 2003 and 2007, and by 2008 about $2 trillion of such loans were outstanding."[44] LCFIs securitized most of those nonprime loans, and securitization encouraged a steady decline in lending standards between 2003 and 2006.[45] LCFIs believed—mistakenly—that they could successfully transfer the risks of nonprime loans by bundling the loans into mortgage-backed securities ("MBS") and selling the MBS to far-flung investors. LCFIs had powerful incentives to originate (or buy) and securitize nonprime loans because they earned large fees from securitizing the loans and selling the MBS.[46]

Thus, LCFIs financed a huge surge in nonprime lending that helped to generate a massive boom-and-bust cycle in the U.S. housing market.[47] "Housing prices rose rapidly from 2001 to 2005, stopped rising in 2006, and began to fall sharply in 2007."[48] As I have previously explained, LCFIs played a central role in this disastrous credit cycle:

> [B]y 2007, the health of the U.S. economy relied on a massive confidence game—indeed, some might say, a Ponzi scheme—operated by its leading financial institutions. This confidence game, which sustained the credit boom, could continue only as long as investors were willing to keep buying new debt instruments [underwritten by LCFIs] that would enable overstretched borrowers to expand their consumption and service their debts. In the summer of 2007, when investors lost confidence in the ability of subprime borrowers to meet their obligations, the game collapsed and a severe financial crisis began.[49]

The rapid decline in home prices after 2006 triggered an abrupt shutdown in nonprime lending and cut off refinancing options for many borrowers.[50] Borrowers defaulted on their mortgages in rapidly increasing numbers, which led to widespread foreclosures. Lenders foreclosed on five million homes by the end of 2010, and 4 million additional foreclosures are expected to occur in 2011 and 2012.[51]

Accelerating defaults on home mortgages inflicted major losses on holders of MBS and other mortgage-related investments. Cascading losses on mortgage-related investments triggered a flight by investors from risky assets of all kinds, and that "flight to safety" unleashed a systemic financial crisis.[52] The financial crisis caused the failures or near-failures of many LCFIs and inflicted severe distress on the U.S. economy.[53] To prevent the onset of a second Great Depression, the U.S. government spent $800 billion on economic stimulus and provided more than $6 trillion of assistance to financial institutions in the form of central bank loans and other government extensions of credit, guarantees, asset purchases and capital infusions.[54] Notwithstanding these extraordinary measures, the U.S. economy is still struggling to escape a prolonged period of slow growth and high unemployment.[55]

By giving prudential regulators an enhanced veto over CFPB's regulations, the House bill would effectively put responsibility for consumer protection back in the hands of the same agencies that failed to protect both consumers and our financial markets during the past decade.[56] The Senate committee report on Dodd-Frank pointed out "the spectacular failure of the prudential regulators" to protect consumers from predatory nonprime mortgages.[57] As the report explained, regulators failed to crack down on mortgages with "exploding" adjustable rates and other abusive features.[58] Instead, "regulators 'routinely sacrificed consumer protection for short-term profitability of banks' . . . and Wall Street investment firms, despite the fact that so many people were raising the alarm about the problems these loans would cause."[59] Moreover, OCC and OTS preempted state anti-predatory lending laws and state enforcement efforts and thereby "actively created an environment where abusive mortgage lending could flourish without state controls."[60]

Numerous studies have confirmed the Senate committee report's findings concerning the shortcomings of federal prudential regulators.[61] For example, FRB had authority under a 1994 federal statute to adopt rules to prohibit unfair or deceptive lending practices by all types of mortgage lenders.[62] However, notwithstanding proposals for action by FRB staff members and many others, FRB failed to promulgate effective regulations until 2008, a year after the subprime mortgage market collapsed.[63] Similarly, FRB declined to exercise its authority to regulate high-risk mortgage lending by nonbank subsidiaries of bank holding companies until 2007, again despite calls for action by FRB staff members and others.[64]

When indisputable evidence of the risks of subprime and Alt-A loans emerged in 2005, FRB, FDIC, OCC and OTS responded not with binding rules, but instead with weak "guidance" that urged banks to follow prudent lending policies. The agencies' guidance encouraged—but did not require—banks to verify each borrower's ability to pay the fully-amortized rate on adjustable-rate mortgages. Federal regulators did not take meaningful steps to ensure compliance with their guidance until after the subprime crisis broke out.[65]

In the absence of effective federal regulation, more than thirty states passed laws to restrain predatory lending practices. However, OCC and OTS quickly issued a series of preemptive rulings that blocked the states from applying those laws to national banks, federal thrifts and their subsidiaries.[66] In combination, federal regulatory inaction and federal preemption helped LCFIs that controlled national banks and federal thrifts to capture the lion's share of the subprime and Alt-A mortgage lending markets during the peak of the housing boom between 2005 and 2007.[67] Several of those federally-supervised LCFIs subsequently failed or required federal assistance to avoid failure.

. . .

2. CFPB Is Likely to Be More Resistant to Regulatory Capture Than the Federal Banking Agencies

In view of the financial services industry's success in securing extensive forbearance from federal bank regulators during the past two decades, why should we expect CFPB to be more resistant to industry pressure? There are at least two major reasons for optimism. First, CFPB's unified mission makes it different from most federal banking agencies. As described above, prudential regulators typically gave short shrift to consumer protection and instead focused on increasing the banking industry's "safety and soundness" by adopting policies that promoted higher short-term profits for banks.[68] In contrast, CFPB has a single clear mandate to protect consumers from unfair, deceptive, abusive or discriminatory practices.[69] While Dodd-Frank requires CFPB to consider the potential costs and benefits of its proposed rules, and to respond to safety-and-soundness concerns raised by prudential regulators, CFPB's consumer protection mission remains paramount. The unambiguous primacy of that mission should motivate CFPB to take its statutory responsibilities seriously.

Second, CFPB's institutional safeguards—including its policymaking autonomy and its assured source of funding—make it substantially more insulated from industry capture compared to OCC, CFTC, SEC and FRB. As shown above, OCC relies for most of its funding on assessments paid by national banks, and OCC could lose significant funding if major national banks converted to state-chartered banks. OCC therefore has powerful budgetary incentives to please its largest regulatory constituents. . . .

Researchers have confirmed that banks have received material benefits while their executives served as directors of Reserve Banks. Two academic studies found that banks were significantly more likely to receive capital assistance under the Troubled Asset Relief Program ("TARP") if their executives served as directors of either Reserve Banks or Reserve Bank branches.[70] A third study determined that (i) banks whose executives were elected as Reserve Bank Class A directors between 1990 and 2009 experienced significant abnormal gains in their stock market values, and (ii) banks whose executives served as Reserve Bank directors during that twenty-year period were significantly less likely to fail (compared with other banks), and none of those banks failed after receiving government assistance. The foregoing evidence indicates that large financial institutions have exerted substantial influence on Fed policies through their election of bank executives and client executives as Reserve Bank directors. Thus, despite the Fed's political and financial autonomy, the Fed's governance structure evidently has made it vulnerable to considerable industry influence.

In contrast to OCC and the Fed, FDIC has demonstrated a significantly higher degree of independence from industry influence. Like CFPB, FDIC has a clearly defined mission and an assured source of funding. FDIC views its fundamental purpose as protecting bank depositors and defending the integrity of the Deposit Insurance Fund ("DIF"). FDIC also has a guaranteed funding source that is not subject to congressional control or vulnerable to charter competition. FDIC collects risk-adjusted assessments from FDIC-insured institutions, and virtually all banks operate with FDIC insurance.

. . .

III. Conclusion

Congress decided to establish CFPB after concluding that federal bank regulators repeatedly failed to protect consumers during the credit boom leading up to the financial crisis. Because of the prudential regulators' systematic failures to protect consumers, Congress vested CFPB with sole responsibility and clear accountability for implementing effective consumer safeguards. Title X of Dodd-Frank authorizes CFPB to issue regulations, conduct investigations and prosecute enforcement proceedings to protect consumers against unfair, deceptive, abusive and discriminatory financial practices. Title X promotes CFPB's independence from political influence by granting CFPB autonomy in its policymaking, rulemaking and enforcement functions and by giving CFPB an assured source of funding from the Fed.

The financial services industry and most Republican members of Congress vehemently opposed CFPB's creation, and they have sought to prevent CFPB from implementing its mandate under Title X. In July 2011, the Republican-controlled House passed legislation that would fundamentally change CFPB's governance, authority and funding. That legislation would seriously undermine CFPB's autonomy and effectiveness by (i) changing CFPB's leadership structure from a single Director to a five-member commission, (ii) giving federal prudential regulators a greatly enhanced veto power over CFPB's rules, and (iii) requiring CFPB to obtain congressional appropriations to fund its operations. Similarly, Republican Senators declared that they would block confirmation of any CFPB Director until the Senate approved legislation making the same three changes. Without a lawfully-appointed Director, there are substantial doubts about CFPB's ability to regulate nondepository providers of financial services and to exercise many of the other powers delegated to CFPB by Title X.

The financial services industry and Republican leaders have justified their campaign against CFPB by claiming that the bureau has unprecedented powers as well as a unique structure that is unaccountable to the political branches. In fact, as shown above, CFPB's structure and powers closely resemble those of other federal financial regulators, particularly FHFA and OCC. Major banks and their legislative supporters strongly supported the creation of FHFA in 2008 and emphasized FHFA's need for sweeping powers and an independent funding source that would *not* be subject to congressional control. Similarly, large banks and Republican leaders have consistently and vigorously defended OCC's authority and autonomy.

Moreover, CFPB is hardly an unaccountable agency. CFPB must consult with a wide variety of outside parties before issuing regulations. Congress has extensive powers to oversee CFPB's operations, and FSOC may review and set aside CFPB's regulations. Accordingly, it seems clear that the financial services industry and its political allies oppose CFPB because of its statutory mission, not its structure.

Large financial firms evidently fear that they cannot exercise the same degree of political influence over CFPB that they have successfully deployed in the past with regard to prudential regulators. In the financial industry's view, CFPB is likely to act independently and conscientiously in carrying out its mandate to protect consumers from predatory financial practices. Congress should want that result. The financial crisis has shown convincingly that a systematic failure to protect consumers will eventually threaten the stability of our financial system as well as our general economy. Congress should therefore preserve CFPB's existing authority and autonomy despite the determined attacks of the financial services industry and its Republican allies.

Notes

1. Dodd-Frank Wall Street Reform and Consumer Protection Act, Pub. L. No. 111–203, 124 Stat. 1376 (2010) [hereinafter Dodd-Frank].
2. *Preamble* to Dodd-Frank, *supra* note 1, at 1376.
3. President Barack H. Obama, Remarks on Signing the Dodd-Frank Wall Street Reform and Consumer Protection Act (July 21, 2010), *available at* http://www.whitehouse.gov/the-press-office/remarks-president-signing-dodd-frank-wall-street-reform-and-consumer-protection-act [hereinafter Presidential Dodd-Frank Statement].
4. Dodd-Frank § 1011(a); *see also* H.R. Rep. No.111–517, at 874 (2010) (Conf. Rep.), *reprinted in* 2010 U.S.C.C.A.N. 722, 730 ("Title X establishes the Bureau of Consumer Financial Protection (Bureau), which will be an independent bureau within the Federal Reserve System.").
5. Presidential Dodd-Frank Statement, *supra* note 3.
6. S. Rep. No. 111–176, at 11 (2010).
7. Rachel E. Barkow, *Insulating Agencies: Avoiding Capture Through Institutional Design*, 89 Tex. L. Rev. 15, 18 (2010).
8. S. Rep. No. 111–176, at 11 (2010).
9. *Id.* at 15; *see also* H.R. Rep. No. 111–517, at 874 (2010) (Conf. Rep.), *reprinted in* 2010 U.S.C.C.A.N. 722, 730 ("The Bureau will have the authority and accountability to ensure that existing consumer protection laws and regulations are comprehensive, fair, and vigorously enforced.").
10. Senate Report No. 111–176, at 15–16 (2010) (quoting congressional testimony of Patricia McCoy on Mar. 3, 2009). For additional analysis of failures by federal bank regulators to protect consumers during the housing boom that led to the financial crisis, *see, e.g.,* Kathleen Engel & Patricia A. McCoy, The Subprime Virus 157–205 (2011); Simon Johnson & James Kwak, 13 Bankers: The Wall Street Takeover and the Next Financial Meltdown 120–32, 141–44 (2010) ("The Federal Reserve sidestepped its consumer protection responsibilities by claiming it lacked jurisdiction. . . . While the Federal Reserve was neglecting to protect consumers, other regulatory agencies were neglecting to ensure the soundness of the banks they supervised," *id.* at 142, 143); Oren Bar-Gill & Elizabeth Warren, *Making Credit Safer*, 157 U. Pa. L. Rev. 1, 81–95 (2008) ("The problem is deep and systemic. These agencies are designed with a primary mission to protect the safety and soundness of the banking system. This means protecting banks' profitability. Consumer protection is, at best, a lesser priority," *id.* at 90); Adam J. Levitin, *Hydraulic Regulation: Regulating Credit Markets Upstream*, 26 Yale J. On Reg. 143, 151–69 (2009) ("The events of the past year have laid bare the shortcomings of our current system of financial-institution regulation. These shortcomings have played out on two levels: consumer protection and systemic risk," *id.* at 151); Arthur E. Wilmarth, Jr., *The Dodd-Frank Act's Expansion of State Authority to Protect Consumers of Financial Services*, 36 J. Corp. L. 893, 897–919 (2011) ("Federal regulatory inaction and federal preemption encouraged federally-chartered depository institutions and their affiliates to become leading participants in nonprime mortgage lending. Ultimately, the regulatory failures of the FRB, the OCC, and the OTS contributed to defaults and foreclosures on millions of nonprime loans," *id.* at 898).
11. S. Rep. No. 111–176, at 166 (2010).
12. Melissa B. Jacoby, *Dodd-Frank, Regulatory Innovation, and the Safety of Consumer Financial Products*, 15 N.C. Banking Inst. 99, 100 (2011).
13. On January 4, 2012, President Obama invoked his constitutional power of recess appointment and appointed Richard Cordray as CFPB's first Director. Helene Cooper & Jennifer Steinhauer, *Bucking Senate, Obama Appoints Consumer Chief*, N.Y. Times, Jan. 5, 2012, at A1; Laura Litvan & Kathleen Hunter, *Cordray Appointment Signals Obama's Readiness to Campaign Against Congress*, Bloomberg, Jan. 5, 2012, http://www.bloomberg.com/news/2012-01-05/obama-s-naming-of-cordray-signals-readiness-for-brawling-election-campaign.html. Republican members of Congress and some analysts challenged the validity of Mr. Cordray's appointment. They maintained that the Senate was not in recess when President Obama issued the appointment. They pointed to the Senate's scheduling of brief pro forma sessions that were explicitly designed to prevent President Obama from making recess appointments. The Obama Administration released an opinion of the Justice Department declaring that the Senate's pro forma sessions did not prevent the President from determining that (i) the Senate was unavailable to act as a body in performing its advise-and-consent function on Presidential appointments and was therefore in recess and (ii) in those circumstances the President could exercise his constitutional authority to make recess appointments. Cheryl Bolen, *Appointments and Nominations: Justice Department Releases Opinion Finding Recess Appointments Lawful*, 98 BNA's Banking Report 95 (Jan. 17, 2012); Cheryl Bolen, *Appointments and Nominations: White House Asserts Legal Rationale for Presidential Recess Appointments*, 98 BNA's Banking Report 99 (Jan. 17, 2012). Analysis of the validity

of Mr. Cordray's recess appointment as CFPB Director is beyond the scope of this article.

14. Dodd-Frank § 1011(a); *see generally* Michael B. Mierzewski et al., *The Dodd-Frank Act Establishes the Bureau of Consumer Financial Protection as the Primary Regulator of Consumer Financial Products and Services*, 127 BANKING L. J. 722 (2010) (providing a helpful overview of CFPB's authority under Title X).

15. Dodd–Frank § 1021(a).

16. Mierzewski et al., *supra* note 59, at 724–25; *see also* Dodd-Frank § 1002(14) (defining "Federal consumer financial law" to include Title X of Dodd-Frank, eighteen federal consumer protection statutes that are enumerated in Dodd-Frank § 1002(12), and certain other laws).

17. Dodd-Frank § 1011(b)(1). As previously discussed, President Obama invoked his constitutional power of recess appointment and appointed Richard Cordray as CFPB's first Director in January 2012. However, the validity of that appointment was disputed by Republican members of Congress and some analysts. *See supra* notes 13, 51.

18. *Id.* § 1011(c). The Supreme Court has observed, in the context of a similar removal statute, that the quoted terms "are very broad and . . . could sustain removal of a [federal official] for any number of actual or perceived transgressions." Bowsher v. Synar, 478 U.S. 714, 729 (1986).

19. Dodd-Frank § 1022(a).

20. *Id.* §1013(a).

21. Dodd-Frank §§ 1022(b), 1031(b).

22. *Id.* § 1032(a).

23. Depository institutions with assets of $10 billion or less will be examined by federal banking agencies to assess their compliance with consumer financial protection laws. Mierzewski et al., *supra* note 59, at 731–32. CFPB has authority (i) to obtain reports from smaller depository institutions, (ii) to include one of CFPB's examiners on the examination teams for such depository institutions, and (iii) to provide input to the primary regulators of such institutions with regard to the scope and conduct of examinations, the contents of examination reports and examination ratings. Dodd-Frank, § 1026.

24. Dodd-Frank, §§ 1002(12), 1031, 1036(a)(1)(B), 1052–1055. CFPB may not bring an administrative enforcement hearing to enforce an enumerated federal consumer financial law to the extent that the law in question specifically limits CFPB's authority to do so. *Id.* § 1053(a)(2).

25. *Id.* §§ 1052–56; *see* Mierzewski et al., *supra* note 59, at 732–35 (describing CFPB's enforcement powers). CFPB has authority to represent itself in the Supreme Court if it submits a request to the Attorney General and the Attorney General concurs or acquiesces in that request. Dodd-Frank § 1054(e).

26. *Id.* §§ 1053–1055.

27. *See infra* notes 103–04 (discussing enforcement powers of federal banking agencies); 15 U.S.C. §§ 45, 57b, 57b-1 (2006) (prescribing the FTC's enforcement authorities).

28. 15 U.S.C. § 57b(b) (prohibiting FTC from assessing punitive damages); Dodd-Frank, § 1055(a)(3) (imposing the same prohibition on CFPB).

29. *See* Dodd-Frank Act §§ 1002(5), (6), (26) (defining "consumer financial product or service," "covered person," and "service provider"); Mierzewski et al., *supra* note 59, at 726 (describing persons, products and services that are regulated under Title X).

30. Dodd-Frank § 1027(f)–(i), (m).

31. *See id.* §§ 1027(a)–(e), 1029 (imposing further restrictions to the CFPB's regulatory authority); H.R. REP. NO. 111–517, at 875 (2010) (Conf. Rep.), *reprinted in* 2010 U.S.C.C.A.N. 722, 731 (discussing exclusions from CFPB's jurisdiction for the above types of firms); S. REP. NO. 111–176, at 160, 169–71 (2010) (same); Mierzewski et al., *supra* note 59, at 727–28 (explaining that the listed exclusions apply "to the extent that the parties are not engaged in offering a consumer financial product or service, or are not separately subject to an enumerated consumer law").

32. *See supra* notes 59–81 and accompanying text (outlining CFPB powers to regulate providers of consumer financial services).

33. Dodd-Frank §1027(o).

34. *Id.* § 1022(b)(2)(A)(i).

35. *Id.* § 1022(b)(2)(A)(ii).

36. *Id.* § 1100G.

37. *See, e.g.,* Business Roundtable v. SEC, 647 F.3d 1146 (D.C. Cir. 2011) (striking down SEC's proxy access rule (Rule 14a-11) because SEC failed to comply with its statutory obligation to perform an adequate analysis of the potential costs and benefits of the rule, including the rule's impact on "efficiency, competition, and capital formation").

38. Dodd-Frank § 1031(c).

39. *Id.* § 1031(d).

40. *See* Levitin, *supra* note 10, at 152 ("The events of 2007–2008 have also shown that . . . [c]onsumer protection must be seen as an essential component of systemic-risk protection. The failure to protect consumers has systemic externalities."); Heidi Mandanis Schooner, *Consuming Debt: Structuring the Federal Response to Abuses in Consumer Credit*, 18 LOY. CONSUMER L. REV. 43, 62 (2005) ("[A] bank that is involved in predatory

lending practices not only harms consumers by charging undisclosed fees, but also may threaten the bank's financial condition by systematically making overly risky loans.").

41. S. Rep. No. 111–176, at 166 (2010) (quoting the views of two senior former bank regulators—Kevin Jacques and Brad Sabel—who denied the existence of any conflict between consumer protection and safety and soundness regulation).

42. S. Rep. No. 111–176, at 9.

43. Arthur E. Wilmarth, Jr., *The Dark Side of Universal Banking: Financial Conglomerates and the Origins of the Subprime Financial Crisis*, 41 Conn. L. Rev. 963, 1046 (2009) [hereinafter Wilmarth, *The Dark Side of Universal Banking*], *quoted in* Wilmarth, *Too-Big-to-Fail Problem, supra* note 57, at 977; *see also* Wilmarth, *supra* note 10, at 897–903, 910–19 (describing regulatory actions that contributed to the failures or government bailouts of several leading LCFIs).

44. Wilmarth, *supra* note 10, at 897; Wilmarth, *The Dark Side of Universal Banking, supra* note 184, at 1011–12, 1015–20, 1022–24 (showing that (i) LCFIs were the primary sources of funding, directly or indirectly, for most nonprime mortgages, (ii) about $3.7 trillion of subprime and Alt-A mortgages were originated between 2001 and 2006, and (iii) more than half of the nonprime loans originated between 2003 and 2007 were used to refinance existing loans).

45. Wilmarth, *The Dark Side of Universal Banking, supra* note 184, at 1020–27; Wilmarth, *Too-Big-to-Fail Problem, supra* note 57, at 963–67.

46. Wilmarth, *The Dark Side of Universal Banking, supra* note 184, at 995, 1025–26; Wilmarth, *Too-Big-to-Fail Problem, supra* note 57, at 971–72.

47. Wilmarth, *Too-Big-to-Fail Problem supra* note 57, at 963–66, 970–71.

48. Wilmarth, *The Dark Side of Universal Banking, supra* note 184, at 1024.

49. *Id.* at 1008.

50. *Id.* at 1019–20, 1024.

51. Wilmarth, *supra* note 10, at 898; *see also* Nick Timiraos, *Home Forecast Calls for Pain*, Wall. St. J., Sept. 21, 2011, at A1 (reporting that "[o]ne in five Americans with a mortgage owes more than their home is worth, and $7 trillion of homeowners' equity has been lost in the [housing] bust").

52. *See, e.g.,* Gary Gorton & Andrew Metrick, *Securitized Banking and the Run on the Repo* 6–21 (Yale ICF, Working Paper No. 09–14, 2009), *available at* http://ssrn.com/abstract=1440752 (providing data confirming that the repo market dried up quickly once losses on MBS became apparent); Arvind Krishnamurthy, *How Debt Markets Have Malfunctioned in the Crisis*, 24 J. of Econ. Perspectives 3, 4 (2010) ("[losses on MBS] caused debt markets to break down; indeed, fundamental values and market values seemed to diverge across several markets and products that were far removed from the 'toxic' subprime mortgage assets at the root of the crisis."); Lasse Heje Pedersen, *When Everyone Runs for the Exit*, 5 Int'l. J. on Cent. Banking 177, 177–81 (2009) (explaining how investors "ran for the exits" after recognizing the risks inherent in mortgage-related investments).

53. Wilmarth, *The Dark Side of Universal Banking, supra* note 184, at 1027–35, 1044–46; Wilmarth, *Too-Big-to-Fail Problem, supra* note 57, at 957–61, 977–81.

54. Wilmarth, *Too-Big-to-Fail Problem, supra* note 57, at 957–59.

55. *Id.* at 959–61; Kevin J. Lansing, *Gauging the Impact of the Great Recession*, FRBSF Econ. Letter 2011–21 (July 11, 2011), *available at* http://www.frbsf.org/publications/economics/letter/2011/el2011-21.html; Neil Irwin, *Flat job figures stoke fears of stalled recovery*, Wash. Post, Sept. 3, 2011, at A1 (reporting that the U.S. economy was continuing to grow slowly and was hindered by high unemployment).

56. *See* Bivins, *supra* note 31 ("It makes no sense to give the same banking regulators who were asleep at the wheel before the last financial crisis more power to second guess the CFPB.") (quoting Pamela Banks, senior policy counsel for Consumers Union); Davidson & Adler, *supra* note 30 (quoting a similar comment by Rep. Barney Frank).

57. S. Rep. No. 111–176, at 15 (2010).

58. *Id.*

59. *Id.* (quoting testimony of Patricia McCoy on Mar. 3, 2009).

60. *Id.* at 16–17.

61. *See, e.g.,* Engel & McCoy, *supra* note 10, at 157–205 (describing regulatory failures by FRB, OCC and OTS); Johnson & Kwak, *supra* note 10, at 120–32, 141–44 (discussing the shortcomings of federal prudential regulators); Bar-Gill & Warren, *supra* note 10, at 81–95 (same); Levitin, *supra* note 10, at 151–69 (explaining the "failure of the current consumer-protection regime in financial services," *id.* at 151); Wilmarth, *supra* note 10, at 897–919 ("Regulatory inaction and preemption by federal banking agencies played a significant role in allowing abusive nonprime lending to grow and spread during the past decade," *id.* at 897).

62. *See* Wilmarth, *supra* note 10, at 898–99 (discussing FRB's authority to prohibit unfair or deceptive mortgage lending practices under the Home Ownership and Equity Protection Act).

63. *Id.* at 899–900; *see also* ENGEL & MCCOY, *supra* note 10, at 195–96 ("When HOEPA passed, Congress instructed the Fed to implement the [prohibition against unfair and deceptive acts and practices in mortgage lending], but Alan Greenspan was dead set against obeying that Congressional mandate so long as he was chairman."); JOHNSON & KWAK, *supra* note 10, at 141–42 (describing the FRB's failure to enforce HOEPA because of Greenspan's opposition); Sudeep Reddy, "Currents: Fed Faces Grilling on Consumer-Protection Lapses," WALL ST. J., Dec. 2, 2009, at A22 (same).

64. Wilmarth, *supra* note 10, at 900–01; *see also* ENGEL & MCCOY, *supra* note 10, at 198–203 (describing the FRB's failure to regulate mortgage lending by nonbank subsidiaries of bank holding companies, due to Alan Greenspan's belief that such regulation would be counterproductive; JOHNSON & KWAK, *supra* note 10, at 142–43 (same); Binyamin Appelbaum, *As Subprime Crisis Unfolded, Watchdog Fed Didn't Bother Barking,* WASH. POST, Sept. 27, 2009, at A1 (same).

65. Wilmarth, *supra* note 10, at 901–03, 907–08; *see also* ENGEL & MCCOY, *supra* note 10, at 165–66, 168, 174, 176 (discussing the reliance of federal regulators on weak, nonbinding guidance even after they became aware of significant and growing problems with risky nonprime lending); JOHNSON & KWAK, *supra* note 10, at 143 (same).

66. Wilmarth, *supra* note 10, at 909–15; *see also* ENGEL & MCCOY, *supra* note 10, at 157–62 (describing the adverse effects of OCC and OTS rules that preempted state consumer protection laws); JOHNSON & KWAK, *supra* note 10, at 143–44 (same); Robert Berner & Brian Grow, *They Warned Us: The Watchdogs Who Saw the Subprime Crisis Coming—and How They Were Thwarted by the Banks and Washington,* BUS. WK., Oct. 20, 2008, at 36 (same).

67. Wilmarth, *supra* note 10, at 916–19; *see also* ENGEL & MCCOY, *supra* note 10, at 169–71, 176–81, 198–206 (explaining how OCC and OTS preemption helped large national banks and federal thrifts to become leading nonprime lenders); JOHNSON & KWAK, *supra* note 10, at 120–44 (same).

Twelve of the fifteen largest subprime lenders in 2006 were subject to regulation by federal banking agencies, and those twelve lenders "controlled 50 percent of the subprime market." ENGEL & MCCOY, *supra* note 10, at 204; *see also id.* at 205 tbl. 10.1 (showing that OTS had jurisdiction over five of the top 15 subprime lenders in 2006, while FDIC had authority over one, FRB over three, and OCC over three).

68. *See supra* notes 197–20911 and accompanying text; Bar-Gill & Warren, *supra* note 10, at 90–91 ("These agencies are designed with a primary mission to protect the safety and soundness of the banking system. This means protecting banks' profitability. Consumer protection is, at best, a lesser priority . . . ."); Levitin, *supra* note 10, at 155–56 (explaining that "[r]egulators have permitted profitability-protection to trump consumer protection for all but the most egregious behavior").

69. Dodd-Frank § 1021(b); S. REP. NO. 111–176, at 11, 164 (2010).

70. Ran Duchin & Denis Sosyura, *TARP Investments: Financials and Politics* 3–4, 19–20, 31–32, 35 (Ross Sch. of Bus. Working Paper No. 1127, 2010), *available at* http://deepblue.lib.umich.edu /bitstream/2027.42/63451/9/1127_duchin_oct10.pdf; Lei Li, *TARP Funds Distribution and Bank Loan Growth* 3–4, 20 (April 22, 2010), *available at* http:// ssrn.com/abstract=1567073.

ARTHUR WILMARTH is a professor of law at George Washington University's College of Law. He joined the university in 1986, after 11 years in a private law practice. He teaches courses in banking law, contracts, corporations, and American constitutional history. He has served as executive director of the law school's Center for Law, Economics and Finance. He is the author of more than 30 articles and book chapters in the fields of banking law and American constitutional history. He has testified before committees of the U.S. Congress on bank regulatory issues. He was a consultant to the Financial Crisis Inquiry Commission in 2010.

Todd J. Zywicki  **NO**

The Consumer Financial Protection Bureau: Savior or Menace?

. . .

Introduction

A centerpiece of the Dodd-Frank Wall Street Reform and Consumer Protection Act ("Dodd-Frank")[1] was the creation of the new Consumer Financial Protection Bureau ("CFPB") within the Federal Reserve.[2] Indeed, so high profile was the agency that it catapulted its founding mother, Elizabeth Warren, into the United States Senate.[3]

To be sure, the system of consumer financial protection needed streamlining and reform even before the onset of the financial crisis. A patchwork of agencies covered different aspects of the financial system and all of them tended to focus on safety and soundness issues rather than consumer protection. The most obvious federal regulator, the Federal Trade Commission ("FTC"), was prohibited from exercising authority over most of the industry, having jurisdiction over only nonbank lenders.[4] Into this regulatory gap poured politically ambitious state attorneys general and state legislators, suing and legislating with an eye toward buying in-state votes with the money of out-of-state banks while also balkanizing the consumer banking system. These activities subsequently triggered a reprisal by the federal government using its preemption power.[5] On the federal level, decades of class action lawsuits and regulatory sedimentation had eroded the simplicity and coherence of the original Truth in Lending Act[6] by rendering the system increasingly unworkable and incoherent.[7] The original model of disclosure-based regulation had become confused and modified by meddling as the federal government increasingly gravitated toward mandating what it thought consumers should care about rather than regulating what consumers *do* care about.[8] Thus, the need for reform was urgent and the opportunity ripe.

Alas, the creation of the CFPB squandered this historical opportunity for innovative and effective consumer protection reform. Although touted as a great leap forward

for consumer protection, the institutional design of the CFPB is in fact a great leap backward into not only the principles that animated agency design in the New Deal and post-New Deal era, but into an even more archaic model of consumer financial protection.[9] In short, the CFPB's institutional design can be seen as the revenge of Richard Nixon: the return of a discredited view of agency design that, like a creature from *Jurassic Park*,[10] has emerged as if it were frozen in amber during the Nixon administration and thawed out today without recognizing why a bipartisan consensus emerged to move beyond the Nixon-era model of regulation and agency design that the CFPB resuscitates.[11]

Indeed, if one were to sit down and design a policymaking agency that embodied all of the pathologies scholars of regulation have identified over the past several decades, one could hardly do better than the CFPB: an unaccountable body, headed by a single director, insulated from both removal by the President and budgetary oversight by Congress, and charged with a tunnel vision mission to pursue one narrow goal that carries the potential for substantial harm to the economy and consumers.[12] So flawed is the CFPB's design, and so similar is it to the regulatory agencies of an earlier era, that the problems it will manifest and the harm it will impose on the economy are entirely predictable. In fact, based on its early efforts, the Bureau is causing such harm already.[13] Most tragically, unless reformed, the likely result of the CFPB in operation will be a result completely contrary to that intended by its founders: an increase in fraud against consumers, an increase in foreclosures in the event of a future housing market downturn, and an increase in cost and reduction in access to high-quality credit products for consumers.[14] . . .

In 2009, the Obama Administration published a white paper that laid out a framework which later became the basis for the Dodd-Frank financial reform legislation, and which included a proposal for a new consumer financial protection agency.[15] Under this initial proposal, the new agency

From *George Mason University Law and Economics Research Paper Series*, 2013, pp. 856–928 (Edited). Copyright © 2013 by Todd Zywicki. Reprinted with permission of the author.

was modeled on the federal CPSC as a multimember commission funded in part by congressional appropriations.[16] As originally introduced by Congressman Barney Frank in the House of Representatives in July 2009, the agency retained a multimember commission structure but also added an independent revenue stream.[17] The proposal for a new agency, however, drew widespread criticism, especially from Republicans.[18] In response to this criticism, the proposal was made to instead turn the agency into a bureau of the Federal Reserve (the "Fed").[19] Therefore, when Senator Chris Dodd introduced the legislation in the Senate in April 2010, the new consumer protection agency had been converted into a bureau of the Fed with a single director and an independent revenue stream.[20] Eventually the Dodd-Frank financial reform legislation passed Congress and was signed into law in July 2010.[21]

The concept of a new dedicated consumer financial protection agency was one of the centerpieces of the Obama financial regulatory reform program.[22] To a large extent, the critique of the existing federal consumer financial protection system was well founded: consumer financial protection was balkanized among many disparate bank regulatory agencies, many of which had any particular expertise in consumer protection regulation (as opposed to prudential regulation).[23] Issuance of new rules regarding consumer protection often resembled a United Nations meeting: a fractious, multi-agency negotiation process animated as much by bureaucratic turf battles and warring agency cultures as by a desire to promote a rational and efficient consumer protection policy. Moreover, the need for reform of consumer protection laws at the national level predated and was independent from the financial crisis that finally provided the impetus for reform.[24] That there is absolutely no evidence that failures in consumer protection actually contributed in a major way to the crisis—indeed, many of the financial service providers swept under the CFPB's umbrella, such as payday lenders and providers of cash remittances, had nothing at all to do with the financial crisis—does not detract from the fact that greater coherence and rationalization was needed.[25] To concentrate consumer financial protection in one body was a reasonable reform to this system, though the responsibilities given to the CFPB could have been allocated to the already-extant FTC, which had developed deep expertise in consumer protection issues, including certain elements of consumer financial products.[26] The fact that it was not *necessary* to create a new superagency (the CFPB) to perform the task of consumer financial regulation should not, however, be read as suggesting that institutional reform of the consumer financial system was unnecessary.

Nonetheless, almost from the beginning the new Bureau proved to be politically controversial. It was conventionally believed that the Bureau's first Director would be its intellectual godmother, Elizabeth Warren.[27] Warren, however, was too controversial a figure to be confirmed by the Senate.[28] As a result, rather than nominating her to head the Bureau, President Obama instead named her an Assistant to the President and Special Advisor to the Secretary of the Treasury on the Consumer Financial Protection Bureau.[29] In this position, Warren was tasked with setting up the Bureau and preparing it to begin its duties upon the designated transfer date one year after the passage of Dodd-Frank.[30] At the end of that one-year period, however, it remained clear that Warren could not be confirmed.[31] Moreover, Warren herself had apparently decided that she would run as the Democratic nominee for United States Senator from Massachusetts in the meantime, challenging incumbent Scott Brown.[32] She was, therefore, never nominated by the President to head the Bureau.[33]

Instead, on July 18, 2011 President Obama nominated former Ohio Democratic Attorney General Richard Cordray to serve as CFPB Director.[34] Senate Republicans immediately announced that they would filibuster any confirmation vote of Cordray's nomination until certain structural reforms were made to the CFPB.[35] The conditions insisted on by the Republicans included reforming the CFPB into a multimember, bipartisan agency (rather than one with a single director), bringing the CFPB under Congress's appropriations authority, and reducing the required level of consensus for the Financial Stability Oversight Council ("FSOC") to overrule actions by the CFPB from a two-thirds consensus (as required by Dodd-Frank) to a simple majority.[36] The Obama Administration refused to acquiesce in this request, and the position therefore remained vacant.

Then on January 4, 2012, in a surprise move, President Obama took the unprecedented step of naming Cordray as the Director of the Bureau, claiming that the President could do so using his constitutional power to make recess appointments, even though Congress was not actually in recess.[37] The legality of Cordray's status remains unclear and has been contested in a lawsuit that also challenges a number of provisions of Dodd-Frank generally, as well as those related to the CFPB specifically.[38] Moreover, the issue is important not just because of the constitutional questions implicated, but also because the statute itself makes the transfer of certain new powers granted to the CFPB under Dodd-Frank—namely, the power to regulate nonbank lenders such as payday lenders, as well as credit reporting agencies—subject to the presence of a confirmed director.[39] In addition, the statute requires the Director to be nominated by the President and confirmed subject to the advice and consent of the Senate. . . .

The CFPB has four features that distinguish it from most other governmental agencies. First, the CFPB is exempted from the Congressional budgetary and appropriations process. Instead, the CFPB receives from the Fed "the amount determined by the [CFPB] Director to be reasonably necessary" to carry out the CFPB's activities, subject to a ten percent cap of the Fed's total operating expenses in 2011, an eleven percent cap in 2012, and a twelve percent cap in 2013 and each year thereafter.[40] Mandatory 2011 appropriations were $162 million and appeared likely to rise rapidly thereafter: 2012 mandatory appropriations were estimated to climb to $340 million, and 2013 mandatory appropriations are estimated to more than double the 2011 figure, reaching $448 million.[41] In addition, the CFPB is entitled to request further funds from Congress under certain circumstances.[42] Thus, not only does Congress have no real budgetary oversight authority over the CFPB through its appropriations responsibility, the Fed itself essentially has no ongoing budgetary oversight authority either.

Second, the CFPB is headed by a single director who is appointed for a fixed term of five years and who is removable only for "cause," which Dodd-Frank defines as "inefficiency, neglect of duty, or malfeasance in office."[43] Although single individuals head many departments and agencies, most (such as cabinet secretaries) serve at the pleasure of the President and are removable by the same.[44] In contrast, multimember commissions, whose members serve for fixed terms and are removable only for cause, typically head independent agencies.[45] In the rare instances in which a single director, such as the Comptroller of the Currency, serves as the head of an agency with formal de jure protection from removal, it appears that as a de facto matter, such heads serve at the pleasure of the President.[46] Moreover, these single-director agencies usually do not hold broad policymaking responsibilities but instead are involved in expertise-based regulation, such as supervising the safety and soundness of banks or the scientific process of the Food and Drug Administration. By contrast, the CFPB director performs an enormous policymaking function by controlling the flow and terms of consumer credit in the American economy.[47] Such policies carry massive implications.

Third, the CFPB's decisions can be overridden only by a two-thirds vote of the FSOC, a new entity created by Dodd-Frank to supervise the safety and soundness of the American financial system.[48] The FSOC can veto actions by the CFPB only if the actions would seriously threaten the "safety and soundness of the United States banking system or [put] the stability of the financial system of the United States at risk."[49]

Finally, Dodd-Frank expressly provides that for purposes of *Chevron* deference,[50] courts must defer to the CFPB "regarding the meaning or interpretation of any provision of a Federal consumer financial law."[51] This provision ensures that the CFPB's interpretation will trump any contrary interpretation from the Fed, or any other entity, by expressly limiting judicial review of the CFPB's interpretation of any consumer financial protection statute.

The effect of these four interlocking provisions has been to make the CFPB one of the most powerful and publicly unaccountable agencies in American history. It is effectively an independent agency housed inside another independent agency—not only largely immune from congressional appropriations, but immune from oversight by the Fed or the President (either directly or via OIRA) as well.[52] No other branch or agency can control the CFPB's budgetary appropriations, regulations, or enforcement decisions.[53] Moreover, there is no multimember commission to counterbalance the Director's policy initiatives.[54] Finally, substantive checks on the CFPB can be triggered only by the cumbersome supermajority rule required for the FSOC to act, and even then, only under the extreme circumstance of a severe threat to the safety and soundness of the American financial system.[55] It is likely that this extreme test will rarely be satisfied in practice.

In practice, therefore, the CFPB is an extremely independent agency—more so, perhaps, than any other prior agency. Led by a single director with authority to engage in both rulemaking and litigation,[56] immune from budgetary oversight, and largely insulated from substantive review, the agency has extreme independence to carry out its functions. Indeed, this extreme independence was originally touted as one of the Bureau's great virtues, as the purported lack of independence of prior financial regulators had been thought to be a source of the allegedly lax oversight that produced the financial crisis.[57]

Characteristics of Agency Behavior

Scholars of regulation have identified a number of tendencies to which bureaucracies are subject. Several are particularly relevant in understanding the flaws in the CFPB's institutional design: a tunnel vision selection bias and commitment to regulatory mission, systematic risk-averse bias in agency decisionmaking, a tendency toward agency overreach and expansionism, and a heightened risk of regulatory capture by industry participants. Each of these problems is exacerbated in the case of the CFPB by the Bureau's self-proclaimed, narrowly defined, single focus on consumer protection,[58] and each is further worsened by the single-director structure of the CFPB, which makes the Bureau unusually vulnerable to idiosyncratic priorities and decisionmaking by the Agency's head. The problems arising from this single-director structure are exacerbated if that agency head is motivated by political ambition, as seems to be the case with the CFPB's first two leaders, Elizabeth Warren and Richard Cordray, both of whom have pursued (in Warren's case)[59] or expressed interest in pursuing (in the case of Cordray) further political aspirations.[60]

One notable characteristic of agency decisionmaking is a tendency toward a tunnel vision focus on the agency's regulatory mission at the expense of other policy goals.[61] Forty-six years ago, Anthony Downs claimed that bureaucrats' "views are based upon a biased or exaggerated view of the importance of their own positions in the cosmic scheme of things."[62] Because of minimal interagency coordination, independent agencies produce an "uncoordinated stream" of regulation, with each agency pursuing its respective goal through the lens of its tunnel vision.[63] For example, increased environmental protection might conflict with other important goals, such as economic growth or national security.[64] Organizations also attract individuals that self-select for high interest in and commitment to the agency's regulatory function (rather than skepticism towards the function), thus producing a natural tendency to place excessive importance on the agency's particular task relative to other policy objectives.[65] This tendency is likely to be especially pronounced with respect to a new agency such as the CFPB, which was created in response to the financial crisis and was initially staffed by Democratic White House and congressional staffers who were not only "true believers" in the agency's mission,[66] but who were hired by the agency's intellectual godmother, Elizabeth Warren—a consumer advocate with an especially strident and idiosyncratic view of the role of consumer protection issues in spawning the financial crisis.[67] A massive influx of "true believers" into a regulatory agency can dramatically alter the trajectory of the agency with respect to regulatory policy, amplifying the policy initiatives of like-minded leaders and dampening future leaders' efforts at course correction.[68]

This tunnel vision focus is heightened when an agency is expressly tasked with a single-mission focus, as the CFPB is rather than a multifunction mission, as is the FTC's. The FTC balances the twin aims of consumer protection and increased competition, both of which benefit consumers in different ways.[69] This internal tension in

pursuing the end goal of maximizing overall consumer welfare facilitates the reinforcement and counterbalance of each goal against the other.[70] Unlike the FTC, however, the CFPB lacks both a counterbalancing regulatory purpose, as well as a multimember structure to facilitate collegial decisionmaking. Thus, the existence of a single focus, consumer financial protection,[71] and single-director design together create a breeding ground for tunnel vision, favoring one aspect of consumer protection to the detriment of other consumer benefits.

This tunnel vision may be exacerbated by the tendency, observed by William Niskanen, for agencies to be expansionist and imperialistic—not for reasons of mission, but simply because of the agency's leaders' self-interest in expanding the power, influence, and budgets of their agency.[72] Not only will this expansionism be consistent with advancing the bureaucrat's personal interest in increasing power and wealth, but an aggressive and expansionist agency will also tend to increase the bureaucrat's value to the private sector if he or she decides to go through the "revolving door" from government into the private sector.[73] For example, attorneys who participate in regulatory drafting will be in high demand to subsequently advise private clients on compliance, as will those who increase the enforcement activities of the agency.[74] Again, this tendency toward aggressive agency expansionism seems likely to be reinforced where, as appears to be the case with the CFPB, its leaders are using the organization to promote their political career or personal agenda—as seems to have been the case with Elizabeth Warren.[75] Although such obvious use of an agency position as a launching pad for personal ambition is rare, in such cases bureau heads can be predicted to use their agency as a vehicle for promoting their own ambitions by aggressively expanding the agency's activities so as to garner publicity and news headlines. Finally, the CFPB's tendencies toward agency pathology are exacerbated by the fact that Dodd-Frank did not set forth any specifications or restrictions as to who may serve as director.[76] Although most statutes refrain from requiring specific qualifications for appointees, doing so would create greater independence because "the pool of potential candidates from which the President picks is more limited and he or she cannot select solely on the basis of partisan leanings."[77]

A related bureaucratic bias is one towards risk-averse decisionmaking. Although efficient regulatory policy would require bureaucracies to weigh offsetting risks symmetrically, in fact, bureaucratic decisionmakers do not personally experience risk symmetrically.[78] For example, when deciding whether to approve a new drug, the Food and Drug Administration ("FDA") should weight equally the expected number of people who might be injured by premature approval of the drug against the number of people who might be injured by unnecessary delay in approval of the drug.[79] In fact, however, leaders of the FDA (as with other bureaucratic agencies) tend to effectively weigh Type II errors (premature approval) more heavily than Type I errors (unnecessary delay) because the former is easier to observe and thus easier to criticize than the diffuse and seemingly more speculative second kind of cost.[80] As a result, FDA leaders systematically weigh Type II errors more heavily than Type I, resulting in inefficiently risk-averse decisionmaking.[81]

In the context of the CFPB's operations, this bias can be expected to take the form of undue focus on the Bureau's narrowly defined consumer protection mission while discounting the benefits to consumers of lower prices, greater choice and innovation, and more robust competition.[82] Consumers certainly benefit from heightened consumer protection in financial services, including regulations that would impose enforced standardization and simplification on the products that consumers can purchase. For example, consumer protection issues would certainly be simplified if every mortgage, credit card, and agreement were required to have only one term (say, the interest rate) and to be otherwise identical, just as every computer or cell phone manufacturer could be required to offer a uniform simple computer or cell phone. Regulators also could eliminate the risk of foreclosures by requiring home sales to be in cash, thereby eliminating mortgages. But these overly simplified rules would harm consumers as much, if not more, than they would help consumers. Thus, "perfect" consumer protection must be traded off at the margin with other goals, such as lower prices and greater choice, innovation, and competition. The optimal consumer protection policy will weigh all of these goals. Yet the CFPB—deliberately tasked to pursue consumer protection over everything else—simply is not structured to process these tradeoffs in a rational manner. The end result will likely be harm to consumers.

Consider, for example, the tradeoffs involved in regulating mortgage brokers. It is possible that mortgage brokers contributed to the financial crisis by innovating mortgages that created strong incentives for moral hazard on the part of consumers (as with mortgages requiring no down payment) as well as by contributing to agency cost problems in the origination and securitization of mortgages.[83] Critics of mortgage brokers have pounced on these flaws, resulting in new strict regulation of mortgage brokers.[84]

But mortgage brokers have two distinct incentives:

First, mortgage brokers have an incentive to maximize the "spread" between the rate at which they can acquire funds to lend to consumers (essentially the wholesale rate) and the rate at which they can lend to borrowers (the retail price). Second, mortgage brokers face competition from other brokers trying to get a borrower to borrow from them. The net result of these two factors— one pushing toward higher rates and one pushing toward lower rates—is ambiguous as an a priori matter.[85]

Empirical studies have found different results, some finding that brokers offer better terms on average than depository lenders and others finding that brokers charge higher prices on at least some elements of the transaction.[86] The explanation for these conflicting findings appears to result from differences in the number of mortgage brokers competing in a given market.[87] Where mortgage brokers are numerous and thus competition and consumer choice is greater, consumers generally receive lower interest rates from brokers as the competition effect predominates; however, where there are a smaller number of brokers and less competition, consumers typically pay higher interest rates as the broker interest effect predominates.[88] Empirical studies indicate that overly restrictive broker regulations may also lead to a higher number of overall foreclosures on subprime mortgages.[89]

As this simple example shows, when confronted with the potential contribution of mortgage brokers to the financial crisis, a well-intentioned consumer protection regulator could respond by imposing overly strict licensing regulations on mortgage brokers designed to protect consumers.[90] But onerous restrictions would reduce competition, resulting in both higher prices and worse service, while perversely leading to a higher number of foreclosures overall. Although a well-balanced regulatory policy would take all of these factors into account, the CFPB's focus on "consumer protection," narrowly defined, combined with the inherent tendency of agencies toward risk-averse decisionmaking runs the risk of leading to overzealous regulation that overlooks the benefits of competition and lower prices for consumers. This is precisely the sort of Type I versus Type II error tradeoff that tends to be problematic for single-issue agencies.[91]

Similar tradeoffs can be identified for a whole range of issues that the CFPB might have to consider, from unconventional mortgage products to particular credit card terms. For example, although upward increases in the interest rates on adjustable-rate mortgages were the major catalyst for the foreclosure crisis,[92] consumers unquestionably also benefit when interest rates fall. Moreover, fixed-rate mortgages pose extreme risks for consumers and the economy at large because of the interest rate mismatch problem that they potentially create (i.e., banks must raise lending capital in short-term borrowing markets in order to lend on long-term fixed-rate mortgages or securitize mortgages to pass along the risk), as well as the fact that fixed-rate mortgages interfere with the ability of consumers, if they do not have equity in their homes, to refinance at lower interest rates when rates fall.[93]

For example, as a result of the unique primacy of the thirty-year fixed-rate mortgage in the United States,[94] the housing bust has hit U.S. homeowners much worse than elsewhere.[95] Millions of homeowners have been unable to refinance at record-low mortgage interest rates because they are not only underwater but are not sufficiently liquid to come up with the several thousand dollars needed for closing costs, even if they had sufficient wealth to do so.[96] If more U.S. homeowners had adjustable-rate mortgages, as homeowners do in most other countries, their interest rates and monthly payments would have ratcheted downward automatically, reducing payments for many, staving off foreclosure for some, and spurring a housing market recovery for all.[97] Despite the obvious symmetry of consumer risk posed by adjustable-rate mortgages, however, there is a chance that the CFPB might tend to focus on the risks to consumers from upward movements in mortgage interest rates while discounting the benefits to consumers and the economy from downward adjustments, thereby creating rules that inefficiently favor the thirty-year fixed-rate mortgage.[98] This would effectively force millions of homeowners to pay thousands of dollars over the life of their loan for long-term insurance against increasing interest rates twenty-five or thirty years in the future.

In addition to the problems that result from a narrowly focused agency, another bureaucratic predisposition is short-term bias in decisionmaking. Rational political actors (including agency heads) tend to favor policies that produce short-term gains but for which the costs are borne in the long run.[99] Short-term gains permit the political actor to take credit for the policy while subsequent officials are forced to bear the resulting economic and political costs.[100] This will be the case especially with respect to an entity such as the CFPB, which has been headed since its inception by individuals with clear partisan political ambitions (such as Warren and Cordray),[101] and thus can be expected to maximize short-term regulatory activity—such as high-profile lawsuits and regulations—while discounting possible future costs of those activities, such as increased cost and reduced availability of credit. The

ambiguous legality of Cordray's appointment adds further short-term bias, revealed by Cordray's writing to his staff that because of "a chance" that his "appointment would be invalidated by a court . . . . [t]his time period should give to each one of us, and not only me, a fierce urgency to accomplish the work we are doing together."[102] The political process may be prone to short-term bias, because the long-term costs of bad regulation generally fall most heavily on less educated, low income individuals who are less likely to perceive the true source of their lack of credit access and less likely to be politically active. For instance, economists have found that, historically, the unintended consequences of heavy-handed governmental regulation of consumer credit have invariably fallen most harshly on low-income consumers, often with a regressive redistributive effect in favor of richer and middle-class consumers.[103]

A final potential problem created by the CFPB's combination of a single-industry mission with a lack of accountability is the risk of agency capture.[104] Historically, this problem has referred to the tendency of regulatory agencies to be "captured" by members of the industry that they were established to regulate, such as the Civil Aeronautics Board (captured by the airline industry),[105] the Interstate Commerce Commission (captured by the railroad industry),[106] or the Securities Exchange Commission (captured by the securities industry).[107] With respect to the CFPB, the threat of capture seems to be less likely to come from the industry as a whole than from particular segments within it—namely, the biggest banks. The CFPB promises an unprecedented onslaught of regulatory compliance costs that are likely to proportionally fall much harder on smaller banks and community banks than on the largest banks. It is well established that certain types of regulatory compliance costs, such as many paperwork and other oversight costs, are largely invariant to the size or output of a firm, and thus fall proportionately harder on smaller firms in an industry.[108] It is unsurprising, therefore, that community banks and credit unions have expressed grave concerns about Dodd-Frank's and the CFPB's punishing regulatory compliance costs.[109] In addition, smaller banks compete by providing more personalized services, such as designing products specifically tailored to individual needs.[110] Dodd-Frank and the CFPB, however, push toward making consumer credit more like a standardized commodity rather than permitting banks to tailor their consumer credit products to the needs of particular borrowers.[111] As noted above, a similar issue arises with respect to mortgage brokers, who can provide an important competitive check on depository institutions.[112]

This one-size-fits-all regulatory approach thus tends to disadvantage those banks that compete on the margins, for instance, by offering superior customer service, while favoring those with the lowest costs, such as big banks that offer economies of scale and lower capital market costs—a result, in part, of the entrenchment of the Too-Big-To-Fail subsidy in Dodd-Frank.[113] Finally, the big banks will have a comparative advantage in being more readily able to make the expenditures needed to hire lobbyists and other Washington resources to influence CFPB decisionmaking than will smaller banks. As a result, the regulatory compliance costs of the CFPB may have the unintended consequences of promoting its capture by the large banks and promoting consolidation of the United States banking industry. For example, as a response to the financial crisis and Dodd-Frank's enactment, industry consolidation has reached an all-time high: as of the first quarter of 2012, the five largest banks held over 39.1% of all deposits, up from 29.2% in 2005.[114] The combination of heavy regulatory costs and the entrenchment of Dodd-Frank's Too-Big-To-Fail funding subsidy is likely to further accelerate this consolidation, thereby ironically increasing the importance of supposedly systemically risky institutions.

. . .

Notes

1. Dodd-Frank Wall Street Reform and Consumer Protection ("Dodd-Frank") Act, Pub. L. No. 111–203, 124 Stat. 1376 (2010).
2. *Id.* §§ 1001–1100H, 124 Stat. at 1955–2113.
3. *See* Danielle Douglas, *Warren Fights for CFPB Again, but this Time as a Senator*, WASH. POST (Feb. 14, 2013), http://articles.washingtonpost.com/2013-02-14/business/37098356_1_richard-cordray-cfpb-director-senate-republicans.
4. *See* 15 U.S.C. § 45(a)(2) (2006); *id.* § 1607(a), (b).
5. *See* Johnathan Mathiesen, Note, *Dr. Spitzlove or: How I Learned to Stop Worrying and Love "Balkanization"*, 2006 COLUM. BUS. L. REV. 311, 313 (describing this phenomenon); *see also infra* Part V.
6. Consumer Credit Protection Act, Pub. L. No. 90–321, 82 Stat. 146 (1968).
7. *See infra* note 264 and accompanying text.
8. *See infra* Part IV (describing the assumptions underlying the CFPB's regulatory authority).
9. *See infra* Part III.
10. JURASSIC PARK (Universal Pictures 1993).
11. *See infra* Part II.B.
12. *See infra* Part III.B.
13. *See, e.g., infra* notes 275–77 and accompanying text.
14. *See infra* Part III.C.2.
15. *See* DEP'T OF THE TREASURY, FINANCIAL REGULATORY REFORM: A NEW FOUNDATION: REBUILDING FINANCIAL SUPERVISION AND REGULATION 55–75 (2009), [hereinafter TREASURY DEP'T WHITE PAPER], *available at* http://www.treasury.gov/initiatives/Documents/FinalReport_web.pdf (proposing the "Consumer Financial Protection Agency").
16. *See id.* at 58 (suggesting the proposed Consumer Financial Protection Agency's basic structure, which included a Director and a Board, and arguing that the Agency should have a "stable funding stream, which could come in part from fees assessed on entities," but not suggesting that the agency be completely self-funded).
17. H.R. 4173, 111th Cong. § 4103 (2009) (as proposed in the House) (providing for a multi-member structure); *id.* § 4109 (adopting an independent funding source).
18. Carl Hulse, *House Approves Tougher Rules on Wall Street*, N.Y. TIMES, Dec. 12, 2009, at A1 (noting that "Republicans strongly criticized the Democratic legislation").
19. *See* Rich Danker, *How the CFPB Got the Fed's Lunch Money*, CQ ROLL CALL (July 23, 2012, 1:56 PM), http://www.rollcall.com/news/Danker-How-the-CFPB-Got-the-Feds-LunchMoney-216345-1.html.
20. *See* S. 3217, 111th Cong. § 1011(a) (2010) (as introduced in the Senate) (establishing the agency as a Bureau within the Fed); *id.* § 1011(b)(1) (establishing a single Director for the Bureau); *id.* § 1017 (establishing the Bureau's funding source).
21. *See* Dodd-Frank Wall Street Reform and Consumer Protection Act, Pub. L. No. 111–203, 124 Stat. 1376 (2010); Helene Cooper, *Obama Signs Contentious Overhaul of the Financial System*, N.Y. TIMES, July 22, 2010, at B3.
22. *See* TREASURY DEP'T WHITE PAPER, *supra* note 18, at 3; *see also* Robert G. Kaiser, *How a Crusade to Protect Consumers Lost Its Steam*, WASH. POST, Jan. 31, 2010, at G1 (noting that President Obama called consumer protection a priority of the administration and urged the approval a new consumer financial protection agency).
23. *See* TREASURY DEP'T WHITE PAPER, *supra* note 18. at 55 (describing this decentralized, conflicting approach).
24. *See, e.g.,* Laurie A. Burlingame, *A Pro-Consumer Approach to Predatory Lending: Enhanced Protection Through Federal Legislation and New Approaches to Education*, 60 CONSUMER FIN. L. Q. REP. 460, 460, 482–84 (2006) (advocating before the 2008 financial crisis for, inter alia, "federal legislation aimed at curbing predatory practices and terms").

25. For debate on this question, see *Did a Lack of Consumer Protection Cause the Financial Crisis?*, CATO INST., (Mar. 16, 2010, 12:00 PM), http://ne.edgecastcdn.net/000873/archive-2010/cpf-03-16-10.m4v.

26. *See, e.g.,* Burlingame, *supra* note 27, at 469 (noting that the FTC had been the most active agency in taking action against predatory lenders).

27. *See* Kaiser, *supra* note 25, at G1 (noting that "[f]riends and allies say Warren would love to be the first director of a CFPA" and that Rep. Barney Frank, then-Chairman of the House Financial Services Committee, quickly endorsed Warren).

28. *See* Brady Dennis, *Warren Expected to Be Adviser*, WASH. POST, Sept. 16, 2010, at A18 (discussing how Warren's nomination would have caused "a confirmation battle").

29. *See id.*

30. *See id; see also* Designated Transfer Date, 75 Fed. Reg. 57,252, 57,252 (Sept. 20, 2010) (setting the transfer date as July 21, 2011, exactly one year after the passage of Dodd-Frank).

31. David Nakamura & Felicia Sonmez, *Obama Defies Senate, Puts Cordray in Consumer Post*, WASH. POST, Jan. 5, 2012, at A1 ("[T]he White House opted not to nominate Warren" at the same time "as the agency was preparing to open its doors in July [2011].").

32. *See id.*

33. *Id.*

34. *See* Richard Shelby, Op-Ed., *The Danger of an Unaccountable 'Consumer-Protection' Czar*, WALL ST. J., July 21, 2011, at A17.

35. *See id.* (explaining the Republicans' proposed changes); *see also* John H. Cushman Jr., *Senate Stops Consumer Nominee*, N.Y. TIMES, Dec. 9, 2011, at B1 (relating these changes to Senate Republicans' eventual filibuster of Cordray).

36. *See* Shelby, *supra* note 37; Edward Wyatt, *Nominee to Head Consumer Bureau Says He Will Streamline Regulations*, N.Y. TIMES, Sept. 7, 2011, at B3 (noting that Senate Republicans tied their opposition to Cordray's confirmation in part to the FSOC's supermajority vote requirement); *see also, e.g.,* Dodd-Frank Wall Street Reform and Consumer Protection Act, Pub. L. No. 111–203, § 1023, 124 Stat. 1376, 1985 (2010) (requiring two-thirds majority vote for FSOC to set aside a CFPB-issued regulation).

37. *See* Nakamura & Sonmez, *supra* note 34.

38. *See* C. Boyden Gray & Jim R. Purcell, *Why Dodd-Frank Is Unconstitutional*, WALL ST. J., June 22, 2012, at A17. The D.C. Circuit recently issued an opinion that puts Cordray's recess appointment in serious constitutional doubt. *See* Noel Canning v.

NLRB, No. 12–1115, slip-op at 13–44 (D.C. Cir. Jan. 25, 2013).

39. *See* Dodd-Frank Act § 12 U.S.C. § 5586(a) (Supp. IV. 2011); *see also* Joint Response by Inspectors Gen. of Dep't of the Treas. & Bd. of Governors of the Fed. Reserve Sys. to Spencer Bachus, Chairman, H. Comm. on Fin. Servs. & Judy Biggert, Chairman, Subcomm. on Ins., Hous. & Cmty. Opportunity of the H. Comm. Fin. on Servs. 4–7 (Jan. 10, 2011), *available at* http://www.federalreserve.gov/oig/files/Treasury_OIG_Posted_PDF_-_Response_CFPB.pdf.

40. Dodd-Frank Wall Street Reform and Consumer Protection Act, Pub. L. No. 111–203, § 1017(a)(1)–(2)(A), 124 Stat. 1376, 1975 (2010) (codified at 12 U.S.C. § 5497(a)(1)–(2)(A) (Supp. IV 2011)).

41. OFFICE OF MGMT. & BUDGET, OTHER INDEPENDENT AGENCIES 1295 (2012), *available at* http://www.whitehouse.gov/sites/default/files/omb/budget/fy2013/assets/oia.pdf.

42. *See* Dodd-Frank Act § 1017(e)(1)(B)–(2), 124 Stat. at 1979 (codified at 12 U.S.C. § 5497(e)(1)(B)–(2)) (authorizing the CFPB to request up to $200 million in discretionary funds if the Director finds that such funds are necessary and submits a report to Congress stating as much).

43. *Id.* § 1011(c)(3), 124 Stat. at 1964 (codified at 12 U.S.C. § 5491(c)(3)).

44. *See* Kimberly N. Brown, *Presidential Control of the Elite "Non-Agency,"* 88 N.C. L. REV. 71, 77 (2009).

45. *See Recent Legislation, Dodd-Frank Act Creates the Consumer Financial Protection Bureau, Pub. L. No. 111–203, 124 Stat. 1376 (2010)*, 124 HARV. L. REV. 2123, 2128 (2011) [hereinafter *Dodd-Frank Creates the CFPB*].

46. *Who's Watching the Watchmen? Oversight of the Consumer Financial Protection Bureau: Hearing Before the H. Subcomm. on TARP, Fin. Servs. & Bailouts of Pub. & Private Programs of the H. Comm. on Oversight & Gov't Reform*, 112th Cong. 83–84 (2011) [hereinafter *Who's Watching the Watchman? Hearing*] (statement of Andrew Pincus, on behalf of the U.S. Chamber of Commerce) (noting the President's position that both the Comptroller of the Currency and the Director of the Office of Thrift Supervision serve at the pleasure of the President).

47. *See* Dodd-Frank Act § 1011(a), 124 Stat. at 1964 (codified at 12 U.S.C. § 5491(a)) (charging the CFBP with "regulat[ing] the offering and provision of consumer financial products or services").

48. *See id.* § 1023(c)(3)(A), 124 Stat. at 1985 (codified at 12 U.S.C. § 5513(c)(3)(A)). The FSOC is composed of ten voting members—nine federal

financial regulatory agencies and an independent member with insurance expertise—and five nonvoting members. *See id.* § 111(b)(1)–(2), 124 Stat. at 1392–93 (codified at 12 U.S.C. § 5321(b)(1)–(2)).

    Voting Members: The Secretary of the Treasury, who serves as the Chairperson of the FSOC, the Chairman of the Board of Governors of the Federal Reserve System, the Comptroller of the Currency, the Director of the Consumer Financial Protection Bureau, the Chairman of the Securities and Exchange Commission, the Chairperson of the Federal Deposit Insurance Corporation, the Chairperson of the Commodity Futures Trading Commission, the Director of the Federal Housing Finance Agency, the Chairman of the National Credit Union Administration Board, and an independent member with insurance expertise that is appointed by the President and confirmed by the Senate for a six-year term. *Id.* § 111(b)(1), (c)(1).

    Nonvoting Members Who Serve in an Advisory Capacity: The Director of the Office of Financial Research, the Director of the Federal Insurance Office, a state insurance commissioner selected by the state insurance commissioners, a state banking supervisor chosen by the state banking supervisors, and a state securities commissioner designated by the state securities supervisors. *Id.* § 111(b)(2). The state nonvoting members have two-year terms. *Id.* § 111(c)(1).

49. *Id.* § 1023(c)(3)(B), 124 Stat. at 1986 (codified at 12 U.S.C. § 5513(c)(3)(B)).

50. *See* Chevron U.S.A. Inc. v. Natural Res. Def. Council, Inc., 467 U.S. 837 (1984).

51. Dodd-Frank Act § 1022(b)(4)(B), 124 Stat. at 1981 (codified at 12 U.S.C. § 5512(b)(4)(B)) ("[T]he deference that a court affords to the Bureau with respect to a determination by the Bureau regarding the meaning or interpretation of any provision of a Federal consumer financial law shall be applied as if the Bureau were the only agency authorized to apply, enforce, interpret, or administer the provisions of such Federal consumer financial law.").

52. *See supra* notes 93–100 and accompanying text.

53. *See supra* notes 93–95 and accompanying text.

54. *See supra* notes 96–100 and accompanying text.

55. *See supra* notes 101–02 and accompanying text.

56. *Id.* § 1022(b)(1), 124 Stat. at 1980 (codified at 12 U.S.C. § 5512(b)(1)) (granting the CFPB rulemaking authority); *id.* § 1054(a), 124 Stat. at 2028 (codified at 12 U.S.C. § 5564(a)) (granting the CFPB litigation authority).

57. *See* S. Rep. No. 111–176, at 163 (2010).

58. *See About Us*, Consumer Fin. Prot. Bureau, http://www.consumerfinance.gov/thebureau/ (last visited Mar. 5, 2013) (stating that the CFPB's "mission is to make markets for consumer financial products and services work for Americans").

59. *See supra* notes 3, 35 and accompanying text.

60. At least before his 2013 renomination, Richard Cordray was mentioned as a potential candidate for governor of Ohio in 2014. *See* Suzy Khimm, *Who Is Richard Cordray, and What Is He Going to Do?*, Wash. Post (Jan. 4, 2012, 2:13 PM), http://www.washingtonpost.com/blogs/wonkblog/post/who-is-richard-cordray-and-what-is-he-going-to-do/2012/01/04/gIQAV4EraP_blog.html ("Cordray had previously expressed interest in running for Ohio governor in 2014, but since his CFPB appointment, he says that he's abandoned these near-term political ambitions."). Of course, there is nothing wrong with partisan politicians or those with political aspirations serving in agency functions. The difference between the CFPB and other agencies, however, is that the CFPB has been billed as nonpolitical, which is the justification for its extreme level of independence from ordinary checks and balances. *See Consumer Protection Is a Non-Partisan Issue: Warren*, CNBC (Nov. 10, 2010, 4:21 PM), http://www.cnbc.com/id/40114195/Consumer_Protection_Is_a_NonPartisan_Issue_Warren (quoting Elizabeth Warren as saying "I just can't believe there is someone who would want to come after this new agency . . . . We're not a partisan agency—we're here for American families.").

61. *See* Breyer, *supra* note 85, at 10–19 (explaining and giving examples of this phenomenon); DeMuth & Ginsburg, *supra* note 86, at 1081 ("An agency succeeds by accomplishing the goals Congress set for it as thoroughly as possible—not by balancing its goals against other, equally worthy goals.").

62. Anthony Downs, RAND Corp., Inside Bureaucracy 107 (1967) (internal quotation marks omitted).

63. Angel Manuel Moreno, *Presidential Coordination of the Independent Regulatory Process*, 8 Admin. L. Rev. Am. U. 461, 464 (1994).

64. *See* Todd J. Zywicki, *Baptists?: The Political Economy of Environmental Interest Groups*, 53 Case W. Res. L. Rev. 315, 327–33 (2002) (discussing an unwillingness of environmentalists to consider tradeoffs between environmental goals and other important goals).

65. David B. Spence & Frank Cross, *A Public Choice Case for the Administrative State*, 89 Geo. L.J. 97, 119–20 (2000) ("That agencies are systematically more loyal to their basic mission seems persuasive,

even obvious. People who are sympathetic to that mission are more likely to be attracted to work at the agency.") (emphasis omitted).

66. *See* Press Release, Consumer Fin. Prot. Bureau, Consumer Financial Protection Bureau Announces Senior Leadership Hires (Nov. 15, 2011), *available at* http://www.consumerfinance.gov/pressreleases /consumer-financial-protection-bureau-announces -senior-leadership-hires/ (announcing the hiring of three former White House staffers and others who formerly worked for Congress and other agencies).

67. *See* Oren Bar-Gill & Elizabeth Warren, *Making Credit Safer*, 157 U. Pa. L. Rev. 1, 1 (2008) ("These dangerous [consumer financial] products can lead to financial distress, bankruptcy, and foreclosure, and, as evidenced by the recent subprime crisis, they can have devastating effects on communities and on the economy.").

68. *See* Timothy J. Muris, *Regulatory Policymaking at the Federal Trade Commission: The Extent of Congressional Control*, 94 J. Pol. Econ. 884, 888 (1986) (noting the influence on the FTC of a wave of "liberal" employees into the Commission in the 1970s and their contribution to the activist policies of the FTC at the time).

69. *About the Federal Trade Commission*, Fed. Trade Comm'n, http://www.ftc.gov/ftc/about.shtm (last visited Mar. 5, 2013) (describing the FTC's mission as "prevent[ing] business practices that are anticompetitive or deceptive or unfair to consumers; . . . enhanc[ing] informed consumer choice and public understanding of the competitive process; and . . . accomplish[ing] this without unduly burdening legitimate business activity").

70. *See Who's Watching the Watchman? Hearing*, *supra* note 100, at 46 (statement of Todd J. Zywicki, Foundation Professor of Law, George Mason University).

71. *See About Us*, *supra* note 112 (describing the CFPB's self-declared mission).

72. *See* Niskanen Jr., *supra* note 89, at 36–42 ("For a positive theory of bureaucracy, though, the beginning of wisdom is the recognition that bureaucrats are people who are, at least, not entirely motivated by the general welfare or the interests of the state."); *see also* Todd J. Zywicki, *Institutional Review Boards as Academic Bureaucracies: An Economic and Experiential Analysis*, 101 Nw. U. L. Rev. 861, 873 (2007) (discussing Niskanen Jr.'s argument).

73. *See* Zywicki, *supra* note 126, at 873 n.48.

74. *See* Paul J. Quirk, Industry Influence in Federal Regulatory Agencies 143–74 (1981); *see also* Robert A. Katzmann, *Federal Trade Commission*, *in* The Politics of Regulation 152, 175–79 (James Q. Wilson

ed., 1980) (describing the effect of attorney turnover at the FTC); Suzanne Weaver, *Antitrust Division of the Department of Justice*, *in* The Politics of Regulation, *supra*, at 124, 134–35 (describing similar effects in the Department of Justice's Antitrust Division).

75. Consider, for example, the extraordinary interview with Elizabeth Warren for *Vanity Fair* magazine, a seemingly unique event for a Washington bureaucrat. *See* Suzanna Andrews, *The Woman Who Knew Too Much*, Vanity Fair, Nov. 2011, at 184.

76. *See* Dodd-Frank Wall Street Reform and Consumer Protection Act, Pub. L. No. 111–203, § 1011(b)(3), 124 Stat. 1376, 1964 (2010) (codified at 12 U.S.C. § 5491(b)(3) (Supp. IV 2011)) (requiring only that the nominee be a U.S. citizen).

77. Rachel E. Barkow, *Insulating Agencies: Avoiding Capture Through Institutional Design*, 89 Tex. L. Rev. 15, 47 (2010). For example, "at least two members of the three-member Surface Transportation Board must have a professional background in transportation," two of the five members of the Public Company Accounting Oversight Board must be certified public accountants, and members of the Defense Nuclear Facilities Safety Board must be "respected experts in the field of nuclear safety." *Id.* at 47–48 (internal quotation marks omitted). Statutes can also impose restrictions on affiliations with non-agency entities. *See id.* at 48. For example, the Consumer Product Safety Act states that a person "cannot hold the office of Commissioner if he or she is 'in the employ of, or holding any official relation to, any person engaged in selling or manufacturing consumer products' or owns 'stock or bonds of substantial value in a person so engaged' or 'is in any other manner pecuniarily interested in such a person.'" *Id.* at 48 (quoting 15 U.S.C. § 2053(c) (2006)).

78. In technical terms this would require so-called Type I and Type II errors to be treated symmetrically. For a discussion, see Stearns & Zywicki, *supra* note 81, at 358–61.

79. *See id.* at 359.

80. *Id.* at 359–60 (noting that "[e]mpirical studies tend to support the theoretical claim that regulators are unlikely to be risk neutral as between these two kinds of error, and instead that regulation is systematically biased in favor of avoiding the more tangible harm associated with Type II error than the abstract and generally unobservable harm from Type I error").

81. *See* Henry I. Miller, To America's Health: A Proposal to Reform the Food and Drug Administration 42–43 (2000) (making this point and noting that "[t]ype 2 errors in the form of unreasonable governmental

requirements and decisions can delay the marketing of a new product, lessen competition to produce it, and inflate its ultimate price").

82. *See Who's Watching the Watchmen? Hearing, supra* note 100, at 44 (statement of Todd J. Zywicki, Foundation Professor of Law, George Mason University).

83. *See infra* Part III.C.2 (discussing the moral hazards created by combinations of state law and various mortgage terms).

84. *See* Loan Originator Compensation Requirements Under the Truth in Lending Act (Regulation Z), 78 Fed. Reg. 11,280 (Feb. 15, 2013) (to be codified at 12 C.F.R. pt. 1026).

85. *Condition of Small Business and Commercial Real Estate Lending in Local Markets: Joint Hearing Before the H. Comm. on Small Bus. & the H. Comm. on Fin. Servs.*, 111th Cong. 336 (2010) (statement of Todd J. Zywicki, Foundation Professor of Law, George Mason University).

86. *Compare* Amany El Anshasy, Gregory Elliehausen & Yoshiaki Shimazaki, *The Pricing of Subprime Mortgages by Mortgage Brokers and Lenders* 12 (July 2005) (unpublished manuscript), *available at* http:// www.chicagofed.org/digital_assets/others/events/2005 /promises_and_ pitfalls/paper_pricing.pdf (finding that "broker-originated mortgages are less costly to the borrower than lender-originated mortgages after holding other loan terms and borrower characteristics constant"), *and* Gregory Elliehausen & Min Hwang, The Price of Subprime Mortgages at Mortgage Brokers and Lender (Nov. 29, 2010) (working paper), *available at* http://papers.ssrn. com/sol3/papers .cfm?abstract_id=1717013 (updated results confirming initial findings *supra*), *with* Susan E. Woodward, U.S. Dep't of Hous. & Urban Dev., A Study of Closing Costs for FHA Mortgages ix (2008), *available at* http://www.huduser.org/Publications/pdf/FHA_closing _cost.pdf (concluding that loans made by mortgage brokers are more expensive than those made by direct lenders by approximately $300 to $425).

87. *See* M. Cary Collins & Keith D. Harvey, *Mortgage Brokers and Mortgage Rate Spreads: Their Pricing Influence Depends on Neighborhood Type*, 19 J. Housing Res. 153, 168 (2010) ("Our results support our hypothesis that the mortgage broker is a better informed agent and show that in general as mortgage broker density increases, both the likelihood of a rate spread occurring and the size of a rate spread declines, while the loan approval rate increases.").

88. *See id* at 167–68.

89. *See, e.g.*, Morris M. Kleiner & Richard M. Todd, *Mortgage Broker Regulations That Matter: Analyzing Earnings, Employment, and Outcomes for Consumers*

4 (Nat'l Bureau of Econ. Research, Working Paper No. 13684, 2007), *available at* http://www.nber.org /papers/w13684.pdf?new_window=1 (finding that "the requirement in many states that mortgage brokers maintain a surety bond or maintain a minimum net worth[ ] has a significant and fairly robust statistical association with . . . higher foreclosure rates on subprime mortgages").

90. It should be emphasized that the author of this Article is aware of no evidence to indicate that strict licensing of mortgage brokers actually increases the overall average quality of mortgage brokers or their services for consumers.

91. David Hyman and William Kovacic provide a similar example when it comes to the conflict between economics and purported consumer protection goals in responding to so-called price gouging in the wake of a natural disaster such as a hurricane. *See* David A. Hyman & William E. Kovacic, *Government Organization/Reorganization: Why Who Does What Matters* 53–54 (Univ. of Ill. Program in Law, Behavior & Soc. Sci., Research Paper No. LE12-14, 2012) (on file with the George Washington Law Review).

92. *See* Todd J. Zywicki & Gabriel Okloski, *The Housing Market Crash* 27–28 (Mercatus Ctr., Working Paper No. 09-35, 2009), *available at* http:// mercatus.org/sites/default/files/publication/WP0935 _Housing_Market_Crash.pdf.

93. *See* Todd J. Zywicki, *The Behavioral Law and Economics of Fixed Rate Mortgages (And Other Just-So Stories)*, 21 Supreme Ct. Econ. Rev. (forthcoming 2013) (manuscript at 6, 16–17) [hereinafter Zywicki, *The Behavioral Law & Economics of Fixed Rate Mortgages*]; *see also* Michael Lea & Anthony Sanders, *Do We Need the 30-Year Fixed-Rate Mortgage?* 5–9 (Mercatus Ctr., Working Paper No. 11-15, 2011), *available at* http://mercatus.org/sites /default/files/Do-WeNeed-30yr-FRM.Sanders.3.14.11 .pdf.

94. *See* Zywicki, *supra* note 147, at 18–19 (noting that no other country in the world has standardized on this product).

95. *See infra* note 311 (comparing European and American home foreclosure rates).

96. Zywicki, *The Behavioral Law & Economics of Fixed-Rate Mortgages, supra* note 147, at 17.

97. *See id.*

98. Any such additional subsidy would already be on top of existing subsidies for the traditional mortgage, such as the implicit subsidy created by Fannie Mae and Freddie Mac's historic support for the product. *See* Binyamin Appelbaum, *Without Loan Giants, 30-Year Mortgage May Fade Away*, NY Times, Mar. 4, 2011, at A1 (noting that

if Fannie Mae and Freddie Mac were shut down, the thirty-year fixed-rate mortgage would likely disappear from the market).

99. STEARNS & ZYWICKI, *supra* note 81, at 361.

100. Id.

101. *See supra* text accompanying note 114.

102. E-mail from Richard Cordray, Dir., Consumer Fin. Prot. Bureau, to Staff, Consumer Financial Protection Bureau (Feb. 6, 2012), *available at* http://issuu.com/judicialwatch/docs/cordray_weekly _message?mode=window&backgroundColor =%23222222.

103. *See* DURKIN ET AL., *supra* note 61, at 629–78 (surveying political economy and redistributional effects of consumer credit regulation through history).

104. *See* STEARNS & ZYWICKI, *supra* note 81, at 376–78 (describing the theory of agency capture and reactions to it).

105. *See* THOMAS K. McCRAW, PROPHETS OF REGULATION 263–65 (1984).

106. Thomas Frank, Op-Ed., *Obama and 'Regulatory Capture,'* WALL ST. J., June 24, 2009, at A13.

107. Jonathan R. Macey, *Administrative Agency Obsolescence and Interest Group Formation: A Case Study of the SEC at Sixty*, 15 CARDOZO L. REV. 909, 922 (1994).

108. B. Peter Pashigian, *A Theory of Prevention and Legal Defense with an Application to the Legal Costs of Companies*, 25 J.L. & ECON. 247, 268–69 (1982) (finding economies of scale in legal costs related to regulatory compliance and observing that "smaller companies . . . are at a cost disadvantage in legal costs incurred," but noting that "[e]xtrapolating [the] results to still smaller companies may be inappropriate if smaller companies are either exempt from or subject to less stringent enforcement by the regulatory authorities").

109. *See, e.g., Rising Regulatory Compliance Costs and Their Impact on the Health of Small Financial Institutions: Hearing Before the H. Subcomm. on Fin. Insts. & Consumer Credit of the H. Comm. on Fin. Servs.*, 112th Cong. 72 (2012) (statement of Ed Templeton, President, SRP Fed. Credit Union) ("[A]dditional regulatory requirements mandated in this massive overhaul have added to the overwhelming number of compliance burdens for credit unions. Undoubtedly, an immense amount of time, effort, and resources will be expended at credit unions as they struggle to keep up with new regulation."); Letter from Stephen P. Wilson, Chairman, Am. Bankers Ass'n, to Hon. Sheila Bair, Chairman, Fed. Deposit Ins. Corp. (March 21, 2010), *available at* http://www.aba.com/aba/documents/blogs/DoddFrank /ChairmanBairMar212011.pdf [hereinafter Wilson Letter] (identifying Dodd-Frank regulations which could negatively affect community banks and noting that "even if [the CFPB] does not examine community banks, the Bureau will set the rules for nearly all of community bank business (since community banks depend heavily on providing retail banking services)").

110. *See* Wilson Letter, *supra* note 163 (criticizing elements of Dodd-Frank for preventing "all banks—and community banks in particular—to continue to provide the products and services that our customers want and that our communities need for robust and sustained economic growth and prosperity").

111. The original idea proposed by the Obama Administration of creating a preferred set of "plain vanilla" loan products is an example of a tendency toward commoditization of consumer lending products. The proposal, however, was later rejected. *See* TREASURY DEP'T WHITE PAPER, *supra* note 18, at 15 ("We propose that the [CFPB] be authorized to define standards for 'plain vanilla' products that are simpler and have straightforward pricing.").

112. *See supra* notes 140–43 and accompanying text.

113. *See* Dodd-Frank Wall Street Reform and Consumer Protection Act, Pub. L. No. 111–203, §§ 204, 210, 124 Stat. 1376, 1454, 1460 (2010).

114. Press Release, Indep. Cmty. Bankers of Am., Credit Rating Downgrade Highlights Danger of Banking Concentration: Deposit Concentration Is at All-Time High (June 25, 2012), *available at* http://www.icba.org/news/newsreleasedetail .cfm?ItemNumber=128191.

TODD J. ZYWICKI is the George Mason University Foundation Professor of Law at George Mason University School of Law. He is the senior scholar of the Mercatus Center at the university as well as senior fellow at the F.A. Hayek Program for Advanced Study in Philosophy, Politics and Economics. He practiced commercial law prior to his appointment with the university. He is the author of more than 70 articles in law reviews and peer-reviewed economics journals. He is one of the Top 50 Most Downloaded Law Authors at the Social Science Research Network. He has testified several times before Congress on issues of consumer bankruptcy law and consumer credit, and he is a frequent commentator on legal issues in the print and broadcast media, including the *Wall Street Journal, New York Times, Washington Post, Washington Times, Forbes, Nightline, National Review, NBC Nightly News*, and other media outlets.

EXPLORING THE ISSUE

Is the Consumer Financial Protection Bureau (CFPB) a Necessary Regulatory Agency?

Critical Thinking and Reflection

1. Subprime mortgages were cited as one of the causes of the economic crash of 2008? How is the CFPB an appropriate response to this crisis that resulted from the crash?
2. Major investment banks as well as AIG required almost $800 billion to bail out debts due to faulty financial instruments such as derivatives. Explain whether or not the CFPB can help with investment banking concerns.
3. Could you file a complaint against a financial agency with the CFPB? Explain the circumstances in which you might.
4. Many individuals are currently having their cars repossessed. According to documents, the individuals couldn't afford the cars and auto agencies sold the vehicles knowing the owners would not be able to make the payments. Should the CFPB become involved in these problems? Explain.
5. Credit card companies may change rules and regulations in writing to consumers. Do most consumers read the updates sent to them by their credit card companies? Would most consumers know if additional fees or interest rates were being charged? How can the CFPB assist with this? What is the consumer's responsibility?

Is There Common Ground?

Once Dodd-Frank passed in 2010, individuals with the U.S. Department of Treasury began laying the groundwork for the Consumer Financial Protection Bureau (CFPB). In July of 2011, the agency started in the basement of the Treasury, and planned for the new bureau that was ordered to be developed. Many tasked with building the agency were surprised that something like the CFPB didn't already exist. They researched how other federal agencies had begun; most of the information was either not applicable or provided a bad example. According to Richard Cordray, the director of the agency, in its first three years the CFPB has helped refund more than $3.8 billion to consumers. In 2014, he told a congressional committee, "Since we opened our doors, we have been focused on making consumer financial markets work better for the American people, the honest businesses that serve them, and the economy as a whole." Many members of the financial sector see the agency as unnecessary and too autonomous. Criticism has also been made that too many lawyers have been hired to litigate on behalf of the bureau and on behalf of financial institutions who are defendants. Some claims are handled efficiently online at www.consumerfinance.gov or by phone, mail, or in person.

The larger actions, such as a recent Bank of America settlement, were handled by at least two law firms—one for the government, and one for the bank. The result was that Bank of America agreed to pay consumers $727 million for deceptively marketing credit card add-on services. Chase Bank USA, N.A. and JPMorgan Chase Bank paid similar settlements amounting to $309 million. The agency has its detractors and fans, with some individuals predicting it will be President Obama's greatest achievement and others insisting it is his biggest blunder.

Additional Resources

Paul J. Cerutti and Margaret Kolchak (Eds.), *The Consumer Financial Protection Bureau: Overview and Analyses*. Hauppauge, NY: Nova Science Pub. Inc., 2012.

Michael M. Greenfield, *Consumer Transactions* (University Casebook Series), 6th ed., New York, NY: Barrister Books, 2014.

Walters Kluwer Law and Business Attorney-Editors, *Dodd-Frank Wall Street Reform and Consumer Protection Act: Law Explanation and Analysis*. New York, NY: Walters, Kluwer Law and Business Attorney-Editors, 2014.

Internet References . . .

Megan Slack, "Consumer Financial Protection Bureau 101: Why We Need a Consumer Watchdog"

> www.whitehouse.gov/blog/2012/01/04/consumer -financial-protection-bureau-101-why-we-need -consumer-watchdog

Hunter Stewart, "Debt Collection Factory Preyed on Broke Americans: Lawsuit"

> http://www.huffingtonpost.com/2014/07/15 /debt-collection-agency-lawsuit_n_5585264 .html?ir=Business

"Dodd-Frank: Title X-Bureau of Consumer Financial Protection"

> www.law.cornell.edu/wex/dodd-frank_title_X

Zach Carter, "How House Democrats Are Caving on Key Mortgage Rules"

> www.huffingtonpost.com/2014/06/09 /democrats-mortgage-rules_n_5474197.html

Regulatory Reform and Consumer Financial Protection Bureau

> www.nclc.org/issues/regulatory-reform.html

Unit 4

UNIT

Global Objectives

*O*ur reach extends around the globe, both in exports and in manufacturing. Some of our most "American" products are produced in other countries, including such iconic products as baseballs, Barbie dolls, and American flags (Bradford, 2013). How do we want these products to be produced? What is the responsibility of the American corporation in terms of its overseas partners and suppliers?

What is the level playing field for global corporations and for international ethical standards? Does our impact on the world require more or less individual responsibility for the actions of our corporations?

Reference: Bradford, H. (2013). "12 Iconic American Products That Are No Longer Made in the U.S." http://www .huffingtonpost.com/2013/01/24/american-products-not-made-usa_n_2536773.html (retrieved April 21, 2015).

Selected, Edited and with Issue Framing Materials by:
Gina Vega, *Organizational Ergonomics*

ISSUE

Should Hydrofracking Be Permitted?

YES: Danny Hakim, from "Gas Drilling Is Called Safe in New York." *The New York Times* (2013)

NO: Ben Goldfarb, from "Hydrofracking Poses Serious Risks to Human Health," *Policymic* (2012)

Learning Outcomes

After reading this issue, you will be able to:

- Discuss why ethical debates about hydrofracking are important.
- Explain why the economic benefits of hydrofracking are of vital interest and importance to a community that has the resources needed for this industry.
- Distinguish the varieties of health and ecological concerns that are associated with hydrofracking. Are these ethically important concerns?
- Discuss how individual, community leaders, and industry officials can be helped by an understanding of ethics in regard to the practice of hydrofracking.
- Economically, what are the benefits and costs of this practice in the New York communities that are considering approving this industry?

ISSUE SUMMARY

YES: Danny Hakim reports that the New York Health Department will be issuing a report claiming that the practice of hydrofracking is safe as it is practiced in the state of New York; after significant pressure from the drilling industry and landowners, the moratorium on hydrofracking was lifted for the Southern Tier of the state in the summer of 2012.

NO: Ben Goldfarb disagrees, citing a recently released Environmental Protection Agency report that links hydraulic fracturing to contaminated well-water in Wyoming. He also points out that an abundance of clean water is needed for the process—a commodity which is scarce in the western United States.

Most extraction services come with risk; however, when the risk is well managed, the product, the service, and the employment it creates, can be a boon for a community. Hydrofracking is a lesser-known extraction industry. It is a process that is used to force natural gas and petroleum from areas underground where it is trapped. Some hydrofracking enthusiasts point out that the natural gas that comes as a result of this procedure has half the carbon emissions of coal and no mercury, sulfur dioxide, or particulate residue. But this issue isn't merely about the benefits of the product. This issue also revolves around the process of extracting the natural gas and petroleum

through hydrofracking, and the harms that come to communities involved in the processes, including loss of water, contamination of water, and the possibility of increased danger of earthquakes.

Hydrofracking involves the use of high-pressure water and materials, including chemicals and sand to break open cracks in rock deep underground. This is combined with a method called horizontal drilling to extract natural gas. The companies involved in the fracking business have yet to disclose the chemicals that are used in the process or address questions such as contamination of water supplies in areas close to where the process is occurring. However, some U.S. government agencies have also been looking into the practice. A hazard alert was released in 2012 by the Occupational Safety and Health Administration (OSHA) based on collected data, which showed workers could be exposed to dust that contains high levels of silica dioxide and other toxins, including radiation materials, during the hydrofracking process. Additionally, the Department of Energy has released information that indicates there can be as many as 65 chemicals used in the fracking process—some of which have been found to be carcinogenic.

However, the problems with this business have not just stayed at the work sites. The debates about the environment and a strong economic future have led some state and local governments to develop legislation regarding the use of clean water, the disposal of contaminated water, and the elimination of certain toxic chemicals that are believed to be part of the fracking process. The United States has allowed hydrofracking or hydraulic fracturing since 1968, and some countries are following the lead of the United States in developing the process. Other countries such as France have banned the process all together. As mentioned earlier, many communities aren't happy with this industry based in their area. For example in March of 2013, police arrested 10 individuals during an "anti-fracking protest" by New Matamoras, Ohio.

The protesters had latched themselves to drilling equipment.

Economically, in the 1970s American geologists began reporting there were large volumes of gas-saturated sandstones with permeability too low to recover the gas in a traditional method, in an economic manner. Experiments and then production in hydraulic fracturing began in thousands of wells in the western United States such as Green River Basin, Denver Basin, and San Juan Basin. The experimentation also included moving from vertical wells to horizontal wells. In doing so, the companies could extract more of the fluids underneath the surface. According to the International Energy Agency website, through hydrofracking there is still a massive amount of recoverable shale gases. They estimate 208 trillion cubic meters. They also estimate about 76 trillion cubic meters of shale gases are still available utilizing the tight gas method of extraction, and 47 trillion cubic meters are available in coal bed methane.

According to the website of the National Petroleum Institute, hydraulic fracturing and horizontal drilling will stimulate the economy by producing jobs and making available for sale nearly 70 percent of natural gas development in North America. The Institute believes that the United States could lose upwards of 50 percent of the natural gas production without using hydrofracking.

YES ⤶

Danny Hakim

Gas Drilling Is Called Safe in New York

Albany—The state's Health Department found in an analysis it prepared early last year that the much-debated drilling technology known as hydrofracking could be conducted safely in New York, according to a copy obtained by *The New York Times* from an expert who did not believe it should be kept secret.

The analysis and other health assessments have been closely guarded by Gov. Andrew M. Cuomo and his administration as the governor weighs whether to approve fracking. Mr. Cuomo, a Democrat, has long delayed making a decision, unnerved in part by strident opposition on his party's left. A plan to allow a limited amount of fracking in the state's Southern Tier along the Pennsylvania border is still seen as the most likely outcome, should the drilling process receive final approval.

The eight-page analysis is a summary of previous research by the state and others, and concludes that fracking can be done safely. It delves into the potential impact of fracking on water resources, on naturally occurring radiological material found in the ground, on air emissions and on "potential socioeconomic and quality-of-life impacts."

But it remains difficult to discern how much original research the state has done on potential health impacts, and environmentalists worry that the administration's lack of transparency is hiding a lack of rigor in its assessment of public health risks. At the same time, the drilling industry, and landowners who have leased their land in the Southern Tier, have grown increasingly frustrated with delays by the Cuomo administration to announce a final plan. State regulators have now been studying the issue of fracking for about four years.

Emily DeSantis, a spokeswoman for the State Department of Environmental Conservation, said the analysis obtained by *The New York Times* was out of date. "The document you have is merely a summary, is nearly a year old, and there will be substantial changes to that version," she said.

She added that a revised version of the Environmental Impact Statement on hydrofracking—which last ran about 1,500 pages—would include more material delving into health issues. The administration has also turned to three outside experts to review the state's own health assessments.

Fracking—more formally known as high volume hydraulic fracturing—involves injecting large amounts of sand, water, and chemicals deep underground at high pressures to extract natural gas from rock formations. The natural gas industry has aggressively sought to drill in the Marcellus Shale, a deep repository that runs through West Virginia, Ohio, Pennsylvania, and New York.

The assessment obtained by *The New York Times* finds that fracking can be done safely within the regulatory system that the state has been developing for several years.

"By implementing the proposed mitigation measures," the analysis says, "the Department expects that human chemical exposures during normal HVHF operations"—short for high-volume hydraulic fracturing—"will be prevented or reduced below levels of significant health concern."

The analysis also rejects a broad quantitative risk assessment of fracking—the kind of study that would try to project the probability of various hazards—saying it would "involve making a large number of assumptions about the many scenario-specific variables that influence the nature and degree of potential human exposure and toxicity."

Environmental groups have long complained that the state has refused to make documents about its health assessments public.

"The document itself is not a health impact study at all," said Katherine Nadeau, the water and natural resources program director at Environmental Advocates of New York, who has reviewed it. "As drafted it is merely a defense or justification as to why the administration didn't do a rigorous study."

Last September, Ms. Nadeau's group submitted a state Freedom of Information Law request to the Cuomo administration seeking any health impact studies that had been conducted, but has yet to receive any such documents—a common delay tactic by the administration on various issues.

"This is Governor Cuomo saying to the people of New York, once again, trust me on fracking, when on the health impact side of it, the public has been kept completely in the dark," Ms. Nadeau said.

Danny Hakim is a graduate of St. John's College in Annapolis, MD, in philosophy. Hakim has been a correspondent covering state government in *The New York Times* Albany bureau since November 2005. He has been Albany bureau chief since 2007. Hakim was a finalist for the Pulitzer Prize for Public Service in April 2012 and was part of a team that won the 2009 Pulitzer Prize for Breaking News.

Ben Goldfarb

 **NO**

Hydrofracking Poses Serious Risks to Human Health

Earlier this month, the Environmental Protection Agency published a report linking hydraulic fracturing, or fracking, to contaminated well-water in Wyoming. While copious anecdotal evidence has hinted at fracking's dangers, the EPA's report is among the first to conclusively document the presence of industrial pollutants in groundwater. This smoking gun proves that fracking confers risks to human health—risks that justify suspending the practice.

First, a few words on what, exactly, the EPA found. In a nutshell, fracking is the process of injecting pressurized fluid into underground shale deposits to force natural gas out of the rock and up to the surface. The composition of this fluid is a trade secret—by and large, frackers are not required to reveal the ingredients of their strange brews. Thanks to a modicum of voluntary disclosure, however, we do know that fracking fluid can contain up to 29 different carcinogens. We also know that keeping all that fluid safely sealed within the fracking well is very difficult, and that the cocktail often escapes into the surrounding rock.

That, apparently, is what happened in Pavillion, Wyoming, where EPA scientists identified numerous compounds—including benzene in concentrations 78 times higher than safe standards—associated with fracking in nearby pit wells. In response, the Agency for Toxic Substances has recommended that citizens of Pavillion switch to alternate water sources and ventilate their bathrooms to prevent their homes from blowing up. No word yet on whether Pavillionites find this advice reassuring.

Citizens who have followed the fracking debate were likely not surprised by the EPA's findings. Since fracking took off in the early 2000s, it has been implicated in an array of ominous maladies; flammable faucets; and, most recently, earthquakes in Ohio. Yet even as the anecdotal evidence has mounted, fracking has continued apace. The practice has accelerated in states with huge shale deposits

such as Pennsylvania, and New York lifted its moratorium this summer. While the EPA's report may lead some states to rethink their position on fracking, I suspect that hydraulic fracturing will continue unimpeded. Accounts of malodorous water, unexplained headaches and nosebleeds, and the death of livestock have not slowed the drilling of wells; I doubt that finding benzene in groundwater will.

The EPA's discovery may have vindicated the long-standing suspicions of environmentalists, but nobody's rejoicing. Fracking improves companies' ability to access natural gas reserves, and natural gas provides plenty of benefits: It produces fewer carbon emissions than other fossil fuels; it is cheap, plentiful, and not imported from a Middle Eastern dictatorship; and it provides income to poor farming communities. For these reasons, numerous pragmatic environmentalists have embraced natural gas as a transitional fuel that can supplant coal and oil until wind and solar are ready for prime time. If fracking were demonstrably safe, environmentalists would have reason to accept it.

But environmental groups tend to adhere to the precautionary principle: The notion that the burden of proof falls on industry to demonstrate that its practices are not harmful. Shoot later; ask questions first. Environmentalists have long avowed that, in the absence of conclusive scientific evidence either way, we should have refrained from fracking—especially given the abundant anecdotal evidence that suggests it is harmful—and conducted more rigorous tests. Then we should have tested fracking again, and a third time, and however many subsequent trials it took to determine beyond a shadow of a doubt that the practice was safe. (This espousal of the precautionary principle stands in opposition to the Obama administration, which avers that fracking can go ahead while the EPA conducts its review.)

For their caution, green groups are tarred as anti-progress obstructionists who won't be happy until every person in America exchanges their car for a horse. But most mainstream environmental non-profits aren't fundamentally against the exploitation of natural gas—they only oppose industrial practices, like fracking, whose actual or potential costs outweigh their benefits. The Environmental Defense Fund, for example, acknowledges that natural gas will inevitably be part of the U.S.'s energy portfolio, but also believes that fracking, as presently practiced, is too shadowy and dangerous to continue unreformed.

But can fracking be cleaned up, or does it inherently pose "fat-tailed risk"—i.e., seemingly improbable consequences that are more likely than we realize, and so terrible that they aren't worth risking? That's a question currently beyond the purview of this article or any other, since we don't fully understand the connections between fracking and groundwater contamination, methane seepage, and those pesky earthquakes. With extensive modifications to the process, it may be possible to frack reasonably safely; or fracking may be intrinsically dangerous and impermissable. We don't know. But we do know that, in the face of uncertainty, caution pays off.

Time and again throughout modern history, fat-tailed environmental risks have been manifested, with disastrous outcomes. Spraying mosquitoes with DDT seemed like a great idea, until we wiped out most of North America's birds. We went ahead and mined every seam of coal we could find in Appalachia, and discovered only after the fact that we'd caused thousands of deaths through respiratory problems and mercury poisoning. Fukushima and Deepwater Horizon luridly demonstrated the perils of taking on outsized risk. And, of course, climate change is fat-tailed risk writ large: Burning fossil fuels has been fun, but now we're confronting the possibility that global temperatures might rise 6 degrees this century and leave large parts of the Earth uninhabitable.

Right now, we have compelling reasons to believe that fracking contaminates water and presents a danger to human health (and let's not even mention the earthquakes). Those risks are too great to let fracking continue unabated: The precautionary principle commands us to shut the practice down pending further review. Someday, a radically different form of hydraulic fracturing may meet environmental and risk-aversion standards; today, fracking is too dangerous to permit.

BEN GOLDFARB is a graduate of Amherst College and is currently at the Yale School of Forestry and Environmental Studies. Goldfarb has been significantly involved in active and instructive conservation efforts. He has attached satellite tags to sea turtles in North Carolina; eradicated invasive fish in Yellowstone National Park; taught agricultural science in Bangkok, Thailand; and conducted forestry research in the urban jungles of the Bronx. Goldfarb has been publishing work as a freelance environmental journalist since 2011 and serves as coeditor-in-chief of *Sage Magazine*, located at Yale University.

EXPLORING THE ISSUE

Should Hydrofracking Be Permitted?

Critical Thinking and Reflection

1. Is hydrofracking needed for energy independence in the United States? What distinguishes energy independence from energy security?
2. What impact would legislation have that restricts hydrofracking based on health concerns?
3. What impact would the status quo operations in hydrofracking have on water supplies and water pollution?
4. Could alternate energy sources be developed that would serve the needs that are currently serviced through the gas and oil produced through hydrofracking?
5. Describe some public policies that could promote energy security for the United States yet not harm the health and ecology of the communities where the industry is based.

Is There Common Ground?

There are moral and political principles that are referred to as precautionary. Often these principles are introduced when great harms could accompany a public business practice or community policy which could bring great benefits. The potential harms in hydrofracking cited in these articles are to the public health. The benefits are increased jobs, sales, and other commerce for the businesses that are involved in the industry. The potential risks and benefits of hydrofracking have been the subject of ongoing debate among physicians, politicians, the oil and gas industry, and the general public. The debate has many prongs, including economic benefits to states, towns, and the country. It also addresses American self-sufficiency in energy supply, ecology, and public health.

Much of the debate in the articles within this issue center on introducing hydrofracking into areas of New York State. Individuals in this area point out that when the hydrofracking industry is introduced to an area, some existing jobs could be lost in sectors such as agriculture and in businesses that support agriculture and rural communities. It has also been argued that the environment will unavoidably be adversely affected, as industrial expansion urbanizes the rural landscape. From a preventive medicine and family health perspective in New York, the conclusion is that it is not possible to balance potential economic benefits with the risks to health and the environment until the Health Impact Assessment is completed. It appears that more time is needed to assess whether this new industry should dot the skylines of rural New York.

Additional Resources

Felicity Barringer, "Spread of Hydrofracking Could Strain Water Resources in West, Study Finds," *New York Times* (May 2, 2013).

Erica Orden and Joseph De Avila, "New York Fracking Decision Is Put Off," *Wall Street Journal* (February 13, 2013).

Ed Rendell, "Why Cuomo Must Seize the Moment on Hydrofracking," *New York Daily News* (May 21, 2013).

"The Economist Debates Fracking," *The Economist* (March 11, 2013).

Ian Urbina, "Deadlist Danger Isn't on the Rig but on the Road," *New York Times* (May 15, 2012).

Internet References . . .

Lindsay Garten, "Pros and Cons of Hydrofracking, Environmental Leadership and Action," October 14, 2011

> https://edblogs.columbia.edu
> /scppx3335-001-2011-3/2011/10/14/pros
> -and-cons-of-hydrofracking

"Hydrofracking Puts Sullivan County's Ethics Laws Under Scrutiny"

> http://capitalregion.ynn.com/content/video
> _stories/519350/hydrofracking-puts-sullivan
> -county-s-ethics-laws-under-scrutiny

Larry Kahaner, "The Fractured Ethics of Fracking," May 26, 2011

> http://gdacc.org/2011/05/31/the-fractured
> -ethics-of-fracking

"The Risks of Hydrofracking," *Risk Management Magazine,* June 5, 2011

www.natlawreview.com/article/risks-hydrofracking

Selected, Edited and with Issue Framing Materials by:
Gina Vega, *Organizational Ergonomics*

ISSUE

Should the World Continue to Rely on Oil as a Major Source of Energy?

YES: Red Cavaney, from "Global Oil Production about to Peak? A Recurring Myth," *World Watch* (January–February 2006)

NO: James Howard Kunstler, from *The Long Emergency* (Grove/Atlantic, 2005)

Learning Outcomes
After reading this issue, you will be able to:
• Discuss why Red Cavaney believes that oil production is not only vast but also the most effective fuel of the future.
• Distinguish between the ethics behind the use of oil supplies and the ethics behind the concerns of global warming.
• Assess the ethical differences between the two stances.
• Distinguish Cavaney's argument for the oil industry from the ability to make as much money as possible for the industry.
• Discuss how ethical concerns about nature often come in conflict with desires for profits.

ISSUE SUMMARY

YES: Red Cavaney, president and chief executive officer of the American Petroleum Institute, argues that recent revolutionary advances in technology will yield sufficient quantities of available oil for the foreseeable future.

NO: James Howard Kunstler contends that the peak of oil production, Hubbert's Peak, was itself the important turning point in our species' relationship to petroleum. Unless strong conservation measures are put in place, the new scarcity will destroy much that we have come to expect in our lives.

We might begin with the fact that the idea of an "oil crisis" has become part of our lives in the last half century. Suddenly gasoline prices are higher, there are lines at the gas stations, political commentators suddenly discover international affairs, and a mood of panic pervades the country. Resolutions are made, actions begun, but then the whole crisis seems to peter out. What's happening?

First, is oil "running out"? Since the 1930s, energy prognosticators have used a model called Hubbert's Curve (named for geologist M. King Hubbert, who first projected it) that predicted the end of oil as an available resource. As

oil recovery technology has progressed, the curve has been lengthened; Red Cavaney's selection relies heavily on this fact. But the curve is still there, and even a major contraction in the oil supply will have a very significant effect on the way America continues to grow and develop; James Kunstler calls our attention to some of the changes we may expect.

There are two major dimensions to the "oil crisis," both of which affect the business community. The first is a management dilemma, stemming from the interaction of the U.S. economy and a global monopoly: how to control the impact of the decisions of international business consortia in the energy business. Business is all about supply and demand (see the selection by Adam Smith in Issue 1). In the case of petroleum, the lion's share of the supply is controlled by energy consortia that as Smith would approve, consider their own economic interests first, with the result that they rarely have the interests of the people of the United States as a priority. The logic of economic success for the industry, as all oil producers know, requires that the producers reduce the supply available for purchase, causing the price to rise, for an interval of time that will be limited by the customer's perception that he is spending too much for oil, and has recourse to other methods of obtaining energy—for instance, by developing solar energy as a source of power or placing restrictions on the amount of gasoline that automobiles sold in the United States can consume in a mile. At that point, production is raised dramatically, oil prices drop precipitously, and as a result, all investments in alternatives to oil consumption are abandoned. After that point, enough time is allowed to elapse so that investments will have been liquidated and the alternative work-force scattered; then the squeeze begins again. American consumers, on this understanding, are at the mercy of a foreign monopoly in complete control of the price of gasoline and heating oil, and would be well advised to use the periods of inexpensive oil to assemble the capital needed to solve the energy problem once and for all. That gathering of capital can only be done by heavy taxation of oil alone, or of all carbon, sufficient to keep the price of oil level for

the consumer while the capital accumulates. The American public dislikes taxes in general, and the oil industry dislikes oil taxes even more.

The second dimension is an industry crisis caused by an environmental threat: how to adjust our automotive industry, traditionally the heart and pride of our manufacturing capacity, to minimize the damage done to the environment by the burning of all fossil fuels, especially the burning of gasoline in the use of automobiles and trucks for transportation. Our automotive industry is set up like all the others—to provide a healthy return to the shareholders by producing products that the consumers want and will buy and that yield a high profit margin. That requirement does not well describe small, fuel-efficient cars, but it does describe the large, low-fuel-mileage sport utility vehicles (SUVs) introduced in the 1990s and now flooding our highways. As the American public contemplates images of polar bears stranded on vanishing ice, hurricanes in the Caribbean, and expanding deserts in Africa, it becomes increasingly likely that each new administration will insist on conservation measures, starting with the all-too-visible SUVs. How should the automotive industry—and the advertisers, the oil companies, and the consumers—respond?

Bear in mind, as you read these selections, that global business will suffer major disruptions in any initiative to end oil dependence; what advantages might make the sacrifices worth their cost?

YES ↵

Red Cavaney

Global Oil Production about to Peak?
A Recurring Myth

Once again, we are hearing that world oil production is "peaking," and that we will face a steadily diminishing oil supply to fuel the global economy. These concerns have been expressed periodically over the years, but have always been at odds with energy and economic realities. Such is the case today.

Let's look at some history: In 1874, the chief geologist of Pennsylvania predicted we would run out of oil in four years—just using it for kerosene. Thirty years ago, groups such as the Club of Rome predicted an end of oil long before the current day. These forecasts were wrong because, nearly every year, we have found more oil than we have used, and oil reserves have continued to grow.

The world consumes approximately 80 million barrels of oil a day. By 2030, world oil demand is estimated to grow about 50 percent, to 121 million barrels a day, even allowing for significant improvements in energy efficiency. The International Energy Agency says there are sufficient oil resources to meet demand for at least the next 30 years.

The key factor here is technology. Revolutionary advances in technology in recent years have dramatically increased the ability of companies to find and extract oil—and, of particular importance, recover more oil from existing reservoirs. Rather than production peaking, existing fields are yielding markedly more oil than in the past. Advances in technology include the following:

Directional Drilling. It used to be that wellbores were basically vertical holes. This made it necessary to drill virtually on top of a potential oil deposit. However, the advent of miniaturized computers and advanced sensors that can be attached to the drill bit now allows companies to drill directional holes with great accuracy because they can get real-time information on the subsurface location throughout the drilling process.

Horizontal Drilling. Horizontal drilling is similar to directional drilling, but the well is designed to cut horizontally through the middle of the oil or natural gas deposit. Early horizontal wells penetrated only 500 to 800 feet of reservoir laterally, but technology advances recently allowed a North Slope operator to penetrate 8,000 feet of reservoir horizontally. Moreover, horizontal wells can operate up to 10 times more productively than conventional wells.

3-D Seismic Technology. Substantial enhancements in computing power during the past two decades have allowed the industry to gain a much clearer picture of what lies beneath the surface. The ability to process huge amounts of data to produce three-dimensional seismic images has significantly improved the drilling success rate of the industry.

Primarily due to these advances, the U.S. Geological Survey (USGS), in its 2000 *World Petroleum Assessment,* increased by 20 percent its estimate of undiscovered, technically recoverable oil. USGS noted that, since oil became a major energy source about 100 years ago, 539 billion barrels of oil have been produced outside the United States. USGS estimates there are 649 billion barrels of undiscovered, technically recoverable oil outside the United States. But, importantly, USGS also estimates that there will be an *additional* 612 billion barrels from "reserve growth"—nearly equaling the undiscovered resources. Reserve growth results from a variety of sources, including technological advancement in exploration and production, increases over initially conservative estimates of reserves, and economic changes.

The USGS estimates reflected several factors:

- As drilling and production within discovered fields progresses, new pools or reservoirs are found that were not previously known.
- Advances in exploration technology make it possible to identify new targets within existing fields.
- Advances in drilling technology make it possible to recover oil and gas not previously considered recoverable in the initial reserve estimates.
- Enhanced oil recovery techniques increase the recovery factor for oil and thereby increase the reserves within existing fields.

Here in the United States, rather than "running out of oil," potentially vast oil and natural gas reserves remain to be developed. According to the latest published government estimates, there are more than 131 billion barrels of oil and more than 1,000 trillion cubic feet of natural gas remaining to be discovered in the United States. However, 78 percent of this oil and 62 percent of this gas are expected to be found beneath federal lands—much of which are non-park and non-wilderness lands—and coastal waters. While there is plenty of oil in the ground, oil companies need to be allowed to make major investments to find and produce it.

The U.S. Energy Information Administration has projected that fossil fuels will continue to dominate U.S. energy consumption, with oil and natural gas providing almost two-thirds of that consumption in the year 2025, even though energy efficiency and renewables will grow faster than their his torical rates. However, renewables in particular start from a very small base; and the major shares provided by oil, natural gas, and coal in 2025 are projected to be nearly identical to those in 2003.

Those who block oil and natural gas development here in the United States and elsewhere only make it much more difficult to meet the demand for oil, natural gas, and petroleum products. Indeed, it is not surprising that some of the end-of-oil advocates are the same people who oppose oil and natural gas development everywhere.

Failure to develop the potentially vast oil and natural gas resources that remain in the world will have a high economic cost. We must recognize that we live in a global economy, and that there is a strong link between energy and economic growth. If we are to continue to grow economically, here in the United States, in Europe, and the developing world, we must be cost-competitive in our use of energy. We need *all* sources of energy. We do not have the luxury of limiting ourselves to one source to the exclusion of others. Nor can we afford to write off our leading source of energy before we have found cost-competitive and readily available alternatives.

Consider how oil enhances our quality of life—fueling growth and jobs in industry and commerce, cooling and warming our homes, and getting us where we need to go. Here in the United States, oil provides about 97 percent of transportation fuels, which power nearly all of the cars and trucks traveling on our nation's highways. And plastics, medicines, fertilizers, and countless other products that extend and enhance our quality of life are derived from oil.

In considering our future energy needs, we also need to understand that gasoline-powered automobiles have been the dominant mode of transport for the past century—and the overwhelming preference of hundreds of millions of people throughout the world. Regardless of fuel, the automobile—likely to be configured far differently from today—will remain the consumer's choice for personal transport for decades to come. The freedom of mobility and the independence it affords consumers is highly valued.

The United States—and the world—cannot afford to leave the Age of Oil before realistic substitutes are fully in place. It is important to remember that man left the Stone Age not because he ran out of stones—and we will not leave the Age of Oil because we will run out. Yes, someday oil will be replaced, but clearly not until substitutes are found—substitutes that are proven more reliable, more versatile, and more cost-competitive than oil. We can rely on the energy marketplace to determine what the most efficient substitutes will be.

As we plan for our energy future, we also cannot afford to ignore the lessons of recent history. In the early 1970s, many energy policymakers were sure that oil and natural gas would soon be exhausted, and government policy was explicitly aimed at "guiding" the market in a smooth transition away from these fuels to new, more sustainable alternatives. Price controls, allocation schemes, limitations on natural gas, massive subsidies to synthetic fuels, and other measures were funded heavily and implemented.

Unfortunately, the key premises on which these programs were based, namely that oil was nearing exhaustion and that government guidance was desirable to safely transition to new energy sources, are now recognized as having been clearly wrong—and to have resulted in enormously expensive mistakes.

Looking into the distant future, there will be a day when oil is no longer the world's dominant energy source. We can only speculate as to when and how that day will come about. For example, there is an even bigger hydrocarbon resource that can be developed to provide nearly endless amounts of energy: methane hydrates (methane frozen in ice crystals). The deposits of methane hydrates are so vast that when we develop the technology to bring them to market, we will have clean-burning energy for 2,000 years. It's just one of the exciting scenarios we may see in the far-off future. But we won't be getting there anytime soon, and until we do, the Age of Oil will continue.

RED CAVANEY has served as president and chief executive officer of the American Petroleum Institute. He was president, chief executive officer, and a director of the American Plastics Council from 1994 to 1997, immediately following service as president of the American Forest & Paper Association and president of its predecessor, the American Paper Institute. He is a past chairman of the American Society of Association Executives and the current chairman of the American Council on Capital Formation.

James Howard Kunstler

 **NO**

The Long Emergency

A few weeks ago, the price of oil ratcheted above fifty-five dollars a barrel, which is about twenty dollars a barrel more than a year ago. The next day, the oil story was buried on page six of the *New York Times* business section. Apparently, the price of oil is not considered significant news, even when it goes up five bucks a barrel in the span of ten days. That same day, the stock market shot up more than a hundred points because, CNN said, government data showed no signs of inflation. Note to clueless nation: Call planet Earth.

Carl Jung, one of the fathers of psychology, famously remarked that "people cannot stand too much reality." What you're about to read may challenge your assumptions about the kind of world we live in, and especially the kind of world into which events are propelling us. We are in for a rough ride through uncharted territory.

It has been very hard for Americans—lost in dark raptures of nonstop infotainment, recreational shopping and compulsive motoring—to make sense of the gathering forces that will fundamentally alter the terms of everyday life in our technological society. Even after the terrorist attacks of 9/11, America is still sleepwalking into the future. I call this coming time the Long Emergency.

Most immediately we face the end of the cheap-fossil-fuel era. It is no exaggeration to state that reliable supplies of cheap oil and natural gas underlie everything we identify as the necessities of modern life—not to mention all of its comforts and luxuries: central heating, air conditioning, cars, airplanes, electric lights, inexpensive clothing, recorded music, movies, hip-replacement surgery, national defense—you name it.

The few Americans who are even aware that there is a gathering global-energy predicament usually misunderstand the core of the argument. That argument states that we don't have to run out of oil to start having severe problems with industrial civilization and its dependent systems. We only have to slip over the all-time production peak and begin a slide down the arc of steady depletion.

The term "global oil-production peak" means that a turning point will come when the world produces the most oil it will ever produce in a given year and, after that, yearly production will inexorably decline. It is usually represented graphically in a bell curve. The peak is the top of the curve, the halfway point of the world's all-time total endowment, meaning half the world's oil will be left. That seems like a lot of oil, and it is, but there's a big catch: It's the half that is much more difficult to extract, far more costly to get, of much poorer quality and located mostly in places where the people hate us. A substantial amount of it will never be extracted.

The United States passed its own oil peak—about 11 million barrels a day—in 1970, and since then production has dropped steadily. In 2004 it ran just above 5 million barrels a day (we get a tad more from natural-gas condensates). Yet we consume roughly 20 million barrels a day now. That means we have to import about two-thirds of our oil, and the ratio will continue to worsen.

The U.S. peak in 1970 brought on a portentous change in geoeconomic power. Within a few years, foreign producers, chiefly OPEC, were setting the price of oil, and this in turn led to the oil crises of the 1970s. In response, frantic development of non-OPEC oil, especially the North Sea fields of England and Norway, essentially saved the West's ass for about two decades. Since 1999, these fields have entered depletion. Meanwhile, worldwide discovery of new oil has steadily declined to insignificant levels in 2003 and 2004.

Some "cornucopians" claim that the Earth has something like a creamy nougat center of "abiotic" oil that will naturally replenish the great oil fields of the world. The facts speak differently. There has been no replacement whatsoever of oil already extracted from the fields of America or any other place.

Now we are faced with the global oil-production peak. The best estimates of when this will actually happen have been somewhere between now and 2010. In 2004, however, after demand from burgeoning China and India shot up, and revelations that Shell Oil wildly misstated its reserves, and Saudi Arabia proved incapable of goosing up its production despite promises to do so, the most knowledgeable experts revised their predictions and now concur that 2005 is apt to be the year of all-time global peak production.

It will change everything about how we live.

To aggravate matters, American natural-gas production is also declining, at five percent a year, despite frenetic new drilling, and with the potential of much steeper declines ahead. Because of the oil crises of the 1970s, the nuclear plant disasters at Three Mile Island and Chernobyl and the acid-rain problem, the U.S. chose to make gas its first choice for electric-power generation. The result was that just about every power plant built after 1980 has to run on gas. Half the homes in America are heated with gas. To further complicate matters, gas isn't easy to import. Here in North America, it is distributed through a vast pipeline network. Gas imported from overseas would have to be compressed at minus-260 degrees Fahrenheit in pressurized tanker ships and unloaded (re-gasified) at special terminals, of which few exist in America. Moreover, the first attempts to site new terminals have met furious opposition because they are such ripe targets for terrorism.

Some other things about the global energy predicament are poorly understood by the public and even our leaders. This is going to be a permanent energy crisis, and these energy problems will synergize with the disruptions of climate change, epidemic disease and population overshoot to produce higher orders of trouble.

We will have to accommodate ourselves to fundamentally changed conditions.

No combination of alternative fuels will allow us to run American life the way we have been used to running it, or even a substantial fraction of it. The wonders of steady technological progress achieved through the reign of cheap oil have lulled us into a kind of Jiminy Cricket syndrome, leading many Americans to believe that anything we wish for hard enough will come true. These days, even people who ought to know better are wishing ardently for a seamless transition from fossil fuels to their putative replacements.

The widely touted "hydrogen economy" is a particularly cruel hoax. We are not going to replace the U.S. automobile and truck fleet with vehicles run on fuel cells. For one thing, the current generation of fuel cells is largely designed to run on hydrogen obtained from natural gas. The other way to get hydrogen in the quantities wished for would be electrolysis of water using power from hundreds of nuclear plants. Apart from the dim prospect of

our building that many nuclear plants soon enough, there are also numerous severe problems with hydrogen's nature as an element that present forbidding obstacles to its use as a replacement for oil and gas, especially in storage and transport.

Wishful notions about rescuing our way of life with "renewables" are also unrealistic. Solar-electric systems and wind turbines face not only the enormous problem of scale but the fact that the components require substantial amounts of energy to manufacture and the probability that they can't be manufactured at all without the underlying support platform of a fossil-fuel economy. We will surely use solar and wind technology to generate some electricity for a period ahead but probably at a very local and small scale.

Virtually all "biomass" schemes for using plants to create liquid fuels cannot be scaled up to even a fraction of the level at which things are currently run. What's more, these schemes are predicated on using oil and gas "inputs" (fertilizers, weed-killers) to grow the biomass crops that would be converted into ethanol or bio-diesel fuels. This is a net energy loser—you might as well just burn the inputs and not bother with the biomass products. Proposals to distill trash and waste into oil by means of thermal depolymerization depend on the huge waste stream produced by a cheap oil and gas economy in the first place.

Coal is far less versatile than oil and gas, extant in less abundant supplies than many people assume and fraught with huge ecological drawbacks—as a contributor to greenhouse "global warming" gases and many health and toxicity issues ranging from widespread mercury poisoning to acid rain. You can make synthetic oil from coal, but the only time this was tried on a large scale was by the Nazis under wartime conditions, using impressive amounts of slave labor.

If we wish to keep the lights on in America after 2020, we may indeed have to resort to nuclear power, with all its practical problems and eco-conundrums. Under optimal conditions, it could take ten years to get a new generation of nuclear power plants into operation, and the price may be beyond our means. Uranium is also a resource in finite supply. We are no closer to the more difficult project of atomic fusion, by the way, than we were in the 1970s.

The Long Emergency is going to be a tremendous trauma for the human race. We will not believe that this is happening to us, that 200 years of modernity can be brought to its knees by a world-wide power shortage. The survivors will have to cultivate a religion of hope—that is, a deep and comprehensive belief that humanity is worth carrying on. If there is any positive side to stark changes coming our way, it may be in the benefits of close communal relations, of having to really work intimately (and physically) with our neighbors, to be part of an enterprise that really matters and to be fully engaged in meaningful social enactments instead of being merely entertained to avoid boredom. Years from now, when we hear singing at all, we will hear ourselves, and we will sing with our whole hearts.

JAMES HOWARD KUNSTLER is best known for his books *The Geography of Nowhere* (1994), a history of American suburbia and urban development, and the more recent *The Long Emergency* (2005). He has written a science fiction novel describing a future culture, *World Made by Hand* (2008). He is a leading proponent of the movement known as "New Urbanism." He has also written *Home from Nowhere* and *The City in Mind*.

EXPLORING THE ISSUE

Should the World Continue to Rely on Oil as a Major Source of Energy?

Critical Thinking and Reflection

1. What distinguishes oil as the most important source of energy? Can our perceptions be changed on this matter?
2. What impact would legislation that promotes independence from oil have on domestic economic growth and development?
3. Is it possible to move to alternative energy forms before the supply of oil diminishes too significantly?
4. Describe some public policies that could promote energy security for the United States as well as other countries. Discuss some different strategies for energy consumption utilized in other countries.

Is There Common Ground?

Twixt the optimist and the pessimist, the difference is droll: the optimist sees the donut, and the pessimist sees the hole" (Anonymous). The selections you have just finished represent the optimistic and the pessimistic sides of the "oil reserves conflict" as we know it. There is more to this subject. We might ask the optimist if the availability of oil is really at the heart of this consumption of oil just to save the earth, now, even if oil supplies are abundant? But there is a question for the pessimist, too: Granted that our "lifestyles" this minute require lots of oil, does our happiness depend on it too? What would it be like to live in a way that consumes lots less oil because it consumes lots less of any kind of energy? Outside of the field of business ethics (and sometimes inside it, too) explorations into the notions of "simplicity" and "the simple life" continue. The less consumption-oriented life suggested in these explorations does not seem to be significantly lower in quality than our own—in many ways, it seems better. Should some ambitious entrepreneurs be looking into these possibilities, as the wave of America's economic future?

Recent events may make partial changes in our views. On April 20, 2010, the Deepwater Horizon exploded, raising new questions, for at least a few months. The explosion resulted in a massive offshore oil spill in the Gulf of Mexico close to the Louisiana coast. The Deepwater Horizon was a semisubmersible mobile offshore drilling unit that was owned and operated by Transocean and was drilling for BP in the Macondo Prospect oil field. The explosion killed 11 employees and injured 16 others. Offshore drilling is a strong economic and political issue in the United States. A freeze was placed on all new wells shortly after the disaster. The freeze has since been lifted, and offshore drilling continues.

Additional Resources

Thomas Friedman, "Having No Oil May Yield the Best Resource," *New York Times* (March 12, 2012).

Paul Hawken, Amory B. Lovins, and L. Hunter Lovins, *Natural Capitalism: Creating the Next Industrial Revolution* (New York: Little, Brown, 1999).

Lisa Newton, *Ethics and Sustainability* (New York: Prentice Hall, 2002).

Lisa Newton, *Business Ethics and the Natural Environment* (Hoboken, NJ: John Wiley & Sons, Incorporated, 2005).

Lisa Newton, *Business Ethics and the Natural Environment* (Blackwood, NY: Blackwell Publishers, 2005).

Internet References . . .

"BMP Projects," Intermountain Oil and Gas

www.oilandgasbmps.org/resources/index.php

"Gran Tests 3,095 Bopd with Peru Horizontal Well [Gulf Oil & Gas Egypt]," Global Financial Network

www.equities.com/news/headline-story?dt=2013-05-29&val=1454329&cat=energy

Stephen Ko, "Oil and Gas Drilling and Exploration"

www.twst.com/interview/6065

"Where Are Oil and Gas Resources Found?" Oil and Gas Resources in the U.S. Tribal Energy and Environmental Information

http://teeic.anl.gov/er/oilgas/restech/dist/index.htm

Selected, Edited, and with Issue Framing Material by:
Gina Vega, *Organizational Ergonomics*

ISSUE

Is the Foreign Corrupt Practices Act Obsolete?

YES: Joseph W. Yockey, from "Choosing Governance in the FCPA Reform Debate," *Journal of Corporation Law* (2013)

NO: Peter J. Henning, from "Taking Aim at the Foreign Corrupt Practices Act," *New York Times* (2012)

Learning Outcomes

After reading this issue, you will be able to:

- Discuss the impact the Foreign Corrupt Practices Act has had in the U.S. business world.
- Explain the difference between a focus on compliance with statutes and a focus on eradicating corruption.
- Explain why or why not bribery should be considered an unethical practice internationally.
- Determine if a U.S. law can be enforced globally.

ISSUE SUMMARY

YES: Joseph Yockey claims that ambiguity in the statute creates perpetual uncertainty about what constitutes an FCPA violation and that reform is needed urgently. New governance can replace the existing concerns about implementation of the FCPA.

NO: Peter Henning states that "business leaders have long contended that the law is overly broad and too aggressively enforced," but believes that "it does little good to charge someone when there is not a realistic prospect that the person can be brought to the United States."

The Foreign Corrupt Practices Act (FCPA) was passed in 1977 for two primary purposes: to ensure bribery could be contained in international business dealings with U.S. firms and to ensure transparency in accounting practices. This law makes it unlawful to make a payment to bribe foreign government officials to obtain or retain business or to direct business to any individual. FCPA requires the maintenance of detailed and accurate records of all transactions and the maintenance of internal accounting controls that identify any activities with third parties or intermediaries such as partners acting on behalf of a company. In order to avoid being held liable for third party misdeeds, companies must exercise due diligence to ensure that third parties are reputable and qualified partners, and that all are engaged in lawful transactions. The FCPA guidelines were expanded in 1988 to apply to foreign firms and persons who participate in corrupt payments while in the United States and again as the International Bribery Act of 1998.

Why the emphasis on bribery? Bribery is a way of life in many countries, so what is there about bribery that makes the United States so exercised? According to Cornell Law School, bribery is "[c]orrupt solicitation, acceptance, or transfer of value in exchange for official action. Bribery refers to the offering, giving, soliciting, or receiving of any item of value as a means of influencing the actions of an individual holding a public or legal duty. This type of action results in matters that should be handled objectively being handled in a manner best suiting the private interests of the decision maker" (https://www.law.cornell.edu/wex/bribery).

If that were the extent of the opposition to bribery, only dealings by U.S. companies would fall within the limitations of the law. However, in 2004, the United Nations added a 10th principle governing the behavior of its membership to its Global Compact. This 10th principle was about corruption (https://www.unglobalcompact.org /aboutthegc/thetenprinciples/principle10.html). The principle reads as follows: "The adoption of the tenth principle commits UN Global Compact participants not only to avoid bribery, extortion, and other forms of corruption, but also to develop policies and concrete programs to address corruption. Companies are challenged to join governments, UN agencies, and civil society to realize a more transparent global economy."

The three elements that provide guidance as to how members should implement the 10th principle:

- "Internal: As a first and basic step, introduce anticorruption policies and programs within their organizations and their business operations;
- External: Report on the work against corruption in the annual Communication on Progress; and share experiences and best practices through the submission of examples and case stories;
- Collective: Join forces with industry peers and with other stakeholders"

This provides some insight into the how and why of the United States' insistence on transparency and its anti-bribery stance. Of course, participation in the UN Global Compact is purely voluntary, and the compact does not include any legally enforceable restrictions. However, the U.S. Justice Department is committed to fighting corruption at all levels, and an international support group offers a sense of global community in this fight.

It would be too much to expect the global business community to be of one mind on this issue. There are many countries in the world for which bribery is a way of life, not a condemnable misdeed. According to Transparency International, one in four individuals have been involved in a bribery situation. Countries are scored on a scale of 0–10 (10 indicates that companies from that country never bribe abroad and 0 means they always do). Netherlands and Switzerland tied for first place (8.8) and Mexico, China, and Russia brought up the end of the list (7.0, 6.5, and 6.1, respectively). The United States placed squarely in the middle of all the countries, at 8.1, below the United Kingdom and above France.

Some nations maintain national legislation that covers areas similar to the FCPA, but clearly not all do. Even when the legislation is in place, it does not seem to make that much difference. Transparency International has called for nations to put in place anti-bribery legislation and step up enforcement of existing legislation to try to counter international corruption. This call is seconded by compliance organizations in the United States, such as the Society of Corporate Compliance and Ethics, the Ethics and Compliance Association, the Association of Trade and Compliance Professionals, and other similarly named organizations including the publishers of *Compliance Week,* a widely read trade magazine for the growing compliance industry. But the bottleneck always seems to end up at the compliance issue.

In countries where there is little to no rule of law, such as Russia, or with limited rule of law, such as China, compliance is irrelevant. In countries with emerging economies, such as those in Africa which correspondent collectively to the lower scoring countries in the Bribe Payer's Index, compliance is less important than "doing business." Laws without teeth and general recommendations of "good corporate behavior" according to Western democratic standards may have little influence in countries that operate from a different political, economic, and social perspective.

In the YES selection, Joseph Yockey bemoans the fact that the purpose of FCPA seems to be more a matter of compliance and enforcement than one of moral positioning. Legality and morality or social responsibility are not interchangeable terms. When most of the cases brought to the Justice Department result in fines, the sanctions can easily become a cost of doing business. In addition, it generally takes a long time to surface evidence of corruption and bribery, and the statute of limitations can be run out. Without a means of enforcing international law, there is little hope for FCPA.

In the NO selection, Peter Henning claims that the FCPA is still needed and can be strengthened and made viable if we bring acts of corruption to the public attention. However, such attention may limit Congressional action for political reasons, if not ethical ones.

YES

Joseph W. Yockey

Choosing Governance in the FCPA
Reform Debate

Introduction

Corruption is a disease that cannot be cured, only managed. While most agree on this basic point, there is considerable debate about the proper course of treatment. The United States' weapon of choice for combating transnational commercial bribery—the type of corruption under consideration here—is the Foreign Corrupt Practices Act (FCPA).[1] Mostly dormant for its first 25 years, the FCPA is now in the midst of an unprecedented surge in enforcement. More firms are coming under FCPA scrutiny, including several of the largest and most well-known companies in the world, and large criminal and civil sanctions are common.

The rise in enforcement places FCPA compliance at the forefront of any board's agenda. It has also led to an increasingly impassioned debate about the wisdom and viability of FCPA reform. On one side of the debate are critics who claim that ambiguity in the statute creates perpetual uncertainty about what constitutes an FCPA violation.[2] They suggest this problem is compounded by fears of indictment that make it practically impossible for firms to challenge aggressive theories of FCPA liability in court. As a result, advocates for reform maintain that firms are forced to settle FCPA cases prematurely—often for sums that go beyond what is necessary for deterrence—and to overspend on internal compliance programs. . . .

Arguably the most useful aspect of the current debate is that it highlights the limitations of a regulatory model that relies primarily on the threat of sanctions to deter wrongdoing. For one, the same resource limitations and low detection rates that lead regulators to rely on negotiated settlements suggest that, instead of overdeterrence, the current model creates a risk of underdeterrence. This might explain why so many observers in the international community believe that transnational bribery remains a significant problem despite the greater emphasis on enforcement in recent years.[3]

A second problem is more nuanced. An increasing number of firms committed to ethical behavior are less interested in arguing about potential statutory changes and are more focused on making FCPA compliance part of their long-term strategies for risk management.[4] Yet, the current enforcement environment—where negotiated settlements are the norm—encourages these firms to lean primarily on compliance strategies that they can defend later should they happen to come under federal scrutiny. This is worrisome because regulators often lack the resources and expertise necessary to gain context-specific knowledge about how risk manifests itself in different firms. As a result, rather than working to craft innovative compliance solutions capable of responding to the dynamic nature of corruption, compliance efforts will likely devolve into static, one-size-fits-all programs designed to check the boxes that regulators look for.[5]

A final problem with the current FCPA reform debate is that it fails to adequately consider the effects of international enforcement activities on domestic compliance efforts. The United States has been quite successful in convincing other countries to adopt FCPA-like legislation, but enforcement has not always followed adoption. Thus, a lingering concern is that gaps in multilateral enforcement will divert business opportunities to firms from countries that are unreachable by the FCPA or its international counterparts. This raises the possibility that at least some American firms will feel compelled to resort to bribery if they fear that doing otherwise will allow foreign competitors to take their place.[6]

To address these problems, we argue that the time has come to take a step back in order to reorient the reform debate towards greater reliance on regulatory strategies that fall within the category of new governance. Among other things, the public–private collaboration that new governance envisions will facilitate the pooling of information necessary to provide firms with a more

Yockey, Joseph W., "Choosing Governance in the FCPA Reform Debate," *Journal of Corporation Law* 38 (325) January 16, 2013 pp. 326–378.

substantive understanding of anti-corruption norms and industry "best practices" for compliance. This is necessary to internalize good habits within the belly of a firm, which in turn plays a critical role in mitigating the resource and monitoring challenges faced by regulators. . . .

The Reform Debate

Rise in FCPA Enforcement Activity

Congress adopted the FCPA in 1977 as an amendment to the 1934 Securities Exchange Act.[7] It consists of two central parts. First, a series of anti-bribery provisions prohibit the act of "corruptly" making "an offer, payment, promise to pay, or authorization of the payment of any money" to "any foreign official for purposes of . . . obtaining or retaining business."[8] This prohibition applies to U.S. issuers, "domestic concerns," and "any person other than an issuer . . . or a domestic concern" who acts while in U.S. territory.[9] Second, it requires issuers to implement various accounting measures meant to assist with anti-bribery compliance efforts. They must "make and keep books, records, and accounts, which, in reasonable detail, accurately and fairly reflect the transactions and dispositions of the assets of the issuer."[10] The Department of Justice (DOJ) and Securities and Exchange Commission (SEC) both enforce the statute's anti-bribery provisions, whereas only the SEC enforces the accounting and internal control requirements.[11]

The reason FCPA reform is back on the map relates to a recent rise in enforcement activity. At first, enforcement was fairly lax. The statute's first 25 years saw just a handful of actions filed annually, often resulting in only modest sanctions. But if the FCPA was a proverbial "sleeping dog" then, today the dog is wide awake.[12] The DOJ now calls FCPA enforcement one of its highest priorities, second only to combating terrorism, and the past decade has given rise to a dramatic upsurge in enforcement activity.[13] Looking at just the number of individual companies charged with FCPA violations during the past ten years, the rate of enforcement increased slightly between 2002 and 2006 before nearly tripling between 2007 and 2011.[14] Sources estimate that the number of FCPA investigations currently pending is between 120 and 150.[15] Enforcement activity continues to target both domestic and foreign firms,[16] as well as individual agents retained by those firms.

Several reasons may explain the increase in enforcement activity. Part of the story concerns globalization. In the time since the FCPA's passage, State Department officials gradually began to place more emphasis on the need for vigorous anti-corruption enforcement to "nurture stability in democratic institutions and strengthen the rule of law in transitional economies."[17] This position emerged as more firms of all sizes began to seek business opportunities abroad, including in many promising new markets where bribery is endemic. Other possible explanations relate to greater international cooperation with anti-corruption enforcement, as well as regulatory developments like the enactment of the Sarbanes–Oxley Act in 2002[18] and the passage of the Dodd–Frank Wall Street Reform and Consumer Protection Act in 2010.[19]

There has also been a recent shift in investigatory resources and tactics. The Federal Bureau of Investigation (FBI) now maintains an FCPA-specific unit consisting of eight full-time FBI agents. A dedicated group of 20 Assistant U.S. Attorneys in Washington, D.C. handles nearly every FCPA prosecution brought by the DOJ.[20] The SEC, too, recently created its own specialized unit tasked with civil FCPA enforcement.[21] Among other strategies, enforcement personnel now focus their attention on specific industry segments, where the targeting of one firm in a particular industry (e.g., pharmaceutical or extraction) often leads to evidence that affiliated firms are involved in the same underlying bribery scheme.[22] In addition, prosecutors continue to bring tools to bear on FCPA matters that were traditionally reserved for organized crime and drug cases.[23] For example, the first undercover "sting" in an FCPA case came in 2010 and led to the arrests of 22 executives in the arms industry.[24] The operation—which one commentator analogized to a Hollywood crime thriller—involved the use of a cooperating witness, the seizure of evidence in multiple states and two different countries, and widespread collaboration among several domestic and international law enforcement agencies.[25]

Criticisms and Calls for Reform

The rise in FCPA enforcement activity has had several effects. For one, it has moved FCPA compliance to the forefront of most boards' agendas and spawned an "industry" of specialized FCPA defense counsel, consultants, and forensic accountants.[26] It has also led many influential members of the business community to push for reform.

Enforcement Practices

The reform movement has less to do with the FCPA's purpose—deterring foreign corruption—and more to do with how the statute is enforced. Specifically, the FCPA's critics maintain a narrative of overenforcement. They argue that the law is vague, over-broad, and often leads to confusion about what is legal and what is illegal. To take one example, critics make much of the fact that the FCPA's definition of "foreign official" includes "any officer or employee of a foreign government or any . . .

instrumentality thereof."[27] Concerns arise because the statute does not define the term "instrumentality," and some experienced attorneys and managers claim that they have a hard time figuring out who or what comes within its scope.[28] Critics suggest that problems with ambiguity in the statute are compounded by the fact that fears of the negative consequences of indictment or conviction make it practically impossible for firms to challenge aggressive theories of liability in court.

Unpacking these issues requires first taking a look at how a typical FCPA case is resolved. When regulators come into contact with a firm suspected of a possible FCPA violation—either after an independent investigation or through voluntary self-disclosure—they have considerable discretion on what to do next. Internal policy guidelines suggest that their ultimate enforcement decisions should follow from the balancing of several factors: (1) the target's cooperation in the investigation; (2) the existence and perceived adequacy of the target's internal compliance and ethics program; (3) the extent of the harm associated with the wrongdoing; and (4) the pervasiveness of the wrongdoing within the organization.[29] Ostensibly, this means that enforcers could weigh these factors and elect to prosecute a firm or its agents. Practically speaking, though, settlement is the norm in FCPA cases.

A good example of how this plays out is the case of Siemens AG. In 2008, Siemens, a German conglomerate, and three of its subsidiaries pleaded guilty to FCPA-related charges and agreed to pay $1.6 billion in sanctions in what still sets the mark for the largest settlement in FCPA history.[30] According to prosecutors, starting in the mid-1990s, Siemens paid over $1.4 billion in bribes to officials in 65 countries across Europe, Asia, Africa, the Americas, and the Middle East—including $1.7 million in kickbacks to the Iraqi government as part of the United Nation's Oil-for-Food Program.[31]

The sequence of events leading to the discovery of Siemens's questionable payments involved actions by regulators in the United States, Germany, Switzerland, Austria, and Italy.[32] The DOJ and SEC worked especially closely with the Munich Public Prosecutor's office, sharing information and evidence in a cooperative process facilitated by provisions for mutual legal assistance contained in the 1997 Organization for Economic Cooperation and Development (OECD) Convention on Combating Bribery of Foreign Public Officials in International Business.[33] For its part, Siemens spent over $950 million on an internal investigation into the allegations of wrongdoing, later sharing what it learned with the U.S. and German governments.[34] This cooperation, which also included taking disciplinary action against individual employees,

helped persuade regulators to reduce the total sanction level under the company's plea deal.[35] By pleading guilty, Siemens paid approximately $800 million to U.S. authorities and $800 million to German authorities.[36] Had the matter resulted in a conviction at trial, the applicable U.S. Sentencing Guideline range placed Siemens's potential exposure between $1.35 and $2.7 billion.[37]

In another notable development, Siemens consented to several corporate governance reforms as part of its plea agreement. The company agreed to retain an independent compliance monitor for a four-year period to oversee the implementation of a new internal compliance and ethics program and to make continuous progress reports to the DOJ.[38] Siemens also agreed to continue its cooperation with additional ongoing investigations into potentially illegal payments.[39] This cooperation played a crucial role in the DOJ's indictment of eight former Siemens executives and agents in December 2011 on charges of bribery and money laundering.[40]

The settlement structure described above is now common in FCPA cases. A clear majority of all FCPA investigations are resolved either through plea agreements or, even more frequently, through deferred prosecution or non-prosecution agreements (DPAs or NPAs). According to data collected by the OECD, the average annual number of DPAs and NPAs rose from fewer than five per year in 2004 to over 20 per year in 2010 (with a high of 38 in 2007).[41] With respect to FCPA matters specifically, the DOJ used DPAs and NPAs in resolving approximately 77% of all actions initiated between 2004–10.[42] This percentage rose to 82% in 2011, and so far in 2012 *every* corporate FCPA enforcement action has been resolved via DPA or NPA.[43]

Because the parties in the *Siemens* case reached a plea agreement, it led to an actual conviction in addition to the company's agreement to implement governance reforms and help with further investigations. DPAs usually require the same types of reforms but differ from pleas in that they resemble a form of probation. The government files charges but agrees to suspend them as long as a firm agrees to do the types of things that Siemens agreed to do (e.g., disgorge profits, retain an independent compliance monitor, and cooperate in the government's underlying investigation).[44] If the firm complies with its obligations under the agreement, the prosecution will eventually dismiss the charges, usually between two to three years later.[45] DPAs also typically require firms to fully admit facts that establish their wrongdoing, meaning that firms must carry out their part of the bargain or risk near-certain conviction at trial.[46] NPAs are similar to DPAs but do not involve a formal court filing. Instead, prosecutors reserve the right to file charges but refrain from doing so if the firm maintains compliance with the same requirements usually included in a plea agreement or DPA.[47]

Overenforcement?

The trend toward using DPAs or NPAs to resolve cases is not without controversy. In the FCPA context, these devices play a key role in the over enforcement narrative put forward by the statute's critics. Why? Because most firms appear reluctant to litigate claims under the FCPA. This is generally explained by the leverage that regulators hold to drive cases toward settlement.[48] Many firms claim that the negative collateral consequences of indictment or conviction would be disastrous. Firms can suffer tremendous harm to their reputation just from being thought of as "criminal"—even as early as the investigatory stage.[49] Firms in some regulated industries could also lose their licenses or permits to operate, and others could become ineligible to receive U.S. or foreign government contracts or funds from international finance sources.[50] Less visible harms include challenges with recruiting well-qualified employees and maintaining good relationships with existing suppliers or customers. The risk of separate civil shareholder class-action suits underscores all of these concerns.

The other primary driver of settlement is the broad standard of liability in cases of corporate crime. As long as an employee acts within the scope of employment and is motivated to serve the interests of her firm, the legal principle of respondeat superior mandates that a corporation is vicariously liable for the employee's wrongdoing.[51] This is true even where the employee violates express instructions or existing compliance requirements. Given that agency costs are never zero and no company can ensure a perfect compliance record, the specter of respondeat superior liability tends to provide enforcers with considerable bargaining power during settlement negotiations.

To advocates for FCPA reform, all of this adds up to a worrying state of affairs. A common criticism is that federal authorities serve as both "prosecutor and judge" and are effectively using firms' willingness to settle as a means to control the outcome of every FCPA case they initiate.[52] Even though most cooperating firms end up paying fines below those called for by the Federal Organizational Sentencing Guidelines,[53] critics argue that it is problematic for defendants to feel coerced to settle without challenging prosecutorial theories of liability in court.[54]

This concern is usually framed in terms of over enforcement. For example, one argument is that the benefits of cooperation often appear illusory, with the high costs of settling going beyond what is necessary for deterrence. There are several examples where firms paid jaw-dropping sums to settle FCPA-related charges despite providing extensive cooperation.[55] Total criminal and civil sanctions imposed on corporations in FCPA matters since 2008 amount to over $3.5 billion—a figure that does not include related expenditures on internal investigations or government-mandated corporate governance reforms.[56] And these latter amounts can be quite large. Anecdotes abound where firms pay millions to outside counsel as part of their cooperation with authorities, followed by millions more in fines and the expense of hiring a government-mandated compliance monitor as part of a settlement.[57] Thus, the $950 million that Siemens spent on its internal investigation[58] is cited alongside the $150 million Avon has currently spent investigating *possible* FCPA misconduct in China—a figure that may grow following the imposition of sanctions after the company shares the results of its investigation with authorities.[59] These examples lead some FCPA practitioners to wonder "how much worse [firms] would be if they didn't self-report or cooperated only if they got caught."[60]

Efforts to avoid fines and other expenditures can lead to several related problems. If firms cannot realistically challenge prosecutors' interpretation of ambiguous provisions in the FCPA due to the fear of collateral consequences, then the resulting unpredictability in enforcement may cause their agents to become overly risk averse, or it could lead firms to avoid certain markets altogether. A recent Dow Jones survey found that 51% of companies have delayed, and 14% have cancelled, business ventures abroad due to uncertainty over FCPA enforcement.[61] Lack of predictable statutory interpretation can also raise the costs of developing and implementing internal compliance programs, and firms may end up devoting time and resources to monitoring efforts that exceed socially optimal levels. Arguably the most vocal FCPA reform advocate, the U.S. Chamber of Commerce (the Chamber), sums up this argument as follows:

> The result of [current FCPA enforcement policy] has been a chilling effect on legitimate business activity (as companies perceive a real risk of prosecution even in scenarios involving only the most remote and attenuated connection to foreign governments) and a costly misallocation of compliance resources (as companies dedicate resources to policing and investigating even such remote and attenuated situations).[62]

These concerns have not fallen on deaf ears. Vigorous lobbying efforts by prominent corporate advocacy groups continue to gain traction among congressional leaders.[63] In just a three-month period at the end of 2011, the Chamber reportedly spent $400,000 on external lobbyists and $5.6 million on an internal team as part of its push for reform.[64] Though no draft legislation has yet to emerge, there appears to be strong bipartisan support for some type of FCPA reform.[65] The DOJ and SEC recently provided 130 pages of new regulatory guidance, but critics want more.[66] Critics hope Congress will take steps like amending the statute to clarify various provisions or to add a defense to liability based on the existence of an "effective" compliance program. . . .

Risk of Underdeterrence

The first issue that the current enforcement model raises is the risk that, if corruption is not being overly deterred, it is being underdeterred. As we have seen, the current sanction-based approach to FCPA enforcement requires the state to make significant investments in monitoring and detection in order to enforce compliance.[67] The strain that this places on regulatory capacity helps explain the reliance on firm self-disclosure and cooperation. But this dynamic also signals a potential paradox in present FCPA enforcement. As anti-corruption enforcement becomes a higher priority, there is a risk that regulators will focus on bringing smaller, easier actions that they can be sure of settling in order to demonstrate a high enforcement volume—or that they will settle cases against larger firms capable of mounting a defense for only minimal amounts.[68]

To take the DOJ as an example, a staff of 20 prosecutors likely cannot afford the time and risk associated with prosecuting every large firm suspected of wrongdoing. Thus, for every case like *Siemens*, prosecutors may devote the bulk of their energy and resources to pursuing firms that self-report or are less able to mount a vigorous defense. This strategy would be rational for an enforcer that needs to point to a vigorous enforcement record to back up a strong public commitment to fighting corruption.[69] However, if the expense of pursuing firms is too great for regulators with limited resources, they could end up imposing sanctions through settlement that are too low to sufficiently deter wrongdoing. These circumstances likely explain why so many NGOs and other actors in the international community believe that transnational bribery remains a significant problem despite greater attention to enforcement compared to years past.[70] They also undercut the values at the heart of the FCPA and raise questions about the United States' reputation in the international community as a pioneer in spreading anti-corruption norms.

One way to bypass these issues might be to legislate for more severe sanctions in FCPA cases. However, as to enforcement, we are concerned with not only finding the correct level of deterrence, but also the costs to society of enforcing the rule designed to do the deterring. With many criminal statutes, the costs of enforcement consist mainly of the costs of paying for prosecutors, prisons, police, and courts. With respect to the FCPA, though, there is another set of significant costs: the costs incurred by companies to establish internal compliance systems. If sanctions are set too high, there could become a point where the total costs of enforcing the statute—including compliance costs—become socially inefficient as they are passed on to consumers and other end-users of a firm's products or services.[71]

Still another option would be for regulators to devote more energy to prosecuting individual wrongdoers within a firm. At bottom, employees who commit FCPA violations typify the agency cost issue that affects all firms. But many FCPA settlements simply require firms to pay a fine and make various internal governance reforms. As long as bribery is profitable and sanctions are borne primarily at the entity level, managers have little incentive to try to stop it.[72] This is especially true if the results of bribery provide them with career advancement or other personal benefits.[73] Prosecuting the individuals responsible for committing bribery—or those who failed to make a good faith effort to monitor the bribe payers—is one way to counteract the principal-agent problem.[74] As Miriam Baer observes:

> Most corporate chieftains would prefer to avoid fines. But all are horrified by the thought of jail and the prospect of being publicly labeled a criminal. . . . [P]unishment [also] improves compliance . . . [because it] reassures the employees and officers who are inclined not to break rules that we will hold accountable those who do. Punishment signals to law-abiding employees that the trust they have placed in others is reasonable and likely to be reciprocated.[75]

The trouble here is in proportioning blame appropriately. It is extraordinarily difficult to structure sanctions in a way that accurately captures the culpability of responsible parties. This difficulty follows from the organizational complexities inherent in modern corporations that make it challenging to assess internal behavior.[76] Even if these obstacles could be overcome and the "right" people are held accountable, the question remains whether subsequent managers or agents will be sufficiently deterred.[77] This concern highlights the importance of corporate culture. While it is true that FCPA violations can be viewed as part of a corporate principal-agent problem, they are not always the product of rogue individual agents. Prosecuting individual wrongdoers can only go so far in producing sweeping reform in companies where violations stem from issues of organizational culture and practices.[78] Cristie Ford and David Hess cite empirical studies showing that a majority of employees believe that "organizational factors"—such as pressure to meet performance targets or the disregard of internal corporate codes—are more to blame for firm misconduct than employee self-interest.[79] For this reason, many scholars believe that "corporate criminal enforcement ought to focus above all on genuine *institutional* production of wrongdoing," where placing "blame at the institutional rather than individual level is most justified and most likely to send useful messages about how institutions ought to arrange themselves so as not to produce lawbreaking."[80]. . .

For firms that strive to be law-abiding, the issue then becomes how to structure their compliance efforts to minimize the chance of wrongdoing. This is often easier said than done. Corruption comes in many forms and rarely remains static. Corrupt negotiations may occur between low-level government workers and low-level firm employees, or between high-ranking government officials and members of a firm's executive suite. Different markets and industries also present different risks. While commercial participants in some countries see bribes as simply a cost of doing business, in others the request for payment often rises to the level of extortion.[81] Unique cultural norms and business practices can further blur the lines between innocuous gift giving and illegal kickbacks.[82]

Firms also are not immune to the monitoring difficulties that frequently bamboozle law enforcement. Transnational bribery often occurs in secret and remote locations. A company's ability to monitor is extremely limited in these circumstances. This concern is compounded by firms' frequent reliance on foreign agents and intermediaries (a legal requirement in some countries) because these actors operate at the periphery of regular corporate activities and have a variety of tools available for hiding illegal payments.[83] Some foreign officials have even gone so far as to help agents hide their tracks by channeling bribes disguised as fees or commissions through specially created shell entities.[84] Similarly, direct quid pro quo transactions often give way to indirect payments to foundations or educational institutions that mask the specific personal benefit enjoyed by a foreign public official or her relatives.[85] These issues affect firms of all sizes, but can be particularly difficult for small- and medium-sized entities to handle given their frequent lack of resources and expertise. Managers may respond by threatening heavier penalties on agents who participate in bribery, but that only raises the additional danger they will become overly risk averse or will demand too great a risk premium for their services.[86]

It follows, then, that one of the greatest barriers to implementing meaningful compliance measures is not cost or willingness; it is overcoming unique risk assessment and monitoring challenges that arise under the circumstances of each firm. However, one danger posed by the current enforcement climate is that it encourages firms to focus primarily on compliance strategies they can defend later should they happen to come under investigation. This has serious drawbacks. Regulators often lack the resources or expertise necessary to gain context-specific knowledge about how risk manifests itself in different firms.[87] Thus, when crafting structural reform aspects during negotiations over a DPA or NPA, this leads them to generate static, uniform rules that fail to account for the myriad business and compliance variables that firms confront on a daily basis.[88] Firms, in turn, may respond by implementing rigid compliance programs designed to "check the boxes" required by regulators regardless of whether they actually work to deter wrongdoing.[89] Rules and commands are rarely as effective in preventing internal misconduct as a system that hires for and seeks to reward and perpetuate a culture of compliance.[90] Moreover, any lack of experimentation also hinders efforts at developing the type of robust compliance laboratory necessary to find new and innovative ways of mitigating the perpetual risk of corruption.[91]

These considerations call into question the wisdom of adding an express compliance defense to the FCPA—something that many FCPA reform advocates continue to request. Without more, a compliance defense, which would provide firms with a shield to liability if they can demonstrate the existence of an "effective" compliance program, is unlikely to produce meaningful organizational reform. First, employee wrongdoers faced with rigid internal monitoring programs may simply respond by investing more time and energy in detection avoidance.[92] Moreover, regulators or courts with incomplete knowledge and limited expertise would seemingly be charged with judging the effectiveness of each company's program. Thus, a worry is that the process necessary to administer a compliance defense would devolve into the same type of formalized programs outlined above that fail to mesh with the unique situations and risks faced by firms and their agents, while also overlooking the bigger picture of reforming corporate values and internal culture.[93]. . .

Advancing the Debate Through Governance

The concerns about FCPA enforcement identified in this Article do not lend themselves to easy answers, but they do suggest that whatever the FCPA reform discussion is about, at some point it must address the inherent limitations of a traditional regulatory approach that focuses primarily on the risk of sanction to spur compliance. As matters stand, both sides of the FCPA reform debate are largely talking past one another. Some firms likely remain undeterred by the present FCPA enforcement climate, whereas the risk and expense associated with even modest FCPA scrutiny can cause socially responsible firms to seek check-list solutions to compliance challenges that they (and regulators) often do not fully understand. This dynamic does not help firms that seek to remain law-abiding, nor does it help regulators operating with limited capacities find ways to reduce overall levels of bribery. . . .

The International Element

Solving the problem of lax international anti-bribery enforcement arguably poses a more difficult challenge than using governance to administer the FCPA because domestic actors lack control over many of the relevant variables. As we have seen, federal regulators can only do so much to pick up the slack of other signatories to the OECD Anti-Bribery Convention. Still, the application of new governance principles on the domestic front helps to identify ways to address international concerns. Anne-Marie Slaughter stresses that "[s]tates can only govern effectively by actively cooperating with other states."[94] On this point, efforts to promote multilateral collaboration continue to bear fruit. Transnational anti-corruption investigations inherently require international coordination, and U.S. regulators generally operate in an increasingly collaborative and collegial fashion with their international counterparts.[95] The United States Attorneys' Manual makes a point of emphasizing that FCPA investigations require documents and testimony from foreign sources.[96] Without the cooperation of foreign enforcement agencies, obtaining this evidence is almost impossible.

The need to address this issue has led to the creation of a robust set of transnational cooperative networks. The DOJ boasts being a part of approximately 60 mutual legal assistance treaties (MLATs) with foreign governments.[97] These bilateral agreements obligate signatories to provide assistance with ongoing investigations where possible. The DOJ reportedly made at least 25 MLAT requests during 2009.[98] Some countries refused to comply, but the DOJ says that it received the information requested in a majority of cases.[99] For its part, the SEC has signed dozens of memoranda of understanding (MOUs) with foreign securities regulators.[100] MOUs set out "'the terms of information-sharing between and among MOU signatories and create a framework for regular and predictable cooperation in securities law enforcement.'"[101] They are particularly useful in tracing funds spread among hidden foreign bank accounts.[102]

Multilateral collaboration is further facilitated through the OECD Working Group. Representatives of member states who attend Working Group meetings can share success stories about experiments to combat corrupt practices. For example, several countries have experienced success using privatized pre-shipment inspections to deter bribery in customs, and others report positive results through the implementation of online procurement systems.[103] In addition, a large part of the Working Group's agenda is based on helping prosecutors from ratifying states to exchange information and build up feelings of trust.[104] This is an area where greater collaboration between U.S. regulators and firms can facilitate international enforcement. Bribery involves both supply and demand. The supply comes when firms pay bribes; the demand comes when foreign officials solicit and receive bribes. So far this Article has focused mainly on issues of compliance on the supply side. But as firms provide information to the DOJ or SEC about where and in what form bribe requests are made, federal authorities can share that information with their foreign counterparts to bolster domestic enforcement efforts on the demand side. This should ameliorate the resource limitations in some countries by lessening the burden of detection.

Of course, collaboration will prove to be of little use if it is not supported by efforts within each country to reduce corruption. This is where the Working Group's final key function comes into play: external monitoring. The Working Group relies on a process of peer review with multiple layers to encourage compliance.[105] First, experts from governments other than the one under review visit the subject country to meet with prosecutors, members of private industry and the private bar, and representatives from civil society groups.[106] Based on the information collected, the Working Group then compiles three "phased" reports. Phase I reviews the adequacy of the country's legislation implementing the OECD Anti-Bribery Convention.[107] Phase II looks at whether the country applies its implementing legislation effectively.[108] Phase III turns to a review of enforcement practices.[109] The primary bite that comes with the Working Group's peer review process is publicity and the market effects of reputation. Though each state values it to a different degree, most are at least partially concerned about reputation.[110] A state with a reputation for enforcing its anti-corruption laws, particularly on the supply side, will be more likely to attract investment from companies committed to clean business practices.

And in fact, the Working Group's criticisms of implementation efforts in several countries—including the United States, the United Kingdom, France, Japan, and Italy—have already inspired various reforms. NGO activism by Transparency International and others with specialized expertise can fulfill a similar function. Indeed, Transparency International's public condemnation of the United Kingdom's virtually non-existent foreign bribery efforts was one of the key drivers leading to the enactment of the

U.K. Bribery Act of 2010—an anti-corruption instrument that in time may prove more potent than the FCPA.[111] In light of the lack of formal, binding mechanisms to enforce international law, external review in the manner described above may be the best option left for incentivizing countries to commit to multilateral anti-corruption efforts. . . .

Conclusion

When it comes to anti-corruption policy, the regulatory challenge is to design a system flexible enough to address the complexities of foreign bribery while still providing firms with the information and resources necessary for efficient compliance. Though advocates on both sides of the FCPA reform debate are often mistaken about key issues, the conversation they started confirms that finding a solution to this challenge will be difficult under the current sanction-based approach to FCPA enforcement. Fortunately, there is another way. As both a theoretical and practical matter, the complexities inherent in regulating corruption suggest that firms and regulators will be better served by looking at FCPA reform through the lens of new governance. The process of public-private collaboration envisioned by new governance can turn the FCPA's ambiguity and flexibility into a framework for the internalization of anti-corruption norms. This process, in turn, should lead to enhanced self-regulation and corporate compliance programs that are dynamic and sustainable. Furthermore, the lessons learned through the application of new governance tools in the domestic context provide useful guidance for the many ongoing international efforts aimed at deterring transnational bribery.

Notes

1. Foreign Corrupt Practices Act of 1977, 15 U.S.C. § 78dd (2012).
2. *See generally* Letter from U.S. Chamber of Commerce et al., to Honorable Lanny A Breuer, Assistant Attorney Gen. U.S. Dep't of Justice, and Robert Khuzami, Dir. of Enforcement, U.S. Sec. and Exch. Comm'n (Feb. 21, 2012), *available at* http://legaltimes.typepad.com/files/fcpa-guidance-letter-2-21-12_4_.pdf (discussing concerns that the statute is unclear about what amounts to a violation); ANDREW WEISSMANN & ALIXANDRA SMITH, U.S. CHAMBER INST. FOR LEGAL REFORM, RESTORING BALANCE: PROPOSED AMENDMENTS TO THE FOREIGN CORRUPT PRACTICES ACT 3 (2010), *available at* http://www.instituteforlegalreform.com/sites/default/files/restoringbalance_fcpa.pdf (discussing the statute's ambiguities and how to make the statute clearer).
3. *See* David Hess & Cristie L. Ford, *Corporate Corruption and Reform Undertakings: A New Approach to an Old Problem*, 41 CORNELL INT'L L.J. 307, 308–09 (2008).
4. DAVID KENNEDY & DAN DANIELSEN, BUSTING BRIBERY: SUSTAINING THE GLOBAL MOMENTUM OF THE FOREIGN CORRUPT PRACTICES ACT 17–18 (2011).
5. Cristie L. Ford, *New Governance, Compliance, and Principles-Based Securities Regulation*, 45 AM. BUS. L.J. 1, 29 (2008).
6. *See* Hess & Ford, *supra* note 11 (illustrating the cumulative advantage that firms can gain from paying bribes).
7. The FCPA was amended in 1988 and 1998. *See* Omnibus Trade and Competitiveness Act of 1988, Pub. L. No. 100-418, 102 Stat. 1107 (codified as amended in scattered sections of 19 U.S.C.); International Anti-Bribery and Fair Competition Act of 1998, Pub. L. No. 105-366, 112 Stat. 3302 (codified at 15 U.S.C. §§ 78dd-1–3, 78ff(2012)). The 1998 amendments were necessary to bring the FCPA into compliance with the Organization for Economic Cooperation and Development Anti-Bribery Convention and authorized extraterritorial jurisdiction over violations committed by U.S. nationals. *See* International Anti-Bribery and Fair Competition Act of 1998 § 2(c) (covering "[a]lternative jurisdiction over acts outside of the United States").
8. 15 U.S.C. §§ 78dd-2(a)–2(a)(1)(B) (2012). The term "corruptly" is not defined in the FCPA. The statute's legislative history suggests that it means a payment made with the intent to induce the recipient to misuse her official position to wrongfully direct business to the payer. *See* United States v. Kay, 359 F.3d 738, 749 n.40 (5th Cir. 2004).
9. 15 U.S.C. § 78dd-2. The term "issuer" means any firm that has a class of securities registered under section 12 of the Securities Exchange Act of 1934 or that is required to file periodic reports with the SEC (i.e., public companies). *Id.* § 78dd-1. "Domestic concerns" are U.S. citizens, nationals, or residents, as well as firms that have their principal place of business in the United States or that are organized under U.S. law. *Id.* § 78dd-2(h).
10. *Id.* § 78m(b)(2)(A).
11. The DOJ has jurisdiction over criminal and civil enforcement of the FCPA's anti-bribery provisions; the SEC has civil authority over the issuers as well as their officers, directors, and agents.
12. Carolyn Hotchkiss, *The Sleeping Dog Stirs: New Signs of Life in Efforts to End Corruption in International Business*, 17 J. PUB. POL'Y & MARKETING 108, 108 (1998).

13. Joseph W. Yockey, *Solicitation, Extortion, and the FCPA,* 87 Notre Dame L. Rev. 781, 782 (2011).

14. The number of firms prosecuted under the FCPA was 2.4 per year from 1998–2006; since then, the number has risen to 12.6 per year. Stephen J. Choi & Kevin E. Davis, *Foreign Affairs and Enforcement of the Foreign Corrupt Practices Act* 1 (N.Y. Univ. Sch. of Law Pub. Law & Legal Theory Research Paper Series, Working Paper No. 12-35, 2012), *available at* http:///ssrn.com /abstract=2116487. The breakdown of SEC/DOJ matters initiated against individual firms over the past ten years is as follows: 6 in 2002; 6 in 2003; 2 in 2004; 8 in 2005; 9 in 2006; 17 in 2007; 16 in 2008; 42 in 2009; 18 in 2010; and 24 in 2011. Shearman & Sterling LLP, Recent Trends and Patterns in the Enforcement of the Foreign Corrupt Practices Act 3 (2012), *available at* http://www.shearman.com /Shearman—Sterlings-Recent-Trends-and-Patterns -in-the-Enforcement-of-the-Foreign-Corrupt-Practices -Act-FCPA—FCPA-Digest-01-03-2012/. Notably, one initial challenge in discussing the rate of FCPA enforcement is characterizing the data. Many actions involve charges against multiple affiliated companies in a single action. In others, the SEC and DOJ charge the same company. When those matters were consolidated into single corporate cases, there were 11 FCPA actions in 2009, 20 in 2010, and 16 in 2011. *Id.* at 1. No matter how the data is characterized, however, most agree that there has been a dramatic increase in FCPA enforcement in recent years. *See* Mike Koehler, *The Foreign Corrupt Practices Act in the Ultimate Year of Its Decade of Resurgence,* 43 Ind. L. Rev. 389, 389 (2010) ("FCPA enforcement activity in 2009, the ultimate year in the decade of the FCPA's resurgence, suggests that CPA enforcement will remain a prominent feature on the legal landscape throughout this decade.").

15. Brandon L. Garrett, *Globalized Corporate Prosecutions,* 97 Va. L. Rev. 1775, 1832–33 (2011); Nathan Vardi, *How Federal Crackdown on Bribery Hurts Business and Enriches Insiders,* Forbes, May 24, 2010, http://www.forbes.com/forbes/2010/0524 /business-weatherford-kbr-corruption-bribery-racket .html.

16. *See* 15 U.S.C. § 78dd-1(a) (2012) (explaining how foreign firms can be prosecuted by U.S. regulators under the FCPA).

17. U.S. Dep't Of State, Fighting Global Corruption: Business Risk Management 12 (2000).

18. Sarbanes–Oxley Act of 2002, Pub. L. No. 107–204, 116 Stat. 745 (codified at 15 U.S.C. § 724(a) (2012)). Sarbanes–Oxley (SOX) imposed new

reporting and certification obligations that may arise when a firm learns of potential FCPA compliance problems.

19. Dodd–Frank Wall Street Reform and Consumer Protection Act, Pub. L. No. 111–203, 124 Stat. 1376 (codified at 15 U.S.C.A. § 78u-6 (West 2012)). Under Dodd–Frank, qualified whistleblowers who provide original information about potential FCPA violations may be awarded between 10% to 30% of any government-imposed sanctions in excess of $1 million. The whistleblower provisions remain in their infancy, but the SEC's Enforcement Division already reports seeing a sharp increase in the number and quality of FCPA tips received. *See 'Full Regime' of Cooperation Emerging in Anti-Corruption Arena, DOJ Official Says,* Sec. L. Daily (BNA) (Aug. 18, 2011) (discussing the increase in tips as a result of the whistleblower program).

20. Garrett, *supra* note 23, at 1785; Matthew C. Turk, *A Political Economy Approach to Reforming the Foreign Corrupt Practices Act,* 33 Nw. J. Int'l L. & Bus. —(forthcoming) (manuscript at 17).

21. Garrett, *supra* note 23. The SEC's FCPA Unit has 36 staff members. *An "Entrepreneurial" and Restructured SEC Pledges Proactive Enforcement,* Harvard L. Sch. F. on Corp. Governance and Fin. Reg. (Apr. 5, 2012, 9:38 AM), http://blogs.law .harvard.edu/corpgov/2012/04/05/an-entrepreneurial -and-restructured-sec-pledges-proactive -enforcement/.

22. Joseph W. Yockey, *FCPA Settlement, Internal Strife, and the "Culture of Compliance",* 2012 Wis. L. Rev. 689, 693–94 (2012).

23. Garrett, *supra* note 23, at 1799.

24. Yockey, *supra* note 30, at 694.

25. Diana B. Henriques, *F.B.I. Snares Weapons Executives in Bribery Sting,* N.Y. Times, Jan. 21, 2010, at A3.

26. *See, e.g., 28th National Conference on the Foreign Corrupt Practices Act,* Am. Conference Inst., http://www .fcpaconference.com/index.php (last visited Dec. 28, 2012) (announcing the FCPA conference).

27. 15 U.S.C. § 78dd-1 (2012).

28. *See* F. Joseph Warin et al., *FCPA Compliance in China and the Gifts and Hospitality Challenge,* 5 Va. L. & Bus. Rev. 33, 44–45 (2010) (discussing the wide range of foreign officials frequently encountered in the context of international business transactions).

29. *See* David Hess, *Combating Corruption Through Corporate Transparency: Using Enforcement Discretion to Improve Disclosure,* 21 Minn. J. Int'l L. 42, 62–63 (2012) (explaining the criteria that DOJ prosecutors use).

30. Press Release, U.S. Dep't of Justice, Siemens AG and Three Subsidiaries Plead Guilty to Foreign Corrupt Practices Act Violations (Dec. 15, 2008) [hereinafter Siemens AG Pleads Guilty], *available at* http://www.justice.gov/opa/pr/2008/December/08-crm-1105.html.

31. *Id.*

32. *Id.*

33. *Id.*

34. These expenses included $850 million in attorneys' fees, $5.2 million for translation services, and $100 million for information technology services. *See* Vardi, *supra* note 23 (detailing the process and results of Siemens's internal investigation and suggesting that the only "winners" were the attorneys who conducted the investigation).

35. Siemens AG Pleads Guilty, *supra* note 38.

36. *Id.*

37. Plea Agreement, United States v. Siemens Aktiengesellschaft, No. CR-8-367, ¶ 4 (Dec. 15, 2008).

38. Siemens AG Pleads Guilty, *supra* note 38.

39. *Id.*

40. Press Release, U.S. Dep't of Justice, Eight Former Senior Executives and Agents of Siemens Charged in Alleged $100 Million Foreign Bribe Scheme (Dec. 13, 2011), *available at* http://www.justice.gov/opa/ pr/2011/December/11-crm-1626.html.

41. *See* ORG. FOR ECON. COOPERATION & DEV., UNITED STATES: PHASE 3 REPORT ON THE APPLICATION OF THE CONVENTION ON COMBATING BRIBERY OF FOREIGN PUBLIC OFFICIALS IN INTERNATIONAL BUSINESS TRANSACTIONS 32 (2010) [hereinafter OECD PHASE 3 REPORT], *available at* http://www.oecd.org/investment/briberyininternationalbusiness/anti-briberyconvention/46213841.pdf (discussing the change in the number of DPAs and NPAs).

42. *Id.* Both the DOJ and SEC are empowered to enter into DPAs, though the first time the SEC used a DPA was in May 2011. Rob Khuzami, the newly appointed director of the SEC's Division of Enforcement, referred to his agency's use of DPAs as a "potential game changer." SHEARMAN & STERLING LLP, A NEW TOOL AND A TWIST? THE SEC'S FIRST DEFERRED PROSECUTION AGREEMENT AND A NOVEL PUNITIVE MEASURE 2 (2011), *available at* http://www.shearman.com/files/Publication/20b76673-2736-4a55-840f-1f75d518ca93/Presentation/PublicationAttachment/71ecb942-9eab-4482-b786-41522a71af75/LT-052411-A-New-Tool-and-a-Twist.pdf.

43. Catherine Dunn, *The Wait Continues for FCPA Guidance from DOJ*, CORPORATE COUNSEL (Nov. 9, 2012), http://www.law.com/corporatecounsel/PubArticleCC.jsp?id=1202577792246&thepage=2.

44. Lisa Kern Griffin, *Compelled Cooperation and the New Corporate Criminal Procedure*, 82 N.Y.U. L. REV. 311, 322 (2007).

45. Mike Koehler, *The Façade of FCPA Enforcement*, 41 GEO. J. INT'L L. 907, 934 (2010).

46. Samuel W. Buell, *Potentially Perverse Effects of Corporate Civil Liability, in* PROSECUTORS IN THE BOARDROOM 87, 92 (Anthony S. Barkow & Rachel E. Barkow eds., 2011).

47. OECD PHASE 3 REPORT, *supra* note 49.

48. SHEARMAN & STERLING LLP, *supra* note 50, at 3.

49. Buell, *supra* note 54, at 90–91.

50. James R. Doty, *Toward a Reg. FCPA: A Modest Proposal for Change in Administering the Foreign Corrupt Practices Act*, 62 BUS. LAW. 1233, 1237 (2007).

51. Frank C. Razzano & Travis P. Nelson, *The Expanding Criminalization of Transnational Bribery: Global Prosecution Necessitates Global Compliance*, 42 INT'L LAW. 1259, 1275–76 (2008).

52. WEISSMANN & SMITH, *supra* note 2, at 2.

53. *See* SHEARMAN & STERLING LLP, *supra* note 22, at 5–6 (explaining that over the past five years, FCPA-defendants that have voluntarily disclosed potential violations have received discounts from applicable Sentencing Guideline calculations in a range of 3% to 67%, with most falling within a range of 20% to 30%).

54. Sara Sun Beale, *A Response to the Critics of Corporate Criminal Liability*, 46 AM. CRIM. L. REV. 1481, 1491–92 (2009). One FCPA compliance expert argues that "[t]he scope of things companies have to worry about is enlarging all the time as the government asserts violations in circumstances where it's unclear if they would prevail in court . . . [y]ou don't have the checks and balances you would normally have if you had more litigation." Vardi, *supra* note 23.

55. Examples include the $1.6 billion paid by Siemens AG in 2008, *see* Vardi, *supra* note 23; $579 million by KBR/Halliburton in 2009, Zachary A. Goldfarb, *Halliburton, KBR Settle Bribery Allegations*, WASH. POST, Feb. 12, 2009, at D1; $400 million by BAE in 2010, Daniel Michaels & Cassell Bryan-Low, *BAE to Settle Bribery Cases for More than $400 Million*, WALL ST. J., Feb. 6–7, 2010, at B1; $388 million by Technip S.A. in 2010, Press Release, U.S. Dep't of Justice, Technip S.A. Resolves Foreign Corrupt Practices Act Investigation and Agrees to Pay $240 Million Criminal Penalty (June 28, 2010); $356 million by Snamprogetti Netherlands in 2010, Press Release, U.S. Dep't of Justice, Snamprogetti Netherlands B.V. Resolves Foreign Corrupt Practices Act Investigation and Agrees to Pay

$240 Million Criminal Penalty (July 7, 2010); $218 million by JGC Corporation in 2011, Press Release, U.S. Dep't of Justice, JGC Resolves Foreign Corrupt Practices Act Investigation and Agrees to Pay a $218.8 Million Criminal Penalty (April 6, 2011); and $185 million by Daimler AG in 2010, Press Release, U.S. Sec. & Exch. Comm'n, SEC Charges Daimler AG with Global Bribery (Apr. 1, 2010). These figures include the total amount of any civil and/or criminal fine, disgorgement, and interest imposed as part of settling FCPA charges.

56. *See* SHEARMAN & STERLING LLP, *supra* note 22, at 4 (noting specifically, over $508 million was paid in 2011; $1.78 billion in 2010; $579 million in 2009; and $803 million in 2008). Several points about these figures deserve mention. First, in 2008 and 2009, it is important to keep in mind that nearly 100% of the total fines came from just two settlements: Siemens AG in 2008 and KBR/Halliburton in 2009. *Id.* The trend of having a few outliers account for the bulk of total sanctions continues into 2010 and 2011. In 2010, nearly two-thirds ($1.1 billion) of the total penalties came from just three of the year's 20 consolidated matters (Technip, Snamprogetti, and BAE). *See id.* at 5 (listing the penalties for Snamprogetti and Technip as $365 million and $338 million, respectively); Michaels & Bryan-Low, *supra* note 63 (listing the penalties for BAE at $400 million). Adding the next three largest settlements from that year to the mix means that six cases accounted for 80% of all sanctions, with the remaining matters settling for an average of $20 million each. SHEARMAN & STERLING LLP, RECENT TRENDS AND PATTERNS IN THE ENFORCEMENT OF THE FOREIGN CORRUPT PRACTICES ACT 2–3 (2011). Results from 2011 are similar. *Id.* The average penalty paid in 2011 was $33.8 million. SHEARMAN & STERLING LLP, *supra* note 22, at 4. If the high and low outliers are removed, the average falls to $22 million. *Id.* Thus, while these numbers are certainly material, they do not appear as dramatic when compared only to annual totals.

57. *See* Vardi, *supra* note 23 (explaining that the independent monitor retained by Siemens as part of its settlement could reportedly cost the company up to $52 million in fees).

58. Siemens AG Pleads Guilty, *supra* note 38.

59. Peter J. Henning, *The High Price of Internal Inquiries*, N.Y. TIMES DEALBOOK, May 6, 2011, http://dealbook.nytimes.com/2011/05/06/the-high-price-of-internal-investigations/. As discussed in Part III.B,

it is important to keep in mind that these figures mean relatively little in isolation. To be useful, these costs must be compared to the scope of the underlying problem, the benefits that a company stood to gain through the corrupt transactions at issue, and the probability of detection.

60. Vardi, *supra* note 23. The data on mitigating factors is mixed. Hinchey surveyed settled FCPA cases from 2002 to 2009 and found that the ratio of sanctions and the amount of bribes paid is greater for companies that voluntarily disclose FCPA violations. Bruce Hinchey, *Punishing the Penitent: Disproportionate Fines in Recent FCPA Enforcements and Suggested Improvements*, 40 PUB. CONT. L.J. 393, 404–06 (2011). Choi & Davis find that the correlation between mitigating factors (including voluntary disclosure and cooperation with authorities) and total monetary penalties paid is not significant. Choi & Davis, supra note 22, at 21. By contrast, *Shearman & Sterling LLP* find that the DOJ gave discounts ranging from 3% to 67% in FCPA cases involving voluntary disclosure and negotiated settlements. SHEARMAN & STERLING LLP, *supra* note 22, at 5.

61. *See* Amy Deen Westbrook, *Enthusiastic Enforcement, Informal Legislation: The Unruly Expansion of the Foreign Corrupt Practices Act*, 45 GA. L. REV. 489, 498 (2011) (discussing confusion over anti-corruption laws).

62. Letter from U.S. Chamber of Commerce et al., *supra* note 2, at 2.

63. The Chamber hired former Attorney General Michael Mukasey to lobby on its behalf.

64. C.M. Matthews, *Clinton Defends FCPA, as U.S. Chamber Lobbys for Changes to Law*, WALL ST. J. BLOGS (Mar. 23, 2012, 1:51 PM), http://blogs.wsj.com/corruption-currents/2012/03/23/clinton-defends-fcpa-as-us-chamber-lobbys-for-changes-to-law.

65. Tina Chi, *While FCPA Reform Has Bipartisan Support, an Actual Proposal Has Not Yet Surfaced, Rep. Bobby Scott Says*, 10 Corp. Accountability Rep. 32 (BNA) (Jan. 13, 2012). U.S. Senators Amy Klobuchar (D. Minn.) and Chris Coons (D. Del.) say that they plan to introduce legislation to clarify parts of the FCPA. U.S. Representative Jim Sensenbrenner (R. Wis.) has also suggested that he will introduce a similar bill. C.M. Matthews, *Is Bobby Scott Getting Behind FCPA Legislation?*, WALL ST. J. BLOGS (Dec. 2, 2011 3:17 PM), http://blogs.wsj.com/corruption-currents/2011/12/02/is-bobby-scott-getting-behind-fcpa-legislation/.

66. CRIMINAL DIV., U.S. DEP'T OF JUSTICE & ENFORCEMENT DIV., SEC. & EXCHANGE COMM'N, FCPA:

67. Cary Coglianese & Evan Mendelson, *Meta-Regulation and Self-Regulation, in* THE OXFORD HANDBOOK ON REGULATION 146 (Robert Baldwin et al. eds., 2010); *see supra* text accompanying notes 167–68 (noting the modest resources of the government and the need to efficiently monitor and evaluate violations).

68. These actions also typically follow from self-disclosure. *See* Hess & Ford, *supra* note 11, at 314 (noting also that "many convictions relied on actions that the corporation could have easily disguised to avoid detection, suggesting that more careful firms are able to make similar payments without significant fear of prosecution").

69. Park, *supra* note 93, at 147–48. Because of its size and considerable funding,

> the SEC is expected to produce a certain amount of enforcement output. It is easier for the SEC to generate a high volume of cases by bringing rule-enforcement cases. While a significant principle-enforcement action might create a significant amount of deterrence, the effects of the action may be unclear. Given the risk and time involved in enforcing principles, it may be rational for the SEC to focus on rule-enforcement cases that are straightforward and likely to settle quickly.

Id.

70. *See Global Corruption Barometer 2010/11*, TRANSPARENCY INT'L (2010), http://gcb.transparency.org /gcb201011/results/ (averaging the results for question #1 worldwide shows that 56% of world citizens believe that overall levels of corruption have increased in the past three years); *see also* Carrington, *supra* note 133, at 142–43 (showing commitment to increase cracking down on corruption yet doubting the effort's effectiveness). Carrington notes:

> One may admire the sincere efforts of all those who have secured the promulgation and ratification of these international conventions and still question whether they are effective in deterring corruption of public officials, or perhaps merely express "a hollow commitment." A thorough empirical study revealing an effect on the realities of weak governments has not been conducted, but the available data points to a

conclusion that "enforcement must be re-energized."

Id.

71. Ginsburg & Wright, *supra* note 115, at 8.

72. *Id.* at 14 ("Corporate fines are unlikely to efficiently deter conduct by an individual employee because he will internalize almost none of the fine imposed against his employer.").

73. Rose-Ackerman, *supra* note 118, at 234 ("If payoffs help a firm obtain business, managers and owners may hope to facilitate their subordinates' bribery while remaining ignorant of the details. If corporations are held criminally liable for the corrupt acts of their employees and agents, top management may not support an effective monitoring system." (citation omitted)); Jennifer Arlen, *The Potentially Perverse Effects of Corporate Criminal Liability*, 23 J. LEGAL STUD. 833, 834 (1994).

74. Rose-Ackerman, *supra* note 118, at 235.

> One possibility is a negligence rule under which firms are only liable if they have neglected their internal enforcement responsibilities. For such a rule to be workable, however, courts must be able to evaluate internal firm behavior, a difficult task. One solution may be quite precise directives stating what type of internal monitoring is required with checks to be sure it is carried out in good faith.

Id.

75. Baer, *supra* note 151, at 630–31.

76. Rose-Ackerman, *supra* note 118, at 234–35.

77. *See* Carrington, *supra* note 133, at 146 (contemplating whether deterred firms will be able to compete with less constrained firms operating in other countries).

78. Hess & Ford, *supra* note 11, at 311, 317.

79. Cristie Ford & David Hess, *Corporate Monitorships and New Governance Regulation: In Theory, in Practice, and in Context*, 33 LAW & POL'Y 509, 512 (2011).

80. Buell, *supra* note 54, at 105.

81. Yockey, *supra* note 21, at 783.

82. *See generally* Warin et al., supra note 36 (describing the unique cultural norms in China exposing individuals to the risk of anti-bribery laws).

83. Yockey, *supra* note 21, at 811. The FCPA expressly prohibits corrupt payments made through the use of third parties. 15 U.S.C. § 78dd-1(a) (3) (2012); *id.* §§ 78dd-2(a)(3), 78dd-3(a)(3) (prohibiting bribes paid "to any person, while knowing that all or a portion of such money or thing of value will be offered, given, or promised, directly or indirectly," to a foreign official).

84. *See* Steven R. Salbu, *A Delicate Balance: Legislation, Institutional Change, and Transnational Bribery,* 33 Cornell Int'l L.J. 657, 686 (2000).

85. *See* Pricewaterhousecoopers, Confronting Corruption 19 (2008), available at http://www.pwc.com/gx /en/forensic-accounting-dispute-consulting-services /business-case-anti-corruption-programme.jhtml.

86. Alan O. Sykes, *Corporate Liability for Extraterritorial Torts Under the Alien Tort Statute and Beyond: An Economic Analysis,* 100 Geo. L.J. 2161, 2186 (2012).

87. Baer, *supra* note 151, at 638–39; Bamberger & Mulligan, *supra* note 7.

88. Bamberger & Mulligan, *supra* note 7.

89. Ford, *supra* note 13.

90. Bibas, *Prosecutorial Regulation, supra* note 147, at 963.

91. Bamberger & Mulligan, *supra* note 7, at 481; Christie Ford, *Macro and Micro-Level Effects on Responsive Financial Regulation,* 44 U. Brit. Colum. L. Rev. 589, 600 (2011).

92. Miriam Hechler Baer, *Insuring Corporate Crime,* 83 Ind. L.J. 1035, 1057–58 (2008).

93. Orly Lobel, *Orchestrated Experimentalism in the Regulation of Work,* 101 Mich. L. Rev. 2146, 2160–61 (2003) (reviewing Paul Osterman et al., Working in America: A Blueprint For the New Labor Market (2001)).

94. Anne-Marie Slaughter, *Sovereignty and Power in a Networked World Order,* 40 Stan. J. Int'l L. 283, 285 (2004).

95. Garrett, *supra* note 23, at 1861.

96. U.S. Attorneys' Manual § 9-47.110 (2000), *available at* http://www.justice.gov/usao/eousa/foia_reading _room/usam/title9/47mcrm.htm.

97. F. Joseph Warin et al., *Nine Lessons from 2009: The Year-in-Review of Foreign Corrupt Practices Act Enforcement,* 38 Sec. Reg. L.J. 19, 45 (2010).

98. *Id.*

99. U.S. Dep't of Justice, Response of the United States: Questions Concerning Phase 3 Oecd Working Group on Bribery § 3.1(g) (2010); Choi & Davis, *supra* note 22, at 38 (reporting that total FCPA-sanctions are greatest in cases that involve home countries that have entered into cooperation and assistance agreements with the United States, which may reflect a greater ease of gathering evidence in such cases).

100. Choi & Davis, *supra* note 22, at 36.

> Since 2003, the SEC has participated with numerous other countries in the Multilateral Memorandum of Understanding Concerning Consultation and Cooperation (Multilateral MOU) and the Exchange of Information sponsored by the International Organization of Securities Commissions. In addition to the U.S. SEC, signatories to the Multilateral MOU include over 85 financial and securities regulatory authorities including the regulatory authorities from Hungary, Pakistan, and Thailand.

Id.

101. McLean, *supra* note 239, at 1988 (quoting *International Enforcement Assistance,* U.S. Sec. & Exchange Commission, http://www.sec.gov/about/offices/oia/oia _crossborder.shtml (last visited Dec. 28, 2012)).

102. Arthur F. Mathews, *Defending SEC and DOJ FCPA Investigations and Conducting Related Corporate Internal Investigations: The Triton Energy/ Indonesia SEC Consent Decree Settlements,* 18 Nw. J. Int'l L. & Bus. 303, 415 (1998).

103. Rose-Ackerman & Truex, *supra* note 187, at 36.

104. Spahn, *supra* note 86 (manuscript at 7).

105. OECD, Convention on Combating Bribery of Foreign Public Officials in International Business Transactions art. 12, Dec. 18, 1977, 37 I.L.M. 1, *available at* http://www.oecd.org/investment/bribery ininternationalbusiness/anti-briberyconvention /38028044.pdf.

106. Ben W. Heineman, Jr. & Fritz Heimann, *The Long War Against Corruption,* Foreign Aff., May /June 2006, at 75, 80.

107. OECD, Phase 1 Country Monitoring of the oecd Anti-Bribery Convention (1999), *available at* http://www.oecd.org.

108. OECD, Phase 2 Country Monitoring of the Oecd Anti-Bribery Convention (1999), *available at* http:// www.oecd.org.

109. OECD Phase 3 Report, *supra* note 49.

110. Robert Knowles, *A Realist Defense of the Alien Tort Statute,* 88 Wash. U. L. Rev. 1117, 1168–69 (2011); Oona Hathaway, *Do Human Rights Treaties Make a Difference?,* 111 Yale L.J. 1935, 2010–11 (2002).

111. *See* Adrienne Margolis, *Bribery Bill Brings UK Closer to OECD Rules,* Int'l Bar Ass'n, http://www .ibanet.org/Article/Detail.aspx?ArticleUid =dbfdf0e9-074c-4b79-a7f8-1aed7e44b3b8 (last visited Dec. 28, 2012) (discussing concern about adequate guidance for companies and the need to monitor companies' adherence to anti-corruption measures).

Joseph W. Yockey is an associate professor of law at the University of Iowa College of Law. His writing interests are in the areas of corporate governance, social enterprise and corporate social responsibility, and corporate crime.

Peter J. Henning  **NO**

Taking Aim at the Foreign Corrupt Practices Act

The Foreign Corrupt Practices Act has been at the center of a tug of war between business interests and federal authorities.

The United States Chamber of Commerce has led efforts to change the law, in response to ramped up prosecutions by the Justice Department and the Securities and Exchange Commission in the last few years. While the proposed changes are described as a means to "improve" the law, they would also make it more difficult to pursue cases.

But the revelations in *The New York Times* that Wal-Mart Stores squelched an investigation into bribery at its Mexican subsidiary may impel prosecutors to be even more forceful in applying the law and put legislative efforts to change it on the back burner.

Business leaders have long contended that the law is overly broad and too aggressively enforced, while federal authorities view it as a powerful means to police the overseas conduct of American companies.

The Foreign Corrupt Practices Act was adopted in 1977 in the wake of revelations of bribery of foreign officials by more than 400 United States companies. This was a time when misconduct by the Central Intelligence Agency and the Watergate scandal were still fresh in the public consciousness, so efforts to clean up business and government were paramount.

The law contains two parts: it prohibits bribing a foreign official for the purpose of "obtaining or retaining business," and it requires that public companies file proper financial statements and maintain a system of internal controls.

The books and records provision is enforced regularly, most recently in the conspiracy prosecution of a former managing director of Morgan Stanley for hiding deals with a Chinese official. The Justice Department and the S.E.C. share authority over enforcement, which means companies have to deal with two sets of investigators whenever a potential violation comes to light.

For the first 30 years or so after its enactment, the anti-bribery portion of law was used sporadically. Only a handful of cases were brought each year against companies, almost always ending in settlements involving a modest fine, and even fewer involved individuals.

Prosecutors have now made enforcement of the law a priority, and more industries have been caught up in investigations. The Justice Department has filed cases against pharmaceutical manufacturers for dealings with state-run health care programs, and is reported to be pursuing an investigation into the dealings of American movie studios in China.

The push for changes in the statute coincided with its expanded enforcement as companies now have to deal with the vagaries of the law once viewed as a mild nuisance at best.

At a hearing before a House subcommittee last year, a former attorney general, Michael B. Mukasey, represented the United States Chamber of Commerce in supporting changes to restrain use of the law because "more expansive interpretations of the statute may ultimately punish corporations whose connection to improper acts is attenuated or, in some cases, nonexistent."

The revelations about Wal-Mart's conduct, however, show the law's importance as an anticorruption tool for policing large businesses.

Tinkering with the law could send the wrong signal to other countries about the importance of curbing bribery. Support among Congressional leaders for revisions that would make it harder to prosecute companies may dissolve if they could easily be portrayed as being soft on bribery—something that would become fodder for an opponent in an election campaign.

The Justice Department's increased enforcement of the Foreign Corrupt Practices Act has also included more charges against individuals rather than just companies. But that shift has also led to problems. In one of its most prominent cases, prosecutors dismissed charges against 22 defendants from the "Africa Sting" case in which the government used an undercover informant to entice suppliers into agreeing to pay bribes to receive contracts with an African government, all of which was fictitious.

The charges foundered over issues regarding the conduct of the informant that raised questions about whether individuals were unfairly enticed into the deals. Federal juries could not reach a verdict after two trials of a group of the defendants, and the Justice Department decided to forgo further prosecutions.

As James B. Stewart wrote in a *New York Times* column last week, there has been a noticeable absence of corporate employees charged with violations even when it appears that the company condoned foreign bribery.

But while companies have been much more amenable to settling investigations rather than challenging charges in court, prosecuting individuals faces a number of hurdles. Corrupt payments are often made by foreign intermediaries acting on behalf of the company, many of whom have no ties to the United States. It does little good to charge someone when there is not a realistic prospect that the person can be brought to the United States.

Pursuing a case against senior executives for turning a blind eye to questionable payments can be quite difficult. The notion that management "had to be aware of what was going on" may well be true in some instances, but that perception alone is not enough to prove any individual corruptly and willfully violated the Foreign Corrupt Practices Act, which is the required legal intent standard for a conviction.

Foreign bribery can takes years to come to the government's attention, so the five-year statute of limitations can preclude prosecuting those involved in the payments. As I discussed in an earlier piece, the Wal-Mart payments to Mexican officials from 2003 to 2005 probably cannot be pursued against individuals at the company unless something more recent occurred.

Interestingly, in the Dodd-Frank Act, Congress extended the statute of limitations for securities fraud crimes to six years, apparently leaving out violations of the Foreign Corrupt Practices Act. Even that small increase in the time available to pursue a case can help prosecutors in putting together charges. Congress can alter the limitations period for any offense, and the Justice Department may point to Wal-Mart to ask Congress to extend the time frame in which foreign bribery charges can be filed.

The investigation of Wal-Mart has brought the Foreign Corrupt Practices Act to the attention of the public in a way not seen since the 1970s scandals that led to its adoption. Congress may find it politically impossible to adopt changes to the statute that would arguably make it more difficult to pursue cases as long as the allegations of foreign bribery by a leading American company remain in the headlines.

PETER J. HENNING is a professor of law at the Wayne State University Law School. Professor Henning's scholarship focuses primarily on white collar crime, constitutional criminal procedure, and attorney ethics.

EXPLORING THE ISSUE

Is the Foreign Corrupt Practices Act Obsolete?

Critical Thinking and Reflection

1. Why is the FCPA an important piece of legislation? What is its impact on U.S. business?
2. How does a focus on compliance differ from a focus on eradicating corruption?
3. Is opposition to bribery a universal principle? Should it be? Why or why not?
4. What are the challenges of implementing a law in countries without "rule of law?"

Is There Common Ground?

Both our YES and NO selections agree on one important concept: without international collaboration, there is no chance of fighting corruption successfully. The issue needs to shift from one of obtaining compliance to one of finding a place of communication where the positions of all participants are heard. The Western, industrialized nations need to curb their position of ethical superiority and listen more carefully to alternative perspectives.

Although some Western positions do reflect universally accepted values, bribery and transparency do not fall into this category. We in the West may want them to, but it is clear from the data that our goal in this regard is not a universal one. Strengthening the global organizations and NGOs that encourage anticorruption policies is one way forward and can lead to the reduction of corruption without limiting economic development.

Additional Resources

Deborah Hardoon and Finn Heinrich, *Bribe Payer's Index*, Transparency International (2011).

Matt Kelley and Lonnie Keene, "How Do Companies Navigate Bribery and Corruption?" 2015 Anti-Bribery and Corruption Benchmarking Report, Kroll and *Compliance Week* (2015).

OECD, *OECD Foreign Bribery Report: An Analysis of the Crime of Bribery of Foreign Public Officials* (Paris: OECD Publishing, 2014).

Internet References . . .

United Nations Global Compact

https://www.unglobalcompact.org/aboutthegc/thetenprinciples/principle10.html

Transparency International

https://www.transparency.org/

Association of Corporate Counsel

http://www.acc.com/legalresources/publications/topten/SLD-FCPA-Compliance.cfm

Selected, Edited, and with Issue Framing Material by:
Gina Vega, *Organizational Ergonomics*

ISSUE

Should U.S. Companies Take Primary Responsibility for Working Conditions in Their International Suppliers' Factories?

YES: Denis G. Arnold and Norman E. Bowie, from "Sweatshops and Respect for Persons," *Business Ethics Quarterly* (2003)

NO: Charles Duhigg and David Barboza, from "In China, Human Costs Are Built into an iPad," *New York Times* (2012)

Learning Outcomes

After reading this issue, you will be able to:

- Determine the level of U.S. corporate responsibility for the actions of suppliers.
- Identify specific areas of which corporations should be especially mindful.
- Evaluate the acceptability of treating workers in different countries differently.

ISSUE SUMMARY

YES: Arnold and Bowie claim that multinational corporations are responsible for the actions of their suppliers based on the Kantian doctrine of respect for persons. Corporations must ensure minimum safety standards are met, along with living wage and local labor laws.

NO: Duhigg and Barboza report that Apple contends that their industry behavior is governed by market desire for cheaper and more advanced technology. Until market desire changes, factory conditions are secondary.

Throughout the world of nations with emerging economies, often referred to as third-world countries, people work in sweatshops, frequently in horrific conditions, to produce the goods enjoyed by the so-called First World nations. These banal goods (clothing, toys, and electronics), routinely sporting the wholesome and highly valued names of America's largest corporations, have resulted in abuse, injury, and even death of those who are tasked with producing them.

For more two hundred years, since the beginning of the Industrial Revolution, companies have been seeking ways to make goods faster and cheaper. As technology improved, it became apparent to manufacturers that their ability to innovate and improve their products required access to an inexpensive labor market. Gradually,

post-WWII, that inexpensive labor market was located not in the United States, but in less developed countries throughout the world. The trend to moving production offshore accelerated in the 1970s and beyond, as production costs in the United States increased dramatically. By the 1990s, fewer than half of U.S.-based corporations were conducting the majority of their manufacturing within the States, but had begun "partnering" with strategic entities in Asia, the Middle East, and Latin America.

Companies outsource for a variety of reasons, including gaining access to world-class capabilities that they might not have had otherwise, freeing internal resources for other purposes, and sharing risks with a partner company (Handfield, 2006). None of these is as compelling, however, as reducing and controlling operating costs, the greatest of which by far is labor cost. We demand our inexpensive jeans, our iPads and iPods, Barbie dolls, computers, sneakers, T-shirts, and a host of other products that we consider staples of our daily life. But the low price of these items comes with a high price for those who manufacture them for us. Although a typical manufacturing salary in a U.S. clothing company such as American Apparel's Los Angeles plant is $30,000 plus benefits, a person doing similar work in Bangladesh earns $600/year. American Apparel clothing is made in the USA. Jeans range in price from $80–$140, T-shirts from $24–$38. You can buy Levi-Strauss jeans (made in Mexico) at Wal-Mart for under $20 and Danskin T-shirts (made in China) for $5.00. Levi-Strauss and Danskin, prototypical American clothing manufacturers, were founded in 1853 and 1882, respectively. Levi Strauss completed its manufacturing exodus from the United States in 2004, and Danskin closed its last plant in Pennsylvania in 2009. They were far from alone in this process.

With the loss of vertical integration came the loss of control over working conditions in distant factories. Reports of worker abuse began to surface shortly after the major push to offshoring began. Sweatshops in Indonesia, Mexico, the Middle East, India, Southeast Asia, and China fielded accusations of lower-than-poverty-level wages, excessive hours, slave labor conditions, and other human rights violations. Workers' coercion, force, and fraud resulted in charges of human trafficking, and dangerous working conditions put health and lives at risk daily. Fires were frequent due to the various kinds of dust generated in factories and the lack of proper ventilation. Conditions that harked back 100 or more years shocked the world when they came to light, and the UN issued its first Global Principles document in 2000 both to publicize the abuses and gain public and political traction to fight them.

Lack of statistical reliability makes it difficult to determine both exactly how much manufacturing is offshored and how challenging working conditions are in the strategic partners' factories. One thing we know for sure: more than 90 percent of the clothing sold in the United States is made overseas (Consumer Reports, 2013), as is nearly all electronic equipment and toys. The press makes us aware of the most egregious abuses and the worst disasters, but we are protected from learning the facts of the daily experience of sweatshop living.

This is due in part to the culture of secrecy that surrounds strategic partnerships. It is very difficult to learn anything about the contracts, agreements, arrangements, and conventions shared by U.S.-based corporations and their overseas second- and third-party connections. Coupled with secrecy is the so-called race to the bottom in which suppliers are pushed to lower their prices again and again in order to retain the contract, resulting in lowering their own costs each time. The expense that is always negotiable is labor.

But what are the duties of the wealthy and powerful companies that partner with third-world companies toward the foreign labor force? How far down the supply chain does their responsibility extend? Clearly, U.S. companies are constrained from many kinds of worker mistreatment within the United States both by law and union agreement, as well as by cultural and social restrictions. The rule of law that governs working conditions in the United States does not extend to conditions abroad, and it appears, if no one is looking, companies also close their eyes.

In the YES selection, Arnold and Bowie invoke Kantian principles related to human dignity and state unequivocably that companies that stand for wholesome values in the United States have no right to violate those values in other countries. People everywhere must be treated the same, as ends in themselves and as worthy of dignity and respect. This categorically precludes the kinds of abuses that have plagued workers abroad.

In the NO selection, Duhigg and Barboza bemoan the abuses perpetrated in foreign factories, but provide evidence that some companies are aware of the abuses and yet do nothing to correct them. They believe that if the companies wanted to correct the abuses, they could. The suggestion is that they do nothing because there is little consumer push to create the impetus required for change. Until American consumers speak out, nothing will change in the factories.

YES

Denis G. Arnold and Norman E. Bowie

Sweatshops and Respect for Persons

In recent years labor and human rights activists have been successful at raising public awareness regarding labor practices in both American and off-shore manufacturing facilities. Organizations such as Human Rights Watch, United Students Against Sweatshops, the National Labor Coalition, Sweatshop Watch, and the Interfaith Center on Corporate Responsibility have accused multinational enterprises (MNEs), such as Nike, Wal-Mart, and Disney, of the pernicious exploitation of workers. Recent violations of American and European labor laws have received considerable attention.[1] However, it is the off-shore labor practices of North American and European based MNEs and their contractors that have been most controversial. This is partly due to the fact that many of the labor practices in question are legal outside North America and Europe, or are tolerated by corrupt or repressive political regimes. Unlike the recent immigrants who toil in the illegal sweatshops of North America and Europe, workers in developing nations typically have no recourse to the law or social service agencies. Activists have sought to enhance the welfare of these workers by pressuring MNEs to comply with labor laws, prohibit coercion, improve health and safety standards, and pay a living wage in their global sourcing operations. Meanwhile, prominent economists wage a campaign of their own in the opinion pages of leading newspapers, arguing that because workers for MNEs are often paid better when compared with local wages, they are fortunate to have such work. Furthermore, they argue that higher wages and improved working conditions will raise unemployment levels.

One test of a robust ethical theory is its ability to shed light on ethical problems. One of the standard criticisms of Immanuel Kant's ethical philosophy is that it is too abstract and formal to be of any use in practical decision making. We contend that this criticism is mistaken and that Kantian theory has much to say about the ethics of sweatshops.[2] We argue that Kant's conception of human dignity provides a clear basis for grounding the obligations of employers to employees. In particular, we argue that respecting the dignity of workers requires that MNEs and their contractors adhere to local labor laws, refrain from coercion, meet minimum safety standards, and provide a living wage for employees. We also respond to the objection that improving health and safety conditions and providing a living wage would cause greater harm than good.

Respect for Persons

. . .

Kant did not simply assert that persons are entitled to respect, he provided an elaborate argument for that conclusion. Persons ought to be respected because persons have dignity. For Kant, an object that has dignity is beyond price. Employees have a dignity that machines and capital do not have. They have dignity because they are capable of moral activity. As free beings capable of self-governance they are responsible beings, since freedom and self-governance are the conditions for responsibility. Autonomous responsible beings are capable of making and following their own laws; they are not simply subject to the causal laws of nature. Anyone who recognizes that he or she is free should recognize that he or she is responsible (that he or she is a moral being). As Kant argues, the fact that one is a moral being entails that one possesses dignity.

> Morality is the condition under which alone a rational being can be an end in himself because only through it is it possible to be a lawgiving member in the realm of ends. Thus morality, and humanity insofar as it is capable of morality, alone have dignity.[3]

As a matter of consistency, a person who recognizes that he or she is a moral being should ascribe dignity to anyone who, like him or herself, is a moral being.

Although it is the capacity to behave morally that gives persons their dignity, freedom is required if a person is to act morally. For Kant, being free is more than freedom from causal necessity. This is negative freedom. Freedom in its fullest realization is the ability to guide one's actions from laws that are of one's own making. Freedom is not simply a spontaneous event. Free actions are caused, but they are caused by persons acting from laws they themselves have made. This is positive freedom. Onora O'Neill puts the point this way.

> Positive freedom is more than independence from alien causes. It would be absent in lawless or random changes, although these are negatively free, since they depend on no alien causes. Since will is a mode of causality it cannot, if free at all, be merely negatively free, so it must work by nonalien causality . . . it [free will] must be a capacity for self-determination or autonomy.[4]

When we act autonomously we have the capacity to act with dignity. We do so when we act on principles that are grounded in morality rather than in mere inclination. Reason requires that any moral principle that is freely derived must be rational in the sense that it is universal. To be universal in this sense means that the principle can be willed to be universally binding on all subjects in relevantly similar circumstances without contradiction. The fact that persons have this capability means that they possess dignity. And it is as a consequence of this dignity that a person "exacts respect for himself from all other rational beings in the world."[5] As such, one can and should "measure himself with every other being of this kind and value himself on a footing of equality with them."[6]

Respecting people requires honoring their humanity; which is to say it requires treating them as ends in themselves. In Kant's words,

> Humanity itself is a dignity: for a man cannot be used merely as a means by any man . . . but must always be used at the same time as an end. It is just in this that his dignity . . . consists. by which he raises himself above all other beings in the world that are not men and yet can be used, and so over all *things*.[7]

. . .

With respect to the task at hand, what does treating the humanity of persons as ends in themselves require in a business context—specifically in the context of global manufacturing facilities? In an earlier work Bowie has spelled out the implications of the Kantian view for businesses operating in developed countries.[8] Here we apply the same strategy in order to derive basic duties for MNEs operating in developing countries. Specifically, we derive duties that apply to MNEs that are utilizing the vast supplies of inexpensive labor currently available in developing economies. To fully respect a person one must actively treat his or her humanity as an end. This is an obligation that holds on every person *qua* person, whether in the personal realm or in the marketplace. As Kant writes, "Every man has a legitimate claim to respect from his fellow men and is *in turn* bound to respect every other."[9] There are, of course, limits to what managers of MNEs can accomplish. Nonetheless, we believe that the analysis we have provided entails that MNEs operating in developing nations have an obligation to respect the humanity of their employees.

The United Nations utilizes both the Kantian view and the capabilities view as a dual theoretical foundation for its defense of human rights. Among the rights identified by the UN are freedom from injustice and violations of the rule of law; freedom to decent work without exploitation; and the freedom to develop and realize one's human potential. It argues that all global actors, including MNEs, have a moral obligation to respect basic human rights.[10] This general approach to poverty and development has recently been embraced by the World Bank.[11] James Wolfensohn, President of The World Bank, writes:

> A better quality of life for the poor calls for higher incomes. This requires sound economic policies and institutions conducive to sustained growth. Achieving higher incomes and a better quality of life also calls for much more—improved and more equitable opportunities for education and jobs, better health and nutrition, a cleaner and more sustainable natural environment, an impartial judicial and legal system, greater civilian and political liberties, trustworthy and transparent institutions, and freedom of access to a rich and diverse cultural life . . . Poor women and men from around the world [note] emphatically the importance of dignity, respect, security, gender issues, a clean environment, health, and inclusion in addition to material well-being.[12]

Significantly, The World Bank has recognized "crucial gaps" in its efforts to encourage development and eliminate poverty through market liberalization. What has been missing is "adequate attention to the quality and sustainability of growth." The World Bank now explicitly acknowledges that all major stakeholders have important roles to play in this process. "Functioning markets and liberalization are crucial" to poverty reduction. "But so is acknowledging the limits of the market and an essential role for governments *and other stakeholders* in the reform process."[13] MNEs have a significant interests in developing nations as sources of natural resources and inexpensive labor, and as emerging markets. As such, The World Bank properly recognizes MNEs as stakeholders with important moral obligations in the global reform process.

Outsourcing and the Duties of MNEs

One significant feature of globalization that is of particular relevance to our analysis is the increase in outsourcing by MNEs. Prior to the 1970s most foreign production by MNEs was intended for local markets. In the 1970s new financial incentives led MNEs to begin outsourcing the production of goods for North American, European, and Japanese markets to manufacturing facilities in developing countries. Encouraged by international organizations such as The World Bank and the International Monetary Fund, developing nations established "free trade zones" to encourage foreign investment via tax incentives and a minimal regulatory environment. In the 1980s the availability of international financing allowed entrepreneurs to set up production facilities in developing economies in order to meet the growing demand by MNEs for offshore production.[14]

. . .

Outsourcing has been especially popular in consumer products industries, and in particular in the apparel industry. Nike, for example, outsources all of its production.

Are MNEs responsible for the practices of their subcontractors and suppliers? We believe that they are. Michael Santoro has defended the view that MNEs have a moral duty to ensure that their business partners respect employees by ensuring that human rights are not violated in the workplace. Santoro argues as follows:

> [M]ultinational corporations are morally responsible for the way their suppliers and subcontractors treat their workers. The applicable moral standard is similar to the legal doctrine of *respondeat superior,* according to which a principal is "vicariously liable" or responsible for the acts of its agent conducted in the course of the agency relationship. The classic example of this is the responsibility of

employers for the acts of employees. Moreover, ignorance is no excuse. Firms must do whatever is required to become aware of what conditions are like in the factories of their suppliers and subcontractors, and thereby be able to assure themselves and others that their business partners don't mistreat those workers to provide a cheaper source of supply.[15]

First, an MNE, like any other organization, is composed of individual persons and since persons are moral creatures, the actions of employees in an MNE are constrained by the categorical imperative. This means MNE managers have a duty to ensure that those with whom they conduct business are properly respected.[16] Second, as Kant acknowledges, individuals have unique duties as a result of their unique circumstances. One key feature in determining an individual's duties is the power they have to render assistance. For example, Kant famously argues that a wealthy person has a duty of charity that an impoverished person lacks. Corollary duties apply to organizations . . .

MNEs are well positioned to help ensure that the employees of its business partners are respected because of this imbalance of power. In addition, MNEs can draw upon substantial economic resources, management expertise, and technical knowledge to assist their business partners in creating a respectful work environment.

The Rule of Law

Lawlessness contributes to poverty[17] and is deeply interconnected with human and labor rights violations. One important role that MNEs can play to help ensure that the dignity of workers is properly respected is encouraging respect for the rule of law. The United Nations has emphasized the importance of ensuring that citizens in all nations are not subject to violations of the rule of law.

> The rule of law means that a country's formal rules are made publicly known and enforced in a predictable way through transparent mechanisms. Two conditions are essential: the rules apply equally to all citizens, and the state is subject to the rules. How state institutions comply with the rule of law greatly affects the daily lives of poor people, who are very vulnerable to abuses of their rights.[18]

It is commonplace for employers in developing nations to violate worker rights in the interest of economic efficiency and with the support of state institutions.

Violations of laws relating to wages and benefits, forced overtime, health and safety, child labor, sexual harassment, discrimination, and environmental protection are legion. Examples include the following:

1. Human Rights Watch reports that in Mexican maquiladoras, or export processing zones, U.S. companies such as Johnson Controls and Carlisle Plastics require female job applicants to submit to pregnancy screening; women are refused employment if they test positive. Employment discrimination based on pregnancy is a violation of Mexican law.[19]

2. A Guatemalan Ministry of the Economy study found that less than 30 percent of maquiladora factories that supply MNEs make the legally required payments for workers into the national social security system which gives workers access to health care. The report was not made public by the Ministry of the Economy due to its "startling" nature.[20]

3. An El Salvadoran Ministry of Labor study funded by the United States Agency for International Development found widespread violation of labor laws, including flagrant violation of the freedom to organize and unionize, in maquiladora factories that supply MNEs. The report was suppressed by the Ministry of Labor after factory owners complained.[21]

4. In North and Central Mexico widespread violation of Mexican environmental laws by MNEs and their contractors has been documented by both U.S. and Mexican nongovernmental organizations, and local Mexican governmental officials.[22]

5. In Haiti, apparel manufacturers such as L.V. Myles Corporation, producing clothing under license with the Walt Disney Company in several contract factories, paid workers substantially less than the Haitian minimum wage. These clothes were sold in the U.S at Wal-Mart, Sears, J.C. Penney and other retailers. This practice continued until the National Labor Committee documented and publicized this violation of Haitian law.[23]

Furthermore, in many nations in which MNEs operate those responsible for administering justice are violators of the law. Factory workers frequently have no legal recourse when their legal rights are violated.

The intentional violation of the legal rights of workers in the interest of economic efficiency is fundamentally incompatible with the duty of MNEs to respect workers. Indifference to the plight of workers whose legal rights are systematically violated is a denial of respect. At a minimum, MNEs have a duty to ensure that their offshore factories, and those of their suppliers and subcontractors, are in full compliance with local laws. Failure to honor the dignity of workers by violating their legal rights—or tolerating the violation of those rights—is also hypocritical. In Kantian terms, it constitutes a pragmatic contradiction. A pragmatic contradiction occurs when one acts on a principle that promotes an action that would be inconsistent with one's purpose if everyone were to act upon that principle. In this case, the principle would be something like the following: "It is permissible to violate the legal rights of others when doing so is economically efficient." MNEs rely on the rule of law to ensure, among other things, that their contracts are fulfilled, their property is secure, and their copyrights are protected. When violations of the legal rights of MNEs take place, MNEs and business organizations protest vociferously. Thus, MNEs rely on the rule of law to ensure the protection of their own interests. Without the rule of law, MNEs would cease to exist. Therefore, it is inconsistent for an MNE to permit the violation of the legal rights of workers while at the same time it demands that its own rights be protected.

Coercion

. . . The obligation that we respect others requires that we not use people as a means only, but instead that we treat other people as capable of autonomous law guided action. The requirement not to use people can be met passively, by not treating them in certain ways. However, the requirement to treat them as ends-in-themselves entails positive obligations. . . . One common way of doing so recognized by Kant is coercion. Coercion violates a person's negative freedom. Coercion is prima facie wrong because it treats the subjects of coercion as mere tools, as objects lacking the rational capacity to choose for themselves how they shall act.

Are sweatshops in violation of the no coercion requirement? An answer to this question depends both on the definition of the concepts in question and on the facts of the particular case. . . .

For psychological coercion to take place, three conditions must hold. First, the coercer must have a desire about the will of his or her victim. However, this is a desire of a particular kind because it can only be fulfilled through the will of another person. Second, the coercer must have an effective desire to compel his or her victim to act in a manner that makes efficacious the coercer's other regarding desire. The distinction between an other regarding desire and a coercive will is important because it provides a basis for delineating between cases of coercion and, for example, cases of rational persuasion. In both instances a person may have an other regarding desire, but in the case of coercion that desire will be supplemented by an effective first-order desire which seeks to enforce that desire on the person, and in cases of rational persuasion it will not. What is of most importance in such cases is that *P* intentionally attempts to compel *Q* to comply with an other regarding desire of *P*'s own. These are necessary, but not sufficient conditions of coercion. In order for coercion to take place, the coercer must be successful in getting his or her victim to conform to his or her other regarding desire. In all cases of coercion *P* attempts to violate the autonomy of *Q*. When *Q* successfully resists *P*'s attempted coercion, Q retains his or her autonomy. In such cases *P* retains a coercive will.

In typical cases, people work in sweatshops because they believe they can earn more money working there than they can in alternative employment, or they work in sweatshops because it is better than being unemployed. In many developing countries, people are moving to large cities from rural areas because agriculture in those areas can no longer support the population base. When people make a choice that seems highly undesirable because there are no better alternatives available, are those people coerced? On the definition of coercion employed here, having to make a choice among undesirable options is not sufficient for coercion. We therefore assume that such persons are not coerced even though they have no better alternative than working in a sweatshop.

Nonetheless, the use of psychological coercion in sweatshops appears widespread. For example, coercion is frequently used by supervisors to improve worker productivity. Workers throughout the world report that they are forced to work long overtime hours or lose their jobs. In Bangladesh, factory workers report that they are expected to work virtually every day of the year. Overtime pay, a legal requirement, is often not paid. Employees who refuse to comply are fired.[24] In El Salvador, a government study of maquiladora factories found that

> in the majority of companies, it is an obligation of the personnel to work overtime under the threat of firing or some other kind of reprisal. This situation, in addition to threatening the health of the workers, causes family problems in that [the workers] are unable to properly fulfill obligations to their immediate family.

> On some occasions, because the work time is extended into the late hours of the night, the workers find themselves obligated to sleep in the factory facilities, which do not have conditions necessary for lodging of personnel.[25]

Bangladesh, El Salvador, and other developing economies lack the social welfare programs that workers in North America and Europe take for granted. If workers lose their jobs, they may end up without any source of income. Thus, workers are understandably fearful of being fired for noncompliance with demands to work long overtime hours. When a worker is threatened with being fired by a supervisor unless she agrees to work overtime, and when the supervisor's intention in making the threat is to ensure compliance, then the supervisors actions are properly understood as coercive. Similar threats are used to ensure that workers meet production quotas, even in the face of personal injury. For example, a 26-year-old worker who sews steering wheel covers at a Mexican maquila owned by Autotrim reports the following:

> We have to work quickly with our hands, and I am responsible for sewing 20 steering wheel covers per shift. After having worked for nine years at the plant, I now suffer from an injury in my right hand. I start out the shift okay, but after about three hours of work, I feel a lot of sharp pains in my fingers. It gets so bad that I can't hold the steering wheel correctly. But still the supervisors keep pressuring me to reach 100 percent of my production. I can only reach about 70 percent of what they ask for. These pains began a year ago and I am not the only one who has suffered from them. There are over 200 of us who have hand injuries and some have lost movement in their hands and arms. The company has fired over 150 people in the last year for lack of production. Others have been pressured to quit. . . .[26]

We do not claim that production quotas are inherently coercive. Given a reasonable quota, employees can choose whether or not to work diligently to fill that quota. Employees who choose idleness over industriousness and are terminated as a result are not coerced. However, when a supervisor threatens workers who are ill or injured with termination unless they meet a production quota that either cannot physically be achieved by the employee, or can only be achieved at the cost of further injury to the employee, the threat is properly understood as coercive. In such cases the employee will inevitably feel compelled to meet the quota. Still other factory workers report being threatened with termination if they seek medical attention. For example, when a worker in El Salvador who was three months pregnant began hemorrhaging she was not allowed to leave the factory to receive medical attention. She subsequently miscarried while in the factory, completed her long work day, and took her fetus home for burial.[27] Other workers have died because they were not allowed to leave the factory to receive medical attention.[28] In cases where workers suffer miscarriages or death, rather than risk termination, we believe that it reasonable to conclude that the workers are coerced into remaining at work.

According to the analysis provided here, workers choose to work in sweatshops because the alternatives available to them are worse. However, once they are employed coercion is often used to ensure that they will work long overtime hours and meet production quotas. Respecting workers requires that they be free to decline overtime work without fear of being fired. It also requires that if they are injured or ill—especially as a result of work related activities—they should be allowed to consult healthcare workers and be given work that does not exacerbate their illnesses or injuries. Using coercion as a means of compelling employees to work overtime, to meet production quotas despite injury, or to remain at work while in need of medical attention, is incompatible with respect for persons because the coercers treat their victims as mere tools. It is important to note that even if the victim of coercion successfully resisted in some way, the attempted coercion would remain morally objectionable. This is because the coercer acts as if it is permissible to use the employees as mere tools.

Working Conditions

Critics of MNEs argue that many workers are vulnerable to workplace hazards such as repetitive motion injuries, exposure to toxic chemicals, exposure to airborne pollutants such as fabric particles, and malfunctioning machinery. One of the most common workplace hazards concerns fire safety. In factories throughout the world workers are locked in to keep them from leaving the factory. When fires break out workers are trapped. This is what happened in 1993 when a fire broke out at the Kader Industrial Toy Company in Thailand. More than 200 workers were killed and 469 injured. The factory had been producing toys for U.S. companies such as Hasbro, Toys "R" Us, J.C. Penney, and Fisher-Price.[29] In Bangladesh alone, there have been seventeen fires that have resulted in fatalities since 1995. A recent fire at Chowdhury Knitwears claimed 52 lives.[30]

Workers are also exposed to dangerous toxic chemicals and airborne pollutants. For example, a Nike commissioned Ernst & Young Environmental and Labor Practices Audit of the Tae Kwang Vina factory outside Ho Chi Minh City, Vietnam, was leaked to the press. Among the many unsafe conditions reported by Ernst & Young at this 10,000 person facility was exposure to toluene (a toxic chemical used as a solvent in paints, coatings, adhesives, and cleaning agents) at amounts 6 to 177 times that allowed by Vietnamese law.[31] The U.S. Environmental Protection Agency identifies the following acute effects of toluene exposure:

> The central nervous system is the primary target organ for toluene toxicity in both humans and animals for acute (short-term) and chronic (long-term) exposures. CNS dysfunction (which is often reversible) and narcosis have been frequently observed in humans acutely exposed to low or moderate levels of toluene by inhalation; symptoms include fatigue, sleepiness, headaches, and nausea. CNS depression and death have occurred at higher levels of exposure. Cardiac arrhythmia has also been reported in humans acutely exposed to toluene[32]

. . .

If our analysis is correct, then those MNEs that tolerate such health and safety risks have a duty to improve those conditions. Lax health and safety standards violate the moral requirement that employers be concerned with the physical safety of their employees. A failure to implement appropriate safeguards means that employers are treating their employees as disposable tools rather than as beings with unique dignity. . . .

Wages

One of the most controversial issues concerning sweatshops is the demand that employers raise the wages of employees in order to provide a "living wage." Workers from all over the world complain about low wages.

While a living wage is difficult to define with precision, one useful approach is to use a method similar to that used by the U.S. government to define poverty. This method involves calculating the cost of a market basket of food needed to meet minimum dietary requirements and then adding the cost of other basic needs. The Council on Economic Priorities uses this approach to define a wage that meets basic needs in different countries. Their formula is as follows:

1. Establish the local cost of a basic food basket needed to provide 2,100 calories per person.
2. Determine the share of the local household income spent on food. Divide into 1 to get total budget multiplier.
3. Multiply that by food spending to get the total per person budget for living expenses.

Table 1

Types of Poverty	Deficiencies	Measures
Extreme Poverty (also known as Absolute Poverty)	Lack of income necessary to satisfy basic food needs	Minimum caloric intake and a food basket that meets that requirement
Overall Poverty (also known as Relative Poverty)	Lack of income necessary to satisfy basic non-food needs	Ability to secure shelter, energy, transportation, and basic health care, e.g.
Human Poverty	Lack of basic human capabilities	Access to goods, services, and infrastructure, e.g.

4. Multiply by half the average number of house-hold members in the area. (Use a higher share if there are many single-parent households.)
5. Add at least 10% percent for discretionary income.[33]

The United Nations Development Programme employs a similar method to distinguish between three different levels of poverty (see Table 1).[34]

It is our contention that, at a minimum, respect for employees entails that MNEs and their suppliers have a moral obligation to ensure that employees do not live under conditions of overall poverty by providing adequate wages for a 48 hour work week to satisfy both basic food needs and basic non-food needs. Doing so helps to ensure the physical well-being and independence of employees, contributes to the development of their rational capacities, and provides them with opportunities for moral development. This in turn allows for the cultivation of self-esteem.[35] It is difficult to specify with precision the minimum number of hours per week that employees should work in order to receive a living wage. However, we believe that a 48 hour work week is a reasonable compromise that allows employees sufficient time for the cultivation of their rational capacities while providing employers with sufficient productivity. In addition, MNEs and their suppliers have an obligation to pay appropriate host nation taxes and meet appropriate codes and regulations to ensure that they contribute in appropriate ways to the creation and maintenance of the goods, services, and infrastructure necessary for the fulfillment of human capabilities. Anything less than this means that MNEs, or their suppliers, are not respecting employees as ends in themselves.

Economic Considerations

Some of the most compelling evidence in support of the proposition that MNEs can improve workplace health and safety conditions while avoiding "tragic outcomes" comes from MNEs themselves. Companies such as Levis Strauss, Motorola, and Mattel have expended considerable

resources to ensure that employees in their global sourcing operations work in healthy and safe environments. For example, Levis Strauss & Company stipulates that "We will only utilize business partners who provide workers with a safe and healthy environment."[36] Levis is known for acting in a manner consistent with this policy. Motorola explicitly endorses the idea of respect for persons in their Code of Business Conduct. The Code is built on two foundations:

> *Uncompromising integrity* means staying true to what we believe. We adhere to honesty, fairness and "doing the right thing" without compromise, even when circumstances make it difficult.

> *Constant respect for people* means we treat others with dignity, as we would like to be treated ourselves. Constant respect applies to every individual we interact with around the world.[37]

The physical instantiation of these principles can be seen at Motorola's factory in Tianjin, China:

> In the company cafeteria, workers queue up politely for a variety of free and nutritious meals. One area is set aside for a pregnancy well-care program. A booth is open at which appointments can be made with the company medical staff. There is a bank branch dedicated to employee needs. It is a scene that one might expect in a Fortune 500 corporate campus in the United States. The overwhelming sense is of a pleasant, orderly place in which people are fulfilled in their work.[38]

Recently Mattel announced the creation of a global code of conduct for its production facilities and contract manufactures. It has spent millions of dollars to upgrade its manufacturing facilities in order to improve worker safety and comfort. Furthermore, it has invited a team of academics lead by S. Prakash Sethi to monitor its progress in complying with its self-imposed standards and to make their findings public.[39] This is believed to be the first time that a major MNE has voluntarily submitted to external monitoring. The examples set by Levis, Motorola, and Mattel provide evidence that MNEs are capable of improving worker health and safety without causing further hardship in the communities in which they operate. . . .

Put simply, workers whose minimum daily caloric intakes are met, and who have basic non-food needs met, will have more energy and better attitudes at work; will be less likely to come to work ill: and will be absent with less frequency. Workers are thus likely to be more productive and loyal. Economists refer to a wage that if reduced would make the firm worse off because of a decrease in worker productivity as the efficiency wage. Empirical evidence supports the view that increased productivity resulting from better nutrition offsets the cost of higher wages.[40] Thus, if workers are being paid less than the efficiency wage in a particular market there are good economic reasons, in addition to moral reasons, for raising wages. Higher productivity per hour could also help alleviate the need for overtime work and facilitate a 48 hour work week. . . .

Conclusion

As Kant argues, it is by acting in a manner consistent with human dignity that persons raise themselves above all things. Insofar as we recognize the dignity of humanity, we have an obligation to respect both ourselves and others.[41] We have argued that MNE managers who encourage or tolerate violations of the rule of law; use coercion; allow unsafe working conditions; and provide below subsistence wages, disavow their own dignity and that of their workers. In so doing, they disrespect themselves and their workers. Further, we have argued that this moral analysis is not undermined by economic considerations. Significantly, MNEs are in many ways more readily able to honor the humanity of workers. This is because MNEs typically have well defined internal decision structures that, unlike individual moral agents, are not susceptible to weakness of the will.[42] For this reason, MNE managers who recognize a duty to respect their employees, and those of their subcontractors, are well positioned to play a constructive role in ensuring that the dignity of humanity is respected.

Notes

Earlier versions of this essay were presented to the Annual Meeting of the Society for Business Ethics, Washington D.C., August, 2001; and the American Philosophical Association 100th Anniversary Conference, "Morality in the 21st Century," Newark, Del., October, 2001. We are grateful to audience members for their comments on those occasions. Thanks also to George Brenkert, Heather Douglas, Laura Hartman, John McCall, Sara Arnold, and an anonymous reviewer for helpful comments on earlier drafts of this essay. Special thanks to Ian Maitland and Norris Peterson for detailed written comments; although we continue to disagree with them on some matters, their comments lead to several improvements in this essay.

1. See, for example, Susan Chandler, "Look Who's Sweating Now," *BusinessWeek* (October 16, 1995); Steven Greenhouse, "Sweatshop Raids Cast Doubt on an Effort By Garment Makers to Police the Factories," *New York Times* July 18, 1997: and Gail Edmondson et al., "Workers in Bondage," *BusinessWeek*, November 27. 2000.
2. For the purposes of this paper we define the term as any workplace in which workers are typically subject to two or more of the following conditions: income for a 48 hour work week less than the overall poverty rate for that country (see Table 1 below); systematic forced overtime; systematic health and safety risks that stem from negligence or the willful disregard of employee welfare; coercion; systematic deception that places workers at risk; and underpayment of earnings.
3. Kant, *Foundations of the Metaphysics of Morals,* 52.
4. Onora O'Neill, *Constructions of Reason* (Cambridge: Cambridge University Press, 1989), 53.
5. Immanuel Kant, *The Metaphysics of Morals,* Mary Gregor, trans., (Cambridge: Cambridge University Press, 1991), 230.
6. Ibid.
7. Ibid., 255.
8. Kant, *Metaphysics of Morals,* 255.
9. His latest book is *Development as Freedom* (New York: Anchor Books, 1999). Martha Nussbaum has developed her own version of the capabilities approach, one that pays particular attention to the unique circumstances of women's lives. *Women and Human Development: The Capabilities Approach* (Cambridge: Cambridge University Press, 2000).
10. United Nations Development Programme, *Human Development Report 2000* (New York: Oxford University Press, 2000).
11. See, for example, Vinod Thomas et al., *The Quality of Growth* (Washington D.C.: The World Bank, 2000); Deepa Narayan et al., *Voices of the Poor: Crying Out for Change* (Washington D.C.: The World Bank, 2000); and Deepa Narayan et al., *Voices of the Poor: Can Anyone Hear Us?* (Washington D.C.: The World Bank, 2000).
12. Thomas et al., *The Quality of Growth,* xiv.
13. Ibid., xvii–xvii (italics added by authors).

14. Pamela Varley, ed., *The Sweatshop Quandary: Corporate Responsibility on the Global Frontier* (Washington D.C., Investor Responsibility Research Center, 1998), 185–86.
15. Michael A. Santoro, *Profits and Principles: Global Capitalism and Human Rights in China* (Ithaca: Cornell University Press, 2000), 161.
16. For a fuller discussion of this matter see Bowie, *Business Ethics. A Kantian Perspective,* esp. chap. 2.
17. Better rule of law is associated with higher per capita income. See *World Development Report 2000/2001: Attacking Poverty* (New York: Oxford University Press, 2000), 103.
18. Ibid., 102. See also the United National Development Programme's *Human Development Report 2000* (New York: Oxford University Press, 2000), esp. 37–38.
19. Human Rights Watch, "A Job or Your Rights: Continued Sex Discrimination in Mexico's Maquiladora Sector," volume 10, no. 1(B) December 1998. Available at http://www.hrw.org/ reports98/women2/.
20. Varley, ed., *The Sweatshop Quandary.* 131.
21. Republic of El Salvador, Ministry of Labor, Monitoring and Labor Relations Analysis Unit. "Monitoring Report on Maquilas and Bonded Areas," (July 2000). Available at http://www. nlcnet.org /elsalvador/0401/translation.htm.
22. Edward J. Williams, "The Maquiladora Industry and Environmental Degradation in the United States-Mexican Borderlands," Paper presented at the annual meeting of the Latin American Studies Association. Washington. D.C., September, 1995. Available at http://www.natlaw. com/pubs/williams. htm. See also, Joan Salvat, Stef Soetewey, and Peter Breuls, *Free Trade Slaves,* 58 min. (Princeton, N.J.: Films for the Humanities and Sciences, 1999), videocassette.
23. National Labor Committee, "The U.S. in Haiti: How to Get Rich on 11 Cents an Hour." 1995. Available at http://www.nlcnet.org/Haiti/0196/index.htm.
24. Barry Bearak. "Lives Held Cheap In Bangladesh Sweatshops." *New York Times.* April 15, 2001.
25. Republic of EI Salvador, Ministry of Labor, Monitoring and Labor, Relations Analysis Unit, "Monitoring Report on Maquilas and Bonded Areas."
26. Varley, ed., *The Sweatshop Quandary;* 68.
27. Salvat et al., *Free Trade Slaves.* 58 mm. (Pnnceton, N.J.. Films for the Humanities and Sciences. 1999). videocassette.
28. Ibid.
29. Varley, ed., *The Sweatshop Quandary,* 67.
30. Bearak, "Lives Held Cheap in Bangladesh Sweatshops."
31. "Ernst & Young Environmental and Labor Practice Audit of the Tae Kwang Vina Industrial Ltd. Co., Vietnam." Available at http://www. corpwatch .org/trac/nike/ernst/audit.html
32. United States Environmental Protection Agency, Office of Air Quality, Planning, and Standards, "Toluene." Available at http://www.epa.gov/ttnuatw1 /hlthef/toluene.html.
33. Aaron Bernstein, "Sweatshop Reform: How to Solve the Standoff," *BusinessWeek,* May 3, 1999.
34. *Poverty Report 2000: Overcoming Human Poverty* (New York: United Nations Development Programme, 2000).
35. Self-esteem is grounded in the conscious recognition of one's dignity as a rational being.
36. Ibid., 539.
37. Motorola, "Code of Business Conduct." Available at http://www.motorola.com/code/code. html.
38. Santoro, *Profits and Principles,* 6.
39. S. Prakash Sethi, "Codes of Conduct for Multinational Corporations: An Idea Whose Time Has Come," *Business and Society Review* 104 (1999): 225–41.
40. C. J. Bliss and N. H. Stern, "Productivity, Wages, and Nutrition, 2. Some Observations." *Journal of Development Economics* 5 (1978): 363–398. For theoretical discussion, see C. J. Bliss and N. H. Stern, "Productivity, Wages, and Nutrition, 1: The Theory." *Journal of Development Economics* 5 (1978),. 331–362.
41. Kant, *Foundations of the Metaphysics of Morals,* 255.
42. For a fuller defense of this position see Peter A. French, *Corporate Ethics* (Fort Worth, TX.: Hartcourt Brace, 1995), 79–87.

Denis G. Arnold is the Jule and Marguerite Surtman Distinguished Professor in Business Ethics at the University of North Carolina, Charlotte. He is the author of *The Ethics of Global Business* (2010) and the editor of *Ethics and the Business of Biomedicine* (Cambridge University Press, 2009).

Norman E. Bowie is the former Elmer L Andersen Chair in Corporate Responsibility at the University of Minnesota. He has authored or edited 16 books and over 75 articles. Professor Bowie is the leading scholar in the application of Kant's moral philosophy to business.

Charles Duhigg and David Barboza  **NO**

In China, Human Costs Are Built into an iPad

The explosion ripped through Building A5 on a Friday evening last May, an eruption of fire and noise that twisted metal pipes as if they were discarded straws.

When workers in the cafeteria ran outside, they saw black smoke pouring from shattered windows. It came from the area where employees polished thousands of iPad cases a day.

Two people were killed immediately, and over a dozen others hurt. As the injured were rushed into ambulances, one in particular stood out. His features had been smeared by the blast, scrubbed by heat and violence until a mat of red and black had replaced his mouth and nose.

"Are you Lai Xiaodong's father?" a caller asked when the phone rang at Mr. Lai's childhood home. Six months earlier, the 22-year-old had moved to Chengdu, in southwest China, to become one of the millions of human cogs powering the largest, fastest and most sophisticated manufacturing system on earth. That system has made it possible for Apple and hundreds of other companies to build devices almost as quickly as they can be dreamed up.

"He's in trouble," the caller told Mr. Lai's father. "Get to the hospital as soon as possible."

In the last decade, Apple has become one of the mightiest, richest and most successful companies in the world, in part by mastering global manufacturing. Apple and its high-technology peers—as well as dozens of other American industries—have achieved a pace of innovation nearly unmatched in modern history.

However, the workers assembling iPhones, iPads and other devices often labor in harsh conditions, according to employees inside those plants, worker advocates and documents published by companies themselves. Problems are as varied as onerous work environments and serious —sometimes deadly—safety problems.

Employees work excessive overtime, in some cases seven days a week, and live in crowded dorms. Some say they stand so long that their legs swell until they can hardly walk. Under-age workers have helped build Apple's products, and the company's suppliers have improperly disposed of hazardous waste and falsified records, according to company reports and advocacy groups that, within China, are often considered reliable, independent monitors.

More troubling, the groups say, is some suppliers' disregard for workers' health. Two years ago, 137 workers at an Apple supplier in eastern China were injured after they were ordered to use a poisonous chemical to clean iPhone screens. Within seven months last year, two explosions at iPad factories, including in Chengdu, killed four people and injured 77. Before those blasts, Apple had been alerted to hazardous conditions inside the Chengdu plant, according to a Chinese group that published that warning.

"If Apple was warned, and didn't act, that's reprehensible," said Nicholas Ashford, a former chairman of the National Advisory Committee on Occupational Safety and Health, a group that advises the United States Labor Department. "But what's morally repugnant in one country is accepted business practices in another, and companies take advantage of that."

Apple is not the only electronics company doing business within a troubling supply system. Bleak working conditions have been documented at factories manufacturing products for Dell, Hewlett-Packard, I.B.M., Lenovo, Motorola, Nokia, Sony, Toshiba and others.

Current and former Apple executives, moreover, say the company has made significant strides in improving factories in recent years. Apple has a supplier code of conduct that details standards on labor issues, safety protections and other topics. The company has mounted a vigorous auditing campaign, and when abuses are discovered, Apple says, corrections are demanded.

And Apple's annual supplier responsibility reports, in many cases, are the first to report abuses. This month, for the first time, the company released a list identifying many of its suppliers.

But significant problems remain. More than half of the suppliers audited by Apple have violated at least one aspect of the code of conduct every year since 2007, according to Apple's reports, and in some instances have violated the law. While many violations involve working conditions, rather than safety hazards, troubling patterns persist.

"Apple never cared about anything other than increasing product quality and decreasing production cost," said Li Mingqi, who until April worked in management at Foxconn Technology, one of Apple's most important manufacturing partners. Mr. Li, who is suing Foxconn over his dismissal, helped manage the Chengdu factory where the explosion occurred.

"Workers' welfare has nothing to do with their interests," he said.

Some former Apple executives say there is an unresolved tension within the company: executives want to improve conditions within factories, but that dedication falters when it conflicts with crucial supplier relationships or the fast delivery of new products. Tuesday, Apple reported one of the most lucrative quarters of any corporation in history, with $13.06 billion in profits on $46.3 billion in sales. Its sales would have been even higher, executives said, if overseas factories had been able to produce more.

Executives at other corporations report similar internal pressures. This system may not be pretty, they argue, but a radical overhaul would slow innovation. Customers want amazing new electronics delivered every year.

"We've known about labor abuses in some factories for four years, and they're still going on," said one former Apple executive who, like others, spoke on the condition of anonymity because of confidentiality agreements. "Why? Because the system works for us. Suppliers would change everything tomorrow if Apple told them they didn't have another choice."

"If half of iPhones were malfunctioning, do you think Apple would let it go on for four years?" the executive asked.

Apple, in its published reports, has said it requires every discovered labor violation to be remedied, and suppliers that refuse are terminated. Privately, however, some former executives concede that finding new suppliers is time-consuming and costly. Foxconn is one of the few manufacturers in the world with the scale to build sufficient numbers of iPhones and iPads. So Apple is "not going to leave Foxconn and they're not going to leave China," said Heather White, a research fellow at Harvard and a former member of the Monitoring International Labor Standards committee at the National Academy of Sciences. "There's a lot of rationalization."

Apple was provided with extensive summaries of this article, but the company declined to comment. The reporting is based on interviews with more than three dozen current or former employees and contractors, including a half-dozen current or former executives with firsthand knowledge of Apple's supplier responsibility group, as well as others within the technology industry.

In 2010, Steven P. Jobs discussed the company's relationships with suppliers at an industry conference.

"I actually think Apple does one of the best jobs of any companies in our industry, and maybe in any industry, of understanding the working conditions in our supply chain," said Mr. Jobs, who was Apple's chief executive at the time and who died last October.

"I mean, you go to this place, and, it's a factory, but, my gosh, I mean, they've got restaurants and movie theaters and hospitals and swimming pools, and I mean, for a factory, it's a pretty nice factory."

Others, including workers inside such plants, acknowledge the cafeterias and medical facilities, but insist conditions are punishing.

"We're trying really hard to make things better," said one former Apple executive. "But most people would still be really disturbed if they saw where their iPhone comes from."

The Road to Chengdu

In the fall of 2010, about six months before the explosion in the iPad factory, Lai Xiaodong carefully wrapped his clothes around his college diploma, so it wouldn't crease in his suitcase. He told friends he would no longer be around for their weekly poker games, and said goodbye to his teachers. He was leaving for Chengdu, a city of 12 million that was rapidly becoming one of the world's most important manufacturing hubs.

Though painfully shy, Mr. Lai had surprised everyone by persuading a beautiful nursing student to become his girlfriend. She wanted to marry, she said, and so his goal was to earn enough money to buy an apartment.

Factories in Chengdu manufacture products for hundreds of companies. But Mr. Lai was focused on Foxconn Technology, China's largest exporter and one of the nation's biggest employers, with 1.2 million workers. The company has plants throughout China, and assembles an estimated 40 percent of the world's consumer electronics, including for customers like Amazon, Dell, Hewlett-Packard, Nintendo, Nokia and Samsung.

Foxconn's factory in Chengdu, Mr. Lai knew, was special. Inside, workers were building Apple's latest, potentially greatest product: the iPad.

When Mr. Lai finally landed a job repairing machines at the plant, one of the first things he noticed were the almost blinding lights. Shifts ran 24 hours a day, and the factory was always bright. At any moment, there were thousands of workers standing on assembly lines or sitting in backless chairs, crouching next to large machinery, or jogging between loading bays. Some workers' legs swelled so much they waddled. "It's hard to stand all day," said Zhao Sheng, a plant worker.

Banners on the walls warned the 120,000 employees: "Work hard on the job today or work hard to find a job tomorrow." Apple's supplier code of conduct dictates that, except in unusual circumstances, employees are not supposed to work more than 60 hours a week. But at Foxconn, some worked more, according to interviews, workers' pay stubs and surveys by outside groups. Mr. Lai was soon spending 12 hours a day, six days a week inside the factory, according to his paychecks. Employees who arrived late were sometimes required to write confession letters and copy quotations. There were "continuous shifts," when workers were told to work two stretches in a row, according to interviews.

Mr. Lai's college degree enabled him to earn a salary of around $22 a day, including overtime—more than many others. When his days ended, he would retreat to a small bedroom just big enough for a mattress, wardrobe and a desk where he obsessively played an online game called Fight the Landlord, said his girlfriend, Luo Xiaohong.

Those accommodations were better than many of the company's dorms, where 70,000 Foxconn workers lived, at times stuffed 20 people to a three-room apartment, employees said. Last year, a dispute over paychecks set off a riot in one of the dormitories, and workers started throwing bottles, trash cans and flaming paper from their windows, according to witnesses. Two hundred police officers wrestled with workers, arresting eight. Afterward, trash cans were removed, and piles of rubbish—and rodents—became a problem. Mr. Lai felt lucky to have a place of his own.

Foxconn, in a statement, disputed workers' accounts of continuous shifts, extended overtime, crowded living accommodations and the causes of the riot. The company said that its operations adhered to customers' codes of conduct, industry standards and national laws. "Conditions at Foxconn are anything but harsh," the company wrote. Foxconn also said that it had never been cited by a customer or government for under-age or overworked employees or toxic exposures.

"All assembly line employees are given regular breaks, including one-hour lunch breaks," the company wrote, and only 5 percent of assembly line workers are required to stand to carry out their tasks. Work stations have been designed to ergonomic standards, and employees have opportunities for job rotation and promotion, the statement said.

"Foxconn has a very good safety record," the company wrote. "Foxconn has come a long way in our efforts to lead our industry in China in areas such as workplace conditions and the care and treatment of our employees."

Apple's Code of Conduct

In 2005, some of Apple's top executives gathered inside their Cupertino, Calif., headquarters for a special meeting. Other companies had created codes of conduct to police their suppliers. It was time, Apple decided, to follow suit. The code Apple published that year demands "that working conditions in Apple's supply chain are safe, that workers are treated with respect and dignity, and that manufacturing processes are environmentally responsible."

But the next year, a British newspaper, *The Mail on Sunday*, secretly visited a Foxconn factory in Shenzhen, China, where iPods were manufactured, and reported on workers' long hours, push-ups meted out as punishment and crowded dorms. Executives in Cupertino were shocked. "Apple is filled with really good people who had no idea this was going on," a former employee said. "We wanted it changed, immediately."

Apple audited that factory, the company's first such inspection, and ordered improvements. Executives also undertook a series of initiatives that included an annual audit report, first published in 2007. By last year, Apple had inspected 396 facilities—including the company's direct suppliers, as well as many of those suppliers' suppliers—one of the largest such programs within the electronics industry.

Those audits have found consistent violations of Apple's code of conduct, according to summaries published by the company. In 2007, for instance, Apple conducted over three dozen audits, two-thirds of which indicated that employees regularly worked more than 60 hours a week. In addition, there were six "core violations," the most serious kind, including hiring 15-year-olds as well as falsifying records.

Over the next three years, Apple conducted 312 audits, and every year, about half or more showed evidence of large numbers of employees laboring more than six days a week as well as working extended overtime. Some workers received less than minimum wage or had pay withheld as punishment. Apple found 70 core violations over that period, including cases of involuntary labor, underage workers, record falsifications, improper disposal of hazardous waste and over a hundred workers injured by toxic chemical exposures.

Last year, the company conducted 229 audits. There were slight improvements in some categories and the detected rate of core violations declined. However, within 93 facilities, at least half of workers exceeded the 60-hours-a-week work limit. At a similar number, employees worked more than six days a week. There were incidents of discrimination, improper safety precautions, failure to pay required overtime rates and other violations. That year, four employees were killed and 77 injured in workplace explosions.

"If you see the same pattern of problems, year after year, that means the company's ignoring the issue rather than solving it," said one former Apple executive with firsthand knowledge of the supplier responsibility group. "Noncompliance is tolerated, as long as the suppliers promise to try harder next time. If we meant business, core violations would disappear."

Apple says that when an audit reveals a violation, the company requires suppliers to address the problem within 90 days and make changes to prevent a recurrence. "If a supplier is unwilling to change, we terminate our relationship," the company says on its Web site.

The seriousness of that threat, however, is unclear. Apple has found violations in hundreds of audits, but fewer than 15 suppliers have been terminated for transgressions since 2007, according to former Apple executives.

"Once the deal is set and Foxconn becomes an authorized Apple supplier, Apple will no longer give any attention to worker conditions or anything that is irrelevant to its products," said Mr. Li, the former Foxconn manager. Mr. Li spent seven years with Foxconn in Shenzhen and Chengdu and was forced out in April after he objected to a relocation to Chengdu, he said. Foxconn disputed his comments, and said "both Foxconn and Apple take the welfare of our employees very seriously."

Apple's efforts have spurred some changes. Facilities that were reaudited "showed continued performance improvements and better working conditions," the company wrote in its 2011 supplier responsibility progress report. In addition, the number of audited facilities has grown every year, and some executives say those expanding efforts obscure year-to-year improvements.

Apple also has trained over a million workers about their rights and methods for injury and disease prevention. A few years ago, after auditors insisted on interviewing low-level factory employees, they discovered that some had been forced to pay onerous "recruitment fees"—which Apple classifies as involuntary labor. As of last year, the company had forced suppliers to reimburse more than $6.7 million in such charges.

"Apple is a leader in preventing under-age labor," said Dionne Harrison of Impactt, a firm paid by Apple to help prevent and respond to child labor among its suppliers. "They're doing as much as they possibly can."

Other consultants disagree.

"We've spent years telling Apple there are serious problems and recommending changes," said a consultant at BSR—also known as Business for Social Responsibility—which has been twice retained by Apple to provide advice on labor issues. "They don't want to pre-empt problems, they just want to avoid embarrassments."

"We Could Have Saved Lives"

In 2006, BSR, along with a division of the World Bank and other groups, initiated a project to improve working conditions in factories building cellphones and other devices in China and elsewhere. The groups and companies pledged to test various ideas. Foxconn agreed to participate.

For four months, BSR and another group negotiated with Foxconn regarding a pilot program to create worker "hotlines," so that employees could report abusive conditions, seek mental counseling and discuss workplace problems. Apple was not a participant in the project, but was briefed on it, according to the BSR consultant, who had detailed knowledge.

As negotiations proceeded, Foxconn's requirements for participation kept changing. First Foxconn asked to shift from installing new hotlines to evaluating existing hotlines. Then Foxconn insisted that mental health counseling be excluded. Foxconn asked participants to sign agreements saying they would not disclose what they observed, and then rewrote those agreements multiple times. Finally, an agreement was struck, and the project was scheduled to begin in January 2008. A day before the start, Foxconn demanded more changes, until it was clear the project would not proceed, according to the consultant and a 2008 summary by BSR that did not name Foxconn.

The next year, a Foxconn employee fell or jumped from an apartment building after losing an iPhone prototype. Over the next two years, at least 18 other Foxconn workers attempted suicide or fell from buildings in manners that suggested suicide attempts. In 2010, two years after the pilot program fell apart and after multiple suicide attempts, Foxconn created a dedicated mental health hotline and began offering free psychological counseling.

"We could have saved lives, and we asked Apple to pressure Foxconn, but they wouldn't do it," said the BSR consultant, who asked not to be identified because of confidentiality agreements. "Companies like H.P. and Intel and Nike push their suppliers. But Apple wants to keep an arm's length, and Foxconn is their most important manufacturer, so they refuse to push."

BSR, in a written statement, said the views of that consultant were not those of the company.

"My BSR colleagues and I view Apple as a company that is making a highly serious effort to ensure that labor conditions in its supply chain meet the expectations of applicable laws, the company's standards and the expectations of consumers," wrote Aron Cramer, BSR's president. Mr. Cramer added that asking Apple to pressure Foxconn would have been inconsistent with the purpose of the pilot program, and there were multiple reasons the pilot program did not proceed.

Foxconn, in a statement, said it acted quickly and comprehensively to address suicides, and "the record has shown that those measures have been successful."

A Demanding Client

Every month, officials at companies from around the world trek to Cupertino or invite Apple executives to visit their foreign factories, all in pursuit of a goal: becoming a supplier.

When news arrives that Apple is interested in a particular product or service, small celebrations often erupt. Whiskey is drunk. Karaoke is sung.

Then, Apple's requests start.

Apple typically asks suppliers to specify how much every part costs, how many workers are needed and the size of their salaries. Executives want to know every financial detail. Afterward, Apple calculates how much it will pay for a part. Most suppliers are allowed only the slimmest of profits.

So suppliers often try to cut corners, replace expensive chemicals with less costly alternatives, or push their employees to work faster and longer, according to people at those companies.

"The only way you make money working for Apple is figuring out how to do things more efficiently or cheaper," said an executive at one company that helped bring the iPad to market. "And then they'll come back the next year, and force a 10 percent price cut."

In January 2010, workers at a Chinese factory owned by Wintek, an Apple manufacturing partner, went on strike over a variety of issues, including widespread rumors that workers were being exposed to toxins. Investigations by news organizations revealed that over a hundred employees had been injured by n-hexane, a toxic chemical that can cause nerve damage and paralysis.

Employees said they had been ordered to use n-hexane to clean iPhone screens because it evaporated almost three times as fast as rubbing alcohol. Faster evaporation meant workers could clean more screens each minute.

Apple commented on the Wintek injuries a year later. In its supplier responsibility report, Apple said it had "required Wintek to stop using n-hexane" and that "Apple has verified that all affected workers have been treated successfully, and we continue to monitor their medical reports until full recuperation." Apple also said it required Wintek to fix the ventilation system.

That same month, a *New York Times* reporter interviewed a dozen injured Wintek workers who said they had never been contacted by Apple or its intermediaries, and that Wintek had pressured them to resign and take cash settlements that would absolve the company of liability. After those interviews, Wintek pledged to provide more compensation to the injured workers and Apple sent a representative to speak with some of them.

Six months later, trade publications reported that Apple significantly cut prices paid to Wintek.

"You can set all the rules you want, but they're meaningless if you don't give suppliers enough profit to treat workers well," said one former Apple executive with firsthand knowledge of the supplier responsibility group. "If you squeeze margins, you're forcing them to cut safety."

Wintek is still one of Apple's most important suppliers. Wintek, in a statement, declined to comment except to say that after the episode, the company took "ample measures" to address the situation and "is committed to ensuring employee welfare and creating a safe and healthy work environment."

Many major technology companies have worked with factories where conditions are troubling. However, independent monitors and suppliers say some act differently. Executives at multiple suppliers, in interviews, said that Hewlett-Packard and others allowed them slightly more profits and other allowances if they were used to improve worker conditions.

"Our suppliers are very open with us," said Zoe McMahon, an executive in Hewlett-Packard's supply chain social and environmental responsibility program. "They let us know when they are struggling to meet our expectations, and that influences our decisions."

The Explosion

On the afternoon of the blast at the iPad plant, Lai Xiaodong telephoned his girlfriend, as he did every day. They had hoped to see each other that evening, but Mr. Lai's manager said he had to work overtime, he told her.

He had been promoted quickly at Foxconn, and after just a few months was in charge of a team that maintained the machines that polished iPad cases. The sanding area was loud and hazy with aluminum dust. Workers wore masks and earplugs, but no matter how many times they showered, they were recognizable by the slight aluminum sparkle in their hair and at the corners of their eyes.

Just two weeks before the explosion, an advocacy group in Hong Kong published a report warning of unsafe conditions at the Chengdu plant, including problems with aluminum dust. The group, Students and Scholars Against Corporate Misbehavior, or Sacom, had videotaped workers covered with tiny aluminum particles. "Occupational health and safety issues in Chengdu are alarming," the report read. "Workers also highlight the problem of poor ventilation and inadequate personal protective equipment."

A copy of that report was sent to Apple. "There was no response," said Debby Chan Sze Wan of the group. "A few months later I went to Cupertino, and went into the Apple lobby, but no one would meet with me. I've never heard from anyone from Apple at all."

The morning of the explosion, Mr. Lai rode his bicycle to work. The iPad had gone on sale just weeks earlier, and workers were told thousands of cases needed to be polished each day. The factory was frantic, employees said. Rows of machines buffed cases as masked employees pushed buttons. Large air ducts hovered over each station, but they could not keep up with the three lines of machines polishing nonstop. Aluminum dust was everywhere.

Dust is a known safety hazard. In 2003, an aluminum dust explosion in Indiana destroyed a wheel factory and killed a worker. In 2008, agricultural dust inside a sugar factory in Georgia caused an explosion that killed 14.

Two hours into Mr. Lai's second shift, the building started to shake, as if an earthquake was under way. There was a series of blasts, plant workers said.

Then the screams began.

When Mr. Lai's colleagues ran outside, dark smoke was mixing with a light rain, according to cellphone videos. The toll would eventually count four dead, 18 injured.

At the hospital, Mr. Lai's girlfriend saw that his skin was almost completely burned away. "I recognized him from his legs, otherwise I wouldn't know who that person was," she said.

Eventually, his family arrived. Over 90 percent of his body had been seared. "My mom ran away from the room at the first sight of him. I cried. Nobody could stand it," his brother said. When his mother eventually returned, she tried to avoid touching her son, for fear that it would cause pain.

"If I had known," she said, "I would have grabbed his arm, I would have touched him."

"He was very tough," she said. "He held on for two days."

After Mr. Lai died, Foxconn workers drove to Mr. Lai's hometown and delivered a box of ashes. The company later wired a check for about $150,000.

Foxconn, in a statement, said that at the time of the explosion the Chengdu plant was in compliance with all relevant laws and regulations, and "after ensuring that the families of the deceased employees were given the support they required, we ensured that all of the injured employees were given the highest quality medical care." After the explosion, the company added, Foxconn immediately halted work in all polishing workshops, and later improved ventilation and dust disposal, and adopted technologies to enhance worker safety.

In its most recent supplier responsibility report, Apple wrote that after the explosion, the company contacted "the foremost experts in process safety" and assembled a team to investigate and make recommendations to prevent future accidents.

In December, however, seven months after the blast that killed Mr. Lai, another iPad factory exploded, this one in Shanghai. Once again, aluminum dust was the cause, according to interviews and Apple's most recent supplier responsibility report. That blast injured 59 workers, with 23 hospitalized.

"It is gross negligence, after an explosion occurs, not to realize that every factory should be inspected," said Nicholas Ashford, the occupational safety expert, who is now at the Massachusetts Institute of Technology. "If it were terribly difficult to deal with aluminum dust, I would understand. But do you know how easy dust is to control? It's called ventilation. We solved this problem over a century ago."

In its most recent supplier responsibility report, Apple wrote that while the explosions both involved combustible aluminum dust, the causes were different. The company declined, however, to provide details. The report added that Apple had now audited all suppliers polishing aluminum products and had put stronger precautions in place. All suppliers have initiated required countermeasures, except one, which remains shut down, the report said.

For Mr. Lai's family, questions remain. "We're really not sure why he died," said Mr. Lai's mother, standing beside a shrine she built near their home. "We don't understand what happened."

Hitting the Apple Lottery

Every year, as rumors about Apple's forthcoming products start to emerge, trade publications and Web sites begin speculating about which suppliers are likely to win the

Apple lottery. Getting a contract from Apple can lift a company's value by millions because of the implied endorsement of manufacturing quality. But few companies openly brag about the work: Apple generally requires suppliers to sign contracts promising they will not divulge anything, including the partnership.

That lack of transparency gives Apple an edge at keeping its plans secret. But it also has been a barrier to improving working conditions, according to advocates and former Apple executives.

This month, after numerous requests by advocacy and news organizations, including *The New York Times,* Apple released the names of 156 of its suppliers. In the report accompanying that list, Apple said they "account for more than 97 percent of what we pay to suppliers to manufacture our products."

However, the company has not revealed the names of hundreds of other companies that do not directly contract with Apple, but supply the suppliers. The company's supplier list does not disclose where factories are, and many are hard to find. And independent monitoring organizations say when they have tried to inspect Apple's suppliers, they have been barred from entry—on Apple's orders, they have been told.

"We've had this conversation hundreds of times," said a former executive in Apple's supplier responsibility group. "There is a genuine, companywide commitment to the code of conduct. But taking it to the next level and creating real change conflicts with secrecy and business goals, and so there's only so far we can go." Former Apple employees say they were generally prohibited from engaging with most outside groups.

"There's a real culture of secrecy here that influences everything," the former executive said.

Some other technology companies operate differently.

"We talk to a lot of outsiders," said Gary Niekerk, director of corporate citizenship at Intel. "The world's complex, and unless we're dialoguing with outside groups, we miss a lot."

Given Apple's prominence and leadership in global manufacturing, if the company were to radically change its ways, it could overhaul how business is done.

"Every company wants to be Apple," said Sasha Lezhnev at the Enough Project, a group focused on corporate accountability. "If they committed to building a conflict-free iPhone, it would transform technology."

But ultimately, say former Apple executives, there are few real outside pressures for change. Apple is one of the most admired brands. In a national survey conducted by *The New York Times* in November, 56 percent of respondents said they couldn't think of anything negative about Apple. Fourteen percent said the worst thing about the company was that its products were too expensive. Just 2 percent mentioned overseas labor practices.

People like Ms. White of Harvard say that until consumers demand better conditions in overseas factories—as they did for companies like Nike and Gap, which today have overhauled conditions among suppliers—or regulators act, there is little impetus for radical change. Some Apple insiders agree.

"You can either manufacture in comfortable, worker-friendly factories, or you can reinvent the product every year, and make it better and faster and cheaper, which requires factories that seem harsh by American standards," said a current Apple executive.

"And right now, customers care more about a new iPhone than working conditions in China."

CHARLES DUHIGG is a Pulitzer Prize-winning reporter at *The New York Times,* where he writes for the business section. Prior to joining the staff of *The New York Times* in 2006, he was a staff writer of the Los Angeles Times. In 2012, he was part of a team writing a series titled "The iEconomy" about Apple, and the company's influence within the United States and abroad.

DAVID BARBOZA has been a correspondent for *The New York Times* based in Shanghai, China, since November 2004. Mr. Barboza writes primarily for the Business section and reports on Fortune 500 companies operating in China, Chinese trends, and economics.

Should U.S. Companies Take Primary Responsibility for Working Conditions in Their International Suppliers' Factories? by Vega

279

EXPLORING THE ISSUE

Should U.S. Companies Take Primary Responsibility for Working Conditions in Their International Suppliers' Factories?

Critical Thinking and Reflection

1. Which takes precedence: monitoring working conditions in factories or maintaining an efficient supply chain that facilitates production?
2. What is more important to you—cheap clothing and electronics or working conditions abroad?
3. How far down the supply chain does corporate responsibility extend?

Is There Common Ground?

Raising awareness is not sufficient to compel action in this situation, but it is a start. Certainly, if American consumers do not object to purchasing goods manufactured under conditions of slavery, there is no impetus for the corporations to require change by their suppliers. Awareness must be emphasized to the local consumer and must also be emphasized by the corporation itself. When corporations monitor the activities of their suppliers and demand specific standards, they will get them.

Grassroots movements by consumers can make a difference as well. When a significant number of people refuse to purchase items manufactured in unsafe conditions, corporations will feel the economic pressure to enforce safe labor policies instead of tacitly avoiding dealing with them. Because sweatshops overseas have grown to fill the need for cheap labor, consumers must call a halt to the demand for cheap prices if we wish to encourage safe and healthy manufacturing.

Additional Resources

Robert Handfield, "A Brief History of Outsourcing," *Supply Chain Management Newsletter* (June 1, 2006).

Adams B. Nager and Robert D. Atkinson, "The Myth of America's Manufacturing Renaissance: The Real State of U.S. Manufacturing," *The Information Technology & Innovation Foundation* (January 2015).

Charles Kernaghan, "Gap and Old Navy in Bangladesh: Cheating the Poorest Workers in the World," *Institute for Global Labour and Human Rights* (October 2013).

Internet References . . .

Consumer Reports

http://www.consumerreports.org/cro
/magazine/2013/02/made-in-america/index.htm

Marc Gunther

http://www.marcgunther.com/whos-responsible-for
-factory-conditions-in-poor-countries-has-csr
-gone-too-far/

The United Nations Global Compact

https://www.unglobalcompact.org/